Titel/Title

www.ebn24.com

Wirtschaftsstandort Deutschland

Chancen und Perspektiven einer Wirtschaftsnation

Opportunities and prospects of an economic nation

Europäischer Wirtschafts Verlag
Bundesrepublik Deutschland
2005/2006

Vorwort/Foreword

Sehr geehrte Damen und Herren,

Es scheint gerade ein Volkssport zu sein, den Wirtschaftsstandort Deutschland schlecht zu reden. Die Klagen kommen aus allen Parteien, von Unternehmern und natürlich den zahlreichen selbst ernannten Experten. Im Ausland schüttelt man darüber nur den Kopf. Wie kann sich eine anerkannte Wirtschaftsnation so depressiv oder gar selbstzerstörerisch darstellen!

Der französische Schriftsteller Antoine de Saint-Exupéry schrieb einmal sinngemäß: Wenn du ein Schiff bauen willst, fordere die Männer nicht auf, Holz zu beschaffen, Werkzeuge vorzubereiten und Arbeit einzuteilen, sondern lehre die Männer die Sehnsucht nach dem weiten endlosen Meer. Auf den Standort Deutschland bezogen heißt das, eine Aufbruchstimmung zu erzeugen, die – ein großes Ziel vor Augen – ein ganzes Land mitreißt. Mit unseren Projekten wollen wir helfen, diese Euphorie zu entfachen. Wir wollen gemeinsam mit unseren Partnern in Politik, Wirtschaft, Wissenschaft und Gesellschaft definieren, wohin die Reise gehen soll, wo wir in Zukunft im internationalen Wettbewerb stehen wollen und vor allem: was wir leisten müssen, um diese Ziele zu erreichen.

Dabei sollten wir uns, wenn es auch gerade nicht dem Zeitgeist entspricht, auf unsere Stärken besinnen, über die die ganze Welt spricht, nur wir nicht: die hervorragende Ausbildung der meisten Deutschen, ihr Fleiß und ihr Erfindergeist, die erstklassige Infrastruktur Deutschlands und das technische Know-how seiner Unternehmen sowie die in der Welt einmalige Stärke und Kreativität des Mittelstandes. Wer darüber redet, weiß auch die Schwächen einzuordnen und lässt sich nicht überwältigen von den alltäglichen Klagen.

In diesem Sinne konzipieren wir auch unsere Projekte – sachlich stets, auch kritisch, aber immer optimistisch. Ich denke, auch der Leser dieses Bandes wird uns dies bestätigen. Es kommen wieder Experten aus vielen Bereichen der Politik, Wirtschaft und Wissenschaft zu Wort. Mit unterschiedlichen, manchmal konträren Auffassungen, so dass der Leser sich sein Urteil bilden kann. Diese Diskussion ist Voraussetzung für eine wirkliche Aufbruchstimmung.

Wer sich in der Wirtschaft umhört, weiß auch, welche Themen dabei im Vordergrund stehen: der Bürokratieabbau, denn noch immer behindern 5.000 Gesetze und Verordnungen wirtschaftlichen Erfolg, die Föderalismusreform, damit Entscheidungen zügiger fallen können, der Subventionsabbau, weil diese zukunftsfähige Strukturen ver-

hindern, die Förderung von Bildung, Forschung und Entwicklung, weil so unsere Position im internationalen Wettbewerb gestärkt wird, sowie Entscheidungen in Brüssel, die deutschen Unternehmen und Arbeitgebern eine faire Chance bieten.

In diesem Sinne: Begeistern wir uns für das Meer, das Schiff baut sich dann geradezu von selbst!

Dear Reader

It virtually seems to be national sport, to run down Germany as a business location making it look bad. Complaints are coming from all political parties, entrepreneurs and of course from the numerous self-styled experts. Abroad people are just shaking their heads. How is it possible that a recognised economic nation presents itself so depressive or even self-destructive!

The gist of what the French writer Antoine de Saint-Exupéry once wrote says: If you want to build a ship, don't ask the men to bring wood, to prepare tools and to divide up the work between them, instead teach them to feel longing for the wide endless sea. Relating these words to Germany as a business location it means that a sense of commercial optimism must be produced, which – striving to achieve a goal – takes over the whole country.

Through our projects we want to help to arouse this euphoria. Together with our partners in politics, industry, science and society we want to define, where the journey should take us, where we want to position ourselves in the international competition in future and above all: what we have to do to achieve these goals.

We should, even if it does not correspond to the present general spirit, remember our strengths, which the entire world speaks about, only we do not: the excellent training most Germans enjoyed, their industriousness and inventive spirit, the first-class infrastructure available in Germany and the technical know-how of its companies as well as the strength and creativity of its medium-size business sector, which is unique in the world. And whoever talks about these, also knows to consider the weaknesses and will not be overcome by every-day complaints.

This is also the spirit the concepts of our projects contain – always factual, also critical, but constantly optimistic. I think that also the reader of this volume will confirm our view. Again, experts from many fields of politics, industry and science have the word. With differentiating, sometimes contrary opinions, so that the reader can form his or her own view. This discussion is the prerequisite for real commercial optimism to develop.

Whoever asks around in the economy knows, which themes are of priority in this respect: the reduction of bureaucracy, because 5,000 laws and regulations are still hindering economic success, the reform of federal structures, thereby enabling faster decision-making processes, the reduction of subsidies, because they hinder the creation of future-oriented structures, the promotion of education, research and development, because in this way our position in international competition will be strengthened, as well as decisions in Brussels that offer a fair chance to German companies and employers.

In this sense: let us have enthusiasm for the sea, the ship will then almost build itself!

Christian Kirk
CEO of
MEDIEN GRUPPE KIRK AG

Inhalt/Contents

Wirtschaftsstandort Deutschland
Business Location Germany

Christian Kirk Vorstandsvorsitzender der Medien Gruppe Kirk AG	Vorwort Foreword	3
Wolfgang Clement Bundesminister für Wirtschaft und Arbeit	Für mehr wirtschaftliche Dynamik und mehr Beschäftigung in Deutschland For more economic vibrancy and more employment in Germany	6
Dr. Angela Merkel Vorsitzende der CDU Deutschlands und Vorsitzende der CDU/CSU-Fraktion im Bundestag	Chancen erkennen – Deutschland braucht eine neue soziale Marktwirtschaft Recognising chances – Germany needs a new social market economy	14
Jürgen R. Thumann Präsident des Bundesverbandes der Deutschen Industrie e. V.	Für einen attraktiven Standort – Visionen für die deutsche Wirtschaft For an attractive business location – visions for the German economy	22
Michael Sommer Vorsitzender des Deutschen Gewerkschaftsbundes	Für Reformen, gegen soziale Ungerechtigkeit For reforms, against social injustice	32
Dr. h. c. Ludwig Georg Braun Präsident des Deutschen Industrie- und Handelskammertages	Bürokratieabbau – DIHK für die Entlastung der Unternehmen Reducing bureaucracy – DIHK supports reducing the load on businesses	38
Hans Eichel Bundesminister der Finanzen	Sechs Jahre Euro – Erfahrungen und Perspektiven Six years of Euro – experiences and perspectives	46
Roland Koch Ministerpräsident des Landes Hessen	Frankfurt am Main, dynamischer Finanzplatz in der Mitte Europas Frankfurt on the Main, dynamic financial centre in the heart of Europe	54
Prof. Dr. Wolfgang Böhmer Ministerpräsident des Landes Sachsen-Anhalt	Neue Wege in der Wirtschaft – das Beispiel Sachsen-Anhalt New countries and new avenues to build up the economy	62
Prof. Dr. Rudolf Steinberg Präsident der Johann-Wolfgang-Goethe Universität, Frankfurt am Main	Wie schaffen wir Spitzenuniversitäten? How can we create top quality universities?	68
Prof. Dr. Karl Max Einhäupl Vorsitzender des Wissenschaftsrates	Die Reform des Bildungs- und Wissenschaftssystems The reform of the education and science system	78
Joachim Broudré-Gröger Ehem. Deutscher Botschafter in der VR China	Wachstumsmarkt China – Chance für den Standort Deutschland? Growth market China – a chance for the business location Germany?	88
Prof. Dr. Utz Claassen Vorstandsvorsitzender der EnBW Energie Baden-Württemberg AG	Mit Energie Zukunft gestalten Shaping the future with power	96

Inhalt/Contents

Hans-Georg Morawitz Geschäftsführer der Rhein Metall Defence Electronics GmbH Dr. Hanno Brandes Management Engineers GmbH & Co. KG International Consultants	Hohes Innovationstempo sichert Marktanteile High pace of innovation secures market shares	104
Albert Darboven Geschäftsführer der J. J. Darboven GmbH & Co. KG	Loyalität, Engagement und Liebe zum Produkt – Basis wirtschaftlichen Erfolgs Loyalty, engagement and love of the product – the basis of economic success	110
Otto Kentzler Präsident des Zentralverbandes des Deutschen Handwerks	Innovationen im Handwerk erschließen neue Märkte Innovations in skilled trade open up new markets	116
Béla Nikolai Anda Sprecher der Bundesregierung und Chef des Bundespresseamtes	Wie attraktiv ist die Darstellung des Standorts Deutschland in den Medien? How attractive is the presentation of Germany as a business location in the media?	124
Prof. Regina Ziegler Geschäftsführerin der Ziegler Film GmbH & Co. KG	Der deutsche Film – immer wieder ein Fall für ein Happy End German cinema – always a good case for a happy end	130
Prof. Dr. med. Peter Sawicki Leiter des Instituts für Qualität und Wirtschaftlichkeit im Gesundheitswesen	Die Zukunft einer gerechten Gesundheitsversorgung The future of just health care	136
Wolfgang Niersbach Geschäftsführender Vizepräsident des Organisationskomitees der FIFA Fußball-Weltmeisterschaft in Deutschland 2006	Die WM 2006 in Deutschland – was bringt sie der deutschen Wirtschaft? The Football World Championship 2006 in Germany – what benefit will it bring to the German economy?	144
Prof. Dr. Christoph Buchheim Fakultät für Volkswirtschaftslehre der Universität Mannheim	Ein vorübergehendes Formtief – zur Wirtschaftsgeschichte der BRD A momentary loss of form – concerning the economic history of the Federal Republic of Germany	150
	Verzeichnis der vorgestellten Unternehmen List of Companies	158
	Impressum Imprint	160

Reformprozess

Für mehr wirtschaftliche Dynamik und mehr Beschäftigung in Deutschland

For more economic vibrancy and more employment in Germany

Mehr wirtschaftliche Dynamik und Beschäftigung zu schaffen sowie die anhaltend hohe Arbeitslosigkeit zu verringern, sind und bleiben die Hauptziele der Wirtschafts- und Arbeitsmarktpolitik der Bundesregierung. Der durch die Agenda 2010 eingeleitete Prozess der grundlegenden Modernisierung von Wirtschaft und Gesellschaft muss daher konsequent weitergeführt werden.

Viel zu lange wurde an Symptomen kuriert, ohne die eigentlichen Ursachen der Wachstumsschwäche anzugehen. Dies hatte zur Folge, dass die Arbeitslosigkeit nicht ab-, sondern zunahm und das Wirtschaftswachstum im Trend immer geringer wurde. Mit jedem konjunkturellen Abschwung hat sich seit über zwei Jahrzehnten der Sockel der Arbeitslosigkeit erhöht. 2003 waren rund 4,4 Millionen Menschen arbeitslos gemeldet. Die durchschnittlichen jährlichen Wachstumsraten fielen von 2,8 Prozent in den 70ern und 2,3 Prozent in den 80ern auf nur noch 1,6 Prozent in den 90er-Jahren. Ein weiteres Absinken unseres Potenzialwachstums und damit in der Folge eine weiter steigende Arbeitslosigkeit können und dürfen wir nicht zulassen. Dies um so mehr, als der Globalisierungsprozess und die demographische Entwicklung neue Rahmendaten setzen, die den Druck auf strukturelle Reformen weiter erhöhen.

Mit der fortschreitenden weltweiten Öffnung der Güter- und Kapitalmärkte, sinkenden Transportkosten sowie technischem Fortschritt in der Informations- und Kommunikationsindustrie haben insbesondere die Güter- und Kapitalströme sowie die Arbeitskräftewanderung zugenommen. Dadurch verstärkt sich der Wettbewerb zwischen den Unternehmen und der Druck nimmt zu, immer wieder neue und bessere Produkte auf den Markt zu bringen und Produktionsverfahren zu optimieren. Für die Konsumenten bedeutet dies mehr Wahlmöglichkeiten und niedrigere Preise für Waren und Dienstleistungen. Den Investoren und Finanzanlegern eröffnet die Globalisierung Standortalternativen. Dies erhöht den Druck auf die Wirtschaftspolitik, für günstige Standortbedingungen zu sorgen. Die Konsequenzen wirtschaftspolitischer Weichenstellungen, die die Standortattraktivität mindern oder verbessern, werden in Zeiten fortschreitender Globalisierung immer schneller spürbar.

Durch den Globalisierungsprozess verschieben sich die Produktionsstrukturen. Der intensivierte Wettbewerb forciert den Strukturwandel in Richtung derjenigen Güter, die im Inland besonders effizient hergestellt werden können. Für Deutschland als Land, das reichlich mit Kapital und gut ausgebildeten Arbeitskräften ausgestattet ist, bedeutet dies, dass vermehrt kapital- und wissensintensive Produkte und weniger arbeitsintensive Güter hergestellt werden. Damit steigt die Bedeutung von Forschung, Innovation, Bildung und Ausbildung für den Standort Deutschland. Denn die Wettbewerbsfähigkeit unserer Unternehmen kann nur dann aufrechterhalten werden, wenn die Produktivität der Produktionsfaktoren steigt.

Auch die demographische Entwicklung wird zu Veränderungen in Gesellschaft und Wirtschaft führen. Während 2001 noch 28 Personen im Rentenalter 100 Personen im Erwerbsalter gegenüberstanden, werden es im Jahr 2030 nach der 10. koordinierten Bevölkerungsvorausberechnung des Statistischen Bundesamtes schon 47 sein. Dies hat gravierende Konsequenzen insbesondere für unsere sozialen Sicherungssysteme. Die finanziellen Lasten, die aus der veränderten Bevölkerungsstruktur resultieren, können nicht von einer Generation allein getragen werden. Dies würde entweder bedeuten, dass die Beitragssätze – und damit die Lohnnebenkosten mit allen Konsequenzen für Wachstum und Arbeitsplätze – auf ein nicht mehr tragbares Niveau steigen oder das Rentenniveau auf eine nicht hinnehmbare Höhe abgesenkt werden müssten. Beides wären einseitige und unsoziale Lösungen. Es müssen daher Finanzierungsstrukturen gefunden werden, die bei einer alternden und schrumpfenden Bevölkerung nachhaltig sind und die zu einer gleichmäßigen Belastung der Generationen führen. Darüber hinaus hat unsere Wirtschaft nach wie vor enorme finanzielle Belastungen durch die deutsche Wiedervereinigung zu verkraften. Der Transformationsprozess der neuen Länder ist noch nicht abgeschlossen. Diese einzigartige Herausforderung hat kein anderes Land in Europa zu meistern.

Alle diese strukturellen Anforderungen verlangen der nationalen Wirtschaftspolitik eine große Gestaltungskraft ab. Komplexe Probleme erfordern

Wolfgang Clement

Der Autor, 1940 in Bochum geboren, studierte Rechtswissenschaften in Münster. Nach einem Jahr als wissenschaftlicher Assistent am Institut für Prozessrecht in Marburg kehrte er 1968 wieder zur Westfälischen Rundschau zurück, wo er bis zum stellvertretenden Chefredakteur aufstieg. Ab 1987 leitete er knapp zwei Jahre als Chefredakteur die Hamburger Morgenpost, bis er 1989 als Chef der Staatskanzlei in die Politik und nach NRW zurückkehrte. 1995 übernahm er die Leitung des Ministeriums für Wirtschaft und Mittelstand, Technologie und Verkehr von NRW. Von 1998 bis 2002 war Wolfgang Clement Ministerpräsident des Landes Nordrhein-Westfalen, seit 2002 ist er Bundesminister für Wirtschaft und Arbeit.

The author was born in Bochum in 1940. He studied law at the University of Münster. After a year as a research assistant at the Institute of Trial Law in Marburg he returned to the newspaper Westfälische Rundschau in 1968, where he was appointed Deputy Chief Editor. From 1987 he was Chief Editor of the Hamburger Morgenpost for almost two years, then he returned to North Rhine-Westphalia and entered politics as Head of the State Chancellery of the State Government. In 1995 he took over as Head of the State Ministry of Commerce and Medium-Sized Industry, Technology and Transport in North Rhine-Westphalia. Wolfgang Clement was State Premier of North Rhine-Westphalia from 1998 to 2002 and has been Germany's Minister of Commerce and Labour since 2002.

The Process of Reform

Deutschland als Land, das reichlich mit Kapital und gut ausgebildeten Arbeitskräften ausgestattet ist, muss vermehrt kapital- und wissensintensive Produkte und weniger arbeitsintensive Güter herstellen.

As a country well-endowed with capital and a well-trained workforce, Germany must produce more capital and knowledge-intensive products and fewer labour-intensive products.

Creating more economic vibrancy and employment and reducing the high level of unemployment are and will remain the main aims of the German Government's economic and employment policies. The new process of fundamental modernisation of the German economy and society started by the 2010 Agenda must therefore be continued rigorously.

For far too long the symptoms of the economic doldrums were treated without anything being done about the actual causes. This resulted not in a decrease but in an increase in unemployment and in a downwards trend in economic growth. Permanent unemployment has risen with each economic downturn over the past two decades. In 2003 Germany had some 4.4 million registered unemployed. Average annual growth rates fell from 2.8 per cent in the 1970s and from 2.3 per cent in the 1980s to only 1.6 per cent in the 1990s. Germany cannot and must not permit a further downturn in economic growth and hence a further increase in unemployment. This is all the more the case as the globalisation process and demographic development are setting new parameters which further increase pressure on structural reforms.

With the continuing international opening of markets for goods and capital, sinking freight costs and technical progress in the information and communications industry, the flow of goods and capital and labour migration especially have increased. This reinforces inter-firm competition, and the pressure to bring new products and services onto the market and develop new production processes increases apace. For the consumer this means a wider selection and lower prices of goods and services. And globalisation gives investors a wider choice of locations. This increases pressure on economic policies to ensure the creation of favourable location conditions. In these times of progressing globalisation, the consequences of changes in economic direction that reduce or improve the attractiveness of locations are making themselves felt with increasing rapidity.

The process of globalisation is displacing production structures. More intense competition is forcing structural change towards those goods that can be produced particularly efficiently by the domestic market. This means that, as a country which is well-endowed with capital and a well-trained workforce, Germany must produce more capital and knowledge-intensive products and fewer labour-intensive products. This increases the significance of research, innovation, education and vocational training for Germany. The competitiveness of our business sector can only be maintained if the productivity of its production factors increases.

Germany's demographic development will also lead to changes in society and the economy. While there were 28 pensioners for every 100 gainfully employed person in 2001, this former figure will rise to 47 by 2003 according to the 10th coordinated population forecast calculations of the Federal Statistics Office. This will have serious consequences for our social welfare systems. The financial burdens which will result from the altered population structure cannot be borne by one generation alone. This would either mean that the contribution rates to the German social insurance system – and hence associated wage costs, with all the consequences for economic growth and employment – would rise to an impossible level or the level of state pensions would have to be reduced to an unacceptable level. Both would be one-sided and socially irresponsible solutions. Financial systems must be found that can be sustained even with an ageing and shrinking population and which lead to an equal burden for all generations. In addition, our economy still has to bear financial burdens resulting from German reunification. The process of transformation in Eastern Germany is still incomplete and this is a unique challenge that no other country in Europe has to master.

All these structural challenges require a major dose of creativity from Germany's national economic policies. Complex problems demand different solutions. Consequently the German Government's efforts to carry out reform are aimed at all

Reformprozess

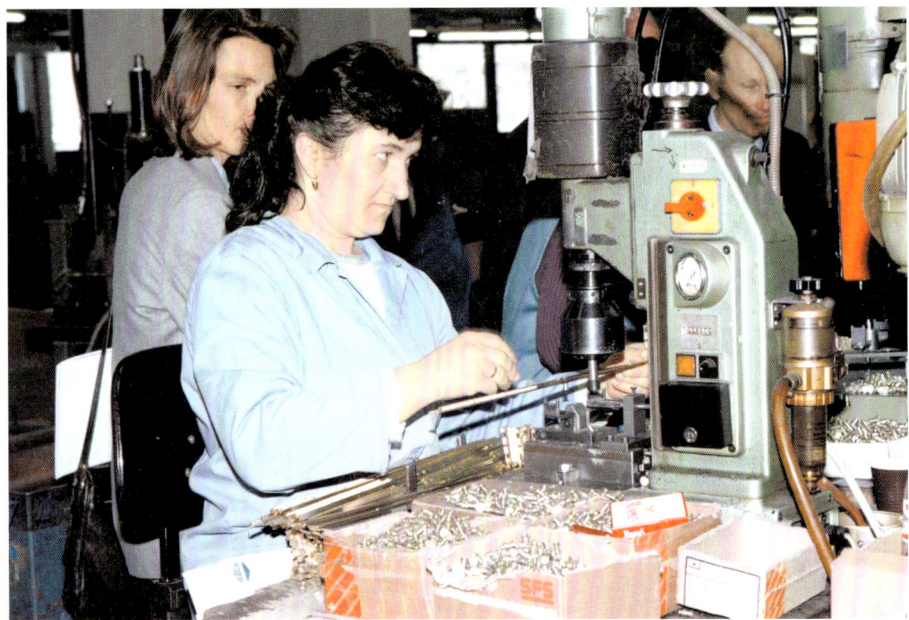

2030 werden 100 Erwerbstätigen 47 Rentner gegenüberstehen.
In 2030 there will be 100 people in the workforce for every 47 pensioners.

differenzierte Lösungsansätze. Daher setzt die Bundesregierung mit ihren Reformanstrengungen den Hebel an allen Faktoren an, die Wachstum und Beschäftigung fördern können. Dazu gehören insbesondere mehr Leistung, mehr Innovationen und mehr Investitionen. Die Agenda 2010 war ein erster Schritt. Sie steht für mutige, zielführende Strukturreformen in Deutschland und markiert einen Wendepunkt in der Wirtschafts- und Arbeitsmarktpolitik. Mit der konsequenten Umsetzung der Reformmaßnahmen hat die Bundesregierung im In- und Ausland die Reformfähigkeit Deutschlands demonstriert.

Die in der Agenda 2010 enthaltenen Maßnahmen zielen darauf ab, Eigenverantwortung, Kreativität und Risikobereitschaft einerseits, Solidarität und soziale Gerechtigkeit andererseits in eine neue Balance zu bringen. Die Agenda 2010 bildet ein Gesamtpaket, mit dem die Lohnnebenkosten gesenkt, Impulse für Investitionen und Konsum gegeben, Anreizmechanismen auf der Angebots- und Nachfrageseite des Arbeitsmarktes verbessert sowie Selbstständigkeit und Eigeninitiative gefördert werden. Dies wird dazu beitragen, das Wachstumspotenzial der deutschen Volkswirtschaft zu erhöhen und damit die Voraussetzungen für mehr Beschäftigung schaffen.

Arbeitsmarkt

Die Reformen auf dem Arbeitsmarkt stehen im Zeichen von mehr Eigenverantwortung und Flexibilität, von Fördern und Fordern, kurz: von Anreizen für mehr Leistung. Mehr Möglichkeiten und verbesserte Anreize zur Aufnahme einer Arbeit entstehen durch Mini- und Midi-Jobs, Ich-AGs, bessere Hinzuverdienstmöglichkeiten für Transferempfänger und die Intensivierung der Arbeitsvermittlung. Mit finanziellen Einbußen bzw. Sanktionen beim Arbeitslosengeld I und II muss dagegen rechnen, wer eine zumutbare Arbeit ablehnt. Die ehemalige Bundesanstalt für Arbeit – jetzt Bundesagentur für Arbeit – wird zu einem modernen Dienstleister umgebaut. Statt Arbeitslosigkeit zu verwalten, wird sie in die Lage versetzt, effizient in Arbeit zu vermitteln. Ziel der Begrenzung der Bezugsdauer des Arbeitslosengeldes auf maximal 12 bzw. 18 Monate für die unter bzw. über 55-Jährigen ist es, die Praxis der Frühverrentung zu beenden. Durch die Zusammenlegung von Arbeitslosen- und Sozialhilfe zum Arbeitslosengeld II wird das bisherige Nebeneinander von zwei staatlichen Fürsorgeleistungen und das damit verbundene Verschieben von Kosten zwischen den Trägern – den Kommunen und dem Bund – beendet. Ziel ist es, die Eingliederungschancen der erwerbsfähigen Hilfebedürftigen in Beschäftigung zu verbessern. Dies soll insbesondere durch eine auf den Einzelfall ausgerichtete intensive Beratung und Betreuung sowie Verbesserung des Betreuungsschlüssels zwischen Fallmanagern und Hilfebedürftigen erreicht werden.

Durch die Änderungen beim Kündigungsschutz und bei der Befristung von Arbeitsverträgen werden arbeitsrechtliche Einstellungshindernisse abgebaut. In Betrieben mit zehn oder weniger Arbeitnehmern gilt der Kündigungsschutz nicht für Arbeitnehmer, die ab Januar 2004 neu eingestellt werden. Für bereits beschäftigte Arbeitnehmer in Betrieben zwischen sechs und zehn Beschäftigten bleibt er erhalten. Im Interesse größerer Rechtssicherheit wird bei betriebsbedingten Kündigungen die Sozialauswahl auf vier Kriterien – die Dauer der Betriebszugehörigkeit, das Lebensalter, die Unterhaltspflichten und die Schwerbehinderung des Arbeitnehmers – beschränkt. Von der Sozialauswahl können Arbeitnehmer ausgenommen werden, deren Weiterbeschäftigung wegen ihrer Kenntnisse, Fähigkeiten und Leistungen oder zur Erhaltung einer ausgewogenen Personalstruktur im berechtigten betrieblichen Interesse liegt. Im Falle einer betriebsbedingten Kündigung erhalten Arbeitgeber und Arbeitnehmer die Möglichkeit einer einfachen und kostengünstigen außergerichtlichen Klärung. Für Existenzgründer wird die befristete Beschäftigung von Arbeitnehmern erleichtert. In den ersten vier Jahren des Bestehens eines neu gegründeten Unternehmens können befristete Arbeitsverträge ohne Sachgrund bis zur Dauer von vier Jahren abgeschlossen werden.

Rente

Das Aussetzen der Rentenanpassung zum 1. Juli 2004, die Absenkung der Schwankungsreserve der Rentenkassen und die volle Übernahme des Beitrags zur Pflegeversicherung durch die Rentner sollen den Beitragssatz zur Rentenversicherung stabil halten. Darüber hinaus wird durch die Einführung eines so genannten „Nachhaltigkeitsfaktors" in die Formel für die Rentenberechnung das sich ändernde Zahlenverhältnis zwischen Rentnern und Beitragszahlern angemessen berücksichtigt. So werden die Lasten aus der demographischen Entwicklung gerecht auf Beitragszahler und Rentner verteilt. Zusätzlich werden die bestehenden Anreize zur Frühverrentung abgebaut, um das tatsächliche Renteneintrittsalter anzuheben.

Gesundheit

Die mit dem GKV-Modernisierungsgesetz durchgeführten Reformen zielen darauf ab, den Beitragssatz und damit die Lohnnebenkosten zu senken. Dies führt insbesondere bei lohnintensiven kleinen und mittleren Betrieben zu Entlastungen. Darüber hinaus verbessern sie Qualität und Wirtschaftlichkeit der Versorgung und stärken die Eigenverantwortung der Patienten.

Zu den wichtigsten Reformmaßnahmen zählen: mehr Wahlmöglichkeiten für freiwillig Versicherte bei Versicherungsumfang und Finanzierung, die Herausnahme nicht verschreibungspflichtiger Arzneimittel aus der Erstattungspflicht, die Zulassung des Versandhandels von Arzneimitteln und des Mehrbesitzes von Apotheken, die Herausnahme bzw. Einschränkung der Erstattung von versicherungsfremden Leistungen, höhere prozentuale

The Process of Reform

factors that can assist growth and employment. These especially include increased performance, more innovation and more investment. The 2010 Agenda was a first step. It stands for courageous effective structural reforms in Germany and marks a turning-point in its economic and employment market policies. With the consistent implementation of the reforms the German Government has demonstrated this country's ability to change.

The steps in the 2010 Agenda are aimed at "re-jigging" personal responsibility, creativity and the readiness to take risks on the one hand and solidarity and social justice on the other. The 2010 Agenda forms an overall package with which associated wage costs can be reduced, stimuli for investment and consumption can be provided, stimuli on the supply and demand side of the employment market can be improved and personal independence and initiative can be promoted. This will contribute to an increase in the potential for growth, thereby creating a favourable environment for more employment.

The employment market

The reforms on the employment market are dominated by more personal responsibility and flexibility and by sanction and support (carrot and stick methods) – in short, by incentives for more effort. More opportunities and improved incentives to take up a job are being developed through the "Mini-Jobs" and the "Midi-Jobs", the so-called "Ich-AGs", or "Me Ltds", the opportunity for state beneficiaries to earn more and the increase in job placement efforts. On the other hand, those refusing to accept a reasonable job offer will have to reckon with financial penalties and reduced benefits in the so-called Unemployment Benefit I and II. The former Federal Employment Service – now renamed the Federal Employment Agency – is being converted into a modern service provider. Instead of administering unemployment, it will be capable of finding work for its clients efficiently. The aim of limiting the eligibility period for unemployment benefit to a maximum of 12 months for those under 55 years of age and to 18 months for those over 55 years of age is end the practice of early retirement, thereby reducing the strain on the state pension coffers. The combining of the former unemployment assistance and social welfare benefits and renaming them Unemployment Benefit II will end the former "side-by-side co-existence" of two similar state benefits and the related shoving of the costs and responsibilities backwards and forwards between the former Federal Employment Service and municipalities. The aim is to improve the chances of reintegration into the workforce for beneficiaries who are able to work.

Die Reform der Handwerksordnung wird den Wettbewerb im Handwerk stärken und das Angebot für die Verbraucher verbessern.

The reform of the Trades and Handicrafts Regulations will strengthen competition in the qualified trades and improve services available to the consumer.

This is to be achieved by intensive advice and assistance directed especially at individual cases as well as improving the level assistance between case managers and their clients.

The barriers to hiring new employees are being broken down by the changes in job protection legislation and temporary employment contracts. In companies with ten or less employees the job protection regulations do not apply to those employees hired on or after 1 January 2004. The regulations still apply to those employed before that date in companies with between six and ten employees. In the interests of greater legal security the criteria for redundancies will be restricted to four factors – the length of service, the age of the employee(s) affected, the number of dependants (if any) and whether the employee is seriously handicapped. These factors do not apply to employees whose skills, knowledge, expertise or performance are of particular value to the company or whom the company wishes to retain in order to maintain a balanced staffing structure. In the eventuality of redundancy both employee and employer will have the opportunity of clarifying the matter in a simple, low-cost conciliation procedure. For those who have formed their own companies it will be easier to employ staff on a temporary basis. In the first four years of a new company's existence, temporary employment contracts can be terminated without reason within the first four years.

State pensions

The decision not to adjust pensions on 1 July 2004, the reduction of the level of the reserves of the state pension organisations and the obligation of pensioners to pay their entire nursing care insurance premiums is intended to keep the social insurance premium for state pensions stable. In addition, the introduction of a so-called "sustainability factor" into the formula for calculating state pensions take adequate account of alter the changing relationship between pensioners and those currently paying into the state retirement insurance scheme. This will distribute the burden of demographic development onto the shoulders of those paying into the system and the pensioners more fairly. As well, current incentives to early retirement will be reduced in order to raise the actual official retirement age and thereby reduce the pressure on the funds in the state pension coffers.

Health

The reforms implemented in the Public Health Insurance Modernisation Law are aimed at lowering the percentage of the premium and hence cutting associated wage costs. This will lead to relief in the financial burden for small and medium-sized wage-intensive companies in particular. The reforms will also improve the quality and economy of medical care and increase the patients' share in the cost of treatment. The most important reforms

Reformprozess

Zuzahlungen sowie die Ausgliederung des Zahnersatzes aus der gesetzlichen Krankenversicherung ab 2005 und die Finanzierung des Krankengeldes ausschließlich durch die Versicherten ab 2006.

Steuern

Die beschlossenen Steuersenkungen zum 1. Januar 2004 und 2005 werden flankierend zu den Strukturreformen Wachstumsimpulse für die Wirtschaft geben, indem sie durch die Entlastung von Unternehmen und Bürgern die Investitions- und Konsumbereitschaft steigern. Der Eingangs- und Höchststeuersatz wurden in zwei Stufen auf 15 Prozent und 42 Prozent abgesenkt und erreichen damit historische Tiefstände. Außerdem werden Subventionen und Steuervergünstigungen abgebaut.

Mittelstand und Bürokratieabbau

Wirtschaftliche Dynamik, die in Deutschland zu einem großen Teil vom Mittelstand ausgeht, kann sich nur entfalten, wenn Innovationen und Investitionen ungehindert getätigt werden können. Dazu bedarf es offener Märkte, Wettbewerb und möglichst geringer Hemmnisse und Belastungen. Mit der „Initiative Bürokratieabbau" zielt die Bundesregierung darauf ab, unnötige Verwaltungs- und Verfahrensvorschriften abzubauen, um die Wettbewerbsfähigkeit des Standorts Deutschland zu stärken. Die Reform der Handwerksordnung, die Teil der „Initiative Bürokratieabbau" ist, wird den Wettbewerb im Handwerk stärken und das Angebot für die Verbraucher verbessern. Der Meisterzwang gilt seit Beginn des Jahres 2004 nur noch in 41 statt bisher 94 Handwerken. Für die Auswahl der Handwerke wurde neben der Gefahrgeneigtheit auch die Ausbildungsleistung berücksichtigt. Darüber hinaus können sich langjährige Gesellen auch ohne Meisterbrief selbstständig machen. Durch den erleichterten Berufszugang im Handwerk können das bestehende Potenzial für Neugründungen und kleinere Handwerksbetriebe mobilisiert und Beschäftigung gefördert werden.

Bildung und Innovationen

Neben dem kontinuierlichen Abbau von Inflexibilitäten auf den Märkten wird es in Zukunft verstärkt darauf ankommen, in Bildung, Innovation, Wissenschaft und Forschung sowie in die öffentliche Infrastruktur und zugunsten von Familien zu investieren. Nur so wird der Standort Deutschland im internationalen Wettbewerb auch weiterhin attraktiv bleiben. Denn die wichtigsten Ressourcen unseres Landes sind die Menschen mit ihren Fähigkeiten und ihrem Erfindungsreichtum sowie die Innovationskraft seiner Unternehmen, zu deren ureigenen Aufgaben Forschung und die Entwicklung neuer marktfähiger Produkte zählen. Die Bundesregierung setzt mit ihrer Politik an diesen Stellen an: Sie gestaltet innovationsgerechte Rahmenbedingungen und fördert Forschung und Entwicklung. Sie hat 2004 zum „Jahr der Innovation" gemacht. Gemeinsam mit Wirtschaft, Wissenschaft und Gewerkschaften hat sie die Initiative „Partner für Innovation" ins Leben gerufen. Ziel ist es, das Innovationssystem auf allen Ebenen zu stärken, Hemmnisse abzubauen und neues Vertrauen in die Leistungsfähigkeit Deutschlands zu wecken.

Die Reformpolitik der Bundesregierung schafft wichtige Voraussetzungen für mehr wirtschaftliche Dynamik und wieder mehr Beschäftigung. Sie kann jedoch nur erfolgreich sein, wenn auch die makroökonomischen Bedingungen stimmen. Denn nur in einem wachstums- und stabilitätsorientierten makroökonomischen Umfeld können sich strukturelle Reformen umfassend in wirtschaftliche Dynamik umsetzen und ihre volle Wirksamkeit entfalten. Strukturreformen müssen daher zusammengehen mit einer glaubwürdigen Finanzpolitik, einer stabilitätsorientierten Geldpolitik und einer beschäftigungsorientierten Lohnpolitik.

Erste Erfolge und Perspektiven

Der zur zweiten Jahreshälfte 2003 in Gang gekommene Abbau der saisonbereinigten Arbeitslosigkeit deutet darauf hin, dass die bereits umgesetzten Reformmaßnahmen zu wirken beginnen. Die Bundesregierung sieht darin eine erste Bestätigung, dass sie den richtigen Kurs für mehr Beschäftigung und weniger Arbeitslosigkeit eingeschlagen hat. Damit ist jedoch der Reformprozess in Deutschland noch nicht abgeschlossen. Angesichts der fortschreitenden Globalisierung und des dadurch zunehmenden Wettbewerbsdrucks sowie der langfristigen Folgen aus der demographischen Entwicklung bleibt es eine wirtschaftspolitische Daueraufgabe, für attraktive wirtschaftliche Rahmenbedingungen zu sorgen.

Die Chancen für ein gutes Gelingen der Reformpolitik sind günstig. Deutschland ist als größte Volkswirtschaft Europas zugleich auch der wichtigste Markt auf dem Kontinent. Am 1. Mai 2004 sind zehn Länder aus Mittel- und Osteuropa sowie dem Mittelmeerraum der EU beigetreten. Damit entstand ein Binnenmarkt von ca. 450 Millionen Einwohnern. Für Deutschland eröffnen sich hierdurch große Chancen. Wegen der Exportstärke seiner Industrie und der räumlichen Nähe zu den Beitrittsländern wird Deutschland besonders von den Gewinnen aus der verstärkten Arbeitsteilung und der damit einhergehenden Wohlstandssteigerung in den Beitrittsländern profitieren. Die Stärke Deutschlands beruht auf nach wie vor guten Rahmenbedingungen für die Ansiedlung von Investitionen: stabiles Preisniveau, niedrige Steuern, sozialer Frieden, vor allem aber gut ausgebildete Arbeitskräfte und eine Führungsposition in der technologischen Entwicklung.

Auf diese Stärken werden wir setzen und unsere Standortvorteile weiter ausbauen. Die Modernisierung unserer Gesellschaft ist in vollem Gange. Den eingeschlagenen Reformprozess gilt es konsequent weiterzuführen, damit wir und die nach uns folgenden Generationen auch in Zukunft von Wachstum, Wohlstand und sozialer Gerechtigkeit profitieren können. ■

Mit der weltweiten Öffnung der Güter- und Kapitalmärkte, sinkenden Transportkosten sowie technischem Fortschritt in der Informations- und Kommunikationsindustrie verstärkt sich der Wettbewerb zwischen den Unternehmen und der Druck nimmt zu, immer wieder neue und bessere Produkte auf den Markt zu bringen und Produktionsverfahren zu optimieren.

The Process of Reform

include more choice for those voluntarily insured in the public system in terms of the extent of insurance and financing, making non-prescription medication non-reimbursable for insurance purposes, permitting mail order purchase of medication and letting pharmacists own more than one pharmacy, restricting reimbursement for non-insurance services or making them totally no-reimbursable, introducing higher co-payments, transferring payment for dentures from the public health insurance system to private insurance (via the public system) from 2005 and making contributors to the social insurance scheme finance their own sick pay 100 per cent through the public system as from 2006.

Taxation

Together with structural reform the tax reductions effective as from 1 January 2004 and 2005 respectively, will provide further stimulus for growth by increasing preparedness to invest and consume

With the international opening of the markets for goods and capital, the reduction in freight costs and with technical progress in the information and communications industry, increasing inter-firm competition and pressure will make for better products and improved production methods.

through the decrease in the tax burden on the citizen and on companies. The initial and top tax rates were reduced in two steps to 15 and 42 per cent respectively, thereby achieving the lowest levels in Germany's history. Subsidies and tax relief will also be reduced.

The medium business sector and the reduction in bureaucracy

Economic dynamism, which springs in large part from Germany's medium-size business sector, can only develop if innovations and investment can be made unhindered. This requires open markets, competition and as few hurdles and burdens as possible. The German Government's "Bureaucracy Reduction" Scheme is aiming at reducing unnecessary administrative and procedural regulations in order to increase Germany's competitiveness. The reform of the Trades and Handicrafts Regulations, which is part of the reduction in bureaucracy, will boost competition in the qualified trades and improve their services to consumers. Since the beginning of 2004 the requirement of a master tradesman's qualification in order to open one's own trades firm has applied to only 41 trades instead of 94. The trades concerned were selected for the degree of danger the work involves and the degree to which they offer apprenticeships and traineeships. As well, journeymen with many years' experience can also set up in business without having to acquire or have a master tradesman's qualification.

Education and innovations

Apart from the continual reduction in inflexibility in the markets, it will be increasingly important to invest in education, innovation, sciences and research in future as well as in public infrastructure and for the benefit of families. This is the only way Germany will continue to remain attractive in the face of international competition. The most important resources of our country are its people, with their skills and their inventiveness, and the innovative power of its business community, whose basic tasks include research into and development of new marketable products. These are the areas where the German Government is applying its policies. It is creating conditions conducive to innovation and promoting research and development, and made 2004 the "Year of Innovation". Together with the business community, the scientific community and the trade unions the Government has created the "Partners for Innovation" scheme, which is aimed at strengthening the innovation system at all levels, removing barriers and awakening new confidence in Germany's capabilities.

The German Government's reform policies are creating significant conditions for more economic dynamism and more employment. But they can only succeed if the macro-economic conditions are right. Only in a macro-economic environment oriented to growth and stability can structural reforms be implemented and develop as effectively as possible. Structural reforms must therefore be accompanied by credible financial policies, stability-oriented fiscal policies and employment-oriented wage policies.

The first successes and perspectives for the future

The drop in seasonally-adjusted unemployment in the second half of 2003 indicated that those reforms already implemented were beginning to take effect. The German Government sees this as the first confirmation that it has taken the right steps to achieve more employment and less unemployment. However this does not mean that the reform process in Germany has been completed. In view of progressing globalisation and the resulting pressure from competition, along with the long-term consequences of Germany's demographic development it will remain a permanent economic and political task to ensure attractive basic economic conditions.

The chances that the Government's reform policies will succeed are favourable. As the largest economy in Europe, Germany is also the most important market on the continent. On 1 May 2004, ten countries from central and eastern Europe and the Mediterranean region joined the European Union. This created a domestic market of some 450 million residents and opened up major opportunities for Germany. Because of the export strength of its industry and its geographical proximity to these new members, Germany will benefit especially from the profits gained from the increased division of labour and the accompanying increases in prosperity in these countries. Germany's strength is still based on good basic business conditions for establishing investment – stable prices, low taxes, social peace, but in particular well-trained employees and a leading position in technological development.

We will concentrate on these strengths and continue to expand the advantages of our location. The modernisation of German society is in full swing and the already-commenced reform process must be continued rigorously in order that we and the generations that follow us can benefit from growth, prosperity and social justice in future as well. ■

Company Profile

Mit regionaler Kompetenz zum internationalen Erfolg

International success through regional competence

Der DPD sorgt dafür, dass jeden Tag mehr als 1,4 Millionen Pakete ihr Ziel erreichen. Als einer der führenden Logistik-Dienstleister Europas ist der DPD eine Franchise-Organisation und bietet seinen Kunden eine Vielzahl spezifischer Services – von Nachnahmesendungen bis zu individuellen, speziell zugeschnittenen Produkten für die Beschaffungslogistik. Aschaffenburg ist der Hauptsitz eines nahtlosen Netzwerks, das aus rund 470 Depots in mehr als 30 Ländern besteht und eine Flotte von ca. 13.500 Fahrzeugen unterhält. Mehr als 200.000 Geschäftskunden zeugen von der anhaltenden Erfolgsstory des DPD.

Diese nahm ihren Anfang, als vor einem Vierteljahrhundert die klassischen Versandformen Kleingut, Postpaket und Bahnexpress den Anforderungen des wachsenden Marktes nicht mehr genügten. 18 mittelständische deutsche Spediteure erkannten den neuen Bedarf und legten im April 1976 den Grundstein für Deutschlands ersten privaten Paketdienst. Die Philosophie dieser Pioniere war denkbar einfach und doch visionär: Pakettransport im Auftrag gewerblicher Kunden – unkompliziert, schnell und sicher.

Das neue Angebot stieß auf rege Nachfrage. Die Zahl der beförderten Pakete stieg binnen kurzer Zeit beträchtlich an, sodass der DPD Mitte der 80er-Jahre schließlich die Marktführerschaft unter den privaten deutschen Paketdiensten errang. Anfangs war das System auf Deutschland beschränkt, wurde aber schon bald auf Europa ausgedehnt. Zunehmenden Konzentrationsprozessen im Markt begegneten die Verantwortlichen des DPD Anfang der 90er-Jahre mit der Einführung eines Franchisesystems.

Ende der 90er-Jahre wurden die Kontinuität, Stabilität und Zukunftsfähigkeit des DPD erneut gestärkt. Nach erfolgreichen Gesprächen mit der französischen La Poste erwarb deren Tochter GeoPost sukzessive rund 85 Prozent der DPD GmbH & Co. KG und damit auch die Stimmenmehrheit im Aufsichtsrat. Die Verbindung bringt für beide Partner starke Vorteile und Synergieeffekte – für den einen die mittelständische Struktur des DPD, für den anderen die Konzernstruktur der GeoPost.

Das Ziel ist klar: Der DPD wird zum führenden Paketdienstleister auf den Straßen Europas und forciert den Ausbau seines weltweiten Netzwerks, um sich als Spezialist für KEP-Dienstleistungen noch stärker international zu etablieren. Die Qualität der angebotenen Leistungen will die Geschäftsführung um CEO Dr. Claude Béglé garantieren, indem der DPD sein Service- und Paketportfolio auch zukünftig ausschließlich an den Bedürfnissen seiner Kunden ausrichtet.

Im Vordergrund steht dabei die persönliche Kundenbetreuung vor Ort, kombiniert mit den Vorteilen eines europaweiten Netzwerks. Kunden in der Region profitieren von der Nähe des jeweiligen DPD Standortes unter anderem durch die konstanten und sehr guten Paketlaufzeiten. Zusätzliche Leistungen, beispielsweise Nachnahme- und Expressversand sowie andere individuelle Services, runden das Angebot des DPD ab. ■

Company Profile

DPD CEO Dr. Claude Béglé.

DPD Deutscher Paket Dienst, ensures that more than 1.4 million parcels reach their destination daily. Being one of the leading providers of logistic services in Europe, DPD is a franchise organisation that offers its clients a number of specific services – ranging from cash-on-delivery parcels through to individually, especially tailored products for procurement logistics. The headquarters of a seamless network consisting of around 470 depots in more than 30 countries and a fleet of approx. 13,500 vehicles is located in Aschaffenburg. More than 200,000 corporate clients give evidence of DPD's ongoing success story.

It all started when about a quarter of a century ago, the classical forms of dispatch like small items, postal package and rail express goods did not meet with the requirements of growing markets any longer. 18 medium-size German forwarding agents recognised the newly upcoming demand and laid the foundation for Germany's first private parcel service in April 1976. The philosophy these pioneers had was rather simple and yet visionary: delivering parcels on behalf of commercial clients – uncomplicated, fast and safe.

The new provision had a great demand. Within a short time, the number of forwarded parcels rose tremendously, so that DPD finally grew to be the market leader among private German parcel services. In the beginning, the system was only limited to cover Germany, but soon it was extended throughout Europe. Responsible players at DPD confronted increasing processes of concentration in the market by introducing a franchise system at the beginning of the nineties.

At the end of the nineties, DPD's continuity, stability and future-oriented outlook was strengthened again. After successful negotiations with the French La Poste, its subsidiary GeoPost acquired successively about 85 per cent of DPD GmbH & Co. KG and thereby also the majority in the supervisory board. This connection bears strong advantages for both partners and also considerable synergy effects – for some the medium-sized structure of DPD, for others the corporate structure of GeoPost.

However, the aim is clear: DPD will become the leading parcel service on Europe's roads and is pushing the expansion of its global network, in order to position itself internationally as specialist for CEP services (courier, express and postal delivery services) even stronger. Management led by CEO Dr. Claude Béglé guarantees the quality of services provided by orienting DPD's services and parcel portfolio exclusively towards the needs of its clients also in future.

A local personal customer service combined with the advantages of a European-wide network is of utmost priority in this connection. Customers in the region benefit from proximity of their relevant DPD location, also because of the constant and excellent delivery times for parcels. DPD rounds off its offering by providing additional services, for example cash on delivery and express dispatch as well as other individual services. ■

In time with business.

DPD Deutscher Paket Dienst GmbH & Co.KG

CEO & Sprecher der Geschäftsführung/
CEO & Spokesman of the Board:
Dr. Claude Béglé

Geschäftsführer/Management Board:
Rainer Braun [Operations and Quality Control]
Dr. Armin Bohnhoff [Technology]
Peter Burmeister [Finance and Administration]
Wolfgang Lehmacher [Marketing & Sales]
Marek Zulawski [International Network]

Aufsichtsrat/Supervisor:
Arnold Schroven [Vorsitzender]/[Chairman]

Gesellschafter/Shareholders:
- GeoPost International Management
  & Development Holding GmbH
  (Mehrheitsgesellschafterin mit 83,32 Prozent)
- DPD Systemlogistik GmbH & Co. KG
  (Minderheitsgesellschafterin mit 10,47 Prozent)
- DPD Zeitfracht GmbH & Co. KG
  (Minderheitsgesellschafterin mit 6,21 Prozent)
- GeoPost International Management
  & Development Holding GmbH
  [majority shareholder with 83.32%]
- DPD Systemlogistik GmbH & Co.KG
  [minority shareholder with 10.47%]
- DPD Zeitfracht GmbH & Co.KG
  [minority shareholder with 6.21%]

Mitarbeiter/Employees:
über 22.000 Personen, more than 22,000 people

Umsatz/Turnover (2004):
EUR 1,3 Milliarden (geschätzt)
EUR 1.3 billion (estimate)

Kerngeschäft/Core business:
Paneuropäische Standard- und Expressdienstleistungen
Pan-European parcel and express services

Paketvolumen/Parcel volume (2004):
mehr als 1,4 Millionen Pakete pro Tag
more than 1.4 million parcels a day

Depots/Depots:
mehr als 470 in Europa
more than 470 in Europe

Fahrzeuge/Vehicles: 13.500 in Europa/Europe

Anschrift/Address:
Wailandtstraße 1
D-63741 Aschaffenburg
Telefon +49 (6021) 492 7074
Telefax +49 (6021) 492 7099
E-Mail pr@dpd.de
Internet www.dpd.net

Chancen

Chancen erkennen – Deutschland braucht eine neue soziale Marktwirtschaft

*Recognising chances –
Germany needs a new social market economy*

Deutschland ist ein starkes Land mit einem enormen Zukunftspotenzial. Angesichts der vielen leistungsfähigen Menschen und der großen Reputation Deutschlands in Europa und der Welt – „Made in Germany" ist zu einem weltweiten Markenzeichen geworden – haben wir deshalb auch weiterhin eine gute Ausgangsbasis.

Wer hätte nach 1945 geglaubt, dass Deutschland dies erreichen kann? Es war die soziale Marktwirtschaft Ludwig Erhards, die den Ordnungsrahmen schuf, in dem sich der Fleiß, die Leistungsbereitschaft und der Aufbruchswille vieler Deutscher zu dem Erfolg des Wiederaufbaus bündeln konnten. Markt und wirtschaftlicher Wettbewerb einerseits, gemeinsame Solidarität und soziale Sicherheit andererseits konnten in eine wirkungsvolle Balance gebracht werden. In dieser ersten Gründerzeit der Bundesrepublik Deutschland wurden die Grundlagen für den „Wohlstand für alle" (Ludwig Erhard) gelegt. Die Erfolge der sozialen Marktwirtschaft halfen auch, die Wiedervereinigung Deutschlands als gemeinsame Aufgabe aller Deutschen zu schultern.

Doch mit der Aufhebung der jahrzehntelangen Teilung Deutschlands und Europas zeigten sich auch deutliche Anzeichen eines tiefgreifenden Wandels in Wirtschaft und Gesellschaft. Der Wertewandel verändert tradiertes Verhalten in der Gesellschaft, die Umstrukturierung der Arbeitswelt führt zu erheblich gestiegenen Anforderungen an (Weiter-)Bildung, Flexibilität und Unternehmenskommunikation, neue Technologien ermöglichen weltweite Kommunikation und verändern grundlegend bisheriges Wissen über unsere Welt, die Globalisierung führt zu weltweitem Kapitalexport, wirtschaftlicher Standortkonkurrenz und Wettbewerb auf international zugänglichen Märkten, und die Erweiterung der Europäischen Union schafft einen Binnenmarkt mit knapp 450 Millionen Konsumenten. Auf diese veränderten Bedingungen – und der Wandel geht immer schneller weiter – muss sich Deutschland einstellen. Konkret heißt das: Deutschland braucht weit tiefer gehende strukturelle Reformen, damit die Wachstumsraten wieder größer werden und Deutschland wieder mit zu den Ländern gehört, die an der Spitze des wirtschaftlichen Fortschritts die Zukunftsgesellschaft des 21. Jahrhunderts gestalten. Und um es gleich vorwegzunehmen: Ich bin davon überzeugt, dass Deutschland dazu die Kraft hat.

Das gelingt aber nur, wenn wir uns der Realität stellen: Zwar haben wir in unserem Land einen nach wie vor hohen Lebensstandard, aber in immer mehr Bereichen beginnen wir, von der Substanz zu leben. Das reicht vielleicht für die Gegenwart aus, aber nicht für das Morgen. Wie wollen wir in Zukunft unser Geld verdienen? Wie halten wir stand in der globalen Standortkonkurrenz? Wie sichern wir wieder neu Wohlstand und soziale Sicherheit? Wie können Freiheit und Gerechtigkeit in eine neue Balance gebracht werden? Die Antwort auf diese Fragen kann nur heißen: Wir müssen die unser Land tragenden Strukturen der Sozialen Marktwirtschaft auf eine qualitativ neue Stufe heben – wir brauchen eine neue soziale Marktwirtschaft. Mit ihr wird deutlich, dass wir uns in Deutschland angesichts von Globalisierung, Digitalisierung und Wertewandel in einer zweiten Gründerzeit befinden. Die Industriegesellschaft wird von der Wissens- und Dienstleistungsgesellschaft abgelöst. Wissenschaft, Forschung und die darauf basierende Produktion neuer Güter bekommen eine entscheidende strategische Bedeutung für die Positionierung auf den neuen Märkten. Dienstleistungen machen bereits rund 70 Prozent des Bruttosozialproduktes aus.

Sämtliche der alten Industriegesellschaft entsprechenden Formen und Instrumentarien müssen einer Überprüfung unterzogen werden mit dem Ziel, sie zu reformieren und zu modernisieren im Hinblick auf die entstehenden neuen Strukturen und Erfordernisse in Wirtschaft und Gesellschaft. Dazu gehört vor allem die deutlich höhere Förderung von Wissenschaft und technologischem Fortschritt, von Forschung und Entwicklung (FuE), von Bildung und lebenslangem Lernen. Zwar werden wir wohl immer ein Hochlohnland bleiben. Aber gerade deshalb muss die Förderung von Spitzenleistungen in Wissenschaft und Technik und deren Umsetzung in neue Produkte die Grundlage dafür bilden, dass wir auch in Zukunft materiellen Wohlstand, individuelle Lebensweisen und soziale Sicherung finanziell sichern können. Ein Blick auf

Dr. Angela Merkel

Die Autorin ist Vorsitzende der CDU Deutschlands, Vorsitzende der CDU/CSU-Fraktion im Bundestag und Bundesministerin a. D. Seit 1990 gehört sie dem Deutschen Bundestages an. Angela Merkel wurde 1954 in Hamburg geboren und ist von Beruf Dipl.-Physikerin. 1986 promovierte sie am Zentralinstitut für Physikalische Chemie an der Akademie der Wissenschaften in Berlin zum Dr. rer. nat.
The author is chairwoman of the German conservative party CDU, chairwoman of the parliamentary faction of the CDU/CSU in the German Parliament and retd. Minister of the German government. Since 1990, she has been a Member of the German Parliament, the Bundestag. Angela Merkel was born in Hamburg in 1954 and is a certified physicist. She graduated from the Central Institute for Physical Chemistry at the Academy of Sciences in Berlin with a PhD in 1986.

die Jahrhundertwende um 1900, als der Staat finanziell großzügig die Spitzenforschung unterstützte, zeigt: Bis 1918 ging jeder dritte naturwissenschaftliche Nobelpreis an die Deutschen. Heute sind die meisten Nobelpreisträger in den USA beheimatet.

Das sollte uns ein Ansporn sein, das Ziel zu setzen, die deutsche Wirtschafts- und Innovationskraft im europäischen Maßstab wieder ganz nach vorne zu bringen. Dazu gehören vier Punkte:

Erstens: Damit Forschungsergebnisse schnell in Produkte und Dienstleistungen umgesetzt werden können, müssen die Rahmenbedingungen in Deutschland wesentlich innovationsfreundlicher

Prospects

Germany is a strong country with an enormous growth potential for the future. Considering its many efficient and capable people as well as the great reputation Germany enjoys in Europe and the world – "Made in Germany" has become a worldwide trademark – we continue to have an excellent basis for growth.

After 1945, who would have believed that Germany could achieve this? Ludwig Erhard's social market economy created the necessary structural framework, which served to concentrate the industriousness, the willingness to be efficient and the readiness to press ahead of many Germans that led to the success of the reconstruction. Market conditions and economic competition on the one hand, common solidarity and social security on the other were able to provide an effective balance. During this first economic boom that the Federal Republic of Germany experienced the foundation was laid to have "prosperity for all" (Ludwig Erhard). The success of the social market economy also helped to cope with the reunification of Germany as a mutual task of all Germans.

However, while the decades of division in Germany and Europe were abolished also clear signs of significant change in the economy and society have become visible. The change of values has transformed traditional behaviour in society, restructuring within the world of labour is leading to considerably increased requirements in terms of (further) education, flexibility and communication in companies, new technologies enable worldwide communication and are profoundly changing what we have known about our world so far, globalisation is leading to a worldwide export of capital, economic competition among business locations and competition in internationally accessible markets, and the enlargement of the European Union creates a home market with just less than 450 million consumers. Germany must be prepared for these changed conditions – and the change is increasing faster every year. This means in concrete terms: Germany needs more profound structural reforms so that its growth rates can rise again and Germany can be among those countries again that are shaping the societies of the future for the 21st century as a leading vanguard of economic development. To come to the most important point: I am convinced that Germany does have the power to achieve this.

But we can only succeed in this if we confront reality: it is true, we still have a high standard of living in our country, but we are beginning to live from our substance in more and more areas. It may be sufficient for present times, but not for the future. How do we want to earn our money in future? How can we stand our ground in the global competition of business locations? How will we guarantee new well-being and social security? How can freedom and justice be brought back into a new balance? The answer to these questions can only be: we have to elevate the structures of the social market economy on which our country is built to a new qualitative level – we need a new social market economy. The industrial society is replaced by that of a knowledge and service-based society. Science, research and the production of new goods resulting from them acquire a decisive strategic importance for policies of positioning in new markets. Services already make up around 70 per cent of the gross national product.

All instruments and structures pertaining to the old industrial society must be examined with the aim to reform and modernise them with respect to new emerging structures and requirements of the economic sector and society. This includes above all a considerably increased support of science and technological progress, of research and development (R&D), of education and life-long learning. We will probably always be a country with high wage costs. But especially because of this the support of first-rate performances in science and technology and their application in new products must provide the basis for us to secure material prosperity, individual lifestyle and social security financially also in future. Let's take a look back on the turn of the century around 1900, when the state supported top research generously with finance: until 1918 every third Nobel Prize for natural science went to the Germans. Today, most Nobel Prize winners come from the USA.

Erforderlich ist die deutlich höhere Förderung von Wissenschaft und technologischem Fortschritt, von Forschung und Entwicklung (FuE), von Bildung und lebenslangem Lernen – Lehrausbildung bei der BASF in Ludwigshafen.

A markedly greater support is required of science and technological progress, of research and development (R&D), of education and life-long learning – training apprentices at BASF in Ludwigshafen.

This should be enough motivation to set ourselves the goal to bring German economic power and strength of innovation in the European context to the foremost front again. This includes four points:

First: In order to convert research findings rapidly into products and services, frame conditions in Germany must acquire a considerably more innovation-driven profile. The prerequisites to invest in innovations are increased freedom, legal security and less regulation. Indeed, there still exist "lone" inventors and individual creative engineers. But given the amount and the complexity of knowledge, top scientists work in collaborative teams today and render top technological performances. This requires detailed planning and reliable forecasts. More and more countries and large research institutes elaborate those leading innovations that determine our future through a number of products.

Chancen

ausgestaltet werden. Voraussetzungen für Investitionen in Innovationen sind mehr Freiheit, Rechtssicherheit und weniger Reglementierung. Zwar gibt es auch heute noch den „einsamen" Erfinder und individuellen Tüftler. Technologische Spitzenleistungen werden aber heute in der Regel angesichts der Fülle und der Komplexität des Wissens von vielen Spitzenwissenschaftlern in gemeinsamen Teams erbracht. Das erfordert Planung und Vorausschau. Immer mehr Länder und große Forschungsinstitute arbeiten diejenigen Leitinnovationen heraus, die unsere Zukunft in einer Vielzahl von Produkten bestimmen. Dazu gehören die Lebenswissenschaften – insbesondere die rote, grüne und weiße Gentechnik-Nanotechnologien, optische Technologien, neue Multimedia- und Internetformen, digitale Medizin, Sicherheitstechniken, Navigations-, Logistik- und Verkehrstechniken, elektronische Assistenz, Entwicklungen im Bereich des Klimaschutzes, Virtuelle-Realitäts-Techniken und all das, was sich im Großbereich Nachhaltigkeit entwickeln wird. Viele Techniken sind bereits zur Anwendungs- und Produktreife gediehen: flache Supermonitore, drahtlose Verbindungen, Biochips, Leuchtdioden, Brennstoffzellen für Kleingeräte, nanotechnologisch bearbeitete „saubere" Oberflächen oder Treibstoffe aus Biomasse. Für Deutschland ist es notwendig, sich an diese internationale Entwicklung so anzukoppeln, dass es nicht nur mithalten kann, sondern in den vorderen Rängen dabei ist.

Zweitens: Deutschland muss vor allem mehr als bisher in Wissenschaft, Forschung und Technik investieren. Zwar verfügt unser Land nach wie vor über eine gute Grundlagenforschung. Aber der Schritt in die anwendungsorientierte Forschung und Entwicklung marktfähiger Produkte gelingt oft nicht. Das liegt an den traditionellen Strukturen unserer Bildungslandschaft und Universitätsstruktur, der geringen Bereitschaft zu Risikoübernahme, einem Übermaß an bürokratischen Vorschriften und an mangelndem Wagniskapital. Es liegt aber auch an einem zu geringen Einsatz des Staates im FuE-Bereich. Der internationale Vergleich zeigt, dass Deutschland im Ranking nur noch an siebter Stelle hinter den Ländern USA, Japan, Schweden, Schweiz, Niederlande und Finnland steht. So wurden in Deutschland von 2000 bis 2002 die Forschungsausgaben um 6 Prozent angehoben, während sie in Japan um 15 Prozent, in den USA um 25 Prozent und in Schweden um 30 Prozent erhöht wurden. Damit Deutschland nicht weiter hinterherhinkt, sind in den nächsten Jahren erhebliche Anstrengungen notwendig, damit Weltmarktanteile nicht verloren gehen und neue erobert werden können.

Drittens: Vorfahrt für neue Technologien – das kann nur gelingen im Rahmen eines umfassenden Konzeptes für ein stärkeres Wirtschaftswachstum. Denn sonst werden die durch Wissenschaft, Forschung und Technik induzierten Erkenntnisvorsprünge schnell dahinschmelzen. Innovation und Wirtschaftswachstum sind deshalb zwei Seiten einer Medaille – als Fundament eines auch künftig international wettbewerbsfähigen Standorts Deutschland. Nach wie vor verzeichnen wir in Deutschland zu geringe Wachstumsraten. Neben einer guten Wirtschaftspolitik müssen deshalb Reformen in weiten Teilen von Politik und Gesellschaft den technologischen und ökonomischen Wandel begleiten. Priorität sehe ich hierbei in folgenden Bereichen:

• Flexibilisierung des Arbeitsmarktes, insbesondere durch betriebliche Bündnisse für Arbeit, einen modernen Kündigungsschutz, weniger Re-

Skyline der Finanzmetropole Frankfurt am Main.
Skyline of the financial centre Frankfurt on the Main.

Prospects

These include: life sciences, particularly red, green and white genetic engineering, nano-technologies, optical technologies, new forms of multimedia and the Internet, digital medicine, security system technologies, navigational, logistics and transport technologies, electronic assistance, developments in the field of climate protection, virtual reality technologies and all that will still emerge in the greater field of sustainability. Many technologies have already been developed to maturity for application and production: flat super monitors, wireless connections, bio-chips, light-emitting diodes, fuel cells for small appliances, "clean" surfaces treated with nano-technology processes or fuel made from bio-mass. It is imperative for Germany to link up with this international development in such way that we not only can keep pace with it, but also play a major role in upper rankings.

Second: Germany must above all increase investments in science, research and technology. It is true that our country still has excellent pure research. But we often do not manage the step forward towards application-oriented research and development for marketable products. This is due to the traditional structures of our education landscape and of our universities, the low willingness to take on risks, an excessive amount of bureaucratic regulations and a lack of risk capital. Another reason is also the little engagement from the part of the state in the field of R&D. The international comparison shows that Germany is only ranking on seventh place behind the USA, Japan, Sweden, Switzerland, The Netherlands and Finland. For instance in the years from 2000 to 2002, expenditure for research was increased by six per cent in Germany, while in Japan it was raised by 15, in the USA by 25 and in Sweden by 30 per cent. For Germany not to be lagging behind continuously there are considerable efforts necessary in the coming years so that world market shares do not get lost and new ones can be conquered.

Third: Giving way to new technologies – this can only be achieved successfully within the framework of an extensive concept for increased economic growth. Otherwise, the advantages of findings induced by science, research and technology will melt away rapidly. Innovation and economic growth are therefore two sides of the same coin, which are to serve as foundation for an internationally competitive business location Germany also in future. We are still registering growth rates in Germany that are too low.

Besides a good economic policy we must therefore also initiate reforms in wider parts of political sectors and of society to accompany technological and economic change. In this respect, I consider the following areas to be of utmost priority:

- Transition to a more flexible labour market, particularly through company agreements for securing jobs, a modern protection against dismissal, less regulation of limited employment contracts and support of the low wage sector. On the whole, we must work longer hours in Germany, this is the only way we can reduce costs of goods or services and become more competitive.
- Reduction of bureaucracy
- Cutback on state subsidies
- Reform of the tax system
- Renewal of the education system
- Restructuring of the relationship between the federal government, regional governments and communes within the context of a reform of the federalist system
- Further reforms of the social security systems.

Das Regierungsviertel in der Bundeshauptstadt.
Government district in the federal capital.

Chancen

gulierung der befristeten Arbeitsverhältnisse und eine Förderung des Niedriglohnsektors. Wir müssen in Deutschland insgesamt länger arbeiten, denn nur so können wir die Kosten pro Ware oder Dienstleistung verbilligen und werden damit konkurrenzfähiger.
- Abbau von Bürokratie
- Reduzierung der staatlichen Subventionen
- Reform des Steuersystems
- Erneuerung des Bildungswesens
- Neustrukturierung des Verhältnisses von Bund, Ländern und Gemeinden im Rahmen einer Föderalismusreform
- Weitere Reformen in den sozialen Sicherungssystemen. Dabei muss es vor allem gelingen, die Finanzierung der sozialen Sicherung von den Löhnen und Gehältern zu entkoppeln. Arbeit muss in Deutschland wieder günstiger werden, damit mehr Arbeitsplätze geschaffen werden können.

Zur Verantwortung einer Opposition gehört es, nicht nur zu kritisieren, sondern auch konstruktive Vorschläge zu machen. Die CDU hat in allen oben genannten Bereichen konkrete Vorschläge auf den Tisch gelegt. Die Union hat zudem im Vermittlungsausschuss von Bundestag und Bundesrat Kompromissen beim Arbeitsmarkt und bei der Gesundheitsreform zugestimmt und der Bundesregierung das Angebot unterbreitet, gemeinsam zu einem mutigen Neuanfang bei der Einkommensteuer zu kommen. Für uns gilt: Was in die richtige Richtung geht, das tragen wir mit. Falsche Weichenstellungen machen wir nicht mit. Gerade in der derzeitigen Situation in unserem Land ist es wichtig, dass die Opposition eine besondere Verantwortung übernimmt. Es ist deshalb unsere Aufgabe, als konstruktive Opposition und mit unserer Mehrheit in der zweiten Kammer, dem Bundesrat, noch mehr Verantwortung für das Land zu übernehmen. Denn die Menschen erwarten, dass sie von der Politik nicht im Stich gelassen werden, sondern dass die politischen Kräfte an der Lösung von Problemen arbeiten.

Viertens: All diese strukturellen Reformen nützen nur wenig, wenn sie nicht begleitet werden von einem Wandel der Mentalitäten in unserem Land. Zu sehr haben wir uns inzwischen daran gewöhnt, immer mehr Forderungen an den Staat zu stellen. Das hat nicht nur diesen in seinen Leistungsmöglichkeiten überfordert, sondern auch Problemlösungswege einer freiheitlichen Gesellschaft verkümmern lassen. Zudem hat oftmals einseitige Kritik an manchen modernen Technologien dazu geführt, dass man nicht mehr die damit verbundenen Chancen sieht. Skeptische Grundhaltungen gegenüber der technisierten Welt scheinen bei nicht wenigen zu wachsen. Ohne Zweifel: Kritik ist wichtig, wenn sie Verbesserungen ermöglicht. Aber sie darf nicht dazu führen, dass Deutschland seine technologischen Möglichkeiten nicht richtig nutzt und dadurch zurückfällt. Hier müssen wir umsteuern. Statt des Schürens von Technikängsten brauchen wir das Gegenteil: eine neue Technikbegeisterung, zumindest Aufgeschlossenheit für die Chancen neuer, moderner Technologien und neuer Produkte. Deutschland braucht einen Wechsel hin zu mehr Chancendiskussion und weniger Risikodiskussion. Dies ist einer der Pfeiler zur Schaffung künftigen Wohlstands.

Eine neue soziale Marktwirtschaft – das bedeutet nicht nur Veränderung von Strukturen, es heißt auch Revitalisierung der Mentalitäten und Tugenden, die uns in den ersten Jahrzehnten unserer Republik nach vorne gebracht haben. Zentrale Bedeutung muss für uns die Förderung eines positiven Verständnisses von Wettbewerb und Kooperation erlangen, einer Bejahung von Leistungswillen und Fleiß, Selbstbestimmung und Eigenverantwortung, Gründerwillen und Unternehmertum, Ehrenamt und Freiwilligenengagement.

„Frage nicht, was dein Land für dich tun kann, sondern frage, was du für dein Land tun kannst" – diese Forderung John F. Kennedys trifft auch auf unser Land zu. Die Potenziale sind da – in Wissenschaft und Wirtschaft, in Politik und Bürgergesellschaft. Doch wir müssen mehr für Deutschland tun. Und jeder muss bei sich selber anfangen. Wenn Reformen sinnvoll erklärt und in Politik der Verlässlichkeit und Berechenbarkeit eingebettet werden, dann sind die Bürger und Bürgerinnen unseres Landes auch bereit, Anstrengungen zu unternehmen und einen Neuaufbruch zu wagen.

Deutschland steht vor einer Herausforderung, die dem Wiederaufbau nach dem letzten Krieg in keiner Weise nachsteht. Ich bin davon überzeugt, dass wir diese große Aufgabe meistern können, weil in unserem Land mehr steckt, als zur Zeit daraus gemacht wird. ■

Vorfahrt für neue Technologien – Fortschritte können nur gelingen im Rahmen eines umfassenden Konzeptes für ein stärkeres Wirtschaftswachstum.

Oben:
Bayer-Werk in Leverkusen.

Unten:
Münchner Flughafen: In der Gepäckleitwarte von Siemens laufen die logistischen Fäden zusammen.

Rechte Seite: Das ScienceCenter in Bremen.

Giving way to new technologies – progress can only be achieved successfully within the framework of an extensive concept for increased economic growth.

Below: Bayer works in Leverkusen.

Far below: Munich Airport: the baggage processing centre made by Siemens is the hub of all logistics activities.

Right page: The Science Centre in Bremen.

Prospects

In this respect it must be achieved primarily to detach the financing of social security from salaries and wages. Work must become cheaper in Germany again so that more jobs can be created.

The responsibilities of the opposition include not only to criticise, but also to make constructive proposals. The conservative party CDU has put concrete proposals on the table embracing all above mentioned areas. The conservative party has

moreover agreed to compromises negotiated in the mediation committee of the federal parliament and of the parliament's upper house with respect to the labour market and the reform of the health care system. It has also offered the federal government to draw up mutual new and courageous plans for a renewal of the income tax system. To us is important that: whatever goes in the right direction, we will certainly support. But we do not follow any wrong course anyone may take. Especially given the present situation in our country it is crucial that political opposition forces assume very specific responsibilities. It is therefore our task, being a constructive opposition party and holding the majority in the upper house, the Bundesrat, to assume even more responsibility for our country. Because people expect that politicians do not abandon them and instead find political solutions for the existing problems.

Fourth: All these structural reforms will only be of little use if they are not accompanied by changes in the mentalities within our country. We have meanwhile become too accustomed to making more and more demands towards the state. These excessive demands have not only asked too much of the state, but have also stunted the problem solving capacities of a liberal society. Moreover, one-sided criticism about certain modern technologies has frequently led to not seeing the chances connected with them. Sceptical basic positions against a mechanized world seem to be growing with many. Without a doubt: indeed, criticism is important, if it enables improvements. But it should not lead to a situation, where Germany does not utilize its technological possibilities to the fullest and therefore drops back. This is where we must alter the course of direction. Instead of stirring up the fear of technology we need exactly

the opposite: a new enthusiasm for technology or at least open-mindedness towards the chances new technologies and new products can provide. Germany needs a transformation that is oriented to increased discussion about chances and less about risks. This is one of the pillars for the creation of future prosperity.

A new social market economy – that does not only mean a change of structures, it also signifies the revitalisation of mentalities and values that brought us the development of the first decades in our republic. Supporting a positive understanding of competition and cooperation, the approval of motivation and industriousness, self-determination and self-responsibility, private enterprise and entrepreneurship, honorary offices and voluntary engagement must all be of major importance for us.

"Do not ask what your country can do for you, but ask what you can do for your country" – this demand made by John F. Kennedy also applies to our country. The relevant potentials do exist – in science and industry, in politics and in the society of the citizenry. But we must do much more for Germany. And everyone must start with him or herself. When reforms are explained reasonably and they are embedded in reliable and calculable politics, the citizens of our country will certainly be prepared to make necessary efforts and to risk new changes.

Germany is at the threshold of a new challenge, which in every way can be regarded as equal to the years of reconstruction after the last war. I am convinced that we can master this great task, because we could surely make much more of our country than is currently being done.

Company Profile

Transcom – der größte europäische Anbieter von CRM-Lösungen

*Transcom –
the largest European provider of CRM solutions*

Mehr als 8.000 qualifizierte Mitarbeiter bieten in 36 Zentren in ganz Europa ihre Dienstleistungen an. Mit einem dichten Netzwerk stellen sie von Norwegen bis Marokko an sieben Tagen rund um die Uhr qualitativ hochwertige CRM-Lösungen bereit.

Transcom bietet maßgeschneiderte Kunden-Lösungen, die auf den verschiedensten Kombinationen aus den Schlüsselbereichen beruhen:

Eingehende Kommunikation

Transcom kümmert sich um die gesamte beim Kunden eingehende Kommunikation: per Telefon, E-mail, Internet oder Fax. Schnell, effizient und absolut verlässlich. Seine Größe, Struktur und Technologie sowie die Flexibilität seiner Mitarbeiter ermöglichen Transcom eine extrem schnelle Umkonfigurierung seines Leistungsumfangs. So kann problemlos auf durch Marketing-Kampagnen entstandene Nachfragespitzen reagiert werden. Transcom verfügt außerdem über ein automatisiertes Kontaktmanagement mit IVR-Technologie (Interactive Voice Response) zur Erfassung von Informationen und Bearbeitung von Kundenanfragen.

Telemarketing und ausgehende Kommunikation

Transcom deckt für seine Kunden alle Aspekte des Telemarketings und Kampagnen-Managements ab, von der Lead-Generierung bis zur Umsetzung von Verkaufszielen. Das Unternehmen übernimmt auch andere Outbound-Dienste, zum Beispiel Terminmanagement, Marktanalysen und das Management von Programmen zur Förderung der Kundenloyalität und Zurückgewinnung von Kunden. Transcom-Kunden haben vielfach erfahren, wie wertvoll ein gut informierter und freundlicher Dialog ist, der sich in verringerten Akquisitionskosten und höherer Markentreue niederschlägt.

Verwaltungsaufgaben

Als Teil des Support-Teams für das Back Office seiner Kunden steigert Transcom die Genauigkeit und die Qualität der Arbeit und reduziert die Verwaltungskosten. Das Know-how deckt die gesamte Palette anfallender Aufgaben ab, zum Beispiel die Vorbereitung und den Versand von Produkten und Informationen, die Verwaltung, Sortierung und Verarbeitung der Kommunikation in allen Medien, Eintragungen in Datenbanken und die Bearbeitung von Verträgen.

Webservices

In der vernetzten Welt dreht sich alles um Geschwindigkeit. Durch die schnelle Beantwortung von Anfragen sorgt Transcom dafür, dass die User auf den Webseiten der Kunden verweilen und schafft dadurch echten Mehrwert. Die Webservice-Lösungen leiten schnell und effizient zu den gewünschten Informationen, nehmen Bestellungen an und unterstützen den Zahlungsprozess.

CRM-Beratungsdienstleistungen

Transcom verfügt über umfassende CRM-Erfahrung und stützt sich dabei auf das Lessons Learnt-Prinzip und das Wissen, das bei zahlreichen Kunden bei der Optimierung von Geschäftsprozessen gewonnen worden ist. Der Kunde kann selbst entscheiden, ob das Team bei Inhouse-Bedürfnissen unterstützt oder maßgeschneiderte Transcom-Lösungen eingesetzt werden.

Kontaktautomatisierung

Wenn qualifizierte Fachleute mit den modernsten Technologien arbeiten, führt das häufig zur Optimierung des Kundendienstes. Transcom verfügt über umfassende Kenntnisse bei IVR-Systemen, mit denen erhebliche Kosteneinsparungen bei eingehenden Anrufen erzielt werden können.

Rechtsdienstleistungen

Das Transcom-Team mit lizenzierten Rechtsanwälten ist in einer Vielzahl komplexer rechtlicher Themen bewandert. Die Dienstleistungen reichen von der Beantwortung des rechtlichen Schriftverkehrs bis zur Abwicklung von Eigentumswechseln oder Erbangelegenheiten. Transcom kümmert sich auch um Finanzfragen wie Anleiheemissionen/ISDAS-Verträge, die Verifikation von Vollmachten, die Veröffentlichung rechtlicher Mitteilungen und das Einholen von Informationen über Gesetze, Vertragsabschlüsse und Beratung.

Kreditmanagement

Durch die Integration von CIS Collections in die Transcom-Gruppe steht ein großes Spektrum an verschiedenen Kreditmanagement-Lösungen der nächsten Generation zur Verfügung. Es umfasst u. a. Debitorenmanagement, Front Office, Mahnungswesen, Inkasso- und Rechtsdienstleistungen, Schuldenüberwachung, Forderungsankauf, im Bereich B2C, B2B und auf internationaler Ebene. ∎

Company Profile

Over 8,000 qualified staff members offer their services in 36 centres all over Europe. In a dense network that extends from Norway to Morocco they provide high-quality standard CRM Solutions on seven days around the clock. Transcom offers tailor-made customer solutions based on the most varied combinations from the key areas of:

Inbound communication
Transcom deals with the entire inbound communication received at their clients: By telephone, e-mail, internet or fax. Fast, efficiently and absolutely reliable. Its size, structure and technology as well as the flexibility of its employees enable Transcom to carry out any re-configuration of its service spectrum extremely fast. Thus it is possible to react to emerging peaks of demands without any problem by conducting professional marketing campaigns. Moreover, Transcom disposes of an automated contact management with IVR Technology (Interactive Voice Response) for collecting information and processing customer enquiries.

Telemarketing and outbound communication
Transcom covers all aspects of telemarketing and campaign management for its clients, ranging from lead generation through to the realisation of sales targets. The company also takes on other outbound services, for instance the management of appointment schedules, market analyses and the management of programmes for encouraging customer loyalty and winning back clients. Transcom's clients have experienced many times just how valuable a well-informed and friendly dialogue is, a fact results after all in lower costs for acquisition and a higher brand loyalty.

Administrative tasks
As part of the back office's assistance for clients, the Transcom Support Team increases the precision and quality of work carried out and reduces administrative costs. Our know-how covers the entire spectrum of arising tasks, for example, preparation and dispatch of products and information, administration, sorting and processing of communication in all the media, entries in different databases and the arrangement of contracts.

Web Services
In a completely networked world everything revolves around speed. Through a fast response to incoming enquiries, Transcom ensures that user view-time is prolonged on the client's website and therefore creates a real add-on value. Rapidly and efficiently, Web Service solutions lead directly to the desired information, deal with the taking of orders and support payment processes.

CRM Consultancy Services
Transcom possesses extensive CRM experience and relies on the Lessons Learnt Principle for this and on the knowledge that has been acquired during optimisation of business processes with numerous clients. The customer can decide himself if the Team should provide support for in-house requirements or tailor-made Transcom solutions should be used.

Contact Automation
When qualified experts work with the latest state-of-the-art technologies, frequently an optimisation of customer services is achieved automatically. Transcom disposes of comprehensive expertise regarding IVR Systems, which are capable of generating considerable cost savings for inbound calls.

Legal Services
The Transcom Team with its licensed lawyers is well versed in a great number of complex legal subjects. Services cover the reply of legal correspondence and extend to processing changes of ownership or inheritance matters. Transcom also deals with financial questions like loan issues against fixed interest securities, ISDAS contracts, the certification of power of attorneys, the publication of legal information and obtaining information about laws, elaborating contract agreements and consultancy services.

Credit Management
By integrating CIS Collections into the Transcom Group, a large spectrum of diverse credit management solutions of the next generation have been made available. They comprise debt management, front office, reminders, collection, and legal services, debt monitoring, purchase of claims, in the fields of B2C, B2B and on international level.

TRANSCOM WORLDWIDE

Vorstand/Chairman of the Executive Board: Keith Russel

Geschäftsleiter Deutschland/Managing Director Germany: Nael El Sayed

Gründungsjahr/Year of Foundation: 1995

Mitarbeiter/Employees: ca. 8.500

Geschäftstätigkeit/Business Activities:
Maßgeschneiderte Kunden-Lösungen aus verschiedenen Kombinationen der Schlüsselbereiche:
Eingehende Kommunikation
Telemarketing und ausgehende Kommunikation
Verwaltungsaufgaben
Webservices
CRM-Beratungsdienstleistungen
Kontaktautomatisierung
Rechtsdienstleistungen
Kreditmanagement
Tailor-made customer solutions from several combinations of our key areas of expertise:
Inbound communications
Telemarketing and outbound communications
Administrative tasks
Web services
CRM Consultancy Services
Contact Automation
Legal Services
Credit Management

Anschriften/Addresses:
Germany Düsseldorf
In der Steele 39a
D-40599 Düsseldorf
Telefon +49 (211) 74 00 45 00
Telefax +49 (211) 17 70 40
E-Mail nael.el.sayed@transcomww.com
Internet www.transcom-worldwide.com

Germany Halle
Leipziger Chaussee 191B
D-06142 Halle
Telefon +49 (345) 688 70 00
Telefax +49 (345) 688 70 02
E-Mail nael.el.sayed@transcomww.com
Internet www.transcom-worldwide.com

Germany Rostock
Trelleborger Straße 5
D-18107 Rostock
Telefon +49 (381) 123 13 00
Telefax +49 (381) 123 13 01
E-Mail nael.el.sayed@transcomww.com
Internet www.transcom-worldwide.com

Zentrale/Head Office
Moll DeBarcelona, East tower
S/N World Trade Center, 5a planta
E-08039 Barcelona
Telefon +34 (93) 6 00 41 00
Telefax +34 (93) 6 00 41 50
E-Mail nael.el.sayed@transcomww.com
Internet www.transcom-worldwide.com

Analyse & Vision

Für einen attraktiven Standort – Visionen für die deutsche Wirtschaft

For an attractive business location – visions for the German economy

Der Druck der internationalen Märkte auf den Standort Deutschland hat in den letzten Jahren eine neue Qualität erfahren. Die globalisierte Wirtschaft verändert sich mit zunehmender Geschwindigkeit und Deutschland muss Schritt halten. Verweist man auf die sich daraus ergebenden wirtschaftspolitischen Herausforderungen, so wird immer wieder als Gegenargument angeführt, dass die Bedingungen am Standort alles andere als unattraktiv sein könnten, schließlich sei Deutschland „Export-Weltmeister" und profitiere wie kein anderes Land von den globalen Märkten. Natürlich ist dieser Titel eine Bestätigung für den Erfolg deutscher Produkte und Dienstleistungen. Darauf dürfen wir auch stolz sein. „Made in Germany" ist immer noch auf den Weltmärkten gefragt. Auch in diesem Jahr dürfte sich dieser Trend fortsetzen: Denn trotz der Risiken durch einen starken Euro und trotz hoher Rohstoffpreise erwartet die Industrie für dieses Jahr ein Exportwachstum von 5 bis 6 Prozent und in 2006 sogar von 7 Prozent, so das Ergebnis einer aktuellen BDI-Umfrage.

Bei allem Optimismus: Der Titel „Exportweltmeister" ist zunächst eine rein statistische Größe und sagt eigentlich wenig über die Wettbewerbsfähigkeit des Standortes Deutschland aus. Denn unsere Exporte sind zunehmend vom Standort entkoppelt, ein immer größerer Teil ihrer Wertschöpfung findet woanders statt: in Asien und besonders in den neuen Mitgliedstaaten der EU. Ein deutlicher Beweis hierfür ist die Tatsache, dass der Exportfunke nicht auf die Binnenkonjunktur übergreift und dass die deutsche Wirtschaft seit Jahren nicht genügend wächst. Insofern müssen wir genauer hinsehen. Unsere strukturelle Wachstumsschwäche ist das gravierendste Problem des Standortes. Seit Mitte der 90er-Jahre ist Deutschlands Wirtschaftswachstum alles andere als mus-tergültig. Im Durchschnitt konnten wir nur etwa halb so hohe Wachstumsraten wie Frankreich, Großbritannien, die Niederlande oder wie der gesamte Euro-Raum, ohne Deutschland, erwirtschaften. Auf den Weltmärkten zogen die USA als Wachstumslokomotive in der zweiten Hälfte der 90er-Jahre allen davon. Wenn das schwache Wachstum in Deutschland weiter anhält, würden die USA im BIP pro Kopf bis 2030 auf das 2,2fache des deutschen Niveaus davonziehen, Australien auf das doppelte, Großbritannien, die Niederlande und Schweden auf das 1,5fache. Selbst Spanien läge dann beim 1,4fachen des deutschen BIP pro Kopf.

Es gibt vielerlei Gründe für unsere Wachstumsprobleme. Natürlich ist das Schultern der Lasten aus der Wiedervereinigung ein zentraler Grund, entscheidend sind aber die verschleppten Strukturreformen. Vor allem aber ist es der unbewältigte Strukturwandel, der unsere Wirtschaft lähmt,

Jürgen R. Thumann

Der Autor, 1941 in Schwelm/Westfalen geboren, übernahm mit 19 Jahren als gelernter Groß- und Außenhandelskaufmann die Thumann Stahl-Service Center und baute den elterlichen Betrieb weiter aus. 1966 trat er in die Hille & Müller Gruppe in Düsseldorf als Geschäftsführer und Gesellschafter ein. Gemeinsam mit seinem Cousin gründete er 1978 die Heitkamp & Thumann KG in Düsseldorf. Die Heitkamp & Thumann KG ist eine Gruppe mittelständischer Unternehmen in der Stahl, Metalle und Kunststoffe verarbeitenden Industrie mit zurzeit ca. 2.300 Mitarbeitern an 16 Standorten in Europa, Asien und Nordamerika.
Jürgen R. Thumann ist seit dem 1. Januar 2005 Präsident des Bundesverbandes der Deutschen Industrie e. V. (BDI).

The author was born in 1941 in Schwelm/Westphalia. At the age of 19 he took over the Thumann Steel Service Centre after completing training as wholesale and export trade merchant and expanded the company of his parents. In 1966, he joined the Hille & Müller Group in Düsseldorf as Managing Director and associate. Together with his cousin, he founded the Heitkamp & Thumann KG in Düsseldorf in 1978. Heitkamp & Thumann KG is a group of medium-size businesses of the steel, metal and plastic processing industry presently employing approx. 2,300 staff members at 16 locations in Europe, Asia and North America. Jürgen R. Thumann has been President of Bundesverband der Deutschen Industrie e. V. (BDI)/ (Federal Association of the German Industry) since 1st January 2005.

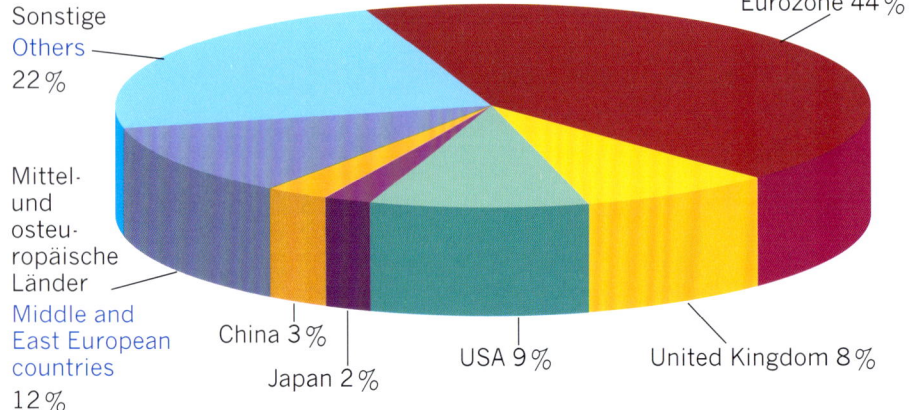

Wichtigste Zielregionen deutscher Exporte
The most important target regions for German exports
Anteile an den Warenausfuhren Januar bis Oktober 2003
Share of goods exported from January to October 2003

- Eurozone 44 %
- Sonstige / Others 22 %
- Mittel- und osteuropäische Länder / Middle and East European countries 12 %
- USA 9 %
- United Kingdom 8 %
- China 3 %
- Japan 2 %

Analysis & Vision

The pressure of international markets on Germany as a business location has acquired a new dimension in recent years. The globalised economy is changing with increasing speed and Germany must be able to keep pace. If one refers to challenges to economic policy that result from this, again and again the counterargument is given claiming that conditions at the location could be everything else than unattractive, since in fact Germany is "World Champion in Exports" and definitely benefits from global markets as no other country does. Of course, this title confirms the success of German products and services. Indeed, we can be proud of it too. "Made in Germany" still is in demand on the world's markets. This trend will certainly be continued also this year: despite the risks that a strong Euro bears and despite high raw material prices, the industrial sector is expecting a growth in exports of 5 to 6 per cent this year and in 2006 even of 7 per cent, according to the result of a current survey conducted by the BDI Bundesverband der Deutschen Industrie (Federal Association of the German Industry).

In spite of all one's optimism: The title of "World Champion in Exports" first of all is of merely statistical significance and really says little about Germany's competitiveness as a business location. In fact our exports are increasingly detached from the location, an ever growing part of its added value is generated elsewhere: in Asia and particularly in the new member states of the EU. Clear proof of this is the fact that the sparks of enthusiasm sent out by export have not infected the domestic economy and that the German economy has not been growing sufficiently for years now. Our structural growth low is the most serious problem the business location has. Since the mid nineties, Germany's economic growth has been everything else but exemplary. On average, we have only been able to generate half the growth rates of countries such as France, Great Britain and The Netherlands or as the entire Euro-Region, without Germany, generates. On global markets, the USA have left behind everyone as growth force in the second half of the nineties. If slow growth continued in Germany, the USA would exceed the German level of GDP per capita until 2030 by 2.2 times, Australia by two times, Great Britain, The Netherlands and Sweden by 1.5 times. Even Spain would then exceed the German GDP per capita by 1.4 times.

There are several reasons for our growth problems. Of course, one of the major reasons is having to bear the brunt of the reunification, but really significant are the delayed structural reforms. Above all however, it is the unresolved structural change that stifles our economy, i. e. high losses of net product in some industrial sectors have not been compensated through corresponding added value in innovative industries and services. On the one hand, structural change has increased considerably in intensity and speed. On the other, Germany has lost its adaptability and capacity of fast reaction. Basically, four mega trends are noticeable, which play a major role in the push of global structural change.

a) Tertiarisation: we are noticing an increasing importance of the service sector. Here, industry related services are the motor of structural change.

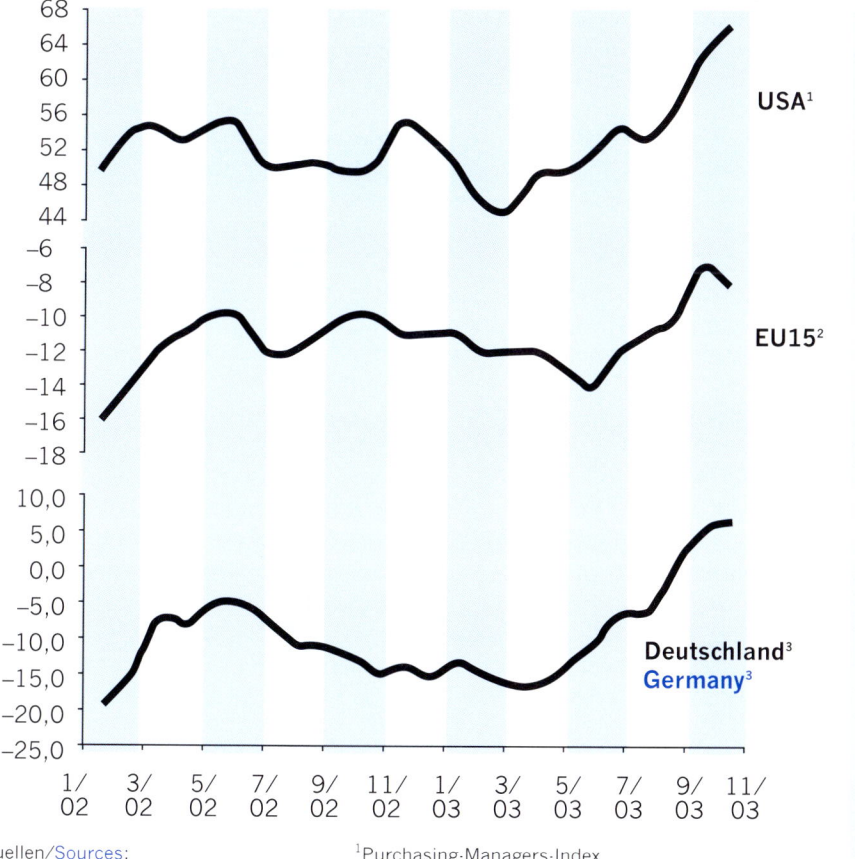

Deutliche Anzeichen für eine Konjunkturerholung/Clear signs of an economic recovery
Stimmungsindikatoren, Salden, saisonbereinigt
Economic climate indexes, balances, seasonally adjusted

	European Index	ifo-balances manufacturing industry	PMI
1/02	−16	−19,2	49,8
2/02	−14	−14,8	53,8
3/02	−12	−7,6	54,7
4/02	−11	−8,0	53,3
5/02	−10	−5,4	54,7
6/02	−10	−5,0	55,2
7/02	−12	−7,6	50,7
8/02	−12	−10,7	50,3
9/02	−11	−11,1	50,7
10/02	−10	−12,2	49,7
11/02	−10	−14,5	50,5
12/02	−11	−13,9	55,2
1/03	−11	−14,9	53,9
2/03	−11	−13,3	50,5
3/03	−12	−15,0	46,2
4/03	−12	−16,3	45,4
5/03	−12	−16,1	49,4
6/03	−13	−13,5	49,8
7/03	−14	−10,3	51,8
8/03	−12	−6,5	54,7
9/03	−11	−5,9	53,7
10/03	−10	0,4	57
11/03	−7	5,4	62,8
12/03	−8	6,6	66,2

Quellen/Sources:
ISM,
Europäische Komission/
European Commission,
Ifo Institut

[1] Purchasing-Managers-Index
[2] Industrial confidence indicator
[3] ifo Geschäftsklima-Index, Verarbeitendes Gewerbe/
Ifo Business Climate Index, Manufacturing industry

Analyse & Vision

Zahlen zur Wirtschaftslage in Deutschland

	2002	2003	2.Vj.02	3.Vj.02	4.Vj.02	1.Vj.03	2.Vj.03	3.Vj.03
Bruttoinlandsprodukt in % gegenüber Vorjahr in Preisen von 1995	0,2	–0,1	0,5	0,9	0,3	0,4	–0,7	–0,2
Produktion[1] in % gegenüber Vorjahr								
Produzierendes Gewerbe	–1,7	–	–2,0	–0,6	0,8	0,7	–0,4	–1,0
davon: Verarbeitendes Gewerbe	–1,5	–	–2,2	–0,4	1,4	1,6	–0,3	–0,6
Bauhauptgewerbe	–5,6	–	–1,6	–3,8	–6,1	–14,3	–6,5	–5,5
Auftragseingang in % gegenüber Vorjahr								
Verarbeitendes Gewerbe:	–0,3	–	1,1	2,6	2,3	2,0	–3,8	–0,1
Inland	–3,4	–	–2,3	–1,4	–0,2	1,0	–2,8	–1,1
Ausland	3,5	–	5,2	7,6	5,2	3,2	–4,9	1,0
Kapazitätsauslastung in der deutschen Industrie in % der betrieblichen Vollauslastung	82,7	–	83,0	82,7	82,8	82,8	81,6	82,5

	2002	2003	07/03	08/03	09/03	10/03	11/03	12/03
GESCHÄFTSKLIMA[2] **Verarbeitendes Gewerbe**								
Geschäftsklima	–	–	–10,3	–6,5	–5,9	0,4	5,4	6,6
Geschäftslage	–	–	–20,6	–18,4	–21,5	–16,1	–11,8	–11,2
Geschäftserwartungen	–	–	0,5	6,1	10,9	18,3	24,1	26,0
Exporterwartungen	–	–	1,0	5,3	6,2	11,7	12,5	12,8
PREISE (1995=100) in % gegenüber Vorjahr								
Lebenshaltung	1,4	1,1	0,9	1,1	1,1	1,2	1,3	1,1
Erzeugerpreise	–0,6	1,7	1,9	2,0	2,0	1,7	2,0	1,8
Importpreise	–2,5	–1,8	–2,0	–1,7	–2,6	–2,5	–1,1	–2,5
Exportpreise	–0,1	0,1	–0,2	–0,2	–0,1	–0,2	0,0	–0,2
Arbeitsmarkt in Tsd.								
Erwerbstätige	38.671	38.279	38.337	38.381	38.578	38.663	–	–
Arbeitslose	4.060	4.376	4.352	4.314	4.207	4.152	4.184	4.317
Arbeitslosenquote[3] (in %)	9,8	10,5	10,4	10,4	10,1	10,0	10,0	10,4
Handelsbilanz in Mrd. Euro								
Saldo	132,8	–	14,2	10,4	14,3	10,8	10,4	–
Euro-Wechselkurse[4] Durchschnittswerte gegenüber US-Dollar	0,9456	1,1312	1,1372	1,1139	1,1222	1,1692	1,1702	1,2286

[1] Arbeitstäglich bereinigt
[2] Salden, saisonbereinigt
[3] Gemessen an allen zivilen Erwerbspersonen
[4] Euro-Referenzkurse der Europäischen Zentralbank

Quelle: Statistisches Bundesamt, Deutsche Bundesbank, Bundesanstalt für Arbeit, ifo Institut, eigene Berechnungen

d. h. hohe Wertschöpfungsverluste in einigen Sektoren der Industrie wurden nicht durch entsprechende Zugewinne bei innovativen Industrien und Dienstleistungen wettgemacht. Der strukturelle Wandel hat einerseits an Intensität und Geschwindigkeit erheblich zugenommen. Andererseits hat Deutschland an Anpassungsfähigkeit und Reaktionsschnelligkeit verloren. Grundsätzlich lassen sich vier Megatrends beobachten, die den strukturellen Wandel weltweit maßgeblich vorantreiben.

a. Tertiarisierung: Wir beobachten eine zunehmende Bedeutung der Dienstleistungen. Dabei sind die industrienahen Dienstleistungen der Motor des Strukturwandels.

b. Globalisierung: Die weltweite Öffnung der Märkte und die Intensivierung der weltweiten Konkurrenz sowie die gestiegene strategische Bedeutung von Direktinvestitionen verändern die weltweite Arbeitsteilung. Ehemals ureigene Domänen deutscher Industriekultur stehen unter enormem Druck der internationalen Märkte.

c. Informatisierung: Die umfassende Durchdringung aller Lebensbereiche von ITK-Technologien bietet gleichzeitig neue strategische Optionen für Unternehmen verbunden mit tief greifenden Veränderungen der Produktionssysteme und der Arbeitswelt.

d. Demografie: Wir Deutschen werden immer weniger und die Wenigen werden immer älter. Im Jahr 2050 könnte nach Berechnungen des Statistischen Bundesamtes die Bevölkerungszahl auf rund 67 Mio. sinken. Bei zunehmendem Durchschnittsalter der Beschäftigten wächst die Gefahr einer Erosion der Wissensbasis und eines Verlus-tes an Innovationsfähigkeit. Hinzu kommt eine sinkende Bereitschaft in der Gesellschaft, neue Wege zu gehen und Reformen vor-

Analysis & Vision

Facts and figures concerning the economic situation in Germany

	2002	2003	2nd Qtr. 02	3rd Qtr. 02	4th Qtr. 03	1st Qtr. 03	2nd Qtr. 03	3rd Qtr. 03
Gross national product in % against previous year in prices of 1995	0,2	–0,1	0,5	0,9	0,3	0,4	–0,7	–0,2
Production [1] in % against previous year								
Manufacturing industry	–1,7	–	–2,0	–0,6	0,8	0,7	–0,4	–1,0
of this: processing industry	–1,5	–	–2,2	–0,4	1,4	1,6	–0,3	–0,6
main construction trade	–5,6	–	–1,6	–3,8	–6,1	–14,3	–6,5	–5,5
Total order value in % against previous year								
Processing industry:	–0,3	–	1,1	2,6	2,3	2,0	–3,8	–0,1
national	–3,4	–	–2,3	–1,4	–0,2	1,0	–2,8	–1,1
abroad	3,5	–	5,2	7,6	5,2	3,2	–4,9	1,0
Capacity utilisation in German the industry in % of operative full capacity	82,7	–	83,0	82,7	82,8	82,8	81,6	82,5

	2002	2003	07/03	08/03	09/03	10/03	11/03	12/03
BUSINESS CLIMATE [2] **Processing industry**								
Business climate	–	–	–10,3	–6,5	–5,9	0,4	5,4	6,6
Business situation	–	–	–20,6	–18,4	–21,5	–16,1	–11,8	–11,2
Business expectation	–	–	0,5	6,1	10,9	18,3	24,1	26,0
Export expectation	–	–	1,0	5,3	6,2	11,7	12,5	12,8
PRICES (1995=100) in % against previous year								
Cost of living	1,4	1,1	0,9	1,1	1,1	1,2	1,3	1,1
Manufacturer's price	–0,6	1,7	1,9	2,0	2,0	1,7	2,0	1,8
Import price	–2,5	–1,8	–2,0	–1,7	–2,6	–2,5	–1,1	–2,5
Export price	–0,1	0,1	–0,2	–0,2	–0,1	–0,2	0,0	–0,2
Labour market in thousands								
Employees	38.671	38.279	38.337	38.381	38.578	38.663	–	–
Unemployed	4.060	4.376	4.352	4.314	4.207	4.152	4.184	4.317
Rate of unemployed [3] (in %)	9,8	10,5	10,4	10,4	10,1	10,0	10,0	10,4
Balance of Trade in billion Euros								
Balance	132,8	–	14,2	10,4	14,3	10,8	10,4	–
Rate of exchange of Euro [4] average values								
against US-Dollar	0,9456	1,1312	1,1372	1,1139	1,1222	1,1692	1,1702	1,2286

[1] daily work adjusted
[2] balances, seasonally adjusted
[3] measured against all civil employees
[4] Euro reference rates of the European Central Bank
Sources: Federal Statistical Office, German Federal Bank, Federal Institute of Labour, ifo Institute, own calculations

b) Globalisation: the opening of markets worldwide and the increasing intensiveness of global competition as well as the grown strategic importance of direct investments change the global division of labour. Domains formerly owned by the German industrial culture are experiencing the enormous pressure of international markets.

c) Informatisation: the extensive penetration into all areas of daily life of ITC technologies at the same time offers new strategic alternatives for companies and is linked with dramatic changes of production systems and in the world of work.

d) Demography: Germans are decreasing in number and the few that still exist are growing ever older. In the year 2050, according to calculations made by the Federal Office of Statistics, the population could decrease to around 67 million people. With an increasing average age of employees, there is a growing danger of erosion of the knowledge base and loss of innovative capacity.

In addition, society is less prepared to tread new paths and push ahead reforms. The greater the share of transfer recipients in the population entitled to vote, the more difficult will it be to modernise transfer systems.

Which challenges must the industrial sector confront?

Consequences of these mega trends characterise the situation at the business location of Germany: insufficient growth, high structural unemployment, growing national debt and impoverished social systems.

We will only be able to face these challenges by creating flexible frame conditions. This is the responsibility of the political sector. But of course, the rapid change also brings about new challenges for us entrepreneurs. Certainly, the industrial sector has lost proportional shares in terms of net

anzutreiben. Je größer der Anteil der Transferempfänger an der Wahlbevölkerung wird, umso schwieriger wird es sein, die Transfersysteme zu modernisieren.

Welche Herausforderungen bestehen für die Industrie?

Die Folgen dieser Megatrends prägen das Bild am Standort Deutschland: unzureichendes Wachstum, hohe strukturelle Arbeitslosigkeit, wachsende Staatsverschuldung und Not leidende Sozialsysteme. Diesen Herausforderungen werden wir nur durch flexible Rahmenbedingungen erfolgreich begegnen können. Da steht die Politik in der Pflicht. Aber natürlich bedeutet der rasante Wandel auch neue Herausforderungen für uns Unternehmer. Gewiss, die Industrie hat im engeren Sinn bei Wertschöpfung und Beschäftigung Anteile verloren. Der Wertschöpfungsanteil der Industrie in Deutschland liegt heute unter 25 Prozent. Doch dieser Anteilsverlust bedeutet nicht automatisch einen Bedeutungsverlust. Denn die enger werdende Verknüpfung zwischen Industrie und industrienahen Dienstleistungen hat einen neuen Kernsektor der Volkswirtschaft, bestehend aus industrieller Produktion und industrienahen Dienstleistungen, entstehen lassen.

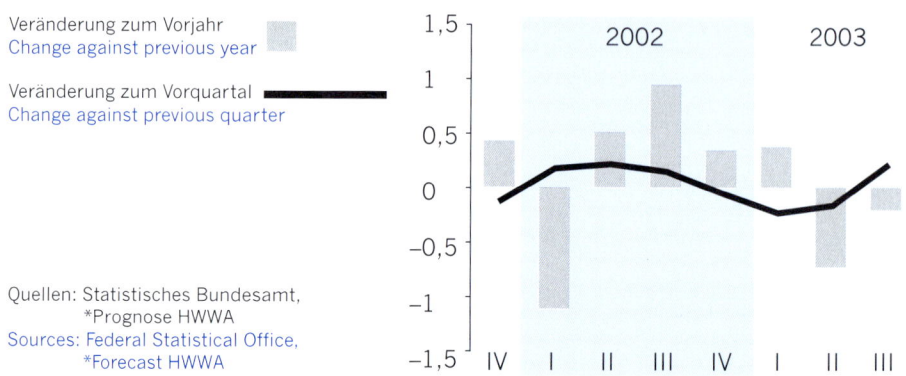

Konjunkturelle Wende geschafft
Economic transition under control
Reales Bruttoinlandsprodukt, Veränderung in Prozent, Deutschland
Real gross national product, change in per cent, Germany

		2003	2004*
BIP	GNP	–0,1	1,7
Privater Konsum	Private consumption	–0,2	1,2
Konsum Staat	State consumption	0,7	–0,2
Anlageinvestitionen	Investments in capital expenditure	–3,3	1,0
Ausrüstungen	Equipments	–4,0	2,0
Bauten	Constructions	–3,4	0,0
Einfuhr	Import	2,0	3,1
Ausfuhr	Export	1,1	4,5

Umfangreiches Outsourcing von unternehmensinternen Dienstleistungen sowie die gestiegene Bedeutung produktbegleitender Dienstleistungen treiben diese Entwicklung an. Die Weltmärkte verlangen heute nicht einfach nur Hardware oder Software, sondern integrierte Problemlösungskonzepte. Der Servicekranz eines Produktes ist entscheidend. Forschung, Entwicklung, Engineering, Logistik, Beratung und Softwareentwicklung sind Beispiele hierfür. Diese Dienstleistungen weisen gleichzeitig die höchste Beschäftigungsdynamik auf. Mehr als vier Millionen Menschen sind heute in Deutschland in dieser Dienstleistungssparte beschäftigt – mit weiter steigender Tendenz. Ohne die Industrie als Fundament wäre diese Dynamik undenkbar. Misst man, wie viel Produktion in der gesamten Volkswirtschaft durch die auf die Industrie gerichtete Endnachfrage hervorgerufen wird, so zeigt sich, dass dieser Anteil seit 1991 bei konstant 39 Prozent liegt. Das bedeutet: Wenn die Industrie anzieht, ziehen die Dienstleister nach. Eine positive wirtschaftliche Entwicklung ist somit ohne eine breite industrielle Basis in Deutschland nicht vorstellbar.

Die Industrie ist derzeit in besonderer Weise im Fokus der Öffentlichkeit: Betriebsschließungen, Offshoring bzw. Standortverlagerungen sind weitere Folgen des strukturellen Wandels. Industrieunternehmen bündeln und optimieren ihre gesamten Wertschöpfungsketten von der Konstruktion bis zum Service. Die Herausforderungen in der Zukunft liegen für die Unternehmen darin, ihr globales Wertschöpfungsportfolio effizient zu managen, alle Prozesse intelligent zu vernetzen und damit eine optimale Ausnutzung der jeweiligen lokalen Ressourcen- und Know-how-Vorteile sicherzustellen – auch in Deutschland. Eine BDI-Umfrage vom Herbst 2004 zu den Motiven für das gestiegene Auslandsengagement der Industrie hat ergeben, dass es in erster Linie drei Gründe sind:
- Erschließen neuer Märkte,
- Optimieren der Kosten entlang der Wertschöpfungskette,
- viele Zulieferer ziehen ihren Kunden nach.

Die deutsche Wirtschaft war schon immer in hohem Maße internationalisiert. Insofern ist diese Entwicklung genau genommen nichts Neues. Neu ist, dass die Unternehmen immer weniger darauf setzen, dass sich die Bedingungen am Standort Deutschland verbessern. Sie ziehen stattdessen Konsequenzen und gehen – still und leise. Manche Region wird derzeit durch massiven Stellenabbau hart getroffen. Doch die Brisanz der Verlagerungen liegt nicht allein im Verlust der vielen hochwertigen Arbeitsplätze. Denn als letzte Konsequenz droht ein umfassender Verlust der in der Zukunft wettbewerbsfähigen Wirtschaftsstrukturen. Seit vielen Jahren wird deutlich, dass die eigentliche wirtschaftliche Dynamik auf den internationalen Märkten hauptsächlich im hochproduktiven Dienstleistungssektor und im Innovationsbereich stattfindet. Der Welthandel verlagert sich kontinuierlich von weniger FuE-intensiven Gütern zu den Bereichen der Hoch- und Spitzentechnologien. Wir brauchen deshalb dringend politische Rahmenbedingungen, die Innovation und Investitionen hier bei uns in Deutschland fördern.

Welche Herausforderungen bestehen für die Wirtschaftspolitik?

Die „Agenda 2010" war und ist ein richtiges Signal für Reformen in Deutschland. Sie kann gleichzeitig aber nur ein Startsignal gewesen sein. Weitere strukturelle Reformen auch in den Bereichen Arbeitsmarkt und Sozialsysteme müssen folgen. Die Notwendigkeit hierfür ist keine Frage des politischen Willens, sondern sie ist eine Frage der ökonomischen Wirklichkeit. So haben sich zum Beispiel die Abgaben für Renten-, Kranken-, Pflege- und Arbeitslosenversicherung in den letzten 50 Jahren verdoppelt. 1950 lagen sie bei 20 Prozent des Bruttoarbeitsentgeltes. Heute sind es 42 Prozent. Zwischen 1991 und 2003 stiegen die Bruttoarbeitskosten um über 20 Prozent, die Nettoverdienste um lediglich fünf Prozent, d. h. der

Analysis & Vision

product and employment. The industrial sector's proportion in the net product in Germany today amounts to less than 25 per cent. But this proportional loss does not automatically mean a loss in importance. Because the intensifying links between industry and industry-relevant services have brought about a new core sector in the national economy, consisting of industrial production and industry-relevant services.

Extensive outsourcing of in-house services as well as the increased significance of product-accompanying services fuel this development. Today, world markets not only require simply hardware or software, but integrated problem solution concepts. The cycle of service a product offers is decisive. Research, development, engineering, logistics, consulting and software development are some examples of this. These services at the same time show the highest dynamism in terms of employment. More than four million people today work in this service sector in Germany – and the proportion is increasing. Without industry as a basis, the present dynamism would be unthinkable. If one considers how much production in the entire national economy results from through the final demand required from industry, one finds that this proportion has remained on the constant level of 39 per cent since 1991. This means: if industry is booming, service providers will follow. Thus, a positive economic development in Germany is unconceivable without a broad industrial basis.

Presently, the industrial sector is particularly at the centre of public attention: company closures, off-shoring or relocations respectively are further consequences of the structural change. Industrial companies harness and optimise their entire value creation chains from construction through to services. For companies the challenges of the future will be to manage their global net product portfolio efficiently, to network all processes intelligently and thereby to ensure an optimal exploitation of the relevant local resource and know-how advantages – also in Germany.

A survey conducted by the BDI in autumn 2004 concerning the motives for the industrial sector's risen engagement abroad found that in the first place there are three reasons for this:
- the development of new markets
- optimisation of costs along the value added chain
- many suppliers relocated following their clients.

The German economy has always been internationalised to a very great extent. That is why this development really is nothing new. But what is new is that companies rely less and less on conditions improving at the business location of Germany. Instead, they take the consequences and disappear – quite discreetly. Many a region is presently hit hard by a massive reduction of jobs. But the explosive nature of relocations rests not only in the loss of many high-quality workplaces. Indeed, the final consequence will be a danger of extensively loosing all competitive economic structures in the future. For many years it has become evident that real economic dynamism on international markets mainly takes place in the highly productive service sector and in the field of innovations. World trade is shifting continuously from less R&D-intensive goods to the fields of high and top-technologies. We therefore urgently need political frame conditions that promote innovation and investments here in Germany.

Which challenges exist for economic policy?

The programme of the "Agenda 2010" has been and still is the correct signal to initiate reforms in Germany. However, it only really served as starting signal. Further structural reforms must follow also in the fields of labour market and social systems. This necessity is not a question of political will; instead it is a question of economic reality. For instance, contributions for pension, health, nursing care and unemployment insurance have doubled in the past 50 years. In 1950 they still amounted to 20 per cent of the gross wages. Today, they amount to 42 per cent. Between 1991 and 2003 gross cost of labour increased by over 20 per cent, net incomes only by five per cent. This means that the gap between gross and net is becoming wider and wider. There must be transparency and reliability about the future political course on federal level. This is the only way to create confidence in politics. And indeed, confidence is more than necessary, not least against the background of the current restrained attitude of consumers and investors. Particularly medium-sized enterprises need consistency in politics and not the hectic pace of every day life or new insecurities. The political economical course in Germany must be just as reliable as the collaboration of medium-sized companies with customers and suppliers. And especially the industrial medium-size business sector contrary to large corporations, does not dispose of expert staff which are able to adapt their company strategy permanently to a constantly changing tax environment. Moreover, the medium-size business sector is not able to provide further capacities to manage excessive administrative and bureaucratic rules and regulations.

Additionally, the political sector must recognise the new dimension of the business location issue. In terms of business location policy it is still too defensive and oriented towards the domestic market. Focussing solely on the structural problems in classical fields like the labour market, social systems, taxes and regulations places too little emphasis on location conditions provided for modern industries and services.

Economic policy in recent years has relied too little on the potentials of added value in knowledge-based, research-intensive, innovative products and services – despite the past "Year of Innovation 2004" and the current "Einstein Year 2005". In these fields of the economy competition is fiercest, this is where comparative advantages of the future are positioned.

The following offensive location factors therefore must be in the focus of politics:
- research, technologies, innovation
- education, science
- infrastructure: information, transport, energy.

With regard to many of these factors Germany is still excellently positioned. One may only think of the high number of patents, the innovative medium-size business sector, the training given to employees and the fully developed infrastructure, which still are valuable points in our balance sum. However, there is much that needs to be improved urgently. Especially knowledge and information are becoming strategic location factors. They are the central motors of economic growth in the 21st century. Work and capital assets will acquire less importance at the same time. We therefore need

Analyse & Vision

Keil zwischen Brutto und Netto wird immer breiter. Es muss Klarheit und Zuverlässigkeit über den künftigen Politikkurs auf Bundesebene geben. Nur so schafft man Vertrauen in die Politik. Und Vertrauen ist mehr als notwendig, nicht zuletzt vor dem Hintergrund der aktuellen Investitions- und Konsumzurückhaltung. Insbesondere mittelständische Unternehmen brauchen Beständigkeit in der Politik und keine Alltagshektik oder neue Verunsicherungen. So zuverlässig wie mittelständische Unternehmen mit Kunden und Lieferanten zusammenarbeiten, so zuverlässig muss der wirtschaftspolitische Kurs in Deutschland sein. Und besonders der industrielle Mittelstand verfügt im Gegensatz zu Großunternehmen nicht über Expertenstäbe, die permanente Anpassungen der Unternehmensstrategie an ein sich ständig veränderndes steuerliches Umfeld vornehmen können. Zudem kann der Mittelstand keine weiteren Kapazitäten zur Bewältigung überbordender administrativer und bürokratischer Auflagen und Regelungen bereitstellen.

Die Politik muss zudem die neue Dimension der Standortfrage erkennen. Sie ist in ihrer Standortpolitik nach wie vor zu defensiv und zu national ausgerichtet. Eine ausschließliche Fokussierung auf die Strukturprobleme in den klassischen Bereichen Arbeitsmarkt, Sozialsysteme, Steuern und Regulierung geht zu wenig auf Standortbedingungen für moderne Industrien und Dienstleistungen ein.

Die Wirtschaftspolitik der letzten Jahre hat zu wenig auf Wertschöpfungspotenziale bei wissensbasierten, forschungsintensiven, innovativen Produkt- und Dienstleistungen gesetzt – trotz des vergangenen „Innovationsjahres 2004" und des diesjährigen „Einstein-Jahres 2005". In diesen Bereichen der Wirtschaft ist der internationale Wettbewerb am schärfsten, hier werden die komparativen Vorteile der Zukunft vergeben.

Folgende offensive Standortfaktoren müssen daher im Fokus der Politik stehen:
• Forschung, Technologie, Innovation,
• Bildung, Wissenschaft,
• Infrastruktur: Information, Verkehr, Energie.

Bei vielen dieser Faktoren steht Deutschland immer noch gut da. Man denke an die hohe Zahl der Patente, den innovativen Mittelstand, die Ausbildung der Arbeitskräfte und die gut ausgebaute Infrastruktur, die nach wie vor wertvolle Aktivposten in unserer Bilanz sind.

Aber: Vieles ist auch dringend verbesserungsbedürftig. Besonders Wissen und Information werden zu strategischen Standortfaktoren. Sie sind

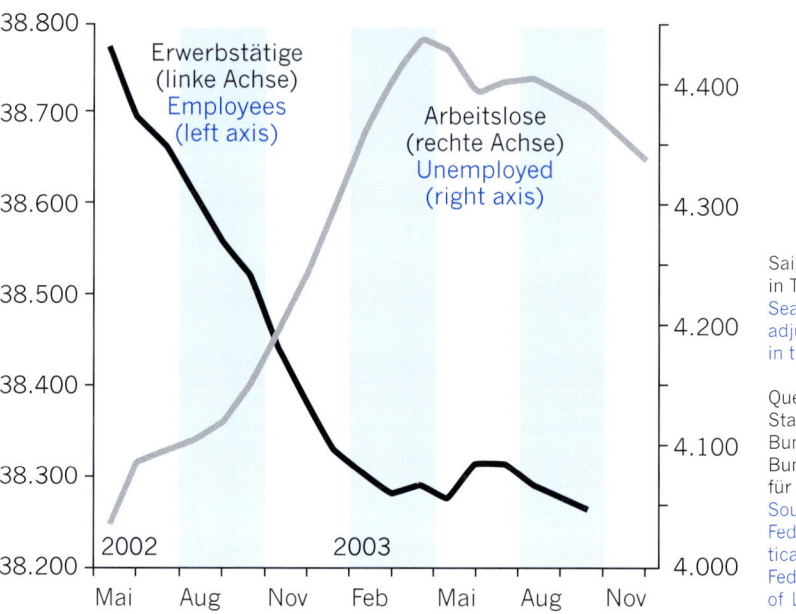

die zentralen Treiber des wirtschaftlichen Wachstums im 21. Jahrhundert. Arbeit und Sachkapital werden gleichzeitig in ihrer Bedeutung zurücktreten. Wir brauchen daher in Deutschland mehr Zukunftsinvestitionen, z. B. in Forschung und Entwicklung. Wir wenden nur 2,4 Prozent unseres Bruttoinlandsproduktes hierfür auf. Davon entfallen zwei Drittel auf die Wirtschaft und ein Drittel auf die öffentliche Hand. Vor 25 Jahren lag das Verhältnis noch bei 50 : 50. Die USA geben insgesamt 2,8 Prozent ihres BIP für FuE aus, in Finnland sind es 3,5 Prozent und in Schweden sogar 4,3 Prozent.

Diese Politik bleibt nicht ohne Folgen. Deutschlands Anteil am Welthandel mit FuE-intensiven Gütern ist gesunken und der Beitrag FuE-intensiver Waren zu unserem Außenhandelssaldo geht seit 1994 zurück. Zwar auf immer noch hohem Niveau, dennoch ist dieser Rückgang deutlich zu beobachten. Vor allem durch die herausragende Stärke im Automobilsektor wird diese Entwicklung noch abgefedert. Wir müssen pragmatisch Prioritäten setzen. Die öffentliche Hand muss wieder mehr in die Zukunft investieren und weniger konsumieren. Die FuE-Haushaltsansätze sind in etlichen Staaten in den letzten Jahren stark nach oben angepasst worden – vielfach entgegen dem herrschenden Konsolidierungsdruck: Zwischen 2000 und 2002 kam ein Plus von etwa sechs Prozent in Deutschland heraus, in Schweden waren es knapp 30 Prozent, in den USA 25 Prozent und selbst im rezessionsgeplagten Japan 15 Prozent.

Richtig ist aber auch: Geld ist nicht alles und Innovationen sind auch immer eine Frage der Geisteshaltung in Gesellschaft und Politik. Wir brauchen einen Mentalitätswechsel. Risikobewusstsein ist wichtig, aber Technologiefeindlichkeit und Skepsis bis hin zu Hysterie bringen uns nicht weiter. Zudem brauchen wir bessere Strukturen im öffentlichen Teil des Innovationssystems. Strukturen, die Wettbewerb ermöglichen – und erzwingen. Das bedeutet mehr Autonomie der Hochschulen und Studiengebühren verbunden mit einem funktionierenden Stipendiensystem. So gewinnen deutsche Hochschulen auf dem globalen Bildungsmarkt wieder mehr Attraktivität für Studenten und Spitzenkräfte aus dem In- und Ausland und so können wir auch den „Brain-Drain" bei deutschen Spitzenforschern stoppen. Nur im Ausbau von Wissensvorsprüngen liegt unsere ökonomische Zukunft. Mit Niedriglohnländern wird Deutschland langfristig kaum konkurrieren können. Die Generierung von Ideen und deren Umsetzung in innovative Produkte und Verfahren sind für den Standort Deutschland der Schlüssel zur Zukunft. Der Forschungs-, Technologie- und Bildungspolitik muss daher im Spektrum der Wirtschaftspolitiken ein höherer Stellenwert eingeräumt werden. Es kommt auf beides an: Wir müssen unsere Schwächen abbauen – runter mit den Kosten, weniger Bürokratie – und wir müssen unsere Stärken stärken, vor allem unsere Innovationsfähigkeit. Nur so sorgen wir für einen attraktiven Standort. Denn nur so werden wir zukunftsfähige Wertschöpfungspotenziale erschließen können. ∎

Analysis & Vision

more investments projects for the future, for example in research and development. We only allocate 2.4 per cent of our gross domestic product to this end. Of these two thirds can be attributed to the economy and one third to the public sector. 25 years ago this proportion was still 50:50. The USA spend a total of 2.8 per cent of their GDP on R&D, Finland 3.5 per cent and Sweden even 4.3 per cent.

This policy will not remain without consequences. Germany's share in world trade with R&D-intensive goods has declined and the contribution of R&D-intensive goods to our export trade balance has been declining since 1994. Indeed, it is still on a high level, but the reduction is clearly visible. Above all, this development is still cushioned by the outstanding strength of the automobile sector. We have to set pragmatic priorities. The public sector must invest more in the future again and consume less. Budgets for R&D have been strongly adjusted upwards in many states in the recent years – often despite the prevailing pressure for consolidation. Between 2000 and 2002 there was a plus of about six per cent in Germany, in Sweden it was just less than 30 per cent, in the USA 25 per cent and even in recession-struck Japan it was 15 per cent.

But the truth is also: money isn't everything and innovations are also always a question of intellectual attitudes in society and politics. We need a change in mentality. It is important to have a consciousness for risks, but animosity towards technology and scepticism bordering on hysteria will not bring us further. Moreover, we need better structures in the public part of the innovation system. Structures that enable – and force – competition. That means an increased autonomy for universities and study fees linked with a functioning system of grants. In this way German universities will be increasingly attractive again for domestic and foreign students and top staff on the global education market and we will be able to stop the "Brain-Drain" of German top researchers. Only by expanding our knowledge advantage we have an economic future. In the long run, Germany will hardly be able to compete with low-wage countries. Generating ideas and applying these results in innovative products and procedures is the key to the future for the business location of Germany. Therefore research, technology and education policy must receive a higher priority in the context of economic policies. Both issues are important: we must reduce our weaknesses – lower the costs, less bureaucracy – and we must increase our strengths, above all our capacity of innovation. This is the only way that we can secure an attractive business location. In fact, this is the only way to develop future-oriented potential of added value. ■

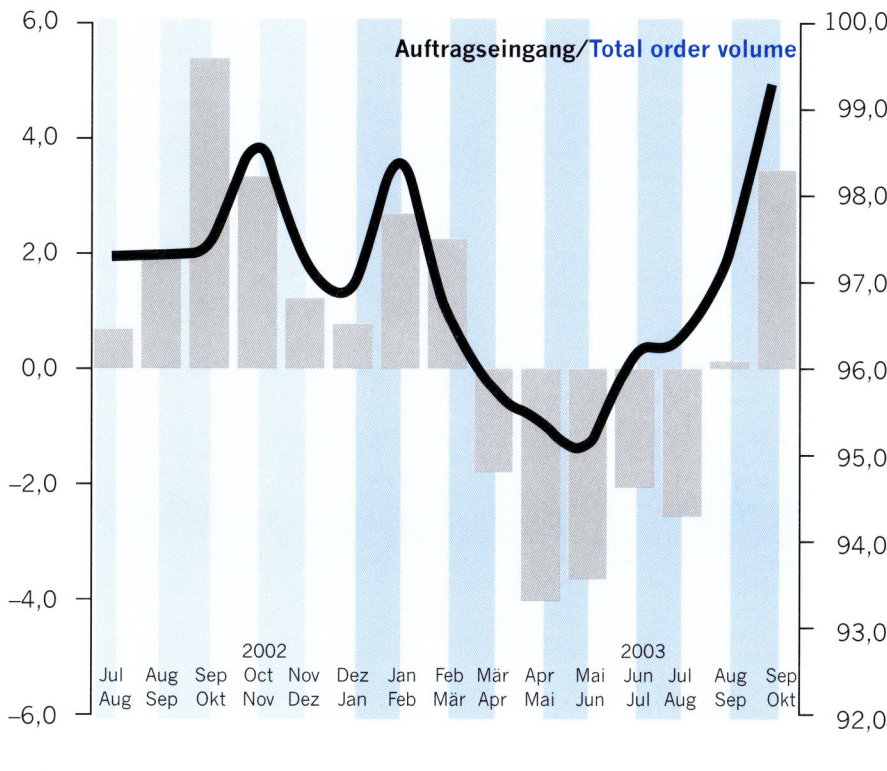

**Ende der Stagnationsphase in der Industrie/
End of the stagnation phase in industry**
Auftragseingang* und Produktion**, 2-Monats-Durchschnitt
Total order volume* and production**, 2-months average

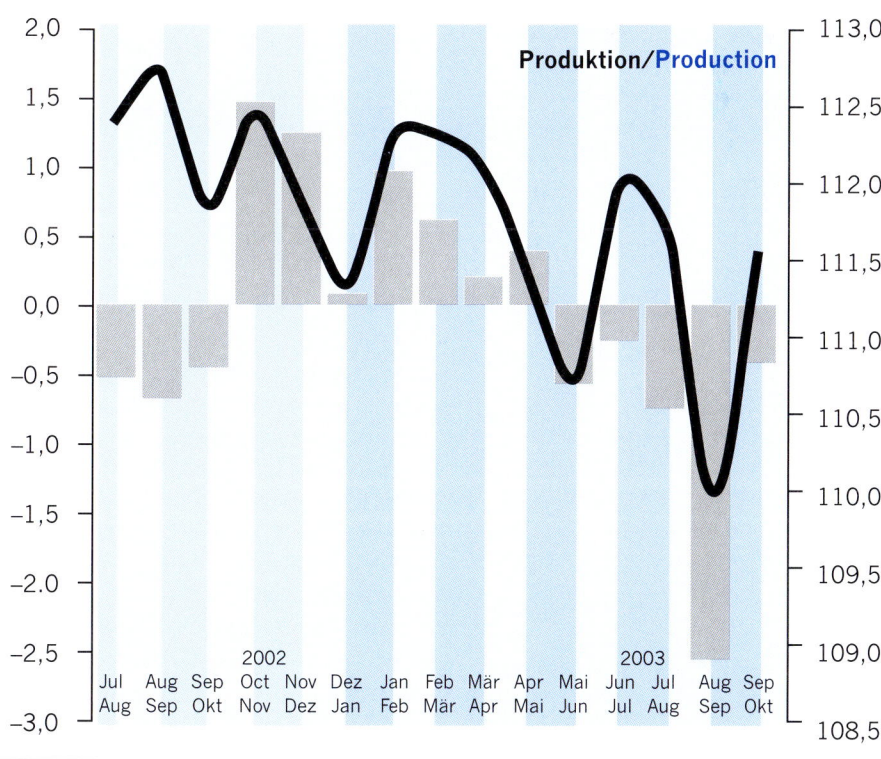

— Index, saisonbereinigt (rechte Achse)/Index, seasonally adjusted (right axis)
▬ Veränderung zum Vorjahr in % (linke Achse)/Change against previous year in % (left axis)

*Verarbeitendes Gewerbe, Volumenindex 200=100/*Manufacturing industry, index volume 200=100
Produzierendes Gewerbe, 1995=100/Producing industry, 1995=100
Quellen: Statist. Bundesamt, Deutsche Bundesbank/Sources: Federal Statistical Office, German Fed. Bank

Premium Bodywear AG

Vorstand/Chief Executive Officer:
Frank K. Markert

Vorsitzender des Aufsichtsrates/Chairman of the Board:
Dr. Torsten Voß

Gründungsjahr/Year of Foundation:
März 2002/March 2002

Mitarbeiter/Employees: 54

Zielgruppen/Target Groups:
marken- und modewusste Menschen
Brand and fashion conscious people

Kunden/Customers:
Facheinzelhandel, selektierte Fachabteilungen von Warenhäusern/
Specialist retail trade, selected special departments of department stores

Produkte/Products:
Damen- und Herrenwäsche/
Ladies and gents underwear

Anschrift/Address:
Chemnitzer Straße 36–38
D-09228 Chemnitz/Germany
Telefon +49 (37200) 860-0
Telefax +49 (37200) 860-314
E-Mail info@prebo.de
Internet www.olafbenz.com

Company Profile

Mit Designerwäsche nach oben: are you ready for red?

To the top with designer underwear: are you ready for red?

Kerngeschäft der Premium Bodywear AG ist die Produktion und der Vertrieb von Designerwäsche.

Das Unternehmen übernahm die Rechte an den erfolgreich platzierten Labels Olaf Benz und Manstore.

Flaggschiff des Unternehmens ist die Marke Olaf Benz. 1989 gestartet, lange bevor die Designer-Szene die Wäsche im gehobenen Genre entdeckte. Das Kollektionsdesign liegt in der Hand des Stilisten Alfons Kreuzer.

Erfolgsbasis ist eine klare Zielgruppen-Denkweise. Olaf Benz bedient junge, intelligente Clubbing-People, modebegeistert, busy, körperbewusst, sportiv. Wäsche gehört zum selbstverständlichen Outfit nach der Devise „nur wer sich gut anzieht, kann sich gut ausziehen". Olaf Benz ist viel eher Überals Unter-Wäsche. Komfortabel für jeden Tag, gleichzeitig proper und fashion und immer mit ausgezeichneten Passformen.

Entscheidend ist die internationale Vermarktung. Von Vorstand Frank K. Markert wurde die strategische Ausrichtung auf den Export präzisiert. Internationale Messen und der Aufbau eines globalen Vertriebsnetzes haben höchste Priorität. Im Ergebnis liegt der Exportanteil über 60 %. Im internationalen Ranking gehört Olaf Benz zu den Top Twenty der Underwear Labels.

Dritter strategischer Faktor ist die aufmerksame Kooperation mit dem Handel. Sichere NOS Programme gehören genauso zur Palette wie gezielte Flächenbewirtschaftung und die Ausstattung des Händlers mit Promotionthemen. „Top-Down" ist die Formel für die Marktentwicklung. Zuerst werden imagebildende Marktführer gewonnen. In Berlin das KaDeWe, Galleries Lafayette in Paris, Bloomingdales in New York sind Beispiele für erfolgreiche Initialzündungen bei der Entwicklung nationaler Märkte. Für die Zukunft sieht Frank K. Markert rot. Rot steht nicht nur für Feuer, Durchsetzung, Innovation und Energie. Rot ist vor allem die CI Farbe von Olaf Benz. ■

Core business of Premium Bodywear AG is the production and sale of designer underwear. The company took over the copyrights of the successfully positioned labels Olaf Benz and Manstore.

The company's flagship is the brand Olaf Benz. It started in 1989, long before the designer scene discovered underwear of the exclusive segment. The collection's design is in the hands of the stylist Alfons Kreuzer.

Basis for our success is a clearly outlined attitude of thinking in target groups. Olaf Benz caters for young, intelligent clubbing people, fashion enthusiasts that are busy, body-conscious and sportive. Underwear is part of their natural outfit just like the slogan "only who dresses well, can undress equally" portrays. Olaf Benz is much more top wear than underwear. Comfortable enough for wearing every day and at the same time proper and fashionable as well as always in the most perfect fitting forms.

Of major importance is our international marketing strategy. CEO Frank K. Markert has given a more precise profile to a strategic orientation towards export. International trade fairs and the building up of a global sales network are of utmost priority. The result shows an export rate of over 60 %. In international ranking, Olaf Benz is one of the top twenty underwear labels.

The third strategic factor is a systematic cooperation with retail trade. Part of the range are secure NOS programmes as well as a targeted coverage of area supplies and the equipment of shops with promotional themes. "Top-Down" as our formula for market development. In the first instance, image-building market leaders are recruited. The KaDeWe department store in Berlin, Galleries Lafayette in Paris and Bloomingdales in New York are examples for successful initial launches when embarking on the development of national markets. Frank K. Markert sees a red future on the horizon. Red stands not only for fire, achievement, innovation and energy. Above all red is the CI colour of Olaf Benz. ■

Company Profile

Bindan: der Pionier für Personaldienstleistungen

Bindan: the personnel service pioneer

Ein einzigartiges Spezialisierungskonzept prägt den Ruf der Bindan-Gruppe.
The Bindan Group is characterised by its unique specialist concept.

Personaldienstleistungen haben auch in Deutschland einen festen Platz in der Wirtschafts- und Arbeitswelt erobert – als unentbehrliches Flexibilisierungs- und Rekrutierungsinstrument für Unternehmen und als Karrieresprungbrett für Arbeitnehmer aller Berufsgruppen.

Als Pionier dieser Dienstleistung gründete Günter Bindan 1960 das erste Zeitarbeitsunternehmen in Deutschland. Seitdem zählt die Bindan-Gruppe zu den TOP-Organisationen der Branche – mit annähernd 100 Niederlassungen und über 4.000 fest beschäftigten Fachkräften (Stand: März 2005).

Bindan hat sich auf die Beschäftigung und Überlassung qualifizierter Berufsgruppen spezialisiert. Dieses konsequent marktbezogene Spartenkonzept zeichnet die Einzigartigkeit der Unternehmensgruppe aus: Jede Niederlassung ist ausschließlich auf nur eine der drei Geschäftssparten spezialisiert: auf „Produktions- und Montagedienste" (gewerbliche Fachberufe für Industrie und Handwerk), „Kaufmännische Dienste" (kaufmännische Fach- und Führungskräfte) oder „Konstruktion und Engineering" (Ingenieure, Techniker, technische Zeichner). Die letztgenannte Sparte firmiert inzwischen unter der eigenständigen Marke „Teccon".

Das „First Class" im Slogan spiegelt den Anspruch der Bindan-Gruppe wider: immer die erstklassige Adresse unter den Top-Anbietern für qualifizierte Personaldienstleistungen zu sein. ∎

Personnel services have fought for and won a firm position in the German economy and employment market. They have proved to be an essential tool for flexible staff and recruiting requirements for companies and a springboard for all kinds of employee career-paths.

Günter Bindan, a pioneer in this sector, founded Germany's first employment agency in 1960. Since then the Bindan Group has been one of the TOP organisations in the sector, with almost 100 branches and over 4,000 qualified permanent employees (as at March 2005).

Bindan specialises in employing and hiring out skilled employee groups. This consistent, market-related sectoral concept is the group's hallmark: every branch office specialises exclusively in just one of three employee groups: skilled industrial staff, skilled office and management staff es well as engineers, technicians and technical drawing staff. The latter sector is based in its own company under the name of "Teccon".

The "First Class" in the slogan reflects the Bindan Group's claim: being the sole top address among the top providers for skilled personnel services. ∎

Bindan-Gruppe

Geschäftsführer/Managers:
Bernd D. Habel
(Vorsitzender/Chairman of the Managing Board)
Rudolf Gabrielczyk
Thomas Schulze

Marketingleiter/Marketing Manager:
Heino Hellmers

Gründungsjahr/Year of Foundation:
1960

Mitarbeiter/Employees:
Über 4.000 Mitarbeiter
in 97 Niederlassungen (Stand März 2005)
Over 4,000 employees
at 97 branches (as at March 2005)

Geschäftstätigkeit/Business Activity:
Personaldienstleistungen:
Zeitarbeit, Temp-to-Hire, Personalvermittlung, On-Site-Service, Outsourcing, Outplacement; Konstruktion und Engineering (nur Teccon)
Personnel services, temporary staff, temp-to-hire, recruiting, on-site services, outsourcing, outplacement;
construction and engineering (Teccon only)

Geschäftsbereiche/Areas of business:
Bindan Produktions- und Montagedienste
Bindan Kaufmännische Dienste
Teccon Konstruktion und Engineering
Bindan Industry Services
Bindan Office Services
Teccon Engineering

Anschrift Hauptverwaltung/
The address of the head office:
Bahnhofstraße 8
D-28816 Stuhr/b.Bremen
Telefon +49 (421) 89 93-0
Telefax +49 (421) 89 93-200
Internet www.bindan.de

Gewerkschaften

Für Reformen, gegen soziale Ungerechtigkeit

For reforms, against social injustice

Deutschland steht vor den komplexen Herausforderungen einer Gesellschaft in der Übergangsphase von der Industriegesellschaft in eine zunehmend wissensbasierte Gesellschaft. Der Wettbewerb hoch entwickelter Volkswirtschaften entwickelt sich immer mehr zu einem Innovationswettbewerb. Die Innovationsfähigkeit der Unternehmen und die Innovationsfähigkeit der Gesellschaft sind entscheidende Voraussetzungen und Basis für das Sichern der vorhandenen Arbeitsplätze, die Schaffung von neuen Arbeitsplätzen und unser aller Wohlstand. Auch wenn die Beschäftigungseffekte von Innovationen aufgrund von Rationalisierungs- und Substitutionseffekten nur schwer zu ermitteln sind, gibt es keine Alternative zu einer konsequenten Innovations-Strategie. Denn in globalisierten Märkten profitieren die innovativen Vorreiter, während bei den Nachzüglern oft die negativen Rationalisierungseffekte überwiegen. Ohne stetige Innovation droht Deutschland der Abstieg in die zweite Liga mit noch weniger Wachstum, noch höherer Arbeitslosigkeit und zunehmenden Modernisierungsdefiziten der gesellschaftlichen Infrastruktur. Doch der Strukturwandel zur Wissensgesellschaft verläuft in Deutschland zu langsam. Defizite zeigen sich bei der Innovationsfähigkeit hinsichtlich der Spitzentechnologie und damit bei den Produkten mit den höchsten Wachstumspotenzialen. Deutschland ist zwar immer noch eine der stärksten Industrienationen, das zeigt sich an den Exporten, doch zugleich Netto-Technologieimporteur. Die technologische Stärke der deutschen Wirtschaft konzentriert sich bisher immer noch in den traditionellen Märkten und herkömmlichen, mittleren Technologien.

Innovation wird in Deutschland vielfach immer noch sehr verkürzt als technischer Fortschritt buchstabiert. Doch Innovation ist ein komplexer sozialer Prozess, in dessen Mittelpunkt der Mensch, seine Qualifikationen, seine Kreativität und seine Motivation als Quelle jeglicher Innovation steht. Die Innovationsfähigkeit der Unternehmen hängt von der Produktivität der Wissens- und Dienstleistungsarbeiter ab. Denn Innovationen werden von Menschen erdacht. Ignoranz gegenüber dem Arbeitsvermögen der Einzelnen ist eine Kernursache nachlassender Innovationskraft.

Ein rohstoffarmes Land wie Deutschland lebt von der Kreativität der Beschäftigten. Ein zukunftsfähiges Innovationskonzept muss deshalb weg von der bisherigen Technologiezentrierung und Innovation als sozialen Prozess eine nachhaltige Innovationsstrategie verstehen deren Kern Ent-

Michael Sommer

Der 1952 in Büderich geborene Autor ist seit 2003 Vorsitzender des Deutschen Gewerkschaftsbundes. Von 1971 bis 1980 absolvierte er ein Politologiestudium an der Freien Universität (FU) Berlin und übte in dieser Zeit bereits verschiedene ehrenamtliche Gewerkschaftsfunktionen aus. Anschließend war er zunächst Dozent im Bildungszentrum der Deutschen Postgewerkschaft (DPG) in Gladenbach und übte ab 1981 verschiedene Gewerkschaftsfunktionen aus. Ab 1997 war er stellvertretender Vorsitzender der DPG, ab 2001 stellvertretender Bundesvorsitzender der Vereinten Dienstleistungsgewerkschaft ver.di. Michael Sommer ist seit 1981 Mitglied der SPD.

The author was born in Büderich in 1952 and has been chairman of the German Association of Unions since 2003. From 1971 until 1980 he studied politics at the Free University (FU) of Berlin, and he served in that period already in several voluntary union functions. Subsequently he worked as lecturer in the Bildungszentrum der Deutschen Postgewerkschaft (DPG/Education Centre of the German Postal Union) in Gladenbach and held various union positions from 1981. From 1997, he served as substitute chairman of DPG; from 2001 substitute national chairman of the Association of Service Sector Unions ver.di. Michael Sommer has been a member of the German socialist party SPD since 1981.

Förderung von Anfang an – für das Leben lernen wir.
Support right from the beginning – we learn for life.

wicklung, Förderung und Pflege des Arbeitsvermögens der Menschen bildet. Wenn wir in Deutschland in unsere Zukunft investieren

Unions

Germany is currently confronting the complex challenges connected with the transition from an industrialised society to an increasingly knowledge-based society. The competition between highly developed national economies is more and more converting into an innovation competition. The companies' capacity of innovation and the society's capacity of innovation are major prerequisites and basis for securing existing workplaces, for creating new jobs and for the prosperity of us all. Even if the effects of innovation on employment can only be established with great difficulty because of the effects of rationalisation and substitution, there is no other alternative but to follow a consistent innovation strategy. Indeed, in globalised markets innovative precursors benefit first, while with late-comers often the negative effects of rationalisation prevail. Without continuous innovation Germany is in danger of being relegated to the second league with even less growth, even higher unemployment and increasing deficits of modernising the social infrastructure.

However, the structural change to becoming a knowledge-based society is progressing too slowly in Germany. Deficits are prevalent in the capacity of innovation with regard to sophisticated technologies and therefore regarding products that have the highest growth potentials. Of course, Germany is still one of the strongest industrialised nations, alone the export figures prove this, but at the same time it is a net technology importer. The technological strength of Germany's economy is still concentrated in the traditional markets and conventional, intermediate technologies.

In Germany, innovation is still often defined in a very short form as technical progress. But innovation is a complex social process, at the centre of which stand the human being, his qualifications, his creativity and his motivation as the source of any innovation. The capacity of innovation in companies depends on the productivity of knowledge and service providers among their employees. In fact, innovations are thought up by people. The ignorance about the individual's ability to work is one of the major causes for the declining power of innovation.

A country that has limited resources of raw materials like Germany thrives on the creativity of its employees. A future-oriented concept of innovation must therefore understand innovation as a social process, parting from the focus on technology so far, and place at its centre the development, support and enhancement of the working ability of the human being. If we do want to invest in the future here in Germany, we must invest considerably more in the human beings.

Investitionen in Menschen sind Investitionen in die Zukunft.
Investments in people are investments for the future.

As the development of popular sports is an undeniable prerequisite for top performances in sports, we need a better general education for all to be able to keep pace. Instead we allow a life-long continuing exclusion, where it is important to invest in life-long accompanying learning. These key words are meanwhile adequately known. There is no deficit of recognition any longer, but a deficit of action.

• Germany is structurally lagging behind in early child development between 10 and 15 years. This is valid for all children, but particularly for those that have a special need of support. Especially with regard to children that have a migration background, with the missing early development a chain of continuous marginalisation starts in the education and employment system, which is undeniably accompanied by increased drop out rates from schools, missing training, higher unemployment rates and missing social integration.
• The lack of children's nursery facilities leads generally to mothers having to stand in, and therefore professional competencies acquired in long years of training are left unexploited. The costs that arise for companies because of the mothers' interruption of employment have now even been calculated.
• The PISA study showed just how enormous the German deficits are in terms of general education and the support of top performances. Countries that develop children without prior selection, achieve the best results in schooling. No other industrialised nation shows such close correlation between social origin and success in school as Germany. The low rankings in university admissions and of university graduates therefore come as no surprise.

Gewerkschaften

Beruf und Familie müssen sich besser vereinbaren lassen.
Profession and family must be more compatible.

wollen, müssen wir wesentlich mehr in die Menschen investieren.

Wie beim Sport die Breitenförderung unabdingbare Voraussetzung für Spitzenleistungen ist, benötigen wir eine bessere Grundlagenausbildung für alle, um in der Spitze mitzuhalten. Stattdessen dulden wir lebenslange fortschreitende Ausgrenzung, wo es darauf ankäme, in lebensbegleitendes Lernen zu investieren. Diese Stichworte sind mittlerweile hinlänglich bekannt. Wir haben längst kein Erkenntnisdefizit mehr, sondern ein Handlungsdefizit:

• In der frühkindlichen Förderung ist Deutschland strukturell 10 bis 15 Jahre im Rückstand. Das gilt für alle Kinder, ganz besonders aber für solche mit besonderem Förderbedarf. Gerade was beispielsweise Kinder mit Migrationshintergrund betrifft, beginnt mit der fehlenden Frühförderung eine Kette von fortgesetzten Ausgrenzungen im Bildungs- und Beschäftigungssystem, die mit erhöhten Schulabbrecherquoten, fehlenden Ausbildungen, höherer Arbeitslosenquote und fehlender sozialer Integration unabweisbar einhergeht.
• Die fehlende Ausstattung mit Kindertageseinrichtungen führt dazu, dass – im Wesentlichen – Mütter einspringen und deshalb in langjährigen Ausbildungen erworbene berufliche Kompetenzen brachliegen lassen müssen. Die Kosten, die Betrieben durch die Unterbrechungen der Erwerbstätigkeit von Müttern entstehen, sind in Studien inzwischen sogar durchgerechnet.
• PISA hat uns gezeigt, wie groß die deutschen Defizite bei der Breitenförderung und bei der Förderung von Spitzenleistungen sind. Länder, die ohne Aussonderung fördern, erreichen die besten schulischen Leistungen. In keinem anderen Industriestaat stehen soziale Herkunft und Schulerfolg in so engem Zusammenhang wie in Deutschland. Über die hinteren Plätze bei der Hochschulzugangsberechtigung und bei den Hochschulabsolventen muss man sich deshalb nicht wundern.

Das Missmanagement beim Umgang mit dem individuellen Arbeitsvermögens setzt sich in den betrieblichen Abläufen fort:
• Es ist nach wie vor nicht gelungen, die Nachfrage nach betrieblichen Ausbildungsplätzen mit dem Angebot ins Gleichgewicht zu bringen. Seit Jahren fehlen in hohem Maß betriebliche Ausbildungsplätze. Für viel zu viele junge Menschen stehen Ausgrenzungen am Beginn ihres Erwachsenenlebens. Bis zu 17 Prozent eines Ausbildungsjahrganges bleiben dauerhaft ohne einen Ausbildungsabschluss. Vor dem Hintergrund der sich wandelnden Beschäftigtenstruktur droht ihnen Arbeitslosigkeit als Lebensschicksal.
• Wir brauchen ein Mehr an innovativer und partizipativer Arbeitszeitgestaltung vor Ort. Die Arbeitsprozesse in den Unternehmen müssen so gestaltet werden, dass die Menschen ihre Fähigkeiten, ihr Wissen und ihre Erfahrungen und nicht zuletzt ihre innovativen Potenziale und Ideen entfalten können.
• Bei lebenslangem Lernen kann es nicht nur um berufliche Bildung gehen. Auch kulturelle und politische Weiterbildung müssen hier als Mitvoraussetzungen für soziale Integration ihren Platz finden. Und wir brauchen lebensbegleitendes Lernen für alle. Nur so kann eine Kette neuer Chancen für alle eröffnet werden. Bildung muss gesellschaftliche Aufgabe mit öffentlicher Verantwortung bleiben. Aktuell brauchen wir eine Offensive für Arbeit, Ausbildung und Qualifizierung. Die Langzeitarbeitslosigkeit kann nur zurückgehen, wenn gering Qualifizierte und besondere Problemgruppen – vor allem in strukturschwachen Regionen – weiterhin gefördert werden.
• Wir brauchen eine bessere Work-Life-Balance: Arbeiten, Leben und Lernen werden in Zukunft stärker verzahnt sein müssen. Das betrifft die Vereinbarkeit von Familie und Erwerbstätigkeit sowie auch für Fragen des altersgerechten Arbeitens. Gerade im Zusammenhang sich wandelnder Erwerbsbiografien erwarten die Menschen soziale Sicherheit. Doch die tradierten sozialen Sicherungssysteme leisten das nicht mehr. Die Einnahmebasis der Sozialversicherungen muss kurz- und mittelfristig durch eine offensive Wachstums- und Beschäftigungspolitik stabilisiert werden. Dies kann durch ein Absenken der Sozialabgaben begleitet werden. Durch eine leistungsgerechte Begrenzung der Ausgaben auf die originären Aufgaben der Sozialversicherung wie durch die Steigerung von Wirtschaftlichkeit und Effizienz könnte die Abgabenbelastung schon kurzfristig gesenkt werden. Dadurch entstünden Wachstums- und Beschäftigungseffekte, die die sozialen Sicherungssysteme stabilisieren würden. Langfristig müssen die sozialen Sicherungssysteme zu einer allgemeinen Erwerbstätigenversicherung umgebaut werden. Neue Lebensrisiken wie wechselnde Zeiten der abhängigen Beschäftigung, der projektförmigen Selbstständigkeit, Familien- oder Bildungsphasen müssen in die sozialen Sicherungssysteme eingepasst werden.

Damit die öffentlichen Hände die beschriebenen Aufgaben erfüllen können, ist es notwendig, eine neue soziale Balance in der Steuerpolitik zu finden. Die Finanzierung der öffentlichen Haushalte kann nicht mehr immer weiter den Arbeitnehmerinnen und Arbeitnehmern aufgebürdet werden. Denn die schlechte Verfassung der öffentlichen Haushalte ist nicht allein eine Folge der wirtschaftlichen Entwicklung, sondern die Folge von massiven Einbrüchen des Steueraufkommens, beispielsweise durch Fehler bei der Reform der Unternehmensbesteuerung. Wir brauchen deshalb eine neue Steuergerechtigkeit zwischen abhängig Beschäftigten und Kapital. Deutschland braucht Reformen. Doch Reform ist, wenn es besser wird. Wir brauchen deshalb dringend ein Umsteuern des Reformprozesses. Vorrangig muss es darauf ankommen, die Menschen dabei zu unterstützen, die Herausforderungen des globalen Strukturwandels mit Zuversicht anzunehmen, durch Innovationen bei Bildung, Qualifizierung und sozialer Sicherheit. Nur so werden wir in Deutschland weiter an der Spitze mithalten können. ∎

Unions

Innovationen werden von Menschen erdacht.

Innovations are thought up by people.

Mismanagement when dealing with the individual ability to work continues in the procedures within companies:

• It has still not been achieved to balance out the demand for training places in companies with provided vacancies. For years, there has been a tremendous lack of training places in companies. The fact of exclusion emerges for far too many young people right at the beginning of their adult life. Up to 17 per cent of youth belonging to one training year will never complete training at all. Against the background of changing employment structures they are threatened by permanent unemployment as their life's destiny.

• We need increased local innovative and participative working hour arrangements. Work processes in companies must be structured in such a way that people are able to develop their capacities, their knowledge and their experiences and ultimately also their potentials for innovation and ideas.

• Life-long learning must not only mean professional education. Also cultural and political continuous education must find their place here as additional condition for social integration. And we need life-accompanying learning for all. This is the only way that a chain of new opportunities can be opened up for all. Education must continue to be a social task of public responsibility. At present, we need an offensive strategy for employment, training and qualification. Long-term unemployment can only be reduced if lowly qualified and special problem groups – particularly in structurally weak regions – are continuously supported.

• We need a better balance between work and life: working, living and learning must be interconnected must stronger in future. This concerns the compatibility of family and employment as well as issues of work suited to appropriate age-groups. Especially in connection with changing employment biographies, people are expecting social security. However, the traditional social security systems do not provide this any longer. The income basis of social insurances must be stabilised in the short and medium term by an offensive growth and employment policy. This can be accompanied by a reduction of social security contributions. The load of contributions could be reduced already without delay through a performance-based limitation of expenditure to the original tasks of social insurance as well as through increasing profitability and efficiency. This would create growth and employment effects, which in turn would stabilise the social security systems. In the long run, social security systems must be remodelled into a general employee insurance. New risks in life, like changing times of dependent employment, of project-like self-employment, family or educational periods, must be integrated into social security systems. In order for local governments to be able to fulfil the described tasks it is necessary to find a new social balance in tax politics. Employees cannot be burdened more and more with the financing of public budgets. In fact, the bad condition of public budgets is not only a consequence of economic development, but the result of massive setbacks in tax income, for instance because of mistakes in the reform of company taxation laws. We therefore need a new justice in taxation laws for dependently working employees and capital gains.

Germany needs reforms. But a reform must make things better. We therefore urgently need a redirection of the process of reform. Primarily the issue must be to support people in accepting the challenges of global structural changes confidently, by providing innovations in education, qualification and social security. This is the only way Germany can continue to keep pace at top level.■

Wir brauchen lebensbegleitendes Lernen für alle.

We need life-accompanying learning for all.

Company Profile

Deutsche Post World Net – drei starke Marken

Deutsche Post World Net – three strong brand names

Deutsche Post World Net zählt zu den größten und leistungsfähigsten Logistikanbietern weltweit und ist das größte Postunternehmen Europas. Mit dem Ziel, die weltweite Nummer 1 in der Logistik zu werden, hat Deutsche Post World Net in den vergangenen Jahren eine rasante Entwicklung durchgemacht.

Vom defizitären Staatsunternehmen Deutsche Bundespost führte der Weg seit 1990 über den profitablen europäischen Brief- und Paketdienstleister zum global agierenden Logistikkonzern. Seit dem Jahr 2000 ist die Deutsche Post AG an der Börse notiert und wird seit März 2001 im DAX 30 geführt.

Die Deutsche Post World Net verfolgt eine konsequente Wachstums- und Internationalisierungsstrategie. Unter dem Dach des Konzerns mit Sitz in Bonn sind heute die drei starken Marken Deutsche Post, DHL und Postbank in einem Leistungsverbund vereint. Insgesamt ist Deutsche Post World Net damit sehr gut positioniert, um die großen Chancen der Globalisierung zu nutzen.

Der Unternehmensbereich BRIEF ist allein in Deutschland Partner für drei Millionen Geschäftskunden und erbringt Leistungen für 39 Millionen Haushalte. Rund 80.000 Zusteller, über 12.000 Filialen, 3.500 Auslieferungsstützpunkte und 108.000 Briefkästen stellen eine flächendeckende Infrastruktur sicher. Gleichzeitig nutzt die Deutsche Post die Chancen auf den Briefmärkten im Ausland, z. B. in den Niederlanden, Großbritannien und den USA. Im Bereich EXPRESS/LOGISTIK setzt das Unternehmen Maßstäbe in Sachen integrierter weltweiter Logistik. DHL ist in mehr als 220 Ländern und Regionen weltweit präsent und bietet seinen Kunden Lösungen entlang der gesamten logistischen Wertschöpfungskette.

Die Postbank ist die Leistungsmarke aus dem Unternehmensbereich FINANZ DIENSTLEISTUNGEN. Sie ist die führende Retailbank in Deutschland mit einem umfassenden Allfinanz-Angebot einschließlich Brokerage, Bausparen und Versicherungen. Fast 12 Millionen Kunden – davon 1,8 Millionen Online-Kunden – sowie 9.000 Filialen bundesweit sprechen für die starke Marktstellung des Finanzdienstleisters. Seit dem 23. Juni 2004 ist die Postbank börsennotiert. Hauptanteilseigner ist Deutsche Post World Net. ∎

Company Profile

Deutsche Post World Net is one of the largest and most efficient logistics services providers worldwide and the largest postal services enterprise in Europe. Pursuing the aim of becoming the global number 1 in logistics, Deutsche Post World Net has experienced an enormous development in recent years.

Formerly Deutsche Bundespost, its path has led from a state-owned company run to a deficit through to a profitable European letter and parcel service since 1990 and finally to a globally active logistics corporation. Since the year 2000, Deutsche Post AG is listed on the stock exchange and since March 2001, it is listed in the DAX 30.

Deutsche Post World Net follows a consistent growth and internationalisation strategy. Under the company's roof with head office in Bonn, today, three strong brand names, namely Deutsche Post, DHL and Postbank are united in service cooperation. On the whole, Deutsche Post World Net is therefore excellently positioned in order to use the great chances of globalisation beneficially.

The company's division of LETTERS alone is in Germany partner to three million corporate clients and generates services for 39 million households. About 80,000 delivering agents, over 12,000 branches, 3,500 distribution centres and 108,000 post boxes ensure complete coverage of the nationwide infrastructure. At the same time, Deutsche Post takes advantage of its chances on the market segments for letters abroad, for instance in the Netherlands, Great Britain and the USA. In the field of EXPRESS/LOGISTICS the company is setting benchmarks with respect to integrated global logistics. DHL is present in more than 220 countries and regions worldwide and offers its clients comprehensive solutions along the entire line of the logistic net product chain.

Postbank is the service trademark of the company's division FINANCIAL SERVICES. It is the leading retail bank in Germany offering comprehensive all-inclusive financial services, like brokerage, saving with a building society and insurances for instance. Almost 12 million customers, of these 1.8 million online customers, as well as 9.000 branches nationwide speak for the strong market position of this financial services provider. Since 23rd June 2004, Postbank is listed on the stock exchange. Main shareholder is Deutsche Post World Net.

Deutsche Post World Net
MAIL EXPRESS LOGISTICS FINANCE

Deutsche Post World Net

Vorstandsvorsitzender/Chairman of the Board of Management:
Dr. Klaus Zumwinkel

Vorstand/Executive Board:
Dr. Edgar Ernst
Walter Scheurle
Dr. Hans-Dieter Petram
Dr. Peter E. Kruse
Uwe R. Dörken
Dr. Frank Appel
Prof. Dr. Wulf von Schimmelmann

Gründungsjahr/Year of Foundation:
1990

Mitarbeiterzahl/Number of Employees:
383.000 (Stand 31.12.2003)

Umsatz 2003/Turnover 2003:
40,017 Milliarden Euro,
EBITA 2,975 Milliarden Euro

Geschäftsfelder/Business Fields:
BRIEF (Marke: Deutsche Post)
EXPRESS/LOGISTIK (Marke: DHL)
FINANZ DIENSTLEISTUNGEN (Marke: Postbank)

Anschrift/Address:
Deutsche Post AG
Charles-de-Gaulle-Straße 20
53113 Bonn
Deutschland/Germany
Telefon   +49 (228) 182-0
Telefax   +49 (228) 182-70 99
Internet   http://www.deutschepost.de

Der Unternehmensbereich BRIEF betreut drei Millionen Geschäftskunden und 39 Millionen Haushalte. DHL ist in mehr als 220 Ländern und Regionen weltweit präsent und die Postbank hat fast 12 Millionen Kunden.

The company's division of LETTERS supports three million corporate clients and 39 million households. DHL is present in more than 220 countries and regions worldwide and the Postbank has almost 12 million customers.

Bürokratieabbau – DIHK für die Entlastung der Unternehmen

Reducing bureaucracy – DIHK supports reducing the load on businesses

Die Summe der Regelungen ist das Problem – Bürokratie kostet Zeit, Geld und Nerven. Mehr als 5.000 Gesetze und Verordnungen mit mehr als 85.000 Einzelvorschriften lähmen in Deutschland die unternehmerische Gestaltungskraft. Dabei ist meist nicht die bürokratische Einzelregelung, sondern vielmehr das undurchsichtige Regulierungsdickicht in seiner Gesamtheit das Problem. Der deutsche Bürokratiedschungel ist über Jahrzehnte gewachsen. Auch die Bilanz der rot-grünen Bundesregierung seit 1998 ist ernüchternd: 95 abgeschafften Bundesgesetzen stehen 396 neue gegenüber. Allein im Steuerrecht gab es seit 1998 wieder 84 neue Gesetze.

Nach einer Untersuchung des Instituts für Mittelstandsforschung (IfM) in Bonn betragen die Bürokratiekosten für die Wirtschaft inzwischen 46 Mrd. Euro im Jahr. Dies ist ein Anstieg von 50 Prozent im Vergleich zum Jahr 1994, als das IfM Bürokratiekosten in Höhe von 30 Mrd. Euro errechnete. Kleinunternehmen müssen dabei höhere bürokratische Lasten schultern als Großunternehmen. Der Zukauf externer Expertise, z. B. von Steuerberatern, ist teuer. Daher bleibt den Chefs kleiner Unternehmen meist gar nichts anderes übrig, als selbst in die bürokratischen Untiefen einzutauchen – zu Lasten unternehmerischer Aktivitäten. Dies zeigt auch die Studie des IfM: Pro Kopf ist der Zeitaufwand infolge bürokratischer Regelungen in Unternehmen mit weniger als fünf Beschäftigten mehr als elfmal höher als in größeren Unternehmen mit mehr als 500 Beschäftigten. Allein die Erledigung bürokratischer Pflichten beansprucht in einem Unternehmen mit vier Mitarbeitern sieben Arbeitswochen im Jahr. So ist nicht verwunderlich, dass 84 Prozent der Bürokratiekosten der Mittelstand tragen muss. Hinzu kommt, dass die immer weiter anwachsende Komplexität von Rechtsvorschriften sowie häufige Gesetzesänderungen den Bürokratieverdruss der Unternehmer steigern. Es ist Zeit zum Umdenken.

Es gibt eine Vielzahl an Gebieten, in denen Bürokratie abgebaut werden müsste. Beispielhaft will ich hier für drei besonders gravierende Handlungsfelder Vorschläge des DIHK zur Beseitigung von bürokratischen Hemmnissen vorstellen.

Arbeitsrecht deregulieren

Das Arbeitsrecht ist für die meisten Unternehmen das größte Bürokratiehemmnis. Existenzgründer kämpfen insbesondere dann mit bürokratischen Belastungen, wenn sie neue Mitarbeiter einstellen. Dann müssen sie die Formalitäten für die Sozialversicherung regeln, Lohnsteuerangelegenheiten erledigen und einen arbeitsmedizinischen Dienst bereitstellen.

Ganz besonders komplex ist der gesetzliche Kündigungsschutz, der in Deutschland zu einem undurchschaubaren Richterrecht entartet ist. Hunderttausende Arbeitsgerichtsurteile zum Kündigungsschutz müssen jedes Jahr gefällt werden. Kein Unternehmer ist in der Lage, sich selbst mit den rechtlichen Grundlagen des Kündigungsschutzes zu befassen. Der einschlägige Kommentar zum Kündigungsschutz ist mit über 3.300 Seiten der Schrecken eines jeden Unternehmers. Daher fordert der DIHK, den Beschäftigtenschwellenwert, ab dem Unternehmen dem Kündigungsschutz unterliegen, von 5 auf 20 Mitarbeiter zu erhöhen. Dies würde mit einem Schlag 90 Prozent aller Unternehmen in Deutschland von einem zentralen Bürokratie- und Beschäftigungshemmnis befreien.

Steuerrecht konsequent vereinfachen

Auch das komplizierte Steuer- und Abgabenrecht mit seinen vielen Ausnahmetatbeständen und Sonderabzugsmöglichkeiten ist eine große Belastung. Es wird geschätzt, dass vom Weltschrifttum zum Steuerrecht 70 Prozent in Deutschland produziert werden. Selbst Steuerexperten müssen manches Mal passen. Wie soll sich da erst ein Unternehmer, der sich im tagtäglichen Wettbewerb bewähren muss, im Steuerdickicht zurechtfinden?

Dr. h. c. Ludwig Georg Braun

Der 1943 in Kassel geborene Autor betrieb nach seiner Ausbildung zum Bankkaufmann bei der Deutschen Bank AG praktische betriebswirtschaftliche Studien in England und den USA. 1968–1971 Geschäftsleitung der Laboratorios Americano S. A. Niteroi, R. J., Brasilien, einer Gesellschaft mit 1.600 Mitarbeitern, 1972 Eintritt in die B. Braun Melsungen AG, Mitglied des Vorstands, seit 1977 kaufmännische Gesamtverantwortung, Bestellung zum Vorstandssprecher, später Vorstandsvorsitzenden der B. Braun Melsungen AG, einem weltweit tätigen Versorger des Gesundheitsmarktes mit ca. 2,75 Milliarden Euro Konzernumsatz und 29.000 Mitarbeitern im Geschäftsjahr 2002. Er ist außerdem Präsident des Deutschen Industrie- und Handelskammertages DIHK.

The author, born in Kassel in 1943, qualified as a bank official with Deutsche Bank AG and subsequently completed practical studies of economics in England and the USA. From 1968–1971, he was in the management of Laboratorios Americano S. A. Niteroi, R. J., Brazil, a company with 1,600 employees. In 1972 he joined B. Braun Melsungen AG as member of the executive board; since 1977, he has been holding the overall commercial responsibility and was appointed speaker of the executive board; later he became chairman of the executive board of B. Braun Melsungen AG, which is a globally active provider of the health care market with approx. 2.75 billion Euros group turnover and 29,000 employees in the business year 2002. Moreover, Ludwig Georg Braun is president of the DIHK Deutscher Industrie- und Handelskammertag (assembly of German chambers of commerce and industry).

Reducing Bureaucracy

Pro Kopf ist der Zeitaufwand infolge bürokratischer Regelungen in Unternehmen mit weniger als fünf Beschäftigten mehr als elfmal höher als in Unternehmen mit mehr als 500 Beschäftigten.

The time taken up per capita due to official regulations in companies with less than five employees is more than eleven times higher than in companies with more than 500 employees.

The problem is the sum of regulations – bureaucracy costs time, money and nerves. More than 5,000 laws and regulations with over 85,000 individual regulations cripple business creativity. But the real problem is usually not individual bureaucratic regulations but rather their opacity in its entirety. Germany's bureaucratic jungle has been growing for decades. Even the record of the SPD/Green coalition government is sobering: it has abolished 95 federal laws but introduced 396 new ones.

According to a study by the Institute for Research into the Medium-Sized Industry Sector (IfM) in Bonn bureaucracy costs the economy now 46 thousand million Euros a year. This is an increase of 50 per cent compared to 1994, when the IfM calculated the cost of bureaucracy at 30 thousand million Euros. And small companies have a higher bureaucratic burden than big companies. Purchasing external expertise, e. g. of tax consultants, is expensive, so the heads of small companies usually have no other choice than to steep themselves in the bureaucratic depths at the expense of their business activities. The IfM study also shows that the time taken per capita supplying information required by the authorities in companies with less than five employees is more than eleven times higher than in larger companies with more than 500 employees. Supplying this information claims seven working weeks a year in companies with four employees. So it is not surprising that the medium-sized industry sector has to foot 84 per cent of the costs of bureaucracy. As well, the increasing complexity of regulations and frequent amendments to the law increase businessmen's annoyance with bureaucracy. It is time to rethink old ideas.

There is a multiplicity of areas in which bureaucracy ought to be reduced. As an example I will present suggestions of the DIHK for getting rid of bureaucratic hindrances in the form of three particularly serious areas of action.

Deregulate employment legislation

The biggest bureaucratic hindrance for most companies is employment law. Especially those starting their own companies have to fight with bureaucratic burdens when they hire new employees. They have to sort out the social insurance formalities, income tax matters and provide an industrial medical service.

The statutory job protection legislation, which has degenerated into an unfathomable body of case law, is particularly complicated. Hundreds of thousands of Employment Court verdicts have to be pronounced in unjustified dismissal cases every year. No businessman is capable of coping with the legal principles of job protection legislation. The relevant commentary on this legislation, with its over 3,300 pages, is the terror of every businessman. The DIHK therefore calls for the maximum number of employees to whom job protection legislation applies to be raised from five per company currently to twenty. This would free 90 per cent of all companies in Germany at a stroke from a central bureaucratic and employment hindrance.

Germany's tax legislation must be simplified rigorously

Germany's complicated tax and levies laws with their many exceptions and provisions for special

Bürokratieabbau

Die Suche nach Ausnahmetatbeständen kostet Zeit. Das Streichen von Sonderregelungen spart daher enorme Kosten. Rechnet man die Zeit für das Erstellen der Einkommensteuererklärung in monetäre Größen um, so kostet die Steuerbürokratie Bürger und Unternehmen, die ihre Gewinne über die Einkommensteuer veranlagen müssen, etwa 10 Mrd. Euro. Hinzu kommt, dass das Streichen von Ausnahmetatbeständen die Basis für eine deutliche Senkung der Steuersätze schafft. Bürokratieabbau im Steuerbereich bringt also eine doppelte Dividende. Der DIHK setzt sich daher für ein einfaches und transparentes Steuersystem ein.

Unternehmen und Bürger kostet die Steuerbürokratie jährlich etwa 10 Mrd. Euro.

Taxation-related bureaucracy matters cost the commercial sector and the taxpayer more than 10 thousand million Euros a year.

Reducing Bureaucracy

deductions are a major burden. It has been estimated that of the world's entire literature on tax legislation, 70 per cent is produced in Germany. If even tax experts give up on it in despair, how is a businessman, who has to keep up with the competition every day, supposed to cope with the tangle of regulations on the subject? The search for exceptions costs time, so the abolition of special regulations would save a lot of money. If one calculates the time required for preparing an income tax declaration in monetary terms, the tax bureaucracy costs the taxpayer and companies – which have to assess their profit via their income tax – about 10 thousand million Euros. As well, the abolition of exceptions would create the basis for a clear reduction in tax rates. The reduction of bureaucracy in the area of taxation would bring a double benefit. The DIHK therefore supports a simple and transparent tax system.

Single out test regions for reducing bureaucracy

A perceptible reduction of bureaucracy is comparable with a radical reduction of subsidies. Everyone is for it at first but when you go into detail resistance builds up. The German economy can no longer afford these delays in reducing its bureaucracy. The DIHK therefore suggests singling out so-called test regions, where bureaucracy can be reduced on a trial basis. The test regions should be able to deviate from federal laws and regulations in order to investigate the effect of flexible approaches on economic growth and employment – as a preliminary stage for a comprehensive reduction of bureaucracy throughout Germany.

This suggestion of the DIHK met with much favourable response. More than 80 regions have submitted their applications for this proposal to the Federal Ministry of Commerce and Labour and in fact the project is being established in the regions of Eastern Westphalia-Lippe, Western Mecklenburg and the State of Bremen. It is intended that this proposal for this relief from bureaucracy also be implemented in other regions during 2004.

Reducing bureaucracy also means assuming personal responsibility

For the urgently necessary reduction of bureaucratic restraints it is not enough to remove the troublesome sections of regulation governing individual cases. Rather, a perceptible reduction of bureaucracy requires a more coordinated approach of political procedures. The reduction of bureaucracy must finally be understood as a comprehensive political task. The bureaucratic restraints for the commercial sector should therefore be examined in all bills introduced into the German Bundestag. Here, particular attention should be paid to the costs and burden of regulations for those starting their own companies and for small companies. The USA and the Netherlands have already set an example. In those countries there is a functioning impact assessment system, and so many laws and regulations have been rejected due to their excessive costs for the business community.

In view of the – in many respects – inflexible and anti-business regulatory culture in Germany, a perceptible reduction in bureaucracy must be oriented to a principle of subsidiarity. The principle of subsidiarity requires the state to assume only those tasks that it can perform demonstrably better than the private sector. In consistently applying the principle of subsidiarity the state should withdraw from many areas currently covered by regulation. Instead of a large number of detailed legal regulations, legislation could also define concrete goals, e.g. industrial safety. The commercial sector would then be obliged to develop and select the best solutions for each company in order to implement these goals. Such regulations could if necessary be agreed on in company alliances. Regulations on subsidiarity should be required particularly for small companies – but would be capable of being extended to the entire commercial community. Successful examples of the implementation of this idea over the last few years have been the business community's self-imposed undertakings in the area of environmental policies.

Reducing bureaucracy means avoiding bureaucracy

All things considered, all promises from government to perceptibly reduce bureaucracy have unfortunately all fizzled out without having any effect at all. Even the Government's campaign is threatening to end up as a paper tiger because it lists the individual bureaucracy reduction projects without any visible systematic plan. However what is needed is a clear, mid-term strategy in order to

Bürokratieabbau

Testregionen zum Bürokratieabbau ausweisen

Spürbarer Bürokratieabbau ist vergleichbar mit einem radikalen Subventionsabbau: Jeder ist zunächst dafür, wenn es jedoch konkret wird, formieren sich die Widerstände. Die deutsche Wirtschaft kann sich diese Verzögerungen beim Bürokratieabbau nicht länger leisten. Der DIHK schlägt daher vor, so genannte Testregionen zum Bürokratieabbau auszuweisen. In den Testregionen sollte von bundesrechtlichen Regelungen abgewichen werden dürfen, um die Wirkungen von Flexibilisierungsansätzen auf Wachstum und Beschäftigung zu untersuchen – als Vorstufe für einen umfassenden Bürokratieabbau in ganz Deutschland.

Dieser Vorschlag des DIHK fand große Resonanz: Mehr als 80 Regionen haben beim Bundesministerium für Wirtschaft und Arbeit ihre Bewerbung eingereicht – und tatsächlich: Das Projekt wird derzeit in den Regionen Ostwestfalen-Lippe, Bremen und Westmecklenburg eingerichtet. Im Laufe des Jahres 2004 soll dann – auch in weiteren Regionen – die Umsetzung der ersten Entlastung folgen.

Bürokratieabbau heißt Eigenverantwortung übernehmen

Für den dringend erforderlichen Abbau bürokratischer Hemmnisse reicht es nicht aus, Einzelfallregelungen zu entschärfen; vielmehr bedarf ein spürbarer Bürokratieabbau einer auch ordnungspolitisch aufeinander abgestimmten Vorgehensweise. Bürokratieabbau muss endlich als umfassende politische Aufgabe verstanden werden. Für alle Gesetzesvorhaben sollten daher die bürokratischen Lasten für Betriebe abgeschätzt werden. Dabei ist explizit die Kosten- und Regulierungsbelastung für Existenzgründer und für Kleinbetriebe zu berücksichtigen. Die USA und die Niederlande machen es vor: Dort gibt es eine funktionierende Folgenabschätzung, und so manche Gesetze und Verordnungen wurden dort bereits angesichts unverhältnismäßig hoher Kosten für die Wirtschaft gekippt.

Mit Blick auf die vielfach unflexible und unternehmensfeindliche Verordnungskultur in Deutschland muss sich ein spürbarer Bürokratieabbau am Subsidiaritätsgrundsatz orientieren: Das Subsidiaritätsprinzip verlangt, dass der Staat nur die Aufgaben übernimmt, die er nachweislich besser lösen kann als der private Sektor. Bei konsequenter Anwendung des Subsidiaritätsprinzips müsste sich der Staat aus vielen Regelungsbereichen zurückziehen. Statt einer Vielzahl detaillierter gesetzlicher und rechtlicher Vorschriften könnte der Gesetzgeber auch konkrete Ziele (z. B. beim Arbeitsschutz) definieren. Die Unternehmen hätten dann die Pflicht, zur Realisierung dieser Ziele betriebsbezogen optimierte Lösungen zu entwickeln und selbst auszuwählen. Solche Regelungen könnten ggf. in betrieblichen Bündnissen getroffen werden. Eine Subsidiaritätsregelung wäre insbesondere für Kleinbetriebe zu fordern – sie wäre aber auch ausweitungsfähig auf alle Unternehmen. Erfolgreiche Beispiele für die Umsetzung dieses Gedankens waren in den letzten Jahren Selbstverpflichtungen der Wirtschaft in der Umweltpolitik.

Bürokratieabbau heißt Bürokratievermeidung

Bisher sind leider alle Versprechen der Politik, Bürokratie spürbar abzubauen, unter dem Strich wirkungslos verpufft. Auch die Initiative „Bürokratieabbau" der Bundesregierung droht als „Papiertiger" zu enden. Denn sie listet nur Einzelprojekte zum Bürokratieabbau auf, ohne dass ein systematisches Konzept zu erkennen wäre. Man braucht jedoch eine klare mittelfristige Strategie, um das ständige Nachwachsen von Bürokratie zu verhindern. Für eine solche Strategie gibt es aus meiner Sicht eine wichtige Leitlinie: Mehr Wettbewerb im Bereich der Kommunen und der öffentlichen Verwaltungen. So wie der Wettbewerb Unternehmen zwingt, auf Märkten effizient zu wirtschaften und neue Geschäftsideen zu entwickeln, so würde der Wettbewerb auch öffentliche Verwaltungen und Gebietskörperschaften motivieren, sich für ihre steuerzahlenden Kunden – Bürger und Unternehmer – ständig zu verbessern.

Der Vorschlag des DIHK, Testregionen einzurichten, zielt genau auf diesen Gedanken des Wettbewerbs ab: Regionen dürfen durch Experimentierklauseln vom Bundesrecht abweichen und können so ihre Attraktivität für unternehmerische Investitionen erhöhen. Dies wiederum wird andere Regionen anregen, ihre Standortbedingungen zu verbessern. In diesem Sinne sind Testregionen die Vorstufe für einen stärker wettbewerblich organisierten Föderalismus. Eine solche Strategie würde auch im öffentlichen Bereich das ökonomische Denken fördern und die vielfach vorherrschende Verordnungskultur aufweichen.

Bürokratie in den Köpfen abbauen

Belässt man es beim Vorschlagen institutioneller Reformen, so wird man die notwendigen Änderungen nicht erreichen. Nur unter drei Voraussetzungen kann eine wirkliche Bürokratiebefreiung gelingen:

1. Zunächst müssen wir Unternehmer selbst verstehen, warum die politischen Entscheider einen immer weiter wachsenden Bürokratieberg zulassen. Politiker und Beamte haben einerseits zumeist nicht lernen können, wie man sich als Unternehmer unter vollem Risiko am Markt behaupten muss. Doch andererseits stehen auch sie oft unter einem großen Druck – wenn auch anderer Art:
   - Politiker müssen Wahlen gewinnen. Und gerade in Deutschland mit seinen vielen obrigkeitsstaatlichen Traditionen lässt sich nur allzu oft Handlungskompetenz mit dem Erlassen neuer Regeln simulieren. Die Diskussion um eine Ausbildungsplatzabgabe ist hierfür ein trauriges Beispiel.
   - Beamte sind für die reibungslose und gerichtsfeste Erledigung von Vorschriften geschult, nicht aber zu deren Beseitigung.

2. Aktivität ist das Gebot der Stunde. Es gilt, Politikern und Verwaltungsbeamten ganz plastisch darzulegen, wie sich Bürokratie auf unseren Betrieb, auf die Personalplanung und auf unternehmerische Standortentscheidungen auswirkt. Wir müssen mit unseren politischen Vertretern vor Ort und in Berlin reden und sie auch in unsere Unternehmen einladen. So können wir das Verständnis der politischen Entscheider für unternehmerische Belange fördern und den Boden für strukturelle Reformen ebnen.

3. Die deutsche „Verordnungskultur" muss einer echten Kultur der Selbstständigkeit weichen. Hierfür braucht Deutschland eine grundlegende Neuorientierung in seinem Bildungssystem und einen langen Atem. Eine Kultur der Selbstständigkeit erfordert, dass das Thema „Unternehmertum" mit all seinen Chancen und Risiken durchgängig – von der Grundschule bis zur Universität – in die Lehrpläne eingeht. Entscheidend ist aber auch die Art des Lernens und Lehrens an unseren Schulen: Schon in frühen Lebensjahren muss die Kreativität und Entdeckungsfreude der Schüler geweckt werden. Das Motto: viel weniger traditionellen Frontalunterricht durchführen, viel mehr aktives Lernen, Teamarbeit und Eigenverantwortung trainieren! Dies fördert in späteren Jahren den Drang nach selbstständigen und zielorientierten Problemlösungen und hemmt das Bedürfnis der Abarbeitung von Problemen streng nach Vorschrift. Die Saat für eine bürokratiearme Gesellschaft wird in der Schule gelegt. Denn die Schüler von heute sind die Politiker, Beamten und Unternehmer von morgen. ∎

Reducing Bureaucracy

prevent the constant regeneration of bureaucracy. In my view there is an important guideline for such a strategy – more competition in municipalities and the public service. As competition forces companies to conduct their businesses efficiently in the market and to develop new business ideas, so competition would motivate the public service and regional authorities to make constant improvements for their tax-paying clients, namely the citizens and the business community.

The DIHK's suggestion of establishing test regions is aimed right at this idea of competition – experimental clauses in the law would permit regions to deviate from federal law and thus increase their attractiveness for commercial investment. This in turn would encourage other regions to improve conditions in their own locations. Having said that, test regions are the preliminary stage for a more competitively organised federalism in Germany.

Such a strategy would also promote economic thinking and soften up the predominant regulatory culture in the area of public administration.

Reducing the bureaucracy mentality

If one merely restricts institutional reform to suggestions, the necessary changes will never be achieved. Real liberation from bureaucracy can only succeed if three conditions are fulfilled:

1. Firstly, we businessmen ourselves have to understand why the political decision-makers keep letting the bureaucratic mountain grow and grow. Politicians and public servants have for the most part never learned how to hold their own in the market under the burden of commercial risk. But on the other hand they, too, are under great pressure – albeit of another sort:

- politicians have to win elections. And in Germany especially, with its many traditions of the authoritarian state, the authority to make decisions and generally assume responsibility can all too often be simulated by making new regulations. The debate on an apprenticeship tax is an unfortunate example of this;
- public servants are trained to administer regulations that function smoothly and which will stand up to challenge in a court of law, not to abolish them.

2. What is required is action. Politicians and public servants must be shown clearly what effects bureaucracy has on our companies, on staff planning and on decisions concerning commercial locations. We must talk with our political representatives locally and in Berlin and invite them to visit our companies. This is the only way we can get the political decision-makers to appreciate the concerns of the commercial community and pave the way for structural reforms.

3. The German regulatory culture must give way to a genuine culture of independence. For this Germany will require a fundamental reorientation in its education system and a good deal of patience. A culture of independence would require the continuous inclusion of entrepreneurship as a subject in the curriculum, with all its opportunities and risks – from primary school to university. But the deciding factor is the type of learning and teaching that is practised at our schools. Creativity and the joy of discovery of the pupils must be awakened. So the motto is: "A lot less traditional 'chalk-and-talk' teaching and train the children in more active learning, teamwork and personal responsibility! In later years this will promote the urge to independent and goal-oriented problem-solving and will restrict the need for working our problems by the book. The seed for a "low-bureaucracy" society would be sown at school because the pupils of today are the businessmen, public servants and politicians of tomorrow. ∎

Statt einer Vielzahl detaillierter gesetzlicher und rechtlicher Vorschriften könnte der Gesetzgeber auch konkrete Ziele, z. B. beim Arbeitsschutz, definieren.

Instead of a multiplicity of detailed official regulations the state could define concrete goals e. g. in industrial safety.

Company Profile

Weltweit rollen Automobile auf ATS-Leichtmetallrädern

Automobiles roll on ATS light alloy wheels worldwide

Die ATS Gruppe produziert Leichtmetallräder für die weltweite Erstausrüstung nahezu aller Automobilhersteller in eigenen Werken in Polen, Deutschland, Südafrika, USA und mit Kooperationspartnern in Brasilien, Indien, Indonesien und dem Zukunftsmarkt China.
Das Werk in Stalowa Wola im Südosten Polens wurde kürzlich als der effektivste Industriebetrieb in der neuesten Liste der 500 besten polnischen Firmen ausgezeichnet. Dieses Werk, das rund 800 Mitarbeiter beschäftigt, hat eine jährliche Produktionskapazität von ca. drei Millionen Rädern und zusätzlichen 500.000 Kurbelwellengehäusen (für General Motors). In die Fabrik wurden bisher rund 50 Millionen Euro investiert.

ATS hat bereits 1967 das Niederdruckgussverfahren eingeführt und 1970 mit dieser Methode die ersten Leichtmetallräder hergestellt. Seitdem steht das Unternehmen an der Spitze der Entwicklung zu immer leichteren Rädern wie dem Hohlspeichenrad – durch ihre intelligente Konstruktion und Fertigung wird ATS den steigenden Anforderungen der Kfz-Industrie gerecht. Auf modernsten, effektiven Fertigungsstraßen werden Produkte in höchster Qualität gefertigt, denn ein Leichtmetallrad verschönert nicht nur das Fahrzeug, sondern entscheidet gleichzeitig über die Sicherheit des Fahrzeuges. Erprobungen wie die Zweiaxialprüfung, die Biegeumlaufprüfung, der Impacttest und die Korrosionsprüfungen werden von ATS-Spezialisten in house durchgeführt.

Die Geschichte der Zulieferung an die Automobilindustrie begann schon 1971 – durch stetige Innovation und Weiterentwicklung bis heute mit ständig wachsenden Stückzahlen von mittlerweile knapp neun Mio. Rädern weltweit.

Seit der Zeit des eigenen ATS-Formel 1-Rennteams blieb die ATS-Gruppe dem Motorsport immer treu. Von der DTM über die DPM, die Formel 3 und die Deutsche Rallyemeisterschaft, von 24-Stunden-Rennen bis Deutschem Berg-Cup – ATS-Räder sind in nahezu jeder Motorsportklasse vertreten und fahren immer wieder als erste ins Ziel.
Diese Zulieferer-Spitzenqualität, hart getestet und bewährt auf Rennstrecken in aller Welt, macht die Räder mit den gelben Buchstaben natürlich auch zur ersten Wahl für Fahrzeugbesitzer, die Wert auf höchste Zuverlässigkeit und erstklassiges Design legen.

In kürzester Zeit hat sich ATS zum Marktführer in der Formel 3 entwickelt. Die weltweit wichtigste Formel-3-Euroserie setzt exklusiv auf die 2002 neu entwickelten Magnesium-Räder von ATS. Im RECARO Formel-3-Cup, der Nachfolgeserie der erfolgreichen Deutschen Formel-3-Meisterschaft, kommt 2004 ein Novum zum Einsatz: das erste Formel-3-Aluminiumrad – entwickelt, konstruiert und gefertigt von ATS.

Individuell auf die verschiedenen Tourenwagen angepasst, jedoch technisch gleich, rollen alle Autos der DMSB Produktionswagen Meisterschaft ebenfalls auf ATS-Rädern. Ein jedes dieser Beispiele über den Einsatz im hochprofessionellen Motorsport beweist: Sieger setzen auf ATS! ■

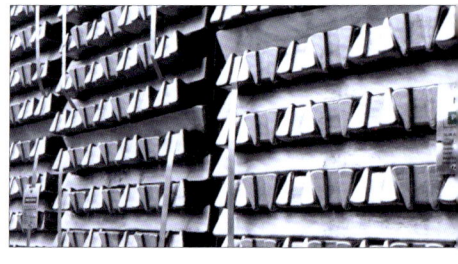

Die ATS Gruppe produziert Orginalausrüstung für folgende Automobilfirmen:
ATS Group produces original equipments for the following automobile companies:

DaimlerChrysler Group
Mercedes	AMG
Smart	Mitsubishi

Ford Group
Ford	Jaguar
Aston Martin	Volvo

General Motors Group
Opel	Vauxhall
OPC	Bertone

Company Profile

ATS Group produces light alloy wheels for the worldwide original equipment of almost all automobile producers in their own plants located in Poland, Germany, South Africa, the USA and with cooperation partners in Brazil, India, Indonesia an the future market China.

The work in Stalowa Wola in the southeast of Poland was recently ranked as one of the most effective industrial companies in the latest list of the 500 best Polish enterprises. This plant that employs around 800 staff members has an annual production capacity of approx. three million wheels and an additional 500,000 crankshaft cases (for General Motors). About 50 million Euros have been invested into this factory so far.

As early as 1967, ATS introduced low pressure technology and in 1970, it produced the first light alloy wheels using this method. Since then the company has been a market leader in the development of ever lighter wheels, like the hollow spokes wheel for instance; because of its intelligent construction and production methods ATS meets the increasing demands of the car industry. Products of the highest quality standards are produced on sophisticated and effective production lines, for a light alloy wheel not only makes the vehicle more stylish, it is also decisive for the safety of the vehicle. Tests like the two-axial test, rotary test under bending conditions, the impact test and the corrosion test are carried out in-house by ATS specialists.

Our history of supplying to the automobile industry started in 1971 with constant innovations and further developments up to today and providing continuously growing figures of just less then nine million wheels worldwide.

Since the times of our own ATS Formula 1 racing team, ATS Group has always been faithful to motor sports. Ranging from DTM across DPM, Formula 3 and the German Rally Championship; from 24-hour races through to the German Mountain Cup, ATS wheels are represented in almost every class of motor sports and pass the goal as number one time and time again.

This top supplier quality, tested on rough grounds and proven on racing tracks in the entire world of course make the wheels with the yellow letters the first choice of any vehicle owner that appreciates a high degree of reliability and first-class design.

ATS has developed into a market leader of the Formula 3 in the shortest of time. The worldwide most important Euro series of the Formula 3 relies exclusively on the magnesium wheels of ATS developed newly in 2002. During the RECARO Formula 3 Cup, the successor series of the successful German Formula 3 Championship, an innovation will be used in 2004: the first Formula 3 aluminium wheel developed, constructed and produced by ATS.

All cars of the DMSB production car championship also roll on ATS wheels, while they are individually adjusted to the different tour vehicles but technically identical.

Each of these examples about application within the highly professional motor sports proves: Winners rely on ATS!

Volkswagen Group
Volkswagen   Audi
Skoda   Seat
Quattro   Votex

PSA Group
Peugeot   Citroen

Nissan/Renault Group
Nissan

Porsche   BMW

MG Rover   Toyota

HWA (Motorsport)   Magna Steyer

ATS Gruppe

Vorstand/Chief Executive Officer:
Siegfried F. Teichert

Geschäftsführer/Managing Directors:
Hans Pfahl
Jürgen Gareis
Adam Kolat
Friedhelm Maiworm

Gründungsjahr/Year of Foundation:
1966

Mitarbeiter/Employees:
1.404 weltweit/worldwide

Geschäftstätigkeit/Business Activities:
Entwicklung, Herstellung und Vertrieb von Leichtmetallrädern und anderen Industriegussprodukten aus Aluminium
Development, production and sale of light alloy wheels and other industrial casting products made of aluminium.

Anschrift/Address:
Bruchstraße 34
D-67098 Bad Dürkheim
Telefon   +49 (6322) 6 04-132
Telefax   +49 (6322) 6 04-290
E-Mail   oem@ats-wheels.com
Internet www.ats-company.com

Finanzpolitik

Sechs Jahre Euro – Erfahrungen und Perspektiven

Six years of euro – experiences and perspectives

Am 1. Januar 1999 übernahm die Europäische Zentralbank die Verantwortung für die einheitliche Geldpolitik eines neuen Wirtschaftsraumes, des Euro-Währungsgebietes. Seitdem ist der Euro die gemeinsame Währung von inzwischen 12 Staaten mit über 300 Millionen Einwohnern. Mit der Einführung der Banknoten und Münzen zu Beginn des Jahres 2002 ist der Euro auch gesetzliches Zahlungsmittel des Euro-Währungsgebietes.

Viele der im Vorfeld der Euro-Einführung geäußerten Befürchtungen über mögliche wirtschaftliche Risiken einer gemeinsamen Währung haben sich als haltlos erwiesen. Mit einer Inflationsrate von 1,9 Prozent im Jahr 2005 verzeichnet der Euroraum heute ein hohes Maß an Preisniveaustabilität. Zudem hat der Euro die Entwicklung des Binnenmarktes entscheidend vorangetrieben und ist ein weiterer Meilenstein zur politischen Integration.

Deutschland ist mit den Mitgliedstaaten des Euro-Währungsgebietes wirtschaftlich besonders eng verflochten. Deshalb lag es von Anfang an im Interesse der Bundesregierung, zu einer stabilen gemeinsamen Währung beizutragen. Nicht nur aufgrund seiner wirtschaftlichen Leistungsfähigkeit, sondern auch wegen seines hohen Maßes an nationaler Preisstabilität spielt Deutschland eine bedeutende Rolle als „Stabilitätsanker" in der Europäischen Union.

Güter- und Kapitalmärkte

Ebenso wie die Einführung der Goldmark im Jahr 1871 dazu beitrug, die Transaktionskosten eines heterogenen Münz- und Währungssystems in Deutschland zu senken, hat der Euro die Effizienz grenzüberschreitender Transaktionen in Europa erhöht und so die Integration der Güter- und Kapitalmärkte beschleunigt. Die Gütermarktintegration, also das Schaffen von Bedingungen für die uneingeschränkte Freizügigkeit von Gütern und Produktionsfaktoren, wird durch die erhöhte Preistransparenz in Europa, einen effektiveren Zahlungsverkehr (Wegfall des Währungsumtausches) sowie den Wegfall von Wechselkursrisiken forciert. Insbesondere Kurssicherungskosten erschwerten in der Vergangenheit den Handel und langfristige grenzüberschreitende Investitionen. Nach aktuellen Studien nahm der Handel innerhalb Europas durch die Euroeinführung um rund 15 bis 20 Prozent zu. Langfristig wird mit einer Zunahme um und 40 Prozent gerechnet. Der dadurch gestiegene Wettbewerbsdruck auf die Unternehmen wird Wachstum und Wohlstand in Europa nachhaltig erhöhen.

Auch die Kapitalmarktintegration, d. h. die Schaffung der Voraussetzungen für die uneingeschränkte Mobilität von Kapital sowie gemeinsamer europäische Institutionen (Bankenaufsicht), wurde durch den Euro weiter beschleunigt. Verstärkte Kapitalmarktintegration – und damit verbunden eine verbesserte Kapitalmarkteffektivität (bessere Allokation des Sparkapitals) – erhöht das Wachstum in Europa. Begleitet wird diese Entwicklung von einer erhöhten Innovationsgeschwindigkeit im Bereich von Finanzierungsinstrumenten. Insbesondere kleine und mittlere Unternehmen erhalten damit neue Möglichkeiten zur Finanzierung ihrer Investitionen. Sichtbares Ergebnis der Kapitalmarktintegration ist bereits heute eine starke Konvergenz der kurz- und langfristigen Zinssätze.

Vertrag von Maastricht und Stabilitäts- und Wachstumspakt

Solide Staatsfinanzen sind zentrale Voraussetzung für eine stabile Währung, für nachhaltiges nichtinflationäres Wachstum und mehr Beschäftigung. Am 1. November 1993 trat der „Maastricht-Vertrag" in Kraft. In ihm schrieben die Staats- und Regierungschefs Konvergenzkriterien fest, die eine Annäherung der wesentlichen makroökonomischen Kennziffern zum Ziel hatten. Um das dauerhafte Funktionieren der Wirtschafts- und Währungsunion zu gewährleisten, wurde von den Mitgliedstaaten im Sommer 1997 der Stabilitäts- und Wachstumspakt beschlossen. Dieser hat das Ziel, die Bestimmungen des EG-Vertrags zur Haushaltsüberwachung und zum Verfahren bei übermäßigen Defiziten zu konkretisieren und zu operationalisieren. Damit sollen insbesondere negative Effekte unsolider Haushaltspolitiken einzelner Länder zu Lasten der gesamten Europäischen Wirtschafts- und Währungsunion dauerhaft verhindert werden. Es ist nicht zuletzt Verdienst des Stabilitäts- und Wachstumspakts, dass die Defizit- und Schulden-

Hans Eichel

Der Autor, 1941 in Kassel geboren, studierte in Marburg und Berlin Germanistik, Philosophie, Politik und Geschichte. Seit 1964 SPD-Mitglied, gehörte er von 1969 bis 1972 als Stellvertreter des Bundesvorsitzenden dem Juso-Bundesvorstand an. Oberbürgermeister seiner Heimatstadt wurde er 1975 im Alter von 33 Jahren und übte das Amt bis 1991 aus.
1991 wurde Hans Eichel zum Ministerpräsidenten des Landes Hessen gewählt, wiedergewählt wurde er 1995. Seit April 1999 ist Hans Eichel Bundesminister der Finanzen.

The author was born in Kassel in 1941. He studied German, philosophy, political science and history at the universities of Marburg and Berlin. An SPD member since 1964, he was vice-president of the management committee of the SPD's Young Socialists wing from 1969 to 1972. He became Lord Mayor of his home town of Kassel in 1975 at the age of only 33 and held that office until 1991.
In that year Hans Eichel was voted State Premier of Hesse and was voted in again in 1995. He has been Federal Minister of Finance since 1999.

rückführung ein zentrales Ziel der Finanzpolitik der EU-Mitgliedstaaten bleibt. Der Pakt ist ein flexibles wirtschaftspolitisches Instrumentarium, das sich als Koordinierungsinstrument der Finanzpolitik in der Europäischen Union grundsätzlich bewährt hat. Der Pakt sieht ganz bewusst vor, dass die jeweilige Lage und Politik eines Landes berücksichtigt werden. Er darf aber nicht zu mechanistisch gehandhabt werden; vielmehr muss er im Sinne einer Einzelfallbeurteilung ökonomisch

Financial Policy

On 1 January 1999, the European Central Bank assumed responsibility for the single monetary policy in a newly established economic region, the euro area. Since then, the euro has been the common currency of what are now 12 states with over 300 million inhabitants. The euro has been the legal tender in the euro area since banknotes and coins were introduced at the beginning of 2002.

Many of the fears voiced before the introduction of the euro about the possible economic risks of a single currency have proved to be unfounded. The 1.9 per cent inflation rate in 2005 reflects a high degree of price level stability within the euro area. Moreover, the euro has played a significant role in advancing the development of the single market, and is a further milestone towards political integration.

The economic ties between Germany and the Member States of the euro area are particularly strong. As a result, it has always been in the interests of the German federal government to contribute to a stable common currency. Its economic efficiency and high level of national price stability mean that Germany has an important role to play as an "anchor of stability" in the European Union.

Goods and capital markets

Just as the introduction of the Goldmark in 1871 helped to reduce the transaction costs of a heterogeneous coin and currency system in Germany, the euro has increased the efficiency of cross-border transactions in Europe and therefore accelerated the integration of the markets for goods and capital. The integration of the goods market, in other words the creation of conditions which allow the unrestricted free movement of goods and factors of production, is being driven by an increased transparency of prices in Europe, more effective payment transactions (elimination of currency exchange) and the elimination of exchange rate risks. In the past, the costs of exchange cover made trade and long-term cross-border investments particularly difficult. According to current surveys, trade within Europe rose by around 15 to 20 per cent following the introduction of the euro. It is estimated that it will increase in the long run by around 40 per cent. The resulting increase in competitive pressure on companies will lead to a sustainable rise in growth and prosperity in Europe.

Capital market integration, i.e. the creation of conditions for the unrestricted mobility of capital as well as the creation of common European institutions (banking supervision), has been accelerated further by the euro. Greater capital market integration – and a related improvement in capital market effectiveness (better allocation of savings capital) – increases growth in Europe. This development is accompanied by an increased rate of innovation in the field of financing instruments. This opens up new opportunities for small and medium-sized enterprises, in particular, to finance their investments. Today, one visible result of capital market integration is the strong convergence of short-term and long-term interest rates.

The Treaty of Maastricht and the Stability and Growth Pact

Sound public finances are the central requirement for a stable currency, for sustainable non-inflationary growth and for more employment. On 1 November 1993, the "Maastricht Treaty" came into force. In it, the heads of states and governments stipulated convergence criteria designed to bring the essential macro-economic indicators more closely together. In order to ensure the permanent functioning of the economic and monetary union, the Member States signed the Stability and Growth Pact in the summer of 1997. Its goal is to specify and to render operational the provisions of the EC Treaty as they relate to budgetary surveillance and the excessive deficit procedure. This is intended, in particular, to offer lasting protection to the European Economic and Monetary Union as a whole from negative effects of unsound budgetary policies of individual countries.

It is due in no small part to the Stability and Growth Pact that deficit and debt reduction remains a central aim of the fiscal policy of the EU Member States. The Pact is a flexible instrument of economic policy which has proven to be a fundamental instrument in coordinating fiscal policies within the European Union. The Pact intentionally provides for a country's respective situation and policies to be taken into consideration. However, application of the Pact must not be too mechanistic; instead it must be interpreted rather to mean that cases are assessed individually in an economically expedient manner. The reform of the Pact reflects this approach.

European monetary policy

The introduction of the D-Mark on 20 June 1948 marked the beginning of an enduring phase of currency stability in Germany. Thanks largely to the D-Mark, the importance of autonomy in monetary policy is today accepted almost unconditionally throughout Europe – a basic condition for the creation of the euro and of the European Central Bank (ECB).

When one reflects on the challenges and experiences of the first years, the overall results of the ECB's monetary policy are positive. This is due above all to the legal principles enshrined in the Maastricht Treaty, namely ECB independence and price stability as the top priority. This strong insti-

Finanzpolitik

sinnvoll interpretiert werden. Die Reform des Paktes trägt diesem Gedanken Rechnung.

Europäische Geldpolitik

Mit der Einführung der D-Mark wurde am 20. Juni 1948 eine andauernde Phase stabiler Währung in Deutschland eingeleitet. Es ist das besondere Verdienst der D-Mark, dass die Bedeutung geldpolitischer Autonomie heute in ganz Europa nahezu uneingeschränkt akzeptiert wird – eine Grundvoraussetzung für die Schaffung des Euro und der Europäischen Zentralbank (EZB).

Blickt man auf die Herausforderungen und Erfahrungen der ersten Jahre zurück, dann fällt die Bilanz für die Geldpolitik der Europäischen Zentralbank positiv aus. Ursächlich hierfür sind vor allem die im Vertrag von Maastricht gelegten rechtlichen Grundlagen: die Unabhängigkeit der EZB und ihr vorrangiges Ziel der Preisstabilität. Dieses starke institutionelle Fundament war unverzichtbar, um die Glaubwürdigkeit der EZB von Beginn an zu gewährleisten. Denn: Als neue Institution konnte die EZB nicht auf eine selbst erworbene Reputation verweisen.

Die EZB nahm ihre Politik im Jahr 1999 in einer günstigen Ausgangsposition stabiler Preise auf. Danach hat allerdings eine ganze Reihe negativer Entwicklungen (u. a. Vervielfachung des Ölpreises, anfängliche Abwertung des Euro) das Preisniveau nach oben getrieben. So wurde die Geldpolitik der EZB schon in den ersten Jahren vor schwierige Herausforderungen gestellt. Es ist deshalb zweifellos ein großer Erfolg, dass Bürger und Investoren aus aller Welt auch zukünftig eine Preissteigerungsrate im Euroraum von weniger als zwei Prozent erwarten. Dies spiegelt sich auch im historisch sehr niedrigen Niveau der langfristigen Zinsen wider.

Internationale Rolle des Euro

Die erfolgreiche Stabilitätsorientierung sowohl der EZB als auch der Mitgliedstaaten hat die Attraktivität des Euro auch auf internationaler Ebene erhöht. Nach nur sechs Jahren hat der Euro seine Bedeutung als zweitwichtigste internationale Währung hinter dem US-Dollar gefestigt:

- Der Anteil des Euro an den internationalen Devisenreserven ist in den letzten Jahren um rund drei Prozentpunkte von 16 Prozent am Jahresende 2000 auf 19 Prozent im Jahr 2002 gestiegen. Damit ist der Euro die zweitwichtigste Reservewährung hinter dem US-Dollar, auf den rund zwei Drittel der weltweiten Devisenreserven entfallen. Der Dollaranteil an den Weltdevisenreserven nahm im gleichen Zeitraum um rund drei Prozentpunkte ab – von 68 Pozent am Ende des Jahres 2000 auf 65 Prozent am Jahresende 2002.

- Der Euro spielt zudem eine bedeutende Rolle als Ankerwährung. In 41 von 150 Staaten mit Währungsbindung ist der Euro Teil des Währungssystems. In den Nachbarregionen der EU verfolgen zahlreiche Länder eine Wechselkurspolitik, für die der Euro Referenzwährung ist. Die Währungsarrangements reichen von kontrolliertem Floating bis hin zu einer festen Wechselkursanbindung. Kosovo und Montenegro haben dem Euro unilateral den Status eines offiziellen Zahlungsmittels eingeräumt. Darüber hinaus ist der Euro in einigen Ländern Mitteleuropas und des westlichen Balkans als Parallelwährung in Umlauf und wird dort sowohl in Form von Bargeld als auch in Gestalt von Einlagen verwendet.

- Auch auf den internationalen Finanzmärkten stößt der Euro auf zunehmende Akzeptanz. Positiv hervorzuheben ist insbesondere der Anstieg des Emissionsvolumens auf Euro lautender Unternehmensanleihen. Mittels dieser Finanzierungsquelle können die Unternehmen in großem Umfang Kapital für Investitionen aufnehmen und damit Wachstum und Beschäftigung steigern.

- Der Anteil des Euro am weltweiten Devisenhandel beläuft sich auf rund 25 Prozent, damit ist er die zweitwichtigste Währung hinter dem Dollar, der mit einem Anteil von rund 50 Prozent nach wie vor dominiert.

- Die Länder des Euroraums nutzen den Euro verstärkt zur Fakturierung im Waren- und Dienstleistungsverkehr mit Staaten außerhalb des Euro-Währungsgebiets. Rund die Hälfte der Im- und Exporte entfallen im Durchschnitt der Mitgliedstaaten auf die Gemeinschaftswährung. Bei der Fakturierung der deutschen Exporte und Importe lässt sich feststellen, dass der Euro den Dollar als Transaktionswährung sowohl im Intra- als auch im Extra-EWU-Handel überrundet hat. Knapp 80 Prozent der deutschen Exporte in alle Länder werden inzwischen in Euro fakturiert, bezogen auf die nicht EWU-Länder sind es 68 Prozent.

Erweiterung des Euroraumes

Mit ihrem EU-Beitritt verpflichten sich die zehn neuen Mitgliedstaaten Estland, Lettland, Litauen, Malta, Polen, Slowakei, Slowenien, Tschechien, Ungarn und Zypern ihre Geld- und Wechselkurspolitik als ein Anliegen von gemeinschaftlichem Interesse anzusehen. Damit ist allerdings nicht automatisch eine zügige Einführung des Euro verbunden. Die Einführung des Euro erfordert – wie für alle derzeitigen Euroländer auch – die Erfüllung der Konvergenzkriterien des Maastricht-Vertrages. So wird gewährleistet, dass neue Mitgliedsländer ihre wirtschaftlichen Strukturen bereits in hohem Maß an die Euroländer angepasst haben. Nur so kann gewährleistet werden, dass die gemeinsame Währung nachhaltig stabil bleibt.

Zu den Konvergenzkriterien zählt neben Preis-, Haushalts- und Zinskriterium insbesondere auch das Wechselkurskriterium. Hiernach kann der Euro nur von den Ländern eingeführt werden, die mindestens zwei Jahre am Wechselkursmechanismus II, dem Nachfolger des Europäischen Währungssystems, teilgenommen haben und in diesem Zeitraum ihren Wechselkurs ohne schwerwiegende Spannungen innerhalb eines engen Bandes um den vereinbarten Leitkurs gehalten haben. Der Konvergenzstand der neuen Mitgliedstaaten unterscheidet sich teilweise erheblich. Insbesondere in den baltischen Staaten werden jedoch Preis-, Haushalts- und Zinskriterium nachhaltig erfüllt. Entsprechend wurden im Juni 2004 Estland und Litauen gemeinsam mit Slowenien in den Wechselkursmechanismus II aufgenommen. Die Länder werden voraussichtlich im Januar 2007 den Euro einführen. Mit dem Beitritt von Lettland, Malta und Zypern zum Wechselkursmechanismus II im Mai 2005 haben nunmehr sechs der zehn neuen Mitgliedstaaten die erste Stufe der monetären Integration vollzogen.

Schlussbemerkungen

Die spürbar positiven Wirkungen der gemeinschaftlichen Währung haben zu einer breiten Akzeptanz des Euro in den anderen Mitgliedstaaten und in Deutschland geführt. Anfängliche Schwierigkeiten mit der Verwendung des neuen Bargeldes sind heute weitgehend ausgeräumt.

Nach sechs Jahren hat der Euro seinen festen Platz im Leben der europäischen Bürger. Er hat zu einer Erhöhung der Preistransparenz beigetragen, Handels- und Investitionshemmnisse reduziert, den Währungsumtausch bei Reisen innerhalb des Euro-Währungsgebietes entfallen lassen und einen wichtigen Beitrag zur weiteren europäischen Integration geleistet. Mit der Erweiterung der EU und einem zukünftig wachsenden Währungsraum nimmt das Potential des Euro noch zu. Damit einhergehende Sorgen über den Verlust an Währungsstabilität sind unbegründet. Wie in der Vergangenheit auch orientiert sich die Erweiterung des Euroraumes an den strengen Regeln des Vertrages von Maastricht. Die interne und externe Stabilität des Währungssystems werden nicht gefährdet. Die Bilanz nach sechs Jahren Euro kann sich sehen lassen. Er ist die gemeinsame Währung für einen international wettbewerbsfähigen Wirtschaftsraum und somit Garant für eine gemeinsame Zukunft in Europa. ∎

Financial Policy

credibility of the ECB right from the beginning. For, as a new institution, the ECB was not in a position to refer to any self-acquired reputation.

The ECB initiated its policy in 1999 in a favourable period of stable prices. Soon after, however, a series of negative developments drove price levels upwards (for instance the strong rise in oil prices, the initial devaluation of the euro). As a result, the early years of the ECB's monetary policy were marked by a number of difficult challenges. It is therefore unquestionably a mark of tremendous success that citizens and investors from across the globe expect a rate of inflation in the euro area of less than two per cent, now and into the future. This is reflected as well in the historically very low level of long-term interest rates.

The international role of the euro

The emphasis placed successfully on stability by both the ECB and the Member States has also increased the attractiveness of the euro at an international level. After only six years, the euro has consolidated its role as the second most important international currency behind the US dollar:

- The share of the euro in international foreign currency reserves increased in recent years by around three per cent from 16 per cent at the end of 2000 to 19 per cent in 2002. This has made the euro the second most important reserve currency behind the US dollar, in which around two thirds of global foreign currency reserves are held. The proportion of global foreign currency reserves held in dollars decreased in the same period by around three per cent from 68 per cent at the end of 2000 to 65 per cent at the end of 2002.
- Furthermore, the euro plays a major role as an anchor currency. The euro forms part of the currency system in 41 out of 150 states that operate with pegged currencies.

In the neighbouring regions of the EU, numerous countries follow an exchange rate policy which has the euro as its reference currency. Currency arrangements extend from controlled floating to fixed exchange rate pegs. Kosovo and Montenegro have unilaterally accorded the euro the status of an official means of payment. Moreover, in some countries of Central Europe and the West Balkans, the euro is circulating as a parallel currency and is used in the form of both cash and deposits.

- The euro is also gaining increasing acceptance on international finance markets. One positive development which can be highlighted in particular is the growth in the volume of company bond emissions issued in euro. Companies can use this source of finance to acquire large volumes of capital for investment and thus increase growth and employment.
- The share of the euro in worldwide foreign currency trade amounts to around 25 per cent and it is therefore the second most important currency behind the dollar, which still dominates this sector with a share of around 50 per cent.
- Countries of the euro area increasingly use the euro for invoicing transactions in goods and services with states outside the euro area. On average, around half of the Member State imports and exports are conducted in the common currency. With regard to billing German exports and imports, the euro has overtaken the dollar as the basis for transactions both in intra-European and in external EMU trade. Almost 80 per cent of German exports worldwide are now invoiced in euro; for non-EMU countries it is 68 per cent.

Enlargement of the euro area

With their accession to the EU, the ten new Member States Cyprus, the Czech Republic, Estonia, Hungary, Latvia, Lithuania, Malta, Poland, Slovakia, and Slovenia have entered into a commitment to treat their monetary and exchange rate policy as a matter of Community interest. However, this does not automatically mean a rapid introduction of the euro. The introduction of the euro requires, as is the case for all current euro countries, the fulfilment of the convergence criteria of the Maastricht Treaty. In this way it is ensured that new Member States have already aligned their economic structures to a large degree to those of the euro countries. This is the only way to guarantee the long-term stability of the single currency.

In addition to price, the convergence criteria include criteria relating to budgets, interest rates and, in particular, exchange rates. These stipulate that the euro can only be introduced by countries which have participated for at least two years in the Exchange Rate Mechanism II - the successor to the European Monetary System - and which during this time have been able to maintain their exchange rate without severe tensions within a narrow band around the agreed central rate. The degree of convergence in the new Member States varies widely in parts. However, particularly in the Baltic States, the price, budget and interest rate criteria are being met continuously. Correspondingly, in June 2004, Estonia and Lithuania were allowed to enter the Exchange Rate Mechanism II together with Slovenia. These countries are due to introduce the euro in January 2007. Following the entry of Cyprus, Latvia and Malta into the ERM II in May 2005, six of the ten new Member States have now completed the first step towards monetary integration.

Concluding remarks

The noticeably positive effects of the common currency have led to broad acceptance of the euro both in Germany and in the other Member States. Initial difficulties in using the new form of cash have since been largely overcome.

After six years, the euro has become a set part of life for European citizens. It has helped to increase the transparency of prices, it has reduced barriers to trade and investment, it has made the need to exchange currency when travelling across the euro area a thing of the past, and it has played a major role in the further integration of Europe. The euro's potential continues to grow with the enlargement of the EU and the currency area set to expand in the future. Accompanying worries about the loss of currency stability are unfounded. As in the past, the enlargement of the euro area is guided by the strict rules set out in the Maastricht Treaty. The internal and external stability of the monetary system is under no threat. Quite a lot has already been achieved in the first six years of the euro. It is the common currency for an internationally competitive economic area and is thus a guarantee for a common future in Europe. ∎

Company Profile

KSM CASTINGS GMBH:
Innovationen in Aluminium- und Magnesiumguss

KSM CASTINGS GmbH: Innovations in aluminium and magnesium castings

Die KSM Castings GmbH mit Sitz in Hildesheim ist weltweiter Partner der Automobilindustrie für Aluminium- und Magnesiumguss-Produkte. Mit der Fokussierung der Geschäftsaktivitäten auf die drei Geschäftsbereiche Chassis, Body und Powertrain richtet sich die Unternehmensgruppe klar an den Kundenanforderungen aus. Sie bietet ihren Kunden maßgeschneiderte Lösungen: vom Design zur Fabrikplanung, als Systemlieferant für Karosserie, Fahrwerk und Antriebsstrang, als Werkzeuglieferant und nicht zuletzt als Logistikkoordinator.

Auf der Basis jahrzehntelanger Erfahrung auf dem internationalen Markt und dank dem in dieser Zeit gewonnenen technologischen Know-how ist die KSM Castings GmbH in der Lage, im direkten Kontakt mit der Automobil- und Automobilzulieferindustrie komplexeste Komponenten und Systeme zu entwickeln und vom Guss bis zur Systemmontage zu fertigen.

Hierfür stehen die sechs Standorte:
- Kloth-Senking Metallgießerei, Hildesheim
- Druckgusswerk Fritz Völkel, Wuppertal
- DGT Druckgießtechnik, Radevormwald
- Concordiahütte, Bendorf
- KSM Castings Wernigerode GmbH
- KSM Castings CZ s.r.o., Hrádek (CZ)

mit ihrer Fertigungs- und Entwicklungskompetenz für Aluminium- und Magnesiumgusskomponenten sowie für Bearbeitung und Montage zur Verfügung.

KSM Castings

Die KSM Castings GmbH ist Entwicklungspartner und Produzent von Leichtmetallgussprodukten für die Automobilzulieferer. Als wachsende internationale Unternehmensgruppe strebt sie nach höchster Kundenzufriedenheit durch wertorientierte Dienstleistung und Partnerschaft mit dem Kunden. Hoch engagierte und qualifizierte Mitarbeiter sind die treibende Kraft zur kontinuierlichen Verbesserung der Prozesse und zusammen mit einer unternehmensweiten Qualitätsphilosophie und Umweltpolitik die grundlegende Basis zur Umsetzung innovativer Technologien. Durch die zentrale Bündelung der Vertriebs- und Entwicklungsaktivitäten in einer Hand und durch die Arbeit des Kompetenzcenters der KSM Castings GmbH im Werk Kloth-Senking Metallgießerei in Hildesheim werden standortübergreifende Synergien konsequent genutzt und standortspezifische Stärken ausgebaut, um so gemeinsam mit dem Kunden die Wettbewerbsfähigkeit im globalen Markt zu stärken. Hierfür steht ein qualifiziertes Team von Ingenieuren und Technikern für einen konsequenten Simultaneous-Engineering-Prozess unter Nutzung einer durchgängigen Prozessdatenkette von der Entwicklung bis zur Festlegung der Fertigungsparameter zur Verfügung.

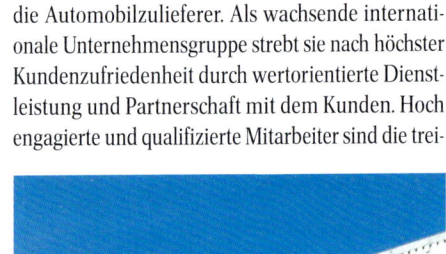

Entwicklung

Simultaneous Engineering steht bei der KSM Castings Gruppe für die gemeinsame Entwicklung mit dem Kunden von der Konzeptidee bis zum einbaufertigen System.

Das bedeutet:
- Blackbox Design
- Packaging Untersuchung
- Simulation
- Prototypenbau und -erprobung
- Serienfreigabe mit dem Kunden
- Serienproduktion

Dabei ist eine durchgängige Prozessdatenkette über die CAD-Daten in Konstruktion, Entwicklung und

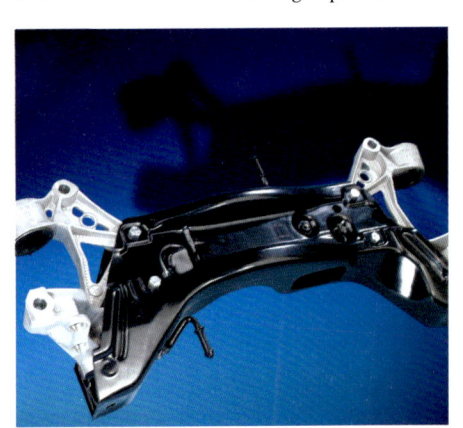

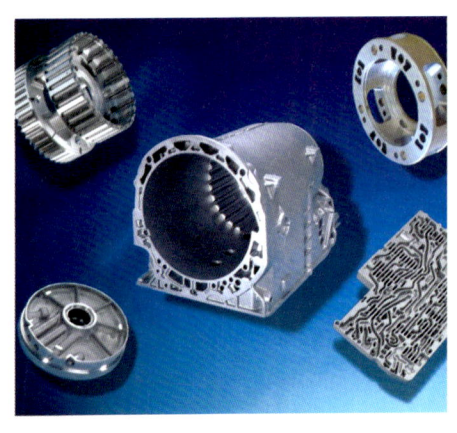

Company Profile

With the focus of its business activities on the three areas of chassis, body and power train, the Hildesheim-based KSM Castings GmbH, an international supplier of aluminum and magnesium castings to the automobile industry, is clearly reacting to customer requirements. It offers its customers custom-made solutions: from design to factory-planning, as systems supplier for body, chassis and power train applications, as tool supplier and last not least as logistics co-ordinator.

Based on decades of experience and technological know-how gained on the international market, KSM Castings GmbH is in the position to develop and manufacture the most complex types of components and systems from castings to systems installation while remaining in direct contact with the automobile manufacturing and component manufacturing industries.

For this the following six locations of
- Kloth-Senking Metallgießerei, Hildesheim
- Druckgusswerk Fritz Völkel, Wuppertal
- DGT Druckgießtechnik, Radevormwald
- Concordiahütte, Bendorf
- KSM Castings Wernigerode GmbH
- KSM Castings CZ s.r.o., Hrádek (Czech Republic)

make available their competence in production and development of aluminum and magnesium castings, processing and installation.

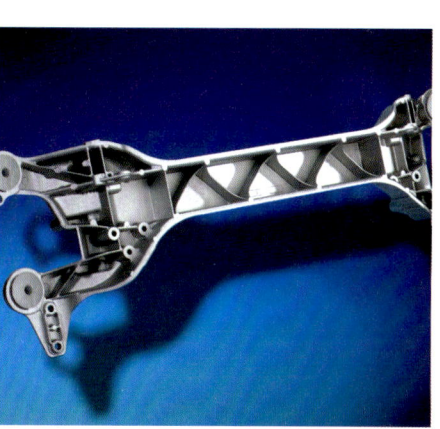

KSM Castings GmbH

KSM Castings is a development partner and producer of light metal products for the automobile industry. As a growing international group of companies it aims to achieve the highest level of customer satisfaction through value-oriented service and partnership with its customers. Highly-motivated and qualified employees are the driving force for continuous improvement of its processes and the implementation of innovative technologies together with a group-wide philosophy of quality and an awareness of environmentally friendly policies. By centrally combining the sales and development activities and through the work of the KSM Castings competence centre at Kloth-Senking Metallgießerei (metal casting company) in Hildesheim, the consistent use of synergies between locations and strengths specific to each location can be expanded to reinforce the ability to compete in the global market together with the customer. A qualified team of engineers and technicians ensures a consistent and simultaneous engineering process by using a continuous process-stream from development to the establishment of production parameters.

Development

At the KSM Castings Group simultaneous engineering stands for the common development with the customer of a conceptual idea to the point where completed systems can be installed:

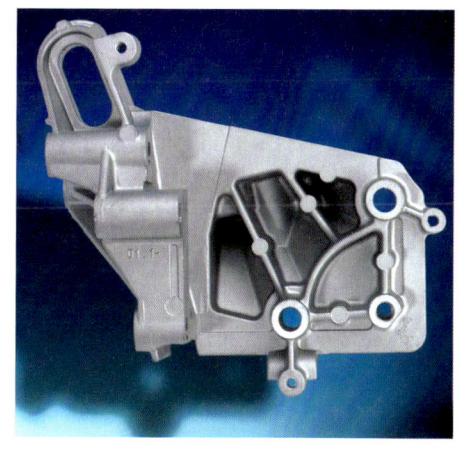

- black-box design
- investigating packaging
- simulation
- making and testing prototypes
- (together with the customer) release for series production
- series production

At the same time, the continuous process stream via CAD data in design, development and production is an important step for the success of the simultaneous engineering process. Through the examination and release of new products it is possible to rapidly test all components and systems integrated in the development process. Goal-oriented project management guarantees adherence to development times and budgets. This also includes consistent supplier management through the whole development process. The process is complemented by permanent R & D work by the "Technical Development" team, which was specially formed for this purpose. The team concentrates on process development and materials development.

Process development

Besides the development of existing process technologies within production, process development also means exploring opportunities for developing new types of casting processes for aluminium and magnesium. This was how the counter-pressure casting process for chassis parts was first developed in Europe as production process for series with more than 400,000 sets per year. Compact high quality chassis parts can be made by combining controlled pressurizing and faster cooling. The achievable mechanical properties of the materials correspond to those of comparable forged parts but are more cost-effective. Particular attention is also given to the continuous development of production technology. The casting mould is the core of series production and an important part in the overall production of parts. This is the reason for dimensional accuracy and metallurgical quality of cast products and why the preparation for series production and tool-making is also integrated in a continuous process stream. The basis of all the de-

Company Profile

Fertigung ein wichtiger Schritt für einen erfolgreichen Simultaneous-Engineering-Prozess. Durch die Prüfung und Freigabe neuer Produkte innerhalb des Entwicklungsprozesses ist eine schnelle, in die Entwicklungsarbeit integrierte Erprobung aller Komponenten und Systeme möglich. Durch ein zielorientiertes Projektmanagement wird die Einhaltung von Entwicklungszeiten und Budgets gewährleistet. Das beinhaltet auch ein konsequentes Lieferantenmanagement über den gesamten Entwicklungsprozess. Ergänzt wird dieser Prozess durch permanente F+E-Arbeit des hierfür speziell eingerichteten Teams „Technologische Entwicklung" mit den Arbeitsschwerpunkten „Verfahrensentwicklung" und „Werkstoffentwicklung."

Verfahrensentwicklung

Verfahrensentwicklung bedeutet neben der Weiterentwicklung der bestehenden Verfahrenstechnologien innerhalb der Fertigung auch das Ausloten von Chancen neuartiger Gießverfahren für Aluminium und Magnesium. So konnte das Gegendruckgießverfahren für Fahrwerksteile als Verfahren in der Serie mit mehr als 400.000 Satz jährlich erstmals in Europa etabliert werden. Durch die Kombination aus gesteuerter Druckbeaufschlagung und hoher Abkühlung entstehen kompakte Fahrwerksteile mit überragender Qualität. Die erreichbaren Werkstoffkennwerte entsprechen denen von vergleichbaren Schmiedebauteilen bei verbessertem Preis-Leistungs-Verhältnis. Besondere Aufmerksamkeit gilt der Weiterentwicklung von Fertigungstechnologien. Die Gießform ist der Kern der Serienfertigung und wichtigster Baustein in der gesamten Herstellung der Produkte. Maßhaltigkeit und metallurgische Qualität der Gussprodukte finden hier ihren Ursprung. Aus diesem Grund sind auch der Bereich der Serienvorbereitung sowie der Werkzeugbau in eine durchgängige Prozessdatenkette integriert. Basis der gesamten Entwicklungsarbeit ist die systematische Absicherung der Ergebnisse mit Hilfe von Six-Sigma-Methodiken und Design-of-Experiment (DoE). Die Anwendung der numerischen Simulationstechnik ist dabei für alle verwendeten Gießverfahren voll etabliert. Alle Prozesse in den Phasen der Entwicklung und Produktion werden durch die Nutzung der Vorteile eines zertifizierten Unternehmensmanagementsystems unterstützt.

Qualitätssicherung

Die Anforderungen der DIN EN ISO 9001, VDA-Band 6.1, der QS 9000 und der ISO/TS 16949 sowie des Umweltzertifikates DIN EN ISO 14001 werden flächendeckend an allen Standorten nachweislich erfüllt. Basis für den kontinuierlichen Verbesserungsprozess ist die permanente Information und Einbeziehung aller Mitarbeiter. Dabei werden kontinuierlich Verbesserungspotenziale ermittelt und zur Steigerung der Wettbewerbsfähigkeit ausgeschöpft. Die Qualitätssicherung im Prozess erfolgt durch automatische Durchleuchtungsanlagen, fluoreszierende Farbeindringprüfung zur Risserkennung, Lecktestprüfungen sowie durch eine Serienüberwachung der Werkstoffkennwerte mit Hilfe von Spektralanalysen und zerstörender Werkstoffprüfung.

Prozesse

Mit modernsten Druckgießanlagen im Schließkraftbereich zwischen 400 und 3.000 Tonnen werden anspruchsvollste Aluminium- und Magnesium-Komponenten für Motor- und Karosserieanwendungen gefertigt. Mit der durch die Kloth-Senking Metallgießerei entwickelten PREMIUM-Druckgießtechnologie steht in der KSM Castings GmbH ein Vakuum-Druckgießverfahren zur Verfügung, durch dessen Anwendung Luft-, Trennmittel- sowie Oxideinschlüsse, die im Gefüge von konventionellen Druckgussteilen zu einer Schädigung des Gefüges führen, sicher vermieden werden. Dies wird durch die Anwendung des Vakuums während der Formfüllphase erreicht. Somit werden prozesssicher mechanisch-technologische Eigenschaften im Bauteil erzielt, die einen Einsatz von Strukturteilen für Anwendungen im gesamten Karosseriebereich und im Fahrwerk ermöglichen. Mit dem Kokillengussverfahren und der weiterentwickelten Gegendruck-Kokillengusstechnologie ist die KSM Castings GmbH besonders auf die Fertigung von crashrelevanten Sicherheitsbauteilen mit hohen Anforderungen an Dehnung und Festigkeit für Fahrwerksanwendungen eingerichtet. Prototypen mit mechanisch-technologischen Eigenschaften, die mit denen der späteren Serienteile vergleichbar sind, werden durch modernste Rapidprototyping-Technologien wie z. B. Stereolithographie gefertigt. Kleinserien werden im Niederdruck-Sandguss hergestellt. Dabei können prozesssicher sowohl Bauteile mit geringsten Wanddicken als auch höchste Werkstoffkennwerte realisiert werden, ein Vorteil, der auch bei hoch belasteten Motorsportkomponenten gern genutzt wird. Bei der Auswahl der verwendeten Werkstoffe können alle Aluminium- und Magnesiumlegierungen verarbeitet werden. Für eine mechanische Bearbeitung der Komponenten werden modernste CNC-Maschinen oder bei entsprechenden Großserien auch Transferanlagen eingesetzt. Dabei werden alle Arbeitsschritte von der Zerspanung über Entgratoperationen bis zur Montage zusammengefasst und mit integrierten Mess- und Regelsystemen überwacht. Zur Dokumentation der Montageschritte stehen integrierte Prozesssteuerungssysteme mit im Fertigungsprozess online überwachten Qualitätsparametern wie z. B. Funktionsmaßen oder Einpress- und Montagekräften zur Verfügung. Diese sind die Garanten für eine stabile Qualität in der Produktion. Durch die konsequente Nutzung von kostengünstigen und rationellen Fertigungstechnologien und die Unterstützung der Fertigung mit modernsten DV-Technologien werden unnötige Pufferbestände vermieden. Durch die gezielte Minimierung jeglicher Bestände und enge, geschlossene Regelkreise wird eine weitere Verbesserung der Prozessqualität erreicht. Darüber hinaus bedeutet die Reduzierung der Umlaufbestände zusammen mit einer punktgenauen Just-in-Time-Belieferung einen zusätzlichen Beitrag zur Absicherung der gemeinsamen Wettbewerbsfähigkeit mit den Kunden. Damit gehört die KSM Castings Gruppe zu den führenden Aluminiumgießereien weltweit und kann sich so erfolgreich entwickeln. ∎

Company Profile

velopment work is the systematic safeguarding of the results with the help of Six-Sigma methods and Design of Experiment (DoE). The use of the numeric simulation technique here is fully established for all casting processes used. All processes in the development and production phases are assisted by the use of the advantages of a certified company management system.

Quality assurance

The requirements of the DIN EN ISO 9001, VDA-Vol. 6.1, the QS 9000 and the ISO/TS 16949 as well as the DIN EN ISO 14001 Environment Certificate are met across the board in all locations. The basis for the continuous improvement process is permanent information and involvement of all employees. Potential for improvement is continuously ascertained and exhausted in order to increase competitiveness. Quality assurance in the process is carried out by automatic x-ray equipment, fluorescent dye penetrant testing to detect any cracks, leak testing and by serial monitoring of the material properties with the help of spectral analysis and destructive material testing.

Processes

The highest quality aluminium and magnesium components for motor, body and chassis applications are produced by means of latest pressure die-casting equipment in the clamping force range of 400 to 3,000 tonnes. With the PREMIUM pressure die-casting technology developed by Kloth-Senking Metallgießerei, the KSM Castings Group can take advantage of a vacuum pressure die-casting technology. By using this technology, inclusions of air, lubrications and oxides, which can lead to structure damage in conventional pressure casting parts, can be avoided. This is achieved through the use of a vacuum during the mould filling phase and ensures process-proof, mechanical-technological characteristics in the part which makes it possible to use structural parts in the whole bodywork and chassis. With the permanent-mould die-casting method and further developed counter-pressure casting technology, KSM Castings GmbH is particularly well equipped for the manufacture of crash-resistant safety parts possessing the highest possible ductility and strength for chassis applications. Prototypes with mechanical characteristics comparable with future series parts are manufactured using Rapid Prototyping technologies such as stereo-lithography. Small-lot products are manufactured using low-pressure sand-casting. At the same time, components of both minimum wall thickness and highest material properties can be manufactured in proven processes – an advantage that is also used with motor sports components which are subject to high levels of stress. All aluminium and magnesium alloys can be processed when selecting the materials to be used. For the machining of the components, the latest CNC machining technology is used. In case of large production lots, transfer equipment is also used. In this process, all steps from machining through deburring to assembling are combined and monitored with integrated measuring and process control systems. To document each stage of assembly, integrated process-control systems are used in the production process with computer-monitored quality parameters such as functional dimensions or assembly parameters. This guarantees a stable production quality. The consistent use of low-cost and rational production technologies and the support of production by means of latest data processing technologies can avoid the unnecessary accumulation of stocks. The targeted minimization of all stocks and tight, closed-loop control circuits will achieve a further improvement of processing quality. In addition, the reduction of cycle stocks together with pin-pointed just-in-time delivery means an additional contribution to the safeguarding of common competitive ability with the customers. This makes the KSM Castings Group one of the leading aluminium casting companies worldwide having the opportunity for successful development and extension. ■

KSM Castings GmbH

Anschrift/Address:
Cheruskerring 38
D-31137 Hildesheim
Telefon +49 (5121) 505-0
Fax +49 (5121) 505-345
E-Mail info@ksmcastings.com
Internet www.ksmcastings.com

Geschäftstätigkeit/Business Activity:
Ihr Partner für Aluminium-und Magnesiumgusskomponenten vom Konzept bis zur Serienfertigung mit mechanischer Bearbeitung und Montage in den Bereichen Body, Chassis, Powertrain
From the concept to series production including machining and assembly, we are your partner for aluminium and magnesium castings in Body, Chassis and Powertrain

KSM Castings – Wernigerode
Fritz Völkel, Wuppertal
Bendorf – CH
DGT Druckgießtechnik, Radevormwald
Kloth-Senking-Metallgießerei
KSM Castings – CZ

Finanzplatz Frankfurt

Frankfurt am Main, dynamischer Finanzplatz in der Mitte Europas

Frankfurt on the Main, dynamic financial centre in the heart of Europe

Frankfurt am Main ist das einzige internationale Finanzzentrum Deutschlands und zugleich das größte in Kontinentaleuropa. Seine Bedeutung geht weit über die Grenzen Europas hinaus. Dieser erfolgreiche Finanzplatz ist Garant für Wachstum, Stabilität und Wohlstand in ganz Deutschland.

Im internationalen Vergleich wird die hohe Konzentration von Bankengruppen, Fondsgesellschaften und damit zusammenhängenden Unternehmen auf der einen und von hochqualifiziertem Personal auf der anderen Seite nach wie vor eine besondere Rolle spielen. Deshalb wird die Hessische Landesregierung unter meiner Führung mit allen ihr zugänglichen Instrumenten dafür sorgen, dass der Finanzplatz Frankfurt seine Stellung im Wettbewerb auch in Zukunft behaupten und seine Vorteile ausbauen kann. Wir wollen den Standort im internationalen Wettbewerb der Finanzmärkte stärken!

Der geborene Finanzplatz

Wenn man Frankfurt am Main einmal charakterisieren soll, dann wird man schnell feststellen, dass Frankfurt für Internationalität und Urbanität steht. Hier bewegen sich Menschen, hier arbeiten Menschen aus allen Kulturkreisen der Welt. Hinzu kommt Frankfurts enorme Wirtschaftskraft. Als Finanzmetropole, als Sitz der Europäischen Zentralbank zumal, hat Frankfurt einen weltweiten Ruf. Mit der Standortentscheidung der Europäischen Zentralbank für Frankfurt ist sie auch zur „Stadt des Euro" geworden. Hier werden für das gesamte „Euroland" die wichtigen währungspolitischen Entscheidungen getroffen. Auch die Deutsche Bundesbank hat seit ihrer Gründung ihren Sitz in Frankfurt. Über 300 Banken, davon alleine 200 ausländische Institute, haben sich in der Mainmetropole niedergelassen, in diesen Banken arbeiten über 70.000 Beschäftigte. Die Wertpapierbörse ist eine der ältesten in Deutschland. Heute hält sie über zwei Drittel des Gesamtumsatzes im deutschen Börsenhandel und ist hinter New York und London die drittgrößte der Welt. Ihre herausragende Leistungsfähigkeit wird von niemand ernsthaft in Zweifel gezogen. In Frankfurt gibt es Finanzdienstleister aller Art und eine Vielzahl anderer Unternehmen, die in enger Beziehung zu den Finanzdienstleistungen stehen. Frankfurt hat aber auch stets von der gesunden Mischung aus Industrie und Handwerk, Handel und Dienstleistungen profitiert. Frankfurt Rhein-Main ist einer der produktivsten und dynamischsten Industriestandorte Deutschlands. Die Region ist Spitzenreiter in Deutschland

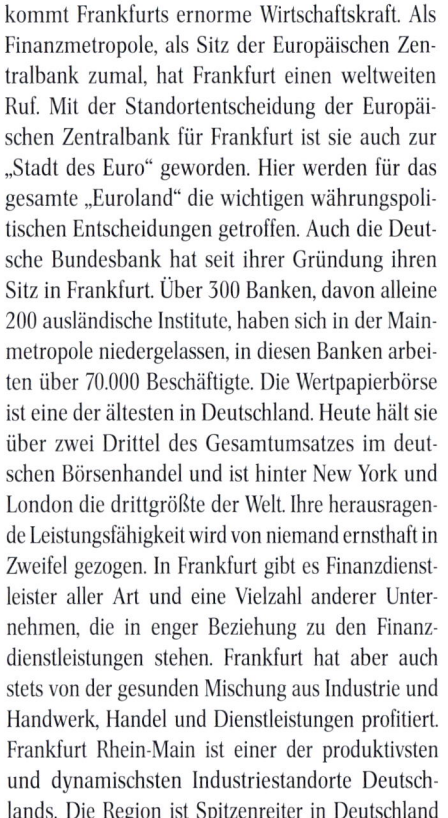

Roland Koch

Der Autor wurde 1958 in Frankfurt/Main geboren. Nach dem Abitur 1977 in Sulzbach/Taunus studierte er Rechtswissenschaften an der Universität Frankfurt/Main. 1982 legte er das erste, 1985 das zweite juristische Staatsexamen ab. Von 1985 bis 1999 war er als selbstständiger Rechtsanwalt mit den Schwerpunkten Wirtschafts- und Wettbewerbsrecht in Eschborn tätig. Seit 1987 ist er als hessischer Landtagsabgeordneter dreimal in direkter Wahl gewählt worden und übte von 1989 bis 1993 das Amt des umweltpolitischen Sprechers seiner Fraktion aus. Seit Januar 1998 ist er Landesvorsitzender der CDU in Hessen. Seit 1999 ist Roland Koch Ministerpräsident des Landes Hessen.

The author was born in 1958 in Frankfurt/Main. After school leaving exams in 1977 in Sulzbach/Taunus he studied law at the University of Frankfurt/Main. In 1982 he passed the first, in 1985 the second state exam in law. From 1985 to 1999 he was a self-employed lawyer in Eschborn, specialised in business and competition law. Since 1987 he has been directly elected three times as a member of the Hessian State Parliament and was environmental spokesman for his faction from 1989 to 1993. From 1991 Roland Koch was deputy chairman, from 1993 until taking office he was chairman of the CDU faction in the State Parliament. Since January 1998 he has been state chairman of the CDU in Hesse. Since 1999 Roland Koch has been Prime Minister of the State of Hesse.

Frankfurt bei Nacht.
Frankfurt at night.

Financial Centre

Knapp eine Stunde dauert die ICE-Fahrt vom Frankfurter Airport nach Köln Hbf.
The Intercity Express ride from Frankfurt Airport to Cologne Central Station takes just less than one hour's journey.

Frankfurt is the only international financial centre in Germany and at the same time the largest of continental Europe. Its significance goes far beyond the limits of Europe. This successful financial centre is a guarantee for growth, stability and prosperity throughout Germany.

On international comparison, the high concentration of banks, investment fund companies and interconnected companies on the one hand and of highly-qualified personnel on the other will continue playing a major role. For this reason, the State Government of Hesse under my leadership will ensure with all possible instruments that the financial centre of Frankfurt maintains its cut-edge position also in future and can expand its advantages. We want to strengthen the business location in the international competition of financial markets!

Born to be a financial centre

If one is to draw a characteristic picture of Frankfurt on the Main, one will rapidly find that Frankfurt is the epitome of internationalism and urbanity. People are mobile here, people coming from all cultural areas of the world work here. In addition, there is Frankfurt's enormous economic power. As financial metropolis, especially as seat of the European Central Bank, Frankfurt enjoys an excellent worldwide reputation. When the European Central Bank decided for Frankfurt as business location, it also became the "City of the Euro". Important decisions of monetary policy are made here for the entire "Eurozone". Since its establishment, also the German Federal Bank has had its seat here. Over 300 banks, of these alone 200 foreign institutes, have settled in the metropolitan city on the Main; more than 70,000 employees work in these banks. The stock exchange is one of the oldest in Germany. Today, it holds over two thirds of the overall turnover of German stock exchange trade and is behind New York and London the third-largest in the world. No one seriously doubts its outstanding efficiency. There are financial services providers of all kind in Frankfurt and a series of other companies that are closely related to financial services. However, Frankfurt has also constantly benefited from a healthy mixture of industry and handicrafts, trade and services. Frankfurt Rhine-Main is one of the most productive and most dynamic industrial locations in Germany. The region is German champion in terms of the "headquarters" of globally oriented companies, and newcomers arrive constantly. Of the 100 largest industrial companies in Germany, every fifth has its head office in Frankfurt. The region's orientation towards the future is clearly evident in that 2,300 high-tech enterprises have chosen Frankfurt as their company seat. In this respect the promising biotech and gene technology enterprises are gaining increasing importance, which are settling in this region to an ever greater extent. In total, almost two million people work in the metropolis on the Main river.

Frankfurt is home to one of the most renowned universities in Germany, the Johann Wolfgang Goethe University. Almost all university disciplines can be studied here. In direct vicinity of Frankfurt

Finanzplatz Frankfurt

bei den „headquarters" weltweit orientierter Unternehmen und ständig kommen neue hinzu. Von den 100 größten Industrieunternehmen in Deutschland hat jedes fünfte seine Firmenzentrale in Frankfurt. Die Zukunftsorientierung der Region wird dadurch deutlich, dass 2.300 Hightech-Unternehmen ihren Firmensitz in Frankfurt gewählt haben. Eine immer stärker werdende Bedeutung gewinnen dabei die zukunftsträchtigen Bio- und Gentechnologieunternehmen, die sich verstärkt in dieser Region niederlassen. Insgesamt arbeiten fast zwei Millionen Menschen in der Mainmetropole.

In Frankfurt ist mit der Johann Wolfgang Goethe Universität eine der renommiertesten Universitäten Deutschlands beheimatet. Nahezu alle universitären Disziplinen sind vertreten. Auch in unmittelbarer Nähe zu Frankfurt gibt es weitere Studieneinrichtungen mit internationalem Ruf: Innerhalb von einer Stunde sind von hier aus mehr als ein Dutzend Universitäten und Fachhochschulen zu erreichen. Eine Dichte, die keine andere Region in Europa bieten kann.

Die Universität Frankfurt, die beteiligten Fachbereiche und Institute sowie die Landesregierung sind sich darin einig, dass durch die Schaffung eines „House of Finance" eine in Deutschland einmalige Bündelung von Wissenschaften der Finanz- und Geldwirtschaft geschaffen werden wird. Die Voraussetzungen in Frankfurt sind in Anbetracht der wirtschaftlichen Institutionen, die sich am Standort befinden, hierfür ideal. Durch das House of Finance sollen nicht zuletzt die bereits jetzt an der Universität Frankfurt bestehenden ausgezeichneten Voraussetzungen weiter verbessert werden, hoch qualifizierte Fach- und Führungskräfte selbst auszubilden und durch die Ausbildung an den Finanzplatz und die dort ansässigen Unternehmen zu binden. Durch die Errichtung eines House of Finance sollen qualifizierter Nachwuchs für den Finanzplatz Frankfurt gewonnen und gefördert werden, ein verstärkter Austausch zwischen Finanzplatz-Community, Wissenschaft und Politik stattfinden und alle bisherigen finanzwirtschaftlichen Aktivitäten an der Universität Frankfurt gebündelt werden.

Dazu zählen die Schwerpunkte „Geld und Währung" und „Finanzen" mit dem Graduiertenkolleg „Money and Finance" aus dem Bereich der Wirtschaftswissenschaften sowie das Institut für Bankrecht, das in Gründung befindliche Institut für Versicherungsrecht und die finanz- und steuerrechtlichen Lehrstühle aus dem Bereich der Rechtswissenschaften. Den Kern des House of Finance bilden die so genannten AnInstitute, also das Center für Financial Studies, das Institute for Law and Finance, das E-Finance-Lab sowie das MathFinance. Die intensive Verflechtung der Institute mit der Finanzplatz-Community soll dabei weiter vertieft werden. Das House of Finance ist ein wesentlicher Bestandteil im Rahmen der geplanten Entwicklung und Gestaltung des neuen zentralen Universitätsstandorts Campus Westend. Der Ausbau des Campus Westend ist eine Investition des Landes mit höchster Priorität.

Die Informationsdrehscheibe

Kein anderer Standort in Deutschland und sogar in Kontinentaleuropa bietet eine vergleichbare Infrastruktur. Im Herzen Europas gelegen, verfügt die größte Stadt Hessens über einen Flughafen, an dem jährlich fast 49 Millionen Gäste ankommen oder abfliegen, von dem aus man nahezu jeden Punkt der Welt erreichen kann. Das Pflegen von internationalen Geschäftskontakten, das Erschließen neuer Märkte im Ausland, aber auch der Zugang ausländischer Unternehmen zum heimischen Markt ist ganz wesentlich abhängig von einer hervorragenden Verkehrsinfrastruktur. Es ist unbestritten, dass keine andere Stadt in Europa solche sehr guten Bedingungen vorzuweisen hat, wie Frankfurt dies kann. Der Rhein-Main Flughafen ist der größte in Kontinentaleuropa und bietet optimale Verbindungen zu den wichtigen Zielen in aller Welt. Innerhalb von zwei Stunden ist nahezu jede europäische Hauptstadt erreichbar. Jede Woche verbinden 4.400 Flüge Frankfurt mit 280 Städten in über 110 Ländern. Mit wöchentlich 390 Direktflügen nach Osteuropa, mehr als London und Paris zusammen, ist der Frankfurter Flughafen das Tor zum Osten. Auch das Verkehrsnetz am Boden entspricht höchsten Ansprüchen die man an die Mobilität stellen kann. Der Hauptbahnhof, der größte in Europa, bietet durch seine Integration in das europäische Netz der Hochgeschwindigkeitszüge einen schnellen Zugang zu deutschen und europäischen Großstädten. Gleiches gilt für den Bahnhof am Flughafen, der eine direkte Anbindung der Schienenverbindungen an den Luftverkehr gewährleistet. Im ganzen Rhein-Main-Gebiet gibt es insgesamt sieben IC/ICE-Haltestellen, von denen aus man die Metropolen Europas erreichen kann. Frankfurt ist in das europäische Fernstraßennetz geradezu optimal eingebunden. Alleine das modern ausgebaute Frankfurter Autobahnkreuz A3/A5 passieren täglich 300.000 Kraftfahrzeuge. Der verkehrsreichste Platz Europas.

Die Stadt ist aber auch eine wichtige Schnittstelle im Bereich der Telekommunikation und des Internets. In Frankfurt kreuzen sich die Datennetze und alle international führenden Telekommunikationsgesellschaften sind zumindest mit Niederlassungen vertreten, ebenso wie die internationalen und nationalen Branchenverbände. Hier werden fast 200 Telekommunikationsunternehmen und Internetprovider gezählt. Zusätzlich zum Netz der Deutschen Telekom hat die Stadt ein rund 700 km langes Glasfasernetz aufgebaut, um dem ständig steigenden Datenverkehr gerecht zu werden. Der De-CIX (Deutsche Commercial Internet Exchange) wickelt über 85 % des deutschen und damit 35 % des europäischen Internetverkehrs mit einem Datendurchsatz von 10 Milliarden Bits pro Sekunde (mit immer weiter steigender Tendenz) ab. Damit ist Frankfurt der Kommunikationsknoten in Europa. Frankfurt ist aber auch Messestadt mit hervorragendem internationalem Ruf: Heute finden rund 50 Messen im Jahr statt, davon sind alleine 15 die

Fast 50 Millionen Fluggäste hat der Frankfurter Airport im Jahr.
Frankfurt Airport has almost 50 million passengers a year.

Financial Centre

Die Alte Oper: ein kulturelles Wahrzeichen Frankfurts.

Alte Oper: Frankfurt's cultural symbol.

there are other tertiary education institutes of international repute: in one hour's drive one can reach about one dozen of universities and universities of applied sciences. This density is unequalled in any other region of Europa.

Frankfurt University, the participating faculties and institutes as well as the state government all agree that through the establishment of a "House of Finance", a concentration of sciences for the finance and money industry will be created here that is unique in Germany. Conditions for this in Frankfurt are ideal in view of the economic institutions present at this location. Through the House of Finance ultimately the already excellent prerequisites existing at Frankfurt University are to be improved further, for providing independent education to highly qualified experts and management personnel and for tying them to the financial centre and to local companies through training.

The establishment of the House of Finance intends to win qualified graduates for the financial centre of Frankfurt and promote them, to increase exchange between the finance-centre community, science and politics, and to concentrate all former financial industry activities at the University of Frankfurt.

This includes the focal points of "Money and Currency" and "Finances" with the Graduate College "Money and Finance" from the field of economics as well as the Institute for Banking Law, the Institute of Insurance Law currently being founded and the finance and tax law chairs from the field of jurisprudence. The main core of the House of Finance will be the so-called AnInstitutes, which are the Center for Financial Studies, the Institute for Law and Finance, the E-Finance Lab as well as the MathFinance. An intensive interconnection between the institutes and the finance-centre community is to be consolidated in this way. The House of Finance is a major component in the context of the planned development and design of the new and central university location Campus Westend. The expansion of Campus Westend is an investment of highest priority to the state government.

The information hub

No other business location in Germany and even in continental Europe offers a comparable infrastructure. Situated in the heart of Europe, Hesse's largest city boasts an airport at which annually almost 49 million passengers arrive or take flights, from which one can nearly reach any point in the world. Maintaining international business contacts, opening up new markets abroad, but also access of foreign companies to the home market depends considerably on the availability of an outstanding infrastructure. It cannot be denied that no other city in Europe possesses such extremely favourable

Finanzplatz Frankfurt

Bulle und...

Bull and ...

in ihren Branchen jeweils weltgrößten Messen. Darunter sind so bekannte Messen wie die IAA-Internationale Automobilausstellung, die traditionsreiche Buchmesse sowie die Ambiente und die Premiere als größte Konsumgütermessen der Welt. Mit 37.000 Ausstellern ist Frankfurt der größte Messeplatz in Europa. Bis zu 2.700.000 Menschen besuchen jährlich die Messen in Frankfurt, die eine Ausstellungsfläche von über 410.000 Quadratmetern zu bieten haben. Der Groß- und Einzelhandel ist nach der Industrie und den Banken der drittgrößte Wirtschaftsfaktor. Deren intensive Handelsbeziehungen haben zu einem immer weiter wachsenden Engagement ausländischer Investoren geführt; so fließen ein Viertel der ausländischen Direktinvestitionen in Deutschland in die Region Frankfurt Rhein-Main.

Frankfurt ist aber auch in anderer Sicht aufregend und multikulturell. Hier leben Menschen aus 180 verschiedenen Ländern und es gibt acht internationale Schulen. Alleine in Frankfurt kommen zu den Städtischen Bühnen mit Oper und Schauspiel und der Alten Oper zwei englische, ein französisches, ein russisches, ein japanisches und ein italienisches Theater. Kreativität und kulturelles Leben sind in Frankfurt genauso ausgeprägt wie international hochkarätige Kultur. Frankfurt ist zu Recht stolz auf sein international hoch angesehenes Museumsufer. Nur ein paar Schritte benötigt man, um in immer neue Welten einzutauchen. Vom Städel mit seiner Sammlung europäischer Malerei zum Liebighaus mit Plastiken der Antike bis zum Barock und weiter zum Museum für Telekommunikation und dem weltweit ersten Filmmuseum, das sich zur Aufgabe gemacht hat Filme in der Originalfassung zu zeigen.

Finanzdienstleistungen werden wichtiger

Eines ist heute abzusehen: Gerade für Finanzdienstleistungen wird Deutschland als größte Volkswirtschaft in der Europäischen Union in den kommenden Jahren ein expandierender und damit attraktiver Markt sein. Die deutsche Wirtschaft befindet sich in einer Phase erheblicher Umstrukturierungen. Unternehmen geben Geschäftsfelder ab, die nicht mehr zu ihren Kernaktivitäten gehören. Und auch auf anderen Feldern sind Änderungen zu erwarten. So wird sich generell die Finanzierung auch mittlerer Unternehmen in Zukunft stärker als in den vergangenen Jahren auf den Kapitalmarkt stützen. Bei diesen Unternehmensgruppen wird die Bedeutung der traditionellen Kreditfinanzierung zurückgehen. Dagegen werden Beteiligungskapital, Anleihen und andere marktorientierte Finanzierungsformen an Bedeutung gewinnen. Die Altersvorsorge wird sich künftig in weit stärkerem Umfang als bisher auf den Kapitalmarkt stützen müssen. Erfahrungen aus angelsächsischen Ländern zeigen, dass es um sehr hohe Beträge und damit um ein für Finanzdienstleistungsunternehmen attraktives Geschäft geht. Auch das allgemeine Anlageverhalten des Publikums hat sich in den letzten Jahren bereits stärker auf den Kapitalmarkt orientiert.

Gerade im Bereich der Finanzdienstleistungen können sich die Verhältnisse sehr schnell ändern. Daher müssen die Rahmenbedingungen immer wieder auf den Prüfstand und angepasst werden. Die Politik darf und wird sich hier keinen Stillstand erlauben. Wir haben dies erkannt und werden unser Handeln danach ausrichten.

Warum müssen also Finanzunternehmen in Frankfurt vertreten sein? Weil es in ihrem eigenen wirtschaftlichen Interesse ist – und die Hessische Landesregierung wird ihnen diese Entscheidung so leicht wie möglich machen. In der weltoffenen Region Frankfurt Rhein-Main finden Investoren Partner mit außerordentlichem Wirtschaftspotential, die gerne gemeinsame Projekte realisieren und in diesen herzlich willkommen sind. Dank dynamischer Wirtschaftskraft, Weltoffenheit und vielfältiger Internationalität herrscht hier ein pulsierendes Klima. Ich lade alle ein, dies in Frankfurt zu erleben und an der Prosperität teilzunehmen. ∎

... Bär vor der Frankfurter Börse.

... Bear in front of the Frankfurt Stock Exchange.

Financial Centre

conditions as Frankfurt. The Rhine-Main Airport is the largest in continental Europe and offers ideal connections to major destinations in the entire world. In a matter of two hours almost any European capital can be reached. Each week, 4,400 flights link Frankfurt with 280 cities in over 110 countries. Frankfurt Airport is the "Gate to the East" with a weekly number of 390 direct flights to East Europe, more than London and Paris together. Also the traffic system on the ground corresponds to the highest standards one can demand of mobility. The Central Station, which is the largest in Europe, provides fast access to German and European cities because of its integration into the European network of high-speed trains. The same goes for the train station at the airport, which guarantees a direct connection of rail transport to air traffic. There are a total of seven Intercity and Intercity Express stops in the entire area of Rhine-Main from which one can easily reach the metropolitan cities of Europe. Frankfurt is virtually ideally integrated in the system of long-distance highways. Daily, 300,000 vehicles pass through the modern development of Frankfurt's motorway crossing A3/A5 alone. It is Europe's busiest traffic location.

But the city is also an important intersection in the field of telecommunications and the Internet. Data networks meet in Frankfurt, and all globally leading telecommunications companies at least have a representative branch, as well as the international and national branch associations. Almost 200 telecommunications companies and Internet providers have been counted here. In addition to the network of Deutsche Telekom the city administration has built up an about 700 km long fibre network to meet the constantly increasing data traffic. The De-CIX (German Commercial Internet Exchange) deals with over 85 % of the German and therefore 35 % of the European Internet traffic with data transmission of 10 billion bits per second (and continuously increasing tendency). This makes Frankfurt the communications hub in Europe.

Moreover, Frankfurt is an exhibition city of excellent international repute. Today, around 50 trade fairs take place each year; of these 15 alone are the worldwide largest fairs of their relevant branch. Among these are such well-known trade fairs as the IAA – International Automobile Exhibition, the traditional Book Fair as well as the Ambiente and the Premiere being the world's largest consumer goods fairs. With 37,000 exhibitors, Frankfurt is the largest exhibition centre in Europe. Up to 2,700,000 people visit the Frankfurt trade fairs each year, which boast an overall exhibition area of over 410,000 square metres. Wholesale and retail trade is after industry and banking the third-largest economic factor. The intensive trade relations these sectors maintain have resulted in continuously growing engagement of foreign investors; in fact, one quarter of foreign direct investments in Germany flow into the region of Frankfurt Rhine-Main.

But also from another point of view Frankfurt is exciting and multicultural. People from 180 different countries live here and there are eight international schools. Frankfurt alone boasts, apart from the state theatres with opera and the playhouses Schauspiel and Alte Oper, two English, one French, one Russian, one Japanese and one Italian theatre. Creativity and cultural life are as pronounced in Frankfurt as international top-class culture. Frankfurt is very proud of its internationally highly renowned Museum Embankment, and rightly so. One only needs a few steps to delve into ever newly created worlds. Starting with the Städel Art Institute and Municipal Gallery and its collection of European paintings, the Liebighaus and its sculptures from ancient through to baroque times and following with the Museum of Telecommunications and the worldwide first Film Museum, which has made it its task to show films in their original version.

Financial services are gaining importance

One thing can be predicted clearly: especially for financial services, Germany, as the largest national economy of the European Union, will be an expanding and therefore attractive market in the coming years. The German economy is currently undergoing a phase of considerable restructuring. Companies are relinquishing business fields that are no longer part of their core activities. And also in other fields one can expect changes. Generally, the financing of medium-sized companies will be supported by the capital market increasingly in future as opposed to recent years. For these groups of companies the importance of traditional financing by way of credit will lessen. In contrast, share capital, bonds and other market-oriented forms of financing will gain importance. Old age pensions will have to lean on the capital market to a much greater extent than so far. Experiences in Anglo-Saxon countries show that extremely high sums are at stake here and therefore an attractive business field for financial services companies is developing. Also the general investment behaviour of the public has changed and has been more oriented towards the capital market in the past years.

Particularly in the financial services sector situations can change very rapidly. For this reason, frame conditions must be tested and adjusted constantly. The political sector cannot and will not take the liberty of standing still in this respect. We have recognised this and will act accordingly.

Why then must financial companies be represented in Frankfurt actually? Because it is in the economic interest of the companies themselves and the Government of the State of Hesse will help to make this decision as simple as possible. In the cosmopolitan region of Rhine-Main investors will find partners with extraordinary economic potentials that would like to realize mutual projects and are very welcome here. Owing to the dynamic economic power, a cosmopolitan attitude and a varied internationalism a pulsating climate prevails here. I invite everyone to come and experience this in Frankfurt and take part in the prosperity.

Messe-Eingang City.

City entrance to Frankfurt's Exhibition Centre.

Company Profile

Der weltweit führende Kreditversicherer – wichtiger Partner der Wirtschaft

The world's leading credit insurer – an important partner for industry

Vor allen Dingen in Westeuropa war die Kreditversicherungsbranche bis weit in die 90er-Jahre hinein auf die jeweiligen nationalen Märkte konzentriert. Im Zuge der danach einsetzenden zunehmenden Internationalisierung und des Konzentrationsprozesses der Branche ist unter dem Dach der Allianz mit der Euler Hermes S.A., Paris, der weltweit führende Kreditversicherer entstanden. Euler Hermes, ein Zusammenschluss der französischen Euler-Gruppe und der Hermes Kreditversicherungs-AG, ist heute weltweit in 40 Ländern vertreten. In den größten Volkswirtschaften Europas, z. B. in Frankreich, England, Italien und Deutschland, ist das Unternehmen Marktführer. Mit einem Anteil von 34 Prozent ist Euler Hermes der weltweit führende Kreditversicherer.

In Deutschland wurde das Unternehmen, für das 2004 etwa 2.100 Mitarbeiter tätig waren, 1917 gegründet und ist seitdem stetig gewachsen. Im Jahr 2004 wurde ein Bruttoumsatz von 650,7 Mio. Euro erreicht. Euler Hermes ist mit den Produkten Delkredere-, Vertrauensschaden- und Kautionsversicherung sowie – über eine Tochtergesellschaft – Inkasso ausschließlich im Firmenkundengeschäft tätig. Außerdem bearbeitet die Euler Hermes Kreditversicherungs-AG als Konsortialführer gemeinsam mit der PricewaterhouseCoopers Aktiengesellschaft Wirtschaftsprüfungsgesellschaft im Auftrag der Bundesrepublik Deutschland die als **Hermesdeckungen** bekannten Exportkreditgarantien des Bundes.

War ursprünglich das Geschäft der Kautionsversicherung die tragende Säule des Unternehmens, so ist mittlerweile die Warenkreditversicherung (Delkredere) mit einem Anteil von etwa zwei Dritteln am gesamten Prämienaufkommen das Kerngeschäft von Euler Hermes. Die Entwicklung in den letzten Jahren verdeutlicht den Stellenwert dieser Dienstleistung für Firmenkunden. Seit dem Ende des durch die Wiedervereinigung ausgelösten Wirtschaftsbooms haben sich die jährlichen Insolvenzzahlen im Zeitraum von 1993 bis 2004 mehr als verdoppelt. Die Insolvenzquote, also das Verhältnis zwischen insolventen Firmen und bestehenden Unternehmen, hat sich von 0,2 Prozent 1970 auf 1,3 Prozent in 2004 mehr als versechsfacht. Seit 2002 ist das Volumen der kurzfristigen Bankkredite rückläufig, während die Inanspruchnahme von Lieferantenkrediten deutlich zugenommen hat. Anders als Banken prüfen und kontrollieren viele Unternehmen die Bonität ihrer Abnehmer jedoch nicht. Darum besteht für diese ein hohes Risiko, mit einem unter Umständen existenzbedrohenden Forderungsausfall konfrontiert zu werden. Insgesamt gingen 2004 Forderungen in Höhe von 26,7 Mrd. Euro verloren.

Mit dem **Schutz vor Forderungsausfall** hilft Euler Hermes Unternehmen, sich gegen dieses Risiko abzusichern. Im Vordergrund steht dabei, Schäden durch eine qualifizierte Bonitätsprüfung zu verhindern. Das Herzstück der Kreditversicherung ist dementsprechend die Kreditprüfung. Durch ein spezielles Bonitätsbewertungssystem ist es möglich, Unternehmen, die sich in einer schwierigen wirtschaftlichen Situation befinden, zu identifizieren und die Kunden frühzeitig zu warnen. Dazu bedient sich Euler Hermes zahlreicher Informationsquellen – national wie international. So kann Euler Hermes beispielsweise auf eine weltweit vernetzte Risikodatenbank zurückgreifen, in der Informationen über mehr als 40 Millionen Unternehmen gespeichert sind. Hinzu kommt das spezielle Know-how der Mitarbeiter über Branchen und Konzerne in fast allen Regionen der Welt. Täglich gehen 16.000 Kreditanträge ein.

Kommt es dennoch zum Zahlungsausfall, wird über ein professionelles Inkasso- und Mahnverfahren versucht, die Not leidenden Forderungen einzutreiben. Gelingt das nicht, tritt nach Ablauf einer Frist oder nach Eintritt der Zahlungsunfähigkeit der Versicherungsschutz ein. 2004 deckte Euler Hermes Forderungen im Wert von mehr als 600 Mrd. Euro.

Diese Dienstleistungen machen Euler Hermes zu einem wichtigen Partner der Wirtschaft. ■

Die Zentrale der Euler Hermes Kreditversicherungs-AG in Hamburg.
The head offices of Euler Hermes Kreditversicherungs-AG in Hamburg.

Company Profile

Primarily in Western Europe the credit insurance industry has been concentrated until far into the nineties in the corresponding national markets. In the course of the following increasing internationalization and of the incipient process of concentration in the industry, the world's leading credit insurer was created with the Paris-based Euler Hermes S.A. under the roof of Allianz AG. Today, Euler Hermes, a merger of the French Euler Group with Hermes Kreditversicherungs-AG, has representative offices in 40 countries worldwide. In the largest national economies of Europe, for instance in France, England, Italy and Germany, the company is absolute market leader. Holding a share of 34 per cent, Euler Hermes is the leading credit insurer worldwide.

In Germany, the company, for which about 2,100 employees worked in 2004, was founded in 1917 and has grown since then continuously. In the year 2004, gross turnover of 650.7 million Euros was generated. Euler Hermes is exclusively dealing with corporate client business with its products trade credit insurance, fidelity insurance and bonds and guarantees as well as – through a subsidiary – with debt collection. Furthermore, Euler Hermes Kreditversicherungs-AG processes as consortium leader together with PriceWaterhouseCoopers Aktiengesellschaft und Wirtschaftsprüfungsgesellschaft export credit guarantees issued by the Federal Republic of Germany known as **Hermes Cover**.

If originally the bond and guarantee business was the major pillar of the company, now the insurance of commercial credits forms the core business of Euler Hermes making up a share of about two thirds of the total premium income. Development experienced in recent years clearly shows the value this service has for corporate clients. Since the end of the economic boom brought about by the reunification, annual insolvency figures have more than doubled in the period between 1993 and 2004. The rate of insolvencies, which is the proportion of insolvent firms against running companies, has more than sextupled from 0.2 per cent in 1970 to 1.3 per cent in 2004. Since 2002, the volume of short-term bank loans has declined, while there has been a marked increase in the drawing on supplier credit facilities. Differently to banks, many companies do not examine and control the creditworthiness of their buyers. Therefore, there is a high risk for them to be confronted with the danger of loosing their livelihood because of bad debts. Overall, debts have been lost in the amount of 26.7 billion Euros in 2004.

By offering **protection against bad debt losses** Euler Hermes helps companies to safeguard themselves against this risk. Of great importance in this respect is to avoid losses by carrying out a qualified credit assessment. Through a special credit assessment system it is possible to identify such companies that are going through a difficult economic situation and to warn policyholders early. To this end, Euler Hermes uses several sources of information – domestically and internationally. In fact Euler Hermes can resort to the worldwide network of a risk database, which stores information of more than 40 million companies. In addition, there is the special know-how employees have about branches of industry and corporations in almost all regions of the world. Each day, 16.000 credit applications are received.

In case of non-payment, however, every effort is made through professional collection and dunning procedures to recover the bed debts. If this should not be successful, after a certain waiting period or after insolvency has been established, an indemnification will be paid under the insurance. In 2004, Euler Hermes covered debts worth more than 600 billion Euros.

These services make Euler Hermes an important partner of industry.

EULER HERMES
Kreditversicherung

Euler Hermes Kreditversicherungs-AG

Vorstand/Executive Board:
Dr. Gerd-Uwe Baden (Vorsitzender/Chairman)
Jochen Dümler
Dr. Hans Janus
Holger Jensen
Juliane Kutter
Dr. Robert Walter

Geschäftsführer der Tochtergesellschaften/
Managing Directors of German subsidiaries:
- Euler Hermes Forderungsmanagement GmbH
  Hans-Hermann Schütt, Herrmann Becker
- Euler Hermes Risk Management GmbH & Co. KG
  Sönke Herrmann, Ulrich Nöthel
- Euler Hermes Rating GmbH
  Ralf Garrn

Gründungsjahr/Year of foundation: 1917

Mitarbeiter/Employees:
2.125 (2004 in Deutschland/in Germany)

Umsatz/Turnover: 650,7 Mio Euro (2004; brutto)

Geschäftsfelder/Business Activity:
- Warenkreditversicherung
  (Schutz vor Forderungsausfall),
- Vertrauensschadenversicherung
  (Schutz vor Veruntreuung),
- Asset-Backed Securities (ABS)
- Inkasso über die Euler Hermes
  Forderungsmanagement GmbH,
- Rating über die Euler Hermes Rating GmbH
Außerdem zusammen mit der
PricewaterhouseCoopers Aktiengesellschaft
Wirtschaftsprüfungsgesellschaft
die Exportkreditgarantien (Hermesdeckungen)
der Bundesrepublik Deutschland
- Trade credit insurance
  (protection against bad debt losses)
- Fidelity insurance
  (protection against embezzlement)
- Asset-Backed Securities (ABS)
- Debt collection through Euler Hermes
  Forderungsmanagement GmbH
- Rating through Euler Hermes Rating GmbH
Furthermore, together with
PriceWaterhouseCoopers Aktiengesellschaf
Wirtschaftsprüfungsgesellschaft, export credit
guarantees (Hermes Cover) issued by the
Government of the Federal Republic of Germany

Vertriebsorganisation/Sales organisation:
7 Niederlassungen und 21 Geschäftsstellen
in ganz Deutschland
7 subsidiaries and 21 branch offices
throughout Germany

Anschrift/Address:
Friedensallee 254
D-22763 Hamburg
Telefon +49 (40) 88 34-0
Telefax +49 (40) 88 34-7744
E-Mail info.de@eulerhermes.com
Internet www.eulerhermes.de

Aufbau Ost

Neue Wege in der Wirtschaft – das Beispiel Sachsen-Anhalt

New countries and new avenues to build up the economy

Um die wirtschaftliche Entwicklung in Ostdeutschland erfolgreich zu gestalten, müssen wir neue Wege betreten. Das tun wir in Sachsen-Anhalt. Wir folgen einem Politikansatz, der alle Politikfelder miteinander vernetzt. Alles wird letztlich dem Ziel untergeordnet, die Rahmenbedingungen für Investitionen zu verbessern. Für die Vernetzung der Ressorts stehen beispielhaft die Investitionserleichterungsgesetze, die die Landesregierung kurz nach ihrem Amtsantritt auf den Weg gebracht hat. Damit wurden u. a. das Vergabegesetz abgeschafft sowie das Bildungsfreistellungsgesetz, das Denkmalschutzgesetz und die Bauordnung geändert.

Die Landesregierung hat einen Generalbevollmächtigten für Investitionen eingesetzt, der potenziellen Investoren unverzüglich als Ansprechpartner zur Verfügung steht. Er garantiert, dass innerhalb von 24 Stunden ein erstes konkretes Angebot vorgelegt werden kann. Unsere Ansiedlungsoffensive trägt inzwischen sichtbare Früchte: Gegenüber 2001 ist die Bruttowertschöpfung im verarbeitenden Gewerbe um 20,7 Prozent gewachsen. Zwischen 2002 und 2004 wurden über 18.000 neue Dauerarbeitsplätze geschaffen. Im Vergleich der neuen Bundesländer schafft die Investitionsförderung damit in Sachsen-Anhalt mit Abstand die meisten Arbeitsplätze je Einwohner. Um das Fördermittelmanagement zu verbessern, hat die Landesregierung im März 2004 eine Investitionsbank errichtet. Sie tritt im Bereich der Wirtschaftsförderung an die Stelle des Landesförderinstitutes. Die Investitionsbank führt die Wirtschaftsförderung in Sachsen-Anhalt in einer Hand zusammen und wickelt sie nach den Grundsätzen eines modernen Dienstleistungsunternehmens ab.

Um auswärtiges Know-how aus Wirtschaft und Politik bei uns in Sachsen-Anhalt zu nutzen, wurde ein Wirtschaftsbeirat beim Ministerpräsidenten eingerichtet. Diesem hochkarätigen Gremium gehören unter dem Vorsitz von Johannes Ludewig eine Reihe von Fachleuten aus überregional tätigen Unternehmen und Banken an.

Dass in Sachsen-Anhalt darüber hinaus in vielen Bereichen Neues geschieht, das den Wirtschaftsstandort stärkt, lässt sich an mannigfaltigen Beispielen belegen:
Im Rahmen ihrer Biotechnologie-Offensive will die Landesregierung in den kommenden Jahren bis zu 150 Millionen Euro investieren. Eines der wichtigsten Projekte ist mit einem Investitionsvolumen von 35 Millionen Euro der Bau des Bioparks Gatersleben, der 2004 startete. Zusammen mit der Automobilzulieferung ist die Biotechnologie das wichtigste Innovationsfeld Sachsen-Anhalts mit zunehmenden Beschäftigungseffekten. In 30 Firmen und Forschungseinrichtungen der „roten" und „grünen" Biotechnologie sind inzwischen rund 2.000 Menschen tätig.

Prof. Dr. Wolfgang Böhmer

Der Autor, geboren 1936 in Dürrhennersdorf (Oberlausitz), studierte Medizin in Leipzig, 1959 Promotion zum Dr. med., 1983 Habilitation. Von 1960 bis 1973 war er Arzt in der Görlitzer Frauenklinik, von 1974 bis 1991 Chefarzt im Krankenhaus Paul-Gerhardt-Stift in der Lutherstadt Wittenberg. Seit 1990 ist Prof. Dr. Böhmer CDU-Mitglied, 1991 bis 1993 war er Minister der Finanzen, 1993 bis 1994 Minister für Arbeit und Soziales des Landes Sachsen-Anhalt. Seit 1998 ist er CDU-Landesvorsitzender und seit Mai 2002 Ministerpräsident des Landes Sachsen-Anhalt.

The author was born in Dürrhennersdorf (Oberlausitz) in 1936 and studied medicine in Leipzig. He graduated as a medical doctor in 1959 and attained his qualification as a professor in 1983. From 1960 until 1973, he served as doctor at the Women's hospital of Görlitz, from 1974 until 1991, as senior consultant at Paul-Gerhardt-Stift hospital in Wittenberg, the City of Luther. Since 1990, Prof. Dr. Böhmer has been a member of the Christian Democratic Party; from 1991 until 1993 he served as Minister of Finances, from 1993 until 1994 as Minister of Labour and Social Issues for the State of Saxony-Anhalt. Since 1998, he has been chairman of the regional section of the Christian Democrats and since May 2002, he has been Prime Minister of the State of Saxony-Anhalt.

Rebuilding East Germany

Trotz Erhöhung der Stundenzahl in Kernfächern wurde in Sachsen-Anhalt die Schulzeit bis zum Abitur wieder auf 12 Jahre verkürzt.

Despite increasing the total hours of lessons in core subjects, the overall school period leading to A-level was reduced to 12 years again in Saxony-Anhalt.

In order to promote economic development in East Germany successfully, we must tread new avenues. We are doing exactly this in Saxony-Anhalt. We are following a political approach that links all fields of politics with each other. Ultimately, everything is subordinate to the goal of improving frame conditions for investments. An example for the integration of this department gives the investment facilitation law brought about by the regional government shortly after taking office. With it, the allocation of funds law was abolished and the law on exemption from education, the protection of historical monuments law and the building regulations were amended among others.

The regional government has installed a plenipotentiary for investments that supports prospective investors directly as contact partner. He guarantees that within 24 hours a first concrete offer can be presented. Our settlement campaign meanwhile bears visible fruits: Compared with 2001, gross value added in processing industry grew by 20.7 per cent. Between 2002 and 2004, over 18,000 new permanent jobs were created. Compared with the new federal states in East Germany investment development efforts in Saxony-Anhalt have therefore by far brought about the greatest number of workplaces per capita.

In order to improve the management of development funds, the regional government established an investment bank at the beginning of 2004. It has replaced the regional development institute in the field of economic development, which was far too paralysed by administrative procedures. The investment bank bundles the programmes of economic development in one agency and deals with them applying the principles of a modern service provider.

To use external know-how from the sectors of economy and politics here in Saxony-Anhalt an economic council was created at the office of the Ministerpräsident. The high-calibre committee is chaired by Johannes Ludewig and includes a number of experts coming from nationally active enterprises and banks.

A diversity of examples proves that new things are happening in many areas in Saxony-Anhalt, which strengthen the state as a business location: In the context of its new biotechnology campaign, the regional government intends to invest up to 150 million Euros in the next year. One of the major projects with an investment volume of 35 million Euros is the construction of the BioPark Gatersleben, started in 2004. Together with the supply of the automobile industry, biotechnology is the most important field of innovation in Saxony-Anhalt showing increasing effects of employment. Around 2,000 people are working now in 30 firms and research institutions of the "red" and "green" branches of biotechnology.

Also the policies of the regional government for the medium-size business sector are treading new paths. The newly established investment bank does not only deal with development applications quicker, it also serves as central consulting office for companies needing information with respect to development programmes. Small and medium-size businesses can now receive up to four million Euros capital-related funds through a silent participation in Mittelständische Beteiligungsgesellschaft Sachsen-Anhalt in combination with a loan from the investment bank. Among other things, this creates cash flow for imminent investments.

The education sector's significance to industry is obvious. Well-trained young people should be made available to the labour market as early as possible. Despite increasing the total hours of lessons in core subjects, the regional government has reduced the overall school period leading to A-level to 12 years again after its predecessor had extended it to 13 years without good cause. Ultimately, also the reduction of A-level education also improves the chances for competition on the labour markets in Europe for these young people.

We are also setting new trends in terms of deregulation and reduction of bureaucracy, as not only the mentioned investment facilitation laws show. Moreover, each public task is scrutinized to whether it can be relinquished or if it can be privatised. Public tasks that can not be privatised are transferred to the communes if communal capacity is ensured and a transferral seems more economical and more purposeful. Furthermore, we have dissolved regional government presidencies and created a regional administration office as new central coordinating and management body of regional administration as of 1st January 2004. In it, 25 independent regional public departments are integrated so far. The creation of the regional administration office allows one to execute administrative processes faster and more congenial for citizens. The new office sees itself as modern service provider for companies, citizens and the communes.

We will continue to pursue determinedly a reduction of bureaucracy also in future. At present we are focussing on strengthening the county districts and increasing their efficiency. Particularly, it is

Aufbau Ost

Auch die Mittelstandspolitik der Landesregierung geht neue Wege. Die neu errichtete Investitionsbank wickelt nicht nur Förderanträge schneller ab, sie ist auch zentrale Beratungsstelle für die Unternehmen, was Förderprogramme betrifft. Kleine und mittlere Unternehmen können nunmehr mit einer stillen Beteiligung der Mittelständischen Beteiligungsgesellschaft Sachsen-Anhalt in Kombination mit einem Darlehen der Investitionsbank eigenkapitalähnliche Mittel von bis zu vier Millionen Euro erhalten. Das schafft u. a. Liquidität für anstehende Investitionen.

Die Bedeutung des Bildungssektors für die Wirtschaft ist offenkundig. Gut ausgebildete junge Menschen sollten möglichst früh dem Arbeitsmarkt zur Verfügung stehen. Trotz Erhöhung der Stundenzahl in Kernfächern hat die Landesregierung die von der Vorgängerin ohne Not auf 13 Jahre verlängerte Schulzeit bis zum Abitur wieder auf 12 Jahre verkürzt. Nicht zuletzt verbessert die Verkürzung der gymnasialen Ausbildung auch die Wettbewerbschancen der jungen Menschen auf dem Arbeitsmarkt in Europa.

Neue Akzente setzen wir auch bei Deregulierung und Bürokratieabbau, wie nicht nur die erwähnten Investitionserleichterungsgesetze zeigen. Darüber hinaus wird jede öffentliche Aufgabe daraufhin überprüft, ob sie verzichtbar ist oder privatisiert werden kann. Nicht privatisierbare staatliche Aufgaben werden auf die Kommunen übertragen, sofern die kommunale Leistungsfähigkeit sichergestellt und eine Übertragung wirtschaftlicher und zweckmäßiger ist. Weiterhin haben wir die Regierungspräsidien aufgelöst und zum 1. Januar 2004 ein Landesverwaltungsamt als zentrale Bündelungs- und Koordinierungsbehörde der Landesverwaltung geschaffen. In ihr sind 25 bisher selbstständige Landesbehörden integriert. Die Errichtung des Landesverwaltungsverwaltungsamtes ermöglicht schnellere, bürgerfreundlichere Verwaltungsabläufe. Die neue Behörde versteht sich als moderner Dienstleister für Unternehmen, Bürger und Kommunen.

Den Bürokratieabbau werden wir auch künftig entschlossen vorantreiben. Im Mittelpunkt steht gegenwärtig die Stärkung der Landkreise sowie die Erhöhung ihrer Leistungsfähigkeit. Insbesondere ist vorgesehen, bis zum Jahr 2007 die Zahl der Landkreise von 21 auf 11 zu reduzieren.

Eng mit dem Bürokratieabbau verbunden ist der Personalabbau, der zügig vorankommt. Durch einen Tarifvertrag, der für Arbeiter und Angestellte Lohnverzicht bei gleichzeitiger Arbeitszeitverkürzung vorsieht, und die Streichung des Weihnachtsgeldes für Beamte konnten die Personalkosten zusätzlich sofort spürbar gesenkt werden.

Eine neue Form der länderübergreifenden Kooperation ist die 2002 mit Sachsen und Thüringen gegründete „Initiative Mitteldeutschland". Unter dem Dach der Initiative wollen die Länder eng zusammenarbeiten, um den Standort Mitteldeutschland zu stärken. Wichtige aktuelle Vorhaben sind der Ausbau der Infrastruktur im Wirtschaftsraum Halle/Leipzig und die Entwicklung der „Metropolregion Mitteldeutschland".

Neue Kooperationsformen praktiziert Sachsen-Anhalt auch auf internationaler Ebene. Auf Initiative des Landes und der ansässigen Chemieindustrie wurde das Netzwerk europäischer Chemieregionen ECRN mit bisher 13 Mitgliedsregionen aus sieben Ländern Europas gebildet. Der Chemiestandort Sachsen-Anhalt ist aufgrund seiner geografischen Lage prädestiniert, Kooperationen mit mittel- und osteuropäischen Staaten aufzubauen. Das Netzwerk gewinnt stetig an Schwung. Schlüsselfelder der Zusammenarbeit sind die europäische Umwelt-, Regional- und Wirtschaftspolitik.

Solche Aktivitäten unterstreichen den Willen Sachsen-Anhalts, die Chancen der Osterweiterung zu nutzen. Auch in Sachsen-Anhalt können wir davon zusätzliche Impulse für den Außenhandel erwarten. Bereits jetzt liegen mit Polen (Platz 5), Tschechien (Platz 8) und Ungarn (Platz 15) drei der Beitrittsländer unter den Top 20 der Außenhandelspartner Sachsen-Anhalts. Allein nach Polen wurden 2004 Waren im Wert von rund 400 Millionen Euro exportiert. Die besondere Bedeutung der Beziehungen zu Polen wird durch eine Regionalpartnerschaft mit der Wojewodschaft Masowien (Warschauer Umland) unterstrichen.

Wir richten unseren Blick aber nicht nur nach Osten. Im Februar 2004 haben wir eine neue Kooperation mit der französischen Region Centre besiegelt.

Die Landesregierung wird auch weiterhin mit Kreativität und Ideenreichtum neue Wege beschreiten, um Investitionen voranzubringen und den Wirtschaftsstandort Sachsen-Anhalt zu stärken. ■

Im Rahmen ihrer neuen Biotechnologie-Offensive will die Landesregierung in den kommenden Jahren bis zu 150 Millionen Euro investieren.
In the context of its new biotechnology initiative, the state government wants to invest up to 150 million euros in the next years.

Rebuilding East Germany

In 30 Firmen und Forschungseinrichtungen der „roten" und „grünen" Biotechnologie sind inzwischen rund 2.000 Menschen tätig.

Meanwhile, there are around 2,000 people working in 30 firms and research institutions of the "red" and "green" fields of biotechnology.

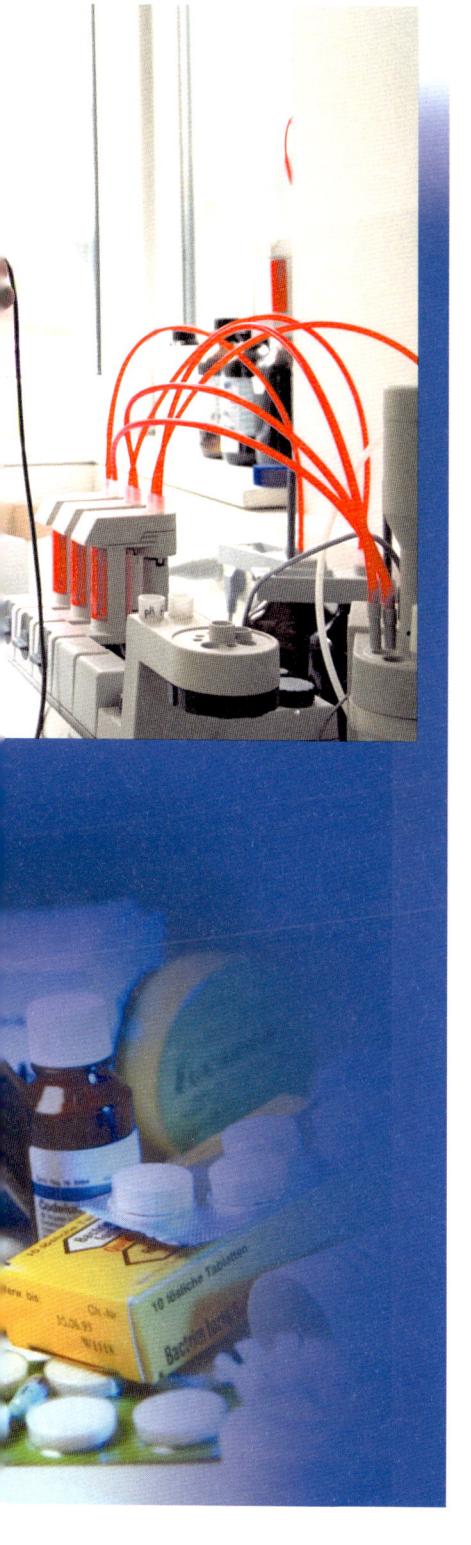

intended to reduce the number of county districts from 21 to 11 until the year 2007. Closely connected with reducing bureaucracy is of course also the reduction of personnel, which is progressing swiftly. A new wage agreement that plans to waive wages for workers and employees while working hours are reduced at the same time as well as cancelling the Christmas bonus for civil servants has additionally lowered personnel costs considerably.

A new form of cross-border cooperation among regional states is the "Initiative for Central Germany", which the state of Saxony-Anhalt has agreed with Saxony and Thuringia in 2002. Under the roof of the initiative, the states intend to work closely together in order to strengthen Central Germany as a business location. Currently important projects are the extension of infrastructure in the economic region Halle/Leipzig and the development of the "Metropolitan Region of Central Germany".

Also on international level Saxony-Anhalt is practising new forms of cooperation in the preliminary stages of the East Enlargement of the European Union. On initiative of the regional government and the local chemical industry, the network of European chemical regions with 13 members so far has been formed. Partners from Poland and The Czech Republic are particularly strong participants.

The chemical business location of Saxony-Anhalt is predestined because of its geographic position to develop collaborations with Central and Eastern European states. The network has continuously increased in dynamism. Key fields of cooperation are the European environment, regional and economic policies.

Such activities underline the strong will of Saxony-Anhalt, to utilize the chances provided by the East Enlargement. We may also expect additional impulses for export trade through this here in Saxony-Anhalt. At present, three of the current accession countries are among the top twenty trade partners of Saxony Anhalt, namely Poland (rank 5), The Czech Rep. (rank 8) and Hungary (rank 15). To Poland alone goods in the value of over 400 million Euros were exported in 2004. The particular importance of our relationship to Poland is stressed by the regional partnership to the Wojewodship Masovia (in the surrounding countryside of Warsaw).

But of course, we are not only looking towards the East now. In February 2004, we closed a cooperation agreement with the French region called Centre.

The regional government shall continue to tread on new paths using creativity and a diversity of ideas to bring about investments and strengthen the business location of Saxony-Anhalt. ■

Company Profile

BIRD & BIRD

BIRD & BIRD

Chairman Deutschland/
Chairman Germany:
Wolfgang von Meibom

Vize Chairman Deutschland/
Vice Chairman Germany:
Dr. Alexander Schröder-Frerkes, LL.M.

Gründungsjahr Deutschland/
Year of Foundation in Germany:
2002 Düsseldorf; 2003 München

Mitarbeiter/Employees:
Deutschland: Anwälte: 65; Insgesamt: 107
International: Anwälte: 450; Insgesamt: 743
Germany: 65 lawyers; in total: 107
Globally: 450 lawyers; in total: 743

Geschäftstätigkeit/Business Activity:
- Gewerblicher Rechtsschutz – Patente und Lizenzen, Marken, Design und Copyright
- Gesellschaftsrecht/Mergers & Acquisitions
- Handelsrecht, Prozessführung und Schiedsgerichtsbarkeit,
- Private Clients
- Arbeitsrecht
- EU- und Wettbewerbsrecht
- Vergaberecht und Privatisierung, Regulierungsrecht
- Sport & Sponsoring
- Medien, Telekommunikation
- Informationstechnologie, E-Commerce
- Life Sciences
- Aviation & Aerospace
- Intellectual Property - Patents and licensing, Trade marks, design and copyright
- Corporate/Mergers & Acquisition
- Commercial contracts & dispute resolution
- Private clients
- Employment
- EU & competition
- Public Procurement & privatisation, regulatory
- Sport & Sponsoring
- Media & Communications
- Information Technology, E-Commerce
- Life Sciences
- Aviation & Aerospace

Anschrift/Address:
BIRD & BIRD Düsseldorf
Karl-Theodor-Straße 6
D-40213 Düsseldorf
Telefon   +49 (211) 20 05 60 00
Telefax   +49 (211) 20 05 60 11
E-Mail   duesseldorf@twobirds.com
Internet www.twobirds.com

Anschrift/Address:
BIRD & BIRD München
Pacellistraße 14
D-80333 München
Telefon   +49 (89) 35 81 60 00
Telefax   +49 (89) 35 81 60 11
E-Mail   muenchen@twobirds.com
Internet www.twobirds.com

Nationale Expertise mit internationaler Erfahrung

National Expertise combined with International Experience

BIRD & BIRD gehört mit über 400 Anwälten zur Spitzengruppe der europäischen Anwaltskanzleien. Die 1846 in London gegründete Anwaltssozietät hat ihre Präsenz in Europa kontinuierlich ausgebaut und verfügt nunmehr über Büros in London, Brüssel, Den Haag, Hong Kong, Mailand, Paris, Peking, Stockholm, Düsseldorf und München. Wir bieten unseren Mandanten nationale Expertise verbunden mit internationaler Erfahrung.

In Deutschland ist BIRD & BIRD in Düsseldorf und München vertreten und verfolgt die Strategie der Fokussierung auf zukunftsorientierte Technologie-Sektoren. BIRD & BIRD ist daher in der Lage mit Marktkenntnis seine Mandanten auf hohem Niveau zu beraten.

In den traditionellen Bereichen Intellectual Property, Corporate/M&A sowie Vergabe- und Regulierungsrecht nimmt BIRD & BIRD eine Spitzenposition in Deutschland ein. Die Sozietät hat sich auf die Sektoren Aviation & Aerospace, Banking & Financial Services, Life Sciences, IT, E-Commerce, Medien, Telekommunikation und Sport & Sponsoring spezialisiert.

Die rund 60 Anwälte, u. a. erfahrene Quereinsteiger aus der Wirtschaft, sind Experten in ihren Fachbereichen und arbeiten im Rahmen von International Sector/Practice Groups eng mit unseren standortübergreifenden Teams in Europa und Asien zusammmen. Hinzu kommen die Erfahrungen einer langjährigen Kooperation mit führenden Kanzleien in weiteren Industrieländern, so vor allem in den USA. Dies garantiert bei nationalen ebenso wie bei grenzüberschreitenden Problemlösungen eine internationale Professionalität auf höchstem Niveau.

Als Anerkennung für unsere erfolgreiche strategische Ausrichtung und unternehmensspezifische Expertise wurde BIRD & BIRD wiederholt von „Global Counsel 3000" zu den „Global 50 Firms" des Jahres 2005 gezählt.

With over 400 lawyers BIRD & BIRD is one of the top groups among European law firms. The lawyer's office was established in 1846 and has expanded its presence continuously throughout Europe. Today it owns offices in London, Brussels, The Hague, Hong Kong, Milan, Paris, Beijing, Stockholm, Düsseldorf and Munich. We offer our clients national expertise linked with international experience.

In Germany, BIRD & BIRD is represented in Düsseldorf and Munich and pursues a strategy of focussing on future-oriented technology sectors. Thus BIRD & BIRD is in a position to provide consulting services with local market expertise to its clients on high quality standard.

In traditional areas like Intellectual Property, Corporate/M&A as well as Public Procurement and Regulatory Law BIRD & BIRD occupies a top ranking position in Germany. The law firm focuses on aviation & aerospace, banking & financial services, life sciences, IT, E-Commerce, media, communications and sport & sponsoring.

About 60 lawyers, including experienced lateral hired specialists from the commercial sector, are experts in their special fields and work in the context of international sector/practice groups closely with local teams across our locations in Europe and Asia. Additionally, there are the experiences of a long-standing collaboration with leading law firms in other industrialised countries, primarily in the USA. This guarantees an international professionalism on the highest level both for domestic and cross-boarder problem solutions.

As recognition for our successful strategic orientation focussing on business-specific expertise BIRD & BIRD has repeatedly been listed among the "Global 50 Firms" of the year 2005 by "Global Counsel 3000".

Company Profile

Folien für die Möbel- und die Türenindustrie weltweit

Coverings for the furniture and door industry worldwide

MFB
Möbelfolien GmbH Biesenthal

Möbelfolien GmbH Biesenthal

Geschäftsführer/Managers:
Johannes la Cour
Telefon: +49 (3337) 48 17
Telefax: +49 (3337) 48 73
E-Mail: Mail@Moebie.de

Christa Lenz
Telefon: +49 (3337) 48 17 und 18
Telefax: +49 (3337) 48 73
Mobil: +49 (172) 901 92 12
E-Mail: Ch.Lenz@Moebie.de

Gesellschafter/Corporate members:
Melaplast Verwaltungs GmbH
in Schweinfurt,
Johannes la Cour,
geschäftsführender Gesellschafter

Mitarbeiter/Employees:
80 Beschäftigte
3 Auszubildende
80 employees
3 trainees

Umsatz/Turnover:
13,0 Mio. Euro/Jahr
13.0 million Euros/year

Geschäftstätigkeit/Business Activity:
Dekordruck, Folien, Kanten und Laminate für die Möbelindustrie, den Objekt- und Innenausbau
Decorative prints, coverings, edges and laminate for the furniture industry, shop-fitting and interior decoration

Anschrift/Address:
Bahnhofstraße 150
D-16359 Biesenthal
Telefon +49 (3337) 48-0
Telefax +49 (3337) 48-34
E-Mail Mail@Moebie.de
Internet www.moebie.de

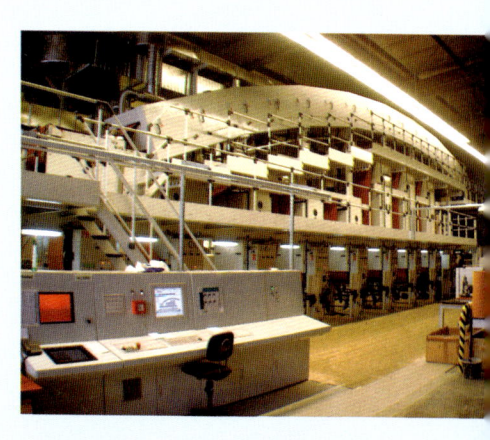

Die Firma Möbelfolien GmbH in Biesenthal ist auf einem historischen Industriegebiet nordöstlich von Berlin angesiedelt.
Holz- und Möbelindustrie waren hier schon immer zu Hause. Seit den 60er-Jahren werden hier Möbelfolien gefertigt. Seitdem ist das Fertigungsprogramm mit den Anforderungen des Marktes stetig gewachsen. Eingebunden in die la Cour–Gruppe – mit den Firmen Melaplast, Melatec, allmilmö und Zeyko – kann heute ein weit gefächertes Fertigungsprogramm Kundenwünsche weltweit erfüllen.
Grundier- und Finishfolien, Kanten, Laminate, Melaminfilme und Phenolharzimprägnierungen können für die Abnehmer in allen Bereichen der Möbelindustrie, des Innenausbaus und des Objektbaus nach deren Vorstellungen und Anforderungen gefertigt werden.
Bei der Firma Möbelfolien stehen Anlagen für alle Fertigungsstufen zur Verfügung, die die gesamte Bandbreite vom Dekordruck bis zum konfektionierten Endprodukt umfassen.
Mit 80 Mitarbeitern werden im Jahr ca. 15 Millionen Quadratmeter Oberflächenveredelung realisiert. ∎

Möbelfolien GmbH in Biesenthal is located in a historic industrial area northeast of Berlin. Biesenthal has always been the home of the woodworking industry and the furniture industry. Since the sixties "furniture foils" are being produced. The production programme has ever since steadily developed in accordance with the needs of the market. Embedded in the la Cour group of companies with Melaplast, Melatec, allmilmö and Zeyko, a wide production range would meet customers' requirements all over the world.
Prime foils and finish foils, edgebandings, laminates, melamine films, and phenolic-resin impregnations can be produced for the customers of all fields of the furniture industry, completion of the interior, as well as for various other kinds of applications matching their ideas and requirements.
For all stages of production we have the necessary equipment to cover the whole range beginning with the printing of decors to the ready-made end product.
Our 80 employees annually manufacture about 15 million square metres of surface refinement. ∎

Wissenschaft und Forschung

Wie schaffen wir Spitzenuniversitäten?

How can we create top quality universities?

Die deutschen Universitäten befinden sich in einer Phase grundlegender Neuorientierung. War das Schlagwort der Reformen der 70er-Jahre das der Demokratisierung, so sind die heutigen Schlüsselbegriffe „Autonomie", „Wettbewerb", „Exzellenz" und „Effizienz". Dem liegt die häufig anzutreffende Feststellung zugrunde, das deutsche Hochschulwesen sei in keiner guten Verfassung. Präziser stellte der Wissenschaftsrat vor kurzem fest, dass das volle Potenzial des Wissenschaftssystems in Deutschland trotz seiner führenden Stellung in der Welt energische Reformen und weit über das jetzige Maß hinausgehende finanzielle Anstrengungen erfordere.

Bei aller Neugestaltung an den Universitäten kann es nützlich sein, sich auf die Grundlagen von Bildung zu besinnen. So gilt auch heute noch das Wort Humboldts und Schleiermachers, wonach Wissenschaft als Bildung zur Individualität verstanden und umgekehrt Bildung durch Wissenschaft angestrebt wird. „Nur die Wissenschaft", so heißt es bei Wilhelm von Humboldt, „die aus dem Innern stammt und ins Innere gepflanzt werden kann, bildet auch den Charakter um, und dem Staat ist es ebenso wenig als der Menschheit um Wissen und Reden, sondern um Charakter und Handeln zu tun." Und genau dies, „die höchste und proportionierlichste Bildung seiner Kräfte zu einem Ganzen", nennt er an anderer Stelle den wahren Zweck des Menschen.

Die Rolle des Studierenden wird in diesem Prozess nicht als die eines passiven Rezipienten verstanden. Ihm wird eine aktive Rolle gerade angesichts des dynamischen Charakters der Universitäten zugeschrieben, welche „die Wissenschaft immer als ein noch nicht ganz aufgelöstes Problem behandeln und daher im Forschen bleiben." Der Schüler kommt, so betont auch Karl Jaspers in seiner Schrift „Die Idee der Universität", zu einer sein Leben bestimmenden wissenschaftlichen Bildung dadurch, dass er an der Forschung teilnimmt. „Die

Prof. Dr. Rudolf Steinberg

Der Autor, geboren 1943 in Cochem/Mosel, verheiratet, studierte Rechts- und Wirtschaftswissenschaften in Freiburg i. Br. und Köln. Nach der Ersten Juristischen Staatsprüfung Studium der Politikwissenschaft an der University of Michigan, Ann Arbor, Mich. (USA). 1970 Promotion, 1977 Habilitation. 1977–1980 Professur für Öffentliches Recht an der Fakultät für Rechtswissenschaften der Universität Hannover. Seit 1980 Professur für Öffentliches Recht, Umweltrecht und Verwaltungswissenschaften in Frankfurt/M. Visiting Professor an der University of Michigan Law School, Ann Arbor, Mich. und der Yale Law School, New Haven, Ct. (USA). 1995–2000 Richter des Thüringer Verfassungsgerichtshofs in Weimar. Seit 2000 ist Rudolf Steinberg Präsident der J. W. Goethe-Universität Frankfurt/Main.

The author was born 1943 in Cochem/Mosel; he is married and studied law and economics in Freiburg i. Br. and in Cologne. After passing his first state examination in law he began studying politics at the University of Michigan, Ann Arbor, Mich. (USA). He achieved his doctoral degree in 1970 and his post-doctoral degree as university lecturer in 1977. From 1977–1980 he held the chair of Public Law at the faculty of law of the University of Hanover. Since 1980 he has held a chair of Public Law, Environment Law and Administration Science in Frankfurt/M. Visiting professor at the University of Michigan Law School, Ann Arbor, Mich. and at Yale Law School, New Haven, Ct. (USA). From 1995–2000 he served as judge at the Thuringian Constitutional Court in Weimar. Since 2000, Rudolf Steinberg has been president of J. W. Goethe University of Frankfurt/Main.

Science and Research

German universities are currently undergoing a phase of basic new orientation. If in the seventies the key word of reforms used to be democratisation, today's key terminology includes words like "autonomy", "competition", "excellence" and "efficiency". This is founded on the frequently existing opinion that the German university system is in no good condition at present. More precisely, the Science Council found shortly that the full potential of Germany's science system requires dramatic reforms despite its leading role globally and furthermore financial efforts, which must go far beyond present limits.

In spite of all the reorganisation at universities, it can surely be of benefit to remember the basic principles of education. For instance the words of Humboldt and Schleiermacher are still valid today, which say that science must be understood as an education towards individuality and in turn the aim is to achieve education through science. "Only that type of science", as Wilhelm von Humboldt says, "which comes from inside and can be transferred into the inside is able to transform the character, and the state is less interested in knowledge and talk than in character and deeds, as is also humanity." And precisely this, "the highest and most appropriate development of his powers into one integral whole", he quotes elsewhere as being the true purpose of man.

In this process, the role of the student is not seen as one of a passive recipient. He is ascribed an active role especially in view of the dynamic character of universities, which "still treat science as a not completely resolved problem and therefore remain within the sector of research". The student achieves, as also Karl Jaspers emphasizes in his paper "The Idea of University", a scientific education that determines his whole life by participating in research actively. "Students, according to the idea, are independent, self-responsible thinkers that follow their teachers critically." And this is where primarily – not, as it often seems, in the ran-domness of lecture visits – lies the freedom of teaching!

Whereas there is excellent support in most natural science subjects, in the small humanities and cultural science subjects, this cannot be said generally about the large faculties, which are driven by ZVS, curricular norms and other bureaucratic ties right up to and above beneficial limits. An encounter with the academic tutor becomes impossible for many. "To provide Humboldt's principles for the universities of the masses is no longer possible", rightly complains the philosopher Jürgen Mittelstraß of Constance. Radical reforms are needed here, which give the university complete autonomy when selecting its students.

Links: Campus der Johann Wolfgang Goethe-Universität Frankfurt am Main. An der Spitze dringender Veränderungen steht eine vollständige Neugestaltung der Auswahl und Zulassung von Studierenden.

Left: Campus site of Johann Wolfgang Goethe University Frankfurt on the Main. Top on the list of urgent changes is a complete reorganisation of students' selection and admission schemes.

Of what nature must these reforms be in detail?

Top on the list of such urgently needed changes is a complete reorganisation of the selection and admission of students. However, it is going to demand extreme efforts on the part of the universities to be able to meet the new task of determining their own selection criteria, the organisation and outline of selection procedures. It could be practical to create a central or also a regional clearing office for this purpose.

The reorganisation would gain characteristic significance if differences were recognised and accepted: different profiles of educational offers that would correspond with different performance and suitability profiles of applying students. Of course, also the universities should not be able to "close doors" arbitrarily. But their autonomy of decision and selection will be limited through new forms of control systems like performance-oriented budgeting systems and target agreements.

New procedures for selection and admission must be accompanied by better information services for applying students about prevailing requirements within the respective courses. Therefore, consulting services for students must begin before studies are taken up so that an optimal "matching" of study and applicant profile can be achieved.

At this point it may already be noted that universities must be allowed to charge general study fees; that is study fees, the amount of which they themselves are able to stipulate, which is possibly varying to that of other universities and differentiated according to study subjects. All experiences have shown that the seriousness and motivation of students is growing. Loyalty to one's own university is thus increased. It is no coincidence that the universities with the highest study fees produce the most faithful alumni in the USA. There should be a number of alternatives to apply for grants open to applicants.

Top level research

As important as good training may be – the scientific ranking of a university is determined by the excellence of its researchers and the research they conduct. In order to achieve top performances in this field, one must remember the special competencies of a university. This makes it indispensable to pursue as much as possible an interdisciplinary concentration of focal points and profiles, collaboration with extra-university research institutions and other science-based institutions, like the research departments of companies for instance.

Wissenschaft und Forschung

Schüler sind der Idee nach selbständige, selbstverantwortliche, ihren Lehrern kritisch folgende Denker." Und vor allem darin – nicht, wie es oftmals scheint, in der Beliebigkeit des Vorlesungsbesuchs – liegt die Freiheit der Lehre!

Während in den meisten naturwissenschaftlichen und den kleinen geistes- und kulturwissenschaftlichen Fächern eine hervorragende Betreuung stattfindet, kann davon in den großen Fachbereichen, die bis an und über den Rand des Zuträglichen durch ZVS, Curricularnormwerte und andere bürokratische Fesseln getrieben werden, generell keine Rede sein. Die Begegnung mit dem akademischen Lehrer wird für viele unmöglich. „Humboldt für die Massenuniversitäten geht nicht mehr" beklagt der Konstanzer Philosoph Jürgen Mittelstraß zu Recht. Hier bedarf es radikaler Reformen, die der Universität Autonomie bei der Auswahl ihrer Studierenden geben.

Wie müssen diese Reformen im Einzelnen aussehen?

An der Spitze dringender Veränderungen steht eine vollständige Neugestaltung der Auswahl und Zulassung von Studierenden. Allerdings wird es von den Hochschulen außerordentliche Anstrengungen erfordern, den neuen Aufgaben einer eigenen Festlegung von Zulassungsvoraussetzungen, der Gestaltung und Organisation von Auswahlverfahren gerecht werden zu können. Hierbei könnte sich die Einrichtung einer zentralen oder aber auch regionaler Clearing-Stelle(n) als hilfreich erweisen.
Prägendes Merkmal einer Umgestaltung wird die Anerkennung und Hinnahme von Differenzen sein: unterschiedliche Profile von Studienangeboten, die mit unterschiedlichen Leistungs- und Eignungsprofilen der Studienbewerber korrespondieren. Natürlich können auch hier die Hochschulen nicht willkürlich „dicht" machen, aber ihre Entscheidungs- und Auswahlautonomie wird durch neue Formen der Steuerung wie leistungsorientierte Budgetierungsysteme und Zielvereinbarungen erweitert.

Neue Verfahren der Auswahl und Zulassung müssen flankiert werden durch bessere Informationen der Studienbewerber über die Anforderungen in den jeweiligen Studiengängen. Studienberatung muss deshalb schon vor dem Studium beginnen, um zu einem optimalen „matching" von Studien- und Bewerberprofil zu gelangen.

Auch an dieser Stelle ist schon darauf hinzuweisen, dass den Universitäten die Erhebung allgemeiner Studiengebühren möglich sein muss; und zwar von Studiengebühren, deren Höhe sie selber und d. h. möglicherweise anders als andere Hochschulen und differenziert nach Fächern festsetzen können. Alle Erfahrungen zeigen, dass die Ernsthaftigkeit und die Motivation der Studierenden steigt. Die Bindung an die eigene Universität wird erhöht. Nicht zufällig bringen in den USA die Universitäten mit den höchsten Studiengebühren die treuesten Alumni hervor. Eine Vielzahl von Stipendienmöglichkeiten sollte den Bewerbern offen stehen.

Spitzenforschung

So wichtig eine gute Lehre auch ist – der wissenschaftliche Rang einer Hochschule wird durch die Exzellenz ihrer Forscher und deren Forschungen bestimmt. Um hier Spitzenleistungen erbringen zu können, bedarf es der Besinnung auf die besonderen Kompetenzen einer Hochschule. Dies macht eine möglichst interdisziplinäre Schwerpunkt- und Profilbildung und die Kooperation mit außeruniversitären Forschungseinrichtungen und anderen wissensbasierten Institutionen – wie den Forschungsabteilungen von Unternehmen – unabdingbar. In ihrem Hochschulentwicklungsplan 2001 hat die Universität Frankfurt derzeit 15 universitäre Forschungsschwerpunkte ausgewiesen. Diese finden sich in allen Bereichen der Forschung von den Geisteswissenschaften über den Bereich Finance bis zu einem breiten Feld von naturwissenschaftlichen und medizinischen Themen.

Science and Research

In ihrem Hochschulentwicklungsplan hat die Universität Frankfurt derzeit 15 universitäre Forschungsschwerpunkte ausgewiesen.

Frankfurt University has presently 15 focal university research projects in its university development plan.

Wissenschaft und Forschung

Bei der Fokussierung auf Spitzenleistungen in der Forschung an der Universität Frankfurt haben die Grundlagenwissenschaften in den Geistes- wie den Naturwissenschaften eine maßgebliche Bedeutung. Das schließt natürlich eine Selbstbesinnung auf die Aufgaben der Grundlagenforschung nicht aus, wie es etwa Mittelstraß gerade auch für die Geisteswissenschaften gefordert hat. Diese könnten ihre Aufgabe der Reflexion der kulturellen Form der Welt nur bewältigen, „indem sie selbst, in ihrer Wahrnehmung der Welt und in ihren Arbeitsformen, den eingeschlagenen Weg der Partikularisierung geisteswissenschaftlicher Orientierung wieder verlassen und eine transdisziplinäre Optik einnehmen." Ihre Stärke an der Frankfurter Universität lässt schon ein Blick auf das Forschungsranking der Deutschen Forschungsgemeinschaft erkennen, wonach die Geisteswissenschaften in Frankfurt auf Platz 2 aller deutschen Hochschulen stehen.

Forschungsschwerpunkte, deren Stärke durch DFG-Sonderforschungsbereiche oder andere Drittmittelforschungsprojekte, durch ein hohes Maß an Kooperation mit außeruniversitären Forschungseinrichtungen und erfolgreiche Arbeit in der Qualifizierung des wissenschaftlichen Nachwuchses erkennbar ist, stellen sich als wissenschaftliche Exzellenznetzwerke dar. In der beträchtlichen Zahl solcher Exzellenznetzwerke im Bereich von geisteswissenschaftlicher Grundlagenforschung, insbesondere in den Geschichtswissenschaften, im Bereich Law, Money and Finance, in der Afrikaforschung, der Materialforschung, der Membrane-Forschung, der Schwerionenforschung, der vasculären Medizin, der Onkologie und der Arzneimittelforschung, erweist sich nicht nur die Forschungsstärke der Frankfurter Universität, sondern auch der Wissensregion Frankfurt-Rhein/Main.

Der Hinweis auf die Graduiertenkollegs, drei International Graduate Schools zusammen mit der Max Planck-Gesellschaft, die neuen internationalen Promotionsprogramme „Gesellschaftswissenschaften" und „Religion im Dialog" und jetzt die Frankfurt International Graduate School for Science beleuchtet die Funktion, bei der die Universitäten ein Monopol besitzen: die Qualifizierung des wissenschaftlichen Nachwuchses. Wie erfolgreich hier die deutschen Universitäten insgesamt, aber auch die Frankfurter Universität mit „ihren" Nobelpreisträgern Selten (Wirtschaftswissenschaften), Blobel (Medizin), Binnig und Störmer (beide Physik) sind, zeigt ihre Beliebtheit vor allem an den amerikanischen Universitäten und Forschungseinrichtungen. Allein 80 Absolventen der Frankfurter Physik bekleiden weltweit 80 Lehrstühle.

Science and Research

The University of Frankfurt outlined in its university development plan 2001 a number of 15 special university research projects at present. These can be found in all areas of research ranging from humanities across finance through to a broad field of natural science and medical subjects.

Bei der Fokussierung auf Spitzenleistungen in der Forschung an der Universität Frankfurt haben die Grundlagenwissenschaften in den Geistes- wie den Naturwissenschaften eine maßgebliche Bedeutung.

Den Universitäten sollte die Erhebung allgemeiner Studiengebühren möglich sein, deren Höhe sie selber differenziert nach Fächern festsetzen können.

When focussing on top performances in research at the University of Frankfurt, the basic sciences in humanities and natural science are of major importance.

Universities should be allowed to charge general study fees, the amount of which they can determine themselves differentiated according to subjects.

When focussing on top performance in research at Frankfurt University, the basic sciences of humanities and natural science are of major importance. This of course does not exclude a reflection on the tasks of pure research as for instance Mittelstraß also demanded for humanities. These would only be able to deal with their task of reflection of the cultural form of the world "by leaving themselves the path of particularisation embarked on, in terms of their perception of the world and in their working methods, for orientation of humanities subjects towards an interdisciplinary perspective." Their strength at Frankfurt University is revealed by a glance on research rankings of the German Research Society, which ranks Frankfurt's humanities faculty on second place of all German universities.

Focal points of research, the strength of which is perceivable in the special research fields of the German Research Society or other third party projects, in the great amount of cooperation projects with extra-university research institutions and in the successful work of qualifying upcoming scientific young professionals, demonstrate the excellence of scientific networks available. Frankfurt University's strength in research and that of the science region of Frankfurt-Rhein/Main are shown in the considerable number of such networks of excellence in the field of pure research in humanities, particularly in the sciences of history, law, money and finance, Africa research, materials research, membrane research, heavy ion research, vascular medicine, oncology and pharmacological research.

Pointing out the graduate colleges, three International Graduate Schools together with the Max Planck Society, the new international PhD programmes "Social Sciences" and "Religion in Dialogue" and now the Frankfurt International Graduate School for Science, throws light on the university's function as a monopolist: its task of qualifying new scientific professionals. Just how successful German universities are on the whole in this respect, but especially Frankfurt University with "its" Nobel prize winners Selten (economics), Blobel (medicine), Binnig and Störmer (both physics), shows in their popularity above all at American universities and research institutions. 80 graduates of Frankfurt's physics faculty alone occupy worldwide 80 university chairs.

Wissenschaft und Forschung

Deregulierung

Die dargestellten Aufgaben bedürfen eines hohen Maßes an Innovations- und Entscheidungsfähigkeit in den Hochschulen. Einen Schritt hierzu stellt eine bürokratische Enthegung aus der Obhut der Ministerialverwaltung dar in Richtung von Autonomie, Globalbudget, leistungsorientierte Mittelzuweisung, Umbau der Gruppenuniversität durch eine Präsidialuniversität, Einführung der kaufmännischen Buchführung, Zielvereinbarungen zwischen Land und Hochschule, aber auch in der Hochschule, Qualitätsmanagement, Evaluation von Lehre und Forschung.

In wichtigen Bereichen bedarf es noch einer Vielzahl von Entscheidungen, um zu einer „Entstaatlichung" zu kommen: beispielsweise bei der Berufung von Professoren, bei dem rigiden und für den Wissenschaftsbereich unpassenden Bundesangestelltentarifvertrag oder beim Bau und der Bauunterhaltung. Einen Durchbruch könnte das von der hessischen Landesregierung geplante Modellgesetz für die Technische Universität Darmstadt bedeuten. Danach zieht sich das Wissenschaftsministerium nahezu vollständig aus den konkreten Entscheidungen der Universität zurück. Wünschenswert wäre es, noch einen Schritt weiter zu gehen und den Hochschulen die Möglichkeit einzuräumen, sich als Stiftungen bürgerlichen Rechts zu organisieren.

Finanzausstattung – Public Private Partnership

Das Ziel, die Wettbewerbsfähigkeit der deutschen Hochschulen in Forschung und Lehre international zu verbessern, ist ohne zusätzliche finanzielle Anstrengungen nicht erreichbar. Denn schon seit langem sind sie – so der Wissenschaftsrat – chronisch unterfinanziert. Wenn sie heute wieder den Anteil am Bruttosozialprodukt des Jahres 1980 erhielten, könnten sie über 6,5 Milliarden Euro mehr verfügen.

Das Land Hessen hat große Anstrengungen unternommen, trotz einer äußerst schwierigen Haushaltssituation die Finanzausstattung der Hochschulen zu erhalten. Beispielhaft für ganz Deutschland hat der Vorsitzende des Wissenschaftsrates, Professor Karl Max Einhäupl, die Pläne des Landes Hessen genannt, weitere 600 Millionen Euro in Neubauten der Universität zu investieren, die damit – so der hessische Finanzminister Weimar – die „modernste Universität Europas" werden soll.

Erkennbar ist aber auch die zunehmende Bereitschaft von Wirtschaft und Gesellschaft, sich für die Universitäten zu engagieren. Voraussetzung hierfür ist allerdings eine Öffnung der Universitäten für die Probleme der Gesellschaft und die Bereitschaft zum Wissensaustausch, von dem – auch in den anwendungsoffenen Grundlagenfächern – beide, also auch die Universitätsforschung, profitieren.

Das reformierte Hochschulrecht erlaubt den Hochschulen aber auch neue Formen der Kooperation mit Privaten im Sinne einer Public Private Partnership. In der Regel werden derartige PPPs der Forschung und der Lehre gleichermaßen zugute kommen. Die Frankfurter Universität hat auf diese Weise hervorragende Projekte realisieren können, wie das House of Finance, mit dem sich die Universität auf dem Kontinent als führende Stätte interdisziplinärer finanzwissenschaftlicher Forschung etabliert, oder das Frankfurt Institute for Advanced Studies (FIAS) als Ort interdisziplinärer Forschung im Bereich der theoretischen Naturwissenschaften.

Diese Projekte vernetzen universitäre und außeruniversitäre Forschung, erleichtern den Informationsaustausch zwischen Wissenschaft und Praxis und bringen zusätzliche Finanzmittel in die Universität, deren Wirkung durch die Verstärkung der staatlichen Grundfinanzierung in exzellenten Bereichen besonders hoch ist. Durch diese Vernetzungen werden Spitzenleistungen in der Forschung und Elitebildung in der Lehre mit relativ bescheidenem Einsatz entscheidend gefördert. Vor allem aber bleiben diese Leistungen im Verbund einer Universität, der immer noch das Ganze der wissenschaftlichen Erkenntnis aufgegeben ist. Spitzenleistungen werden auf diese Weise – und nur so – in Zukunft an Universitäten in Deutschland möglich sein. ■

Science and Research

Deregulation

The tasks described require a high degree of capacity to introduce innovations and new decisions at universities. One step in this direction might be to remove bureaucratic limitations from the administrative ministry with respect to autonomy, global budget, performance-oriented fund allocation, reorganisation of the group university substituted by a presidential university, introduction of commercial bookkeeping, target agreements between the state government and the universities as well as within the universities, quality management, assessment of teaching and research at univer-sities.

Several important areas still require a number of decisive rules in order to arrive at a stage of "denationalisation": for instance the appointment of lecturers, the its rigid and for the field of science inappropriate statutory salary scale or the construction and maintenance of buildings. The model law planned by the Hessian state government could signify a breakthrough for the Technical University of Darmstadt. According to this, the science ministry will almost completely withdraw from concrete decisions made by the university. It would be desirable however, to go one step further and to concede universities the opportunity to organise as incorporated foundations.

Financial funds – public-private partnership

The aim to increase competitiveness of German universities in research and teaching at an international level cannot be achieved without additional financial efforts. Because, according to the Science Council they have been chronically underfinanced for a long time. If they today received the same share of the gross national product as in the year 1980, they would dispose of additional 6.5 billion Euros.

The State of Hesse has made tremendous efforts to keep up financial funds of universities despite a precariously difficult budgetary situation. The chairman of the Science Council, Professor Karl Max Einhäupl, has described the plans of the State of Hesse as exemplary for the whole of Germany, to invest of further 600 million Euros in new buildings for the university, which is designed to become "Europe's most modern university", according to Hesse's Finance Minister Weimar.

But also a growing preparedness on the part of industry and society can be recognised to engage themselves for universities. For this however, the prerequisite is an opening on the part of universities towards the problems of society and the preparedness to engage in scientific exchange, from which both, that is also university research, would benefit in the application-oriented pure research subjects, too.

The reformed university law allows universities also to try new forms of cooperation in public-private partnership schemes. In general, such PPPs are of benefit both to research and teaching equally. Frankfurt University has been able to realize outstanding projects in this way, like the House of Finance for instance, which has established the university as leading place for interdisciplinary financial science research on the continent, or the Frankfurt Institute for Advanced Studies (FIAS) as a place of interdisciplinary research in the field of theoretical natural science.

These projects link up university and extra-university research, facilitate an exchange of information between science and practical work and bring additional financial funds into the university, which have an especially high effect in the fields of excellence because of increased basic state finance. These networks decisively enhance top performance in research and the formation of elites in teaching with relatively moderate means. But above all this performance is rendered within the precinct of a university, which still remains the holder of the entire spectrum of scientific findings. This is the only way indeed in which top performance will be achievable at universities in Germany in future.

Company Profile

Partner für Information und Wissen – Technische Dokumention aus einer Hand

Partner for information and knowledge – Technical Documentation from a one-stop service

Die reinisch AG, Karlsruhe, erstellt und verarbeitet Technische Dokumentationen und bietet Lösungen für das Informationsmanagement. Dazu beraten die Mitarbeiter von reinisch die Kunden und entwickeln und betreiben Prozess- und Systemlösungen. Information und Wissen lassen sich so wirtschaftlich dokumentieren, verwalten und publizieren. Ca. 400 Mitarbeiter sind in zehn Geschäftsstellen im ganzen Bundesgebiet und an Standorten in Spanien, Österreich, in der Schweiz und der Türkei für das Unternehmen tätig.

Breite Leistungspalette
reinisch hat sich auf die Branchen Automotive und Transport, Maschinen- und Anlagenbau fokussiert. Zu den Kunden von reinisch gehören vor allem Unternehmen, die komplexe Produkte für den globalen Markt herstellen. Für sie sind Produktdokumentationen wie Betriebsanleitungen, Kataloge oder Serviceanleitungen und damit verbunden das gesamte Informationsmanagement von entscheidender Bedeutung für den Erfolg eines Produkts.

Mit der zunehmenden Zahl von Medien und insbesondere durch die Integration in unternehmensinterne Prozesse (z. B. in Systeme für ERP/Enterprise-Resource-Planning oder PDM/Produkt-Daten-Management) sind standardisierte Gesamtlösungen gefragt. reinisch bietet hierfür ein umfassendes Leistungsspektrum: Dieses reicht in der klassischen Dokumentationsdienstleistung von der redaktionellen und grafischen Erstellung über die Prozessgestaltung bis hin zur Publikation als Print- oder elektronisches Medium. Darauf aufbauend stellt reinisch Systemlösungen in den Bereichen Dokumenten- und Content-Management, Wissens-Management und Übersetzungs-Management bereit.

Enge Zusammenarbeit
Einer der wichtigsten Erfolgsfaktoren von reinisch ist die konsequente Kundenorientierung. Flache Hierarchien, definierte Ansprechpartner und schneller Zugriff auf Wissen innerhalb des Unternehmens stellen sicher, dass Projekte zuverlässig, kompetent und termingerecht abgeschlossen werden können. Der Kunde steht bei reinisch im Mittelpunkt. Dies wird unter anderem auch dadurch deutlich, dass die Standorte dort sind, wo die Kunden sitzen: in zehn Städten in Deutschland sowie in Spanien, Österreich, der Schweiz und der Türkei.

Um immer das beste Ergebnis zu erzielen, ist reinisch Partnerschaften mit mehreren Unternehmen eingegangen. So kann das Unternehmen als produktunabhängiger Berater evaluieren und sämtliche Standardtools nutzen, die auf dem Markt erhältlich sind. Dabei beherrscht es auch die Tools, die die Kunden schon einsetzen oder noch nutzen möchten.

Dynamische Entwicklung
In vielen Branchen steigt der Bedarf an Technischen Dokumentationen enorm. Das Erstellen von Betriebs- und Bedienungsanleitungen sowie deren Übersetzung in alle Sprachen wird immer mehr Spezialisten wie reinisch überlassen. Außerdem wächst die Nachfrage nach Feedback-Management, damit Reklamationen direkt in die Entwicklung neuer Produkte einfließen.

So stieg der Umsatz des Unternehmens in jüngster Zeit um jährlich 30 Prozent, im Jahr 2004 übertraf er 27 Millionen Euro. ∎

Referenzen/Reference companies
(Auszug/extract)
Buderus
Cooper Power Tools
DaimlerChrysler
Dr. Ing. h.c. F. Porsche
Fuchs-Terex
Glatt Process Technology
Heidelberger Druckmaschinen
IST Instron Structural Testing Systems
Lufthansa
Robert Bosch
Roche Diagnostics
Schlafhorst
Siemens
Springer Verlag
ThyssenKrupp

Company Profile

reinisch

The reinisch AG, Karlsruhe, compiles and processes technical documentation and provides solutions for information management. Staff at reinisch offers consulting, develops and operates process and systems solutions for clients. Thus, information and knowledge can be documented, administered and published economically. Approximately 400 employees work for the group in ten branches nationwide and in locations in Spain, Austria, Switzerland and Turkey.

Broad range of services

reinisch focuses on the branches automotive and transport as well as machine and plant construction. Clients of reinisch include above all companies that produce complex products for the global market. For these, product documentation like operating manuals, catalogues or service instructions are of major importance to ensure a product's success.

With an increasing number of available media and particularly because of their integration into in-house processes (e. g. into systems for ERP/Enterprise-Resource-Planning or PDM/Product-Data-Management) general standardised solutions are popular. reinisch offers a comprehensive service spectrum in this field: it extends within classical documentation services from editorial and graphic compilation across process design through to publication as print or electronic medium. Additionally, reinisch provides systems solutions in the fields of document and content management, knowledge-based management and translation management.

Close cooperation

One of the most important factors for the success of reinisch is its consistent customer orientation. Lean management structures, precisely defined contact partners and fast access to the knowledge available within the company guarantee that projects are completed in a reliable and competent way as well as on schedule. At reinisch, the client is always the main focus. Among other things, this is clearly evident through the fact that our offices are located where the clients are: in ten German cities, as well as in Spain, Austria, Switzerland and Turkey.

To achieve always the best possible result, reinisch has entered partnerships with several companies. Thus, the firm is able to conduct assessment as product-independent consultant and utilize all standard tools that are available on the market. At the same time it also commands the tools that the clients are already using or still intend to apply.

Dynamic development

Many branches are experiencing an enormous increase in demand of technical documentation. The compiling of operating instructions and service manuals as well as their translation into all languages is increasingly left to specialists like reinisch. Moreover, the demand for feedback management is growing and therefore reclamations can be integrated directly into the development of new products.

As a result, the company's turnover sales grew recently by an annual 30 per cent, in the year 2004 it exceeded 27 million Euros. ■

---

reinisch AG

Vorstand/Executive Board:
Franz Reinisch,
Vorstandsvorsitzender/CEO
Anke Wipf,
Vorstand Finanzen/CFO

Gründungsjahr/Year of Foundation: 1991

Mitarbeiter/Employees: 400

Umsatz/Turnover: 27,4 Mio €/27.4 m € (2004)

Geschäftstätigkeit/Business Activity:
- Analyse & Konzeption
- Technische Dokumentation
- Übersetzungsmanagement
- Systemintegration
- Feedback Management
- Analysis & Design
- Technical Documentation
- Translation Management
- System Integration
- Feedback Management

Geschäftsstellen/Branch Offices:
Hamburg, Berlin, Mönchengladbach, Frankfurt, Erlangen, Wörth, Karlsruhe, Freiburg, Stuttgart, München, Österreich, Schweiz, Spanien, Türkei
Hamburg, Berlin, Mönchengladbach, Frankfurt, Erlangen, Wörth, Karlsruhe, Freiburg, Stuttgart, Munich, Austria, Switzerland, Spain, Turkey.

Anschrift/Address:
Emmy-Noether-Straße 9
D-76131 Karlsruhe
Telefon   +49 (721) 66 377-0
Telefax   +49 (721) 66 377-119
E-Mail   info@reinisch.de
Internet www.reinisch.de

Wissenschaft

Die Reform des Bildungs- und Wissenschaftssystems

The reform of the education and science system

Die letzten Jahre haben eines immer deutlicher gemacht: Deutschland braucht richtungsweisende Zukunftskonzepte, weil die Innovationsfähigkeit der Gesellschaft unter den Bedingungen des globalen Wettbewerbs über das Maß an Freiheit, Wohlergehen und Wohlstand der Bürger entscheidet. Um den Anschluss im internationalen Wettbewerb zu halten, der wesentlich von den USA bestimmt wird, muss Deutschland seine Stellung als Innovations- und Wissenschaftsstandort ausbauen und im Zusammenspiel mit den europäischen Partnern eine entsprechende Reformpolitik durchsetzen. Ganz eindeutig kommt der Stärkung des Wissenschaftssystems eine Schlüsselrolle in einer solchen Offensive zu.
Bisher nehmen Bund und Länder im Rahmen der so genannten Gemeinschaftsaufgaben die Wissenschaftsförderung gemeinsam wahr – im Hochschulbau, bei der Deutschen Forschungsgemeinschaft wie auch bei den außeruniversitären Forschungseinrichtungen. Dabei sollte es im Prinzip – allen Erwägungen der letzten Jahre zum Trotz – auch bleiben.

Eine zentrale Aufgabe wird es künftig sein, eine deutschlandweite Perspektive für die Innovations- und Exzellenzförderung zu schaffen. Das setzt voraus, die Situation der Universitäten zu verbessern, damit einzelne von ihnen sich zu international sichtbaren Spitzenuniversitäten entwickeln können, die nicht nur standardbildend für das gesamte deutsche Wissenschaftssystem wirken, sondern auch attraktiv für ausländische Wissenschaftler sind. Gleichzeitig muss unser Ziel dabei aber auch sein, das hohe Qualitätsniveau der deutschen Universitäten in ihrer Gesamtheit nicht nur zu erhalten, sondern so weit möglich auch dieses noch zu steigern. Es ist eine wesentliche Voraussetzung sowohl für die breite Sicherung exzellenter Ausbildung als auch für die Sicherung eines Bewerberfelds um Spitzenplätze. Dafür benötigen die Hochschulen ohne Zweifel zusätzliche Mittel, die durch die Exzellenzinitiative in Höhe von 1,9 Milliarden Euro zur Verfügung stehen. Darüber hinaus müssen die Hochschulen aber auch autonom ihre Strukturen und Inhalte selbst bestimmen können. Im Sinne der angestrebten Leistungssteigerung muss die Zusammenarbeit zwischen Hochschulen und außeruniversitären wie auch industriellen Forschungseinrichtungen intensiviert werden.

Ein für unsere wirtschaftliche und gesellschaftliche Zukunft ebenso wichtiges Thema ist die Gestaltung des Bildungs- und Ausbildungssystems. Es war bisher erfolgreich und hat es vermocht, auf allen Ebenen gute und exzellente Fachleute hervorzubringen. Es ist jedoch nicht zu übersehen, dass dieses System in weiten Teilen diesem Anspruch nicht mehr gerecht wird. Dafür sind verschiedene Ursachen auszumachen, wie es die Pisa-Studie für den Bereich der schulischen Bildung getan hat oder wie es die aktuelle – und schon zu lange währende – Diskussion um Rolle und Qualität der Hochschulen zeigt. Dabei wird immer klarer, dass es nicht ausreicht, die einzelnen Sektoren des Bildungswesens – allgemeinbildende Schulen, berufliche Ausbildung und Hochschulwesen – getrennt voneinander zu analysieren und kurieren zu wollen. Was fehlt, ist ein Gesamtkonzept von Bildung, Wissensvermittlung und Wissensgenerierung, das auf der einen Seite geeignet ist, wieder einem größeren Teil der Jugendlichen einen Start in einen qualifzierten und zukunftsfähigen Beruf, älteren Menschen einen durch Fortbildung gesicherten Verbleib in sich schnell entwickelnden Berufsfeldern zu ermöglichen und das auf der anderen Seite geeignet ist, besonders begabten Menschen ihnen gemäße Wege – d. h. auch manchmal durchaus unkonventionelle Wege – zu öffnen, die ihnen die volle Entfaltung ihrer Begabungen ermöglichen. Gerade in einem solchen, die Begabungen aufnehmenden und fördernden System treffen sich die Interessen des Einzelnen mit denen einer auf Bildung und Wissen angwiesenen Gesellschaft. Der Wirtschaftsstandort Deutschland wird auch nur dann für in- und ausländische Investoren attraktiv bleiben, wenn es hier ein Potenzial an gut und breit ausgebildeten Mitarbeitern und Führungskräften gibt, die geeignet sind, strategische Unternehmensziele zu gestalten und umzusetzen. Zur Standortsicherung gehört dabei ebenso die Ausbildung und Förderung herausragender Wissenschaftler und wissenschaftlicher Einrichtungen.

Ein Problem, das deutlich macht, dass auf allen Ebenen des Bildungssystems Reformen notwendig sind, und das uns in wenigen Jahren massiv beschäftigen wird, ist der Mangel an naturwissenschaftlichem und ingenieurwissenschaftlichem Nachwuchs in Industrie und Wissenschaft. Das fängt an bei der wach-

Prof. Dr. Karl Max Einhäupl

Der Autor, 1947 in München geboren, studierte Medizin an der Ludwig-Maximilians-Universität München und am College of Medicine der Ohio State University. Promotion 1975. Von 1977 bis 1992 wissenschaftliche und klinische Tätigkeit an der Neurologischen Klinik der LMU München, Klinikum Großhadern. Seit 1988 eine C3-Professur mit dem Schwerpunkt Neurologische Intensivmedizin. Seit 1993 Lehrstuhlinhaber an der Medizinischen Fakultät der Humboldt-Universität Berlin und Direktor der Neurologischen Klinik der Charité. 1997 Kooptation in den Wissenschaftsrat, dessen Vorsitzender Einhäupl seit 2001 ist.
Der Wissenschaftsrat berät die Bundesregierung und die Regierungen der Länder in allen Fragen der Wissenschaftspolitik.

The author was born in Munich in 1947 and studied medicine at Ludwig-Maximilians University of Munich and at the College of Medicine of Ohio State University. He graduated as a medical doctor in 1975. From 1977 until 1992, he carried out as scientific and clinical activities for the Clinic of Neurology at LMU Munich, at the Clinic of Großhadern. Since 1988, he has held a C3 chair with focus on neurological intensive medicine. Since 1993, he has held a chair at the Faculty of Medicine of Humboldt University Berlin and has been director of the Clinic of Neurology at the Charité Hospital. In 1997, Prof. Dr. Einhäupl was co-opted to the Federal Science Council and he has been its chairman since 2001.
The Science Council consults the German Federal Government and the governments of all federal states in issues of science policy.

Science

Indeed, the past years have made one thing absolutely more evident: Germany needs a guiding concept for the future, because society's capacity of innovation under the conditions of global competition decides about the degree of freedom, well-being and prosperity of citizens. In order to keep up pace with international competition, which is mainly determined by the USA, Germany must expand its position as a business location for innovation and science and accomplish the implementation of corresponding reform policies in collaboration with European partners. Clearly, strengthening the science sector will play a key role in such a campaign.

So far, the federal and regional governments are assuming tasks of scientific development together within the framework of so-called federal projects – both for university construction as well as for extra-university research institutions and the German Research Society.

Despite all considerations of the past years, things should really stay so in principle. One central task will be in future to create a nationwide perspective also, not only to maintain the high quality standard of German universities in its totality, but also to increase it as much as possible. This is a major prerequisite both for generally securing excellent training as well as for ensuring the availability of applicants for top positions. To this end universities undoubtedly need additional funds, which will be available through the planned Excellence Initiative providing an amount of 1.9 billion Euros. Furthermore, universities also must be capable of determining their structures and contents autonomously. To achieve the pursued increase of efficiency, collaboration between universities and extra-university as well as industrial research institutions must be intensified considerably.

The structure of the education and training system is another very important subject for the future of our economy and society. So far, it has been successful and has accomplished to create good and excellent experts on all levels. However, it cannot be overlooked that in many ways this system is not doing justice to this claim any longer. Several reasons can be found for this, as the Pisa Survey has shown for the field of school education or the current much too long lasting discussion about the role and quality of universities reveals.

It is becoming increasingly more evident that it is not sufficient to analyse the single sectors of the education system separately from each other – schools providing general education, vocational training and university education – and wanting to cure them. What is needed is an overall concept of education as well as the teaching and generation of knowledge, which on the one hand is suitable to enable a larger part of the young population the start into a more qualified and future-oriented professional life and to secure older people the maintenance of jobs in rapidly developing professional environments through continuous training, and on the other hand is capable of opening up appropriate avenues to especially talented people that facilitate the entire enhancement of their abilities – even if this means treading unconventional paths at times. Precisely in such a system that absorbs and promotes talents, the interests of individuals meet with those of a society dependent on education and science. Germany as a business location will only remain attractive for domestic and foreign investors as long as there is a potential of well-trained and extensively qualified employees and management personnel that are capable of formulating strategic company aims and applying the same. Securing the

Mitte: Berliner Humboldt-Universität.
Centre: Humboldt University of Berlin.
Außen: Science Center, Bremen.
Outside: Science Center, Bremen.

for the promotion of innovation and excellence. The prerequisite for this is to improve the situation of universities so that specific ones can develop to internationally visible top universities, which not only serve to form standards for the entire German academic system, but also are attractive for foreign scientists. At the same time our aim must be here business location's competitiveness includes also training and the promotion of outstanding scientists and scientific institutions.

One problem that shows clearly that reforms are necessary on all levels of the educational system and that will occupy us tremendously in a few years,

Wissenschaft

**Studienanfänger- und Absolventenquoten 2001 im Tertiärbereich A[1]
sowie Bildungs- und FuE-Ausgaben nach finanzierenden Sektoren nach OECD-Berechnung
(Angaben für die Jahre 2000, 2001 bzw. 2002 und 2003)**

Quelle: OECD

OECD-Länder	Quoten[2]		Bildungs- und FuE-Ausgaben					Ausgaben für Verteidigung in % der staatlich finanzierten FuE
	Studien-anfänger-quote	Absolventen-quote	Hochschul-ausgaben[3] als Anteil am BIP 2000	FuE-Ausgaben		Finanzierung[4]		
				in Mrd. € (Basis US-$[5])	Anteil am BIP	Darunter Wirtschafts-sektor	Darunter Staats-sektor	
						Anteil in & Gesamtausg.		
Australien	65	42,0	1,6	6,1	1,55	46,3	45,7	7,3
Belgien	32	–	1,3	4,8	2,17	64,3	21,4	0,4
Dänemark	44	38,8	1,6	2,9	2,39	61,7	27,8	1,1
Finnland	72	40,7	1,7	3,6	3,42	70,8	25,5	2,9
Frankreich	37	25,0	1,1	28,2	2,20	54,2	36,9	24,2
Italien	44	20,0	0,9	12,1	1,07	–	–	4,0
Japan	41	32,8	1,1	81,0	3,06	73,0	18,5	4,1
Kanada	–	–	2,6	13,5	1,82	40,0	33,2	4,8
Niederlande	54	–	1,2	6,9	1,89	51,8	36,2	1,9
Norwegen	62	–	1,3	2,1	1,60	51,6	39,8	6,9
Schweden	69	29,6	1,7	7,7	4,27	71,9	21,0	22,2
Schweiz	33	18,7	1,2	4,4	2,63	69,1	23,2	0,7
Spanien	48	32,1	1,2	6,4	0,96	47,2	39,9	37,3
Vereinigtes Königreich	45	37,4	1,0	22,9	1,89	46,2	30,2	30,5
Vereinigte Staaten	42	–	2,7	216,0	2,67	64,4	30,2	53,7
Deutschland[7]	32[6]	19,0	1,0	42,9	2,51[8]	65,3	31,8	6,7
OECD Mittel/Total	47	30,3	1,7	497,8	2,29	63,2	29,1	29,4

[1] Die theoretische Gesamtdauer eines Studiengangs des Tertiärbereichs A beträgt mindestens 3 Jahre, normalerweise jedoch 4 Jahre oder länger

[2] Anteil an der Bevölkerung
[3] Einschließlich Baumaßnahmen nach HBFG; Ausgaben für Forschung und Entwicklung und damit Drittmittel; ohne Krankenversorgung

[4] Restfinanzierung durch privaten Sektor
[5] US-$ Kaufkraftparität
[6] Vgl. Studienanfängerquote nach Berechnung des StBA 2002: 37,1 Prozent

[7] 188 Mrd. € für Bildung, Forschung und Wissenschaft im Jahr 2001
[8] In der Koalitionsvereinbarung zwischen SPD/Grünen 2002 wird als Ziel für das Jahr 2010 ein Anteil von 3 Prozent genannt

senden Zahl von Jugendlichen, die ohne Abschluss von den Schulen gehen. Aber auch diejenigen, die einen Schulabschluss erreicht haben, sind häufig nicht mehr in der Lage, einer auf basalen Kenntnissen der Mathematik und Naturwissenschaften aufbauenden Berufsausbildung zu folgen. Das setzt sich fort in der häufig unzureichenden mathematischen und naturwissenschaftlichen Grundausbildung an den weiterführenden Schulen, die bereits jetzt durch einen eklatanten Mangel an Lehrern, eine mangels Nachwuchs starke Überalterung der Lehrerschaft, einen hohen Stundenausfall und teilweise schlechte und veraltete apparative Ausstattung gekennzeichnet sind. Naturwissenschaftlicher Unterricht berücksichtigt aufgrund dieser schlechten Voraussetzungen häufig nur noch Teilaspekte oder einzelne Fächer, hält mit aktuellen wissenschaftlichen Entwicklungen nicht mehr Schritt und ist häufig nicht in der Lage, die Begeisterung bei Schülern zu wecken, die notwendig ist, um einen wissenschaftlich-technisch anspruchsvollen Lehrberuf zu ergreifen oder gar um ein wissenschaftliches Studium zu beginnen.

Diesem Problem müssen wir uns alle stellen: Schule, Hochschule, Wirtschaft und Politik. Der Wissenschaftsrat hat in den letzten Jahren zwei Empfehlungen erarbeitet, die sich mit Teilaspekten des Problems beschäftigen: mit der Reform der Lehrerbildung (Januar 2001) und des Hochschulzugangs (Januar 2004). Für die Lehrerbildung für das Lehramt an Realschulen und Gymnasien empfiehlt er ein stärker auf die spezifischen Anforderungen von Unterricht und Erziehung im schulischen Kontext zugeschnittenes Bildungsangebot, ein fachwissenschaftlich breit angelegtes BA-Studium und ein auf Vermittlung der pädagogisch-didaktischen Professionalität konzentriertes MA-Studium, den Erwerb von Qualifikationen, die berufliche Einsatzfelder auch außerhalb der Schule eröffnen und eine effektivere Abstimmung zwischen Lehrerarbeitsmarkt und Ausbildungssystem sowie eine Verkürzung der realen Studienzeiten durch eine stärkere fachliche Strukturierung des Studiums. Entsprechend dieser Empfehlung haben bisher einzelne Länder neue Konzepte der Lehrerbildung entwickelt, die sich nun in der Praxis bewähren müssen.

Mit seiner Empfehlung zur Reform des Hochschulzugangs wendet sich der Wissenschaftsrat an die Schulen, die sich verstärkt und professionalisiert um eine gezielte Studien- und Berufsberatung kümmern sollen, da zahlreiche Schulabgänger mit eklatanten Informationslücken auf den Arbeitsmarkt oder in die Hochschulen entlassen werden. Außerdem soll die Bedeutung des Abiturs und der Schulabschlussnote durch die Einführung des Zentralabiturs und von länderübergreifenden Bildungsstandards erhöht werden, so dass beides wieder zu einem verlässlich-

Science

**Proportion of first year students and graduates in 2001 in the tertiary sector A[1])
as well as education and R&D expenditure by financing sectors following OECD calculations
(Statements for the years 2000, 2001 and 2002 or 2003 respectively)**

Source: OECD

OECD countries	Proportions[2])		Education and R&D expenditure					Expenditure for defence in % of state financed R&D
	Share of first year students	Share of graduates	University expendit.[3] as share of GDP 2000	R&D expenditure		Financing[4])		
				in billion € Basis US $[5])	Share in GDP	Economic sector	Public sector	
						Share in % overall expenditure		
Australia	65	42,0	1,6	6,1	1,55	46,3	45,7	7,3
Belgium	32	–	1,3	4,8	2,17	64,3	21,4	0,4
Denmark	44	38,8	1,6	2,9	2,39	61,7	27,8	1,1
Finland	72	40,7	1,7	3,6	3,42	70,8	25,5	2,9
France	37	25,0	1,1	28,2	2,20	54,2	36,9	24,2
Italy	44	20,0	0,9	12,1	1,07	–	–	4,0
Japan	41	32,8	1,1	81,0	3,06	73,0	18,5	4,1
Canada	–	–	2,6	13,5	1,82	40,0	33,2	4,8
The Netherlands	54	–	1,2	6,9	1,89	51,8	36,2	1,9
Norway	62	–	1,3	2,1	1,60	51,6	39,8	6,9
Sweden	69	29,6	1,7	7,7	4,27	71,9	21,0	22,2
Switzerland	33	18,7	1,2	4,4	2,63	69,1	23,2	0,7
Spain	48	32,1	1,2	6,4	0,96	47,2	39,9	37,3
United Kingdom	45	37,4	1,0	22,9	1,89	46,2	30,2	30,5
United States of America	42	–	2,7	216,0	2,67	64,4	30,2	53,7
Germany[7])	32[6])	19,0	1,0	42,9	2,51[8])	65,3	31,8	6,7
OECD Funds/Total	47	30,3	1,7	497,8	2,29	63,2	29,1	29,4

[1]) Theoretical overall term of a course of the tertiary sector A is at last 3 years, but normally 4 years or more
[2]) Proportion of the population
[3]) Including construction projects according to HBFG, expenditure for research and development and therefore third party funds; without care of patients
[4]) Remaining finance covered by private sector
[5]) US $ purchase power parity
[6]) See the proportion of first year students according to calculations of the Federal Statistical Office 2002: 37,1 per cent
[7]) 188 billion € for education, research and science in the year 2001
[8]) The coalition agreement of the Social Socialist Party/The Green Party specifies a target rate of 3 per cent for the year 2010

is the lack of up-coming experts of natural science and engineering in industry and science. It starts with the growing number of school leavers that complete school education without obtaining the final school leavers' certificate. But even those that have achieved the final school leavers' qualification are often not capable any longer to follow vocational education training founded on basic knowledge of mathematics and natural science. It continues with the frequently insufficient basic teaching of mathematics and natural science at continuing schools of further education, a branch that is already now characterised by a striking lack of teachers, a high proportion of old teaching staff because of the lack of young professionals, high levels of cancelled lessons and partly bad and out-of-date technical equipment. Natural science lessons therefore often only considers part aspects or single subjects because of these awful conditions, cannot keep up with current scientific developments and are frequently not capable any more to arouse enthusiasm in schoolchildren, which is necessary to take up a scientific or technically demanding apprenticeship or even to start scientific studies.

We all must face this problem together however: Schools, universities, the economic sector and politics. The Federal Science Council has elaborated two recommendations in the past years that deal with partial aspects of this problem: namely the Reform of Teacher Training (January 2001) and of University Access (January 2004). It recommends for teacher training of teachers at secondary schools and grammar or high schools an education provision that is more targeted to the specific needs of teaching and education within a scholastic context, broadly approached expert and scientific BA studies and MA studies that concentrate on imparting pedagogical and didactical professionalism, the acquisition of qualifications that provide access to professional fields of employment also outside of schools and a more effective coordination between the teacher labour market and the education system as well as shortening the real study time by increasingly structuring study courses in terms of expert subjects. Reacting to this recommendation, so far only individual regional states have developed new concepts of teacher training, which now have to be tested and proven in practical work.

The Science Council is addressing especially those schools with its Reform of University Access that are to become engaged increasingly and more professionally in specific study and vocational consulting,

Wissenschaft

Ausgaben für Forschung und Entwicklung in Mrd. €

Land	1997	1998	1999	2000	2001	2002	Absolute Steigerung	Zuwachsrate in % Jahresdurchschnitt
Deutschland	33,6	35,1	38,4	41,7	42,4	42,9	9,3	4,99
USA	165,8	176,8	190,3	206,8	214,2	216,0	48,4	5,43
Frankreich	21,8	22,4	23,7	25,6	27,9	.	6,1	6,35
Großbritannien	18,2	18,6	20,3	21,2	22,9	.	4,7	5,97
Schweden	5,5	.	6,1	.	7,7	.	2,2	8,78

Ausgaben der Hochschulen für Forschung und Entwicklung (ohne Lehre) in Mrd. €

Land	1997	1998	1999	2000	2001	2002	Absolute Steigerung	Zuwachsrate in % Jahresdurchschnitt
Deutschland	6,0	6,1	6,3	6,7	7,0	7,3	1,3	3,98
USA	23,6	24,7	26,3	28,3	31,0	34,3	7,3	7,71
Frankreich	3,8	3,9	4,1	4,8	5,3	5,5	1,5	8,55
Großbritannien	3,6	3,7	4,0	4,4	4,9	.	1,3	8,18
Schweden	1,2	.	1,3	.	1,5	.	0,1	6,14

Quelle: OECD

eren Indikator für die Studienbefähigung wird. Die schulfachliche Angebotsstruktur sollte durch eine klare Gewichtung der Lerninhalte und eine Begrenzung der Spezialisierung standardisiert werden. Zusätzlich wird die Einführung eines Basisfaches Naturwissenschaften empfohlen. Die Hochschulen sollen künftig aktiver an der Studienzulassung mitwirken. In zulassungsbeschränkten Studiengängen sollen sie Auswahlverfahren durchführen, in nicht zulassungsbeschränkten Studiengängen Eignungsfeststellungsverfahren mit Beratungsfunktion. Im Rahmen des ersten Studienjahres sollte eine fachwissenschaftliche Orientierungsphase etabliert werden.

Gerade für den Bereich der Schule und der Berufswahl hat der Wissenschaftsrat auch Anregungen für eine Beteiligung der Wirtschaft gegeben: Wesentlich wird die Bereitschaft sein, sich über Berufsverbände oder Kammern intensiv an Information und Beratung von Schülerinnen und Schülern zu beteiligen. Denkbar wäre aus meiner Sicht auch, Schulklassen zu Informationsveranstaltungen in Betriebe einzuladen und Praktikumsplätze und Ferienjobs zur Verfügung zu stellen. Dabei darf es natürlich nicht bei Einzelmaßnahmen bleiben, sondern es sollten kontinuierliche und beidseitig geförderte Beziehungen zwischen Schulen und der regionalen Wirtschaft entstehen. Diese sollten auch nicht nur zum Ziel haben, künftige Arbeitskräfte für bestimmte Betriebe zu rekrutieren, sondern den Jugendlichen ein breites Spektrum an Möglichkeiten und Perspektiven zu eröffnen. Darüber hinaus könnten Betriebe der Region in abgestimmten Aktionen helfen, die Ausstattung der Schulen mit naturwissenschaftlichem und informationstechnischem Gerät der letzten oder jeweils vorletzten Generation zu verbessern. Alle diese Anregungen gelten für Hochschulen gleichermaßen.

Ein weiteres Problemfeld ist die Kooperation zwischen Hochschulen und Wirtschaft: (1) die Überbrückung zwischen den immer kürzer werdenden Zyklen industrieller Innovationsstrategien und den eher auf Langfristigkeit angelegten Strategien der Hochschulforschung. (2) die aufgrund mangelnder Grundausstattung der Hochschulen sinkende Attraktivität der Hochschulen für Kooperationen. Was können wir tun, damit die Hochschulen mehr neuartige Ideen und Theorien, Methoden und Technologien hervorbringen?

Innovationsförderung wird häufig auf die Förderung der Anwendung von Wissenschaft in der Praxis verkürzt. Deshalb hat man in Deutschland bisher vor allem die anwendungsbezogene Projektförderung ausgebaut. Diese Strategie hat zahlreichen Unternehmen, Hochschulen und Foschungseinrichtungen ermöglicht, gemeinsam Forschungsprojekte durchzuführen. Die Innovationsfähigkeit der Hochschulen und ihr Beitrag zur gesellschaftlichen und wirtschaftlichen Innovation müssen jedoch noch durch weitere Maßnahmen unterstützt werden. Dabei kann es nicht in erster Linie darum gehen, die Höhe der Drittmittel weiter zu steigern und damit die kreativen Freiräume zu besetzen, über die Hochschulen in besonderem Maße verfügen müssen. Diese Freiräume müssen gestaltet und geschützt werden. Deshalb muss der einzelne Wissenschaftler auch künftig genügend Grundmittel zur Verfügung haben, mit denen er diesen kreativen Raum nutzen und dabei auch etwas riskieren kann. Der Anteil der Grundmittel an der Gesamtausstattung ist jedoch seit Jahren deutlich rückläufig. Ein großer Teil der verbliebenen Grundmittel wird bereits durch laufende Ausgaben gebunden. Dieser Mangel an verfügbaren Grundmitteln wirkt sich in vielerlei Beziehung nachteilig aus. So manifestiert er sich unter anderem in fehlender Geräteausstattung, aber auch in einem Verlust der Attraktivität für exzellente Wissenschaftler. Es ist daher erforderlich, zentrale Forschungs- und Innovationsfonds einzusetzen, aus denen die Hochschulen im Rahmen ihrer Strategie – und mit einer gewissen Unabhängigkeit vom Drittmittelmarkt – Wissenschaftler, die innovative Ideen haben, unterstützen können. Solche Fonds sollten z.T. aus dem Landeszuschuss finanziert werden. Hinzukommen müssen jedoch Einnahmen aus Patenten, aus Ausgründungen und aus Weiterbildungen. Generell wird erfolgreiche Forschung auf Dauer ohne eine Vollkostendeckung, das heißt die Erstattung der mit ihr verbundenen direkten und indirekten Kosten, auf Dauer nicht möglich sein. Verändern müssen sich auch die finanziellen Voraussetzungen für Auftragsforschung für die Wirtschaft. Ein wirklicher Anreiz, Kooperationen mit Unternehmen einzugehen, würde dann entstehen, wenn die Hochschule dafür einen Bonus erhielte, der in den zentralen Fonds einfließt.

Hochschulen müssen zunehmend selbst wirtschaftlich handeln und eine engere Verzahnung mit der Wirtschaft fördern. Eine vielseitigere Einnahmestruktur wird ihnen letztlich ein größeres Maß an Autonomie bescheren. Diese Autonomie muss jedoch auch von Seiten des Staates zugestanden werden: Die Universitäten müssen zusätzliche Ein-

Science

because many school leavers are released with alarming gaps of information onto the labour market or into universities. Furthermore, it is intended to increase the significance of A-levels (Abitur) and the school leaving marks by introducing a "Zentralabitur" as well as cross-regional education standards, so that both can become a reliable indication for admission to university studies again. The structure of school subjects offered should be standardised by clearly weighting the teaching contents and limiting specialisation. Additionally, the introduction of a basic subject of natural science is recommended. Universities will be required to take a more active part in the admission of students. For courses in which the number of admissions is limited they are to carry out selection procedures, for courses in which the number of admissions is not limited aptitude tests including consulting sessions are planned. Within the context of the first study year, an expert and scientifically led orientation phase should be established.

Particularly for schools and job selection, the Science Council has also put forward proposals for an economic sector should be created. These should not only be targeted to recruit a future workforce for specific companies, but should open up a broad spectrum of possibilities and perspectives for the youth. Moreover, companies of the region could support mutually agreed action plans to improve the equipment of schools with natural science and IT devices of the last or previous generation respectively. All these suggestions can equally be applied in universities.

Another problematic field is the cooperation between universities and industry: (1) Bridging the gap between ever shorter cycles of industrial innovation strategies and the strategies of university research rather aimed at longer terms. (2) The declining attractiveness of universities for collaboration because of lacking basic equipments. What can be done for universities to produce increasing numbers of innovative ideas and theories, methods and technologies?

The promotion of innovation frequently is reduced to the promotion of the application of science in which universities must be allowed to pursue to a particularly great extent. This freedom must be structured and protected. For this reason, individual scientists are to dispose of sufficient basic funds also in future that they can use this creative freedom with and that allows them to take certain risks. But the proportion of basic funding in overall equipment of universities has been declining markedly since years now. Great parts of the remaining basic funds are tied up already by running costs. This lack of available basic funds is damaging universities seriously and manifests itself in missing equipments and the failure to attract excellent scientists. It is therefore urgently necessary to use central research and innovation funds from which universities can draw to support scientists within the context of their strategy – and with certain independence from third party funding –who have innovative ideas. Such funds should partly be financed from subsidies of the regional government. To this must be added however income from patents, spin-offs and from continuous education programmes. Generally, successful research will not be possible in the

Expenditure for research and development in billions of €

State	1997	1998	1999	2000	2001	2002	Absolute increase	Growth rate in % annual average
Germany	33,6	35,1	38,4	41,7	42,4	42,9	9,3	4,99
USA	165,8	176,8	190,3	206,8	214,2	216,0	48,4	5,43
France	21,8	22,4	23,7	25,6	27,9	·	6,1	6,35
Great Britain	18,2	18,6	20,3	21,2	22,9	·	4,7	5,97
Sweden	5,5	·	6,1	·	7,7	·	2,2	8,78

Expenditure of universities for research and development (without teaching) in billion €

	1997	1998	1999	2000	2001	2002	Absolute increase	Growth rate in % annual average
Germany	6,0	6,1	6,3	6,7	7,0	7,3	1,3	3,98
USA	23,6	24,7	26,3	28,3	31,0	34,3	7,3	7,71
France	3,8	3,9	4,1	4,8	5,3	5,5	1,5	8,55
Great Britain	3,6	3,7	4,0	4,4	4,9	·	1,3	8,18
Sweden	1,2	·	1,3	·	1,5	·	0,1	6,14

Source: OECD

active participation of the economic sector: Of major importance will be the preparedness to become involved intensively in providing information and advice for schoolchildren through professional associations or chambers. In my opinion it would also be feasible to invite school classes to information events into companies and to make available practical internships and summer jobs. Of course, one-off projects should not be the rule in this respect, instead continuous and mutually promoted relationships between schools and the regional practical work. This is why in Germany above all application-oriented project promotion has been expanded so far. This strategy has enabled numerous companies, universities and research institutions to carry out mutual research projects. However, the innovative capacity of universities and their contribution to societal and economic innovation must be supported through additional measures. The issue in this respect is not only to increase the amount of third party funding further and therefore to block the freedom of creative development, long run without complete cost-effectiveness, that means the reimbursement of directly or indirectly related costs. Furthermore, also financial prerequisites for contract research for industry should be subjected to change. Cost-effective management, i. e. refunding direct and indirect costs, could be a conceivable approach for this. A real stimulation for entering cooperation agreements with companies could be created if universities were to receive a bonus, which would flow into the central fund.

Wissenschaft

nahmen behalten und bewirtschaften dürfen und sie müssen sich stärker als bisher untereinander und intern ausdifferenzieren können. Einzelne Institute oder Fachbereiche werden sich dann stärker auf die Forschung und die Ausbildung des wissenschaftlichen Nachwuchses, andere auf die grundständige Lehre, wieder andere auf Wirtschaftsbeziehungen und Dienstleistungen konzentrieren. Nicht zuletzt müssen arbeits- und tarifrechtliche Hemmnisse abgebaut werden, die eine flexiblere Gestaltung von Arbeits- und Schwerpunktbereichen behindern.

Der Wissenschaftsrat hat hierzu eine Stellungnahme erarbeitet, die das Ziel hat, einerseits verbesserte Beschäftigungsmöglichkeiten für qualifizierte Wissenschaftler nach der Qualifzierungsphase an Hochschulen und Wissenschaftseinrichtungen zu eröffnen und diese dauerhaft anzulegen, andererseits den Hochschulen die notwendige Flexibilität bei der Personalbewirtschaftung zu erhalten. Zu diesem Zweck sollten die Hochschulen künftig ein modifiziertes Kündigungsrecht für unbefristet beschäftigte angestellte Wissenschaftler erhalten, das den dauerhaften Wegfall von Drittmitteln als Grundlage einer betriebsbedingten Kündigung formuliert. Ein vereinfachtes System der Entgeltbestimmung soll es zudem erlauben, hervorragende Leistungen an Wissenschaftseinrichtungen zu honorieren. Die Umsetzung dieser Empfehlungen dürfte es künftig ebenfalls erleichtern, schwerpunktmäßige Wirtschaftskooperationen mit dem entsprechenden Drittmittelpersonal zu etablieren und es Wissenschaftlern ermöglichen, zwischen öffentlichen Wissenschaftseinrichtungen und der Industrieforschung zu wechseln. ∎

Gemeinschaftsaufgabe Forschungsförderung (Art. 91b) und Hochschulbau (Art. 91a) durch Bund und Länder in Mio. €

Quelle: BMBF

Art. 91 b Einrichtung	Anzahl der Institute	Finanzierungs-schlüssel	2003 Ist			2004 Soll		
			Insg.	Bund	Länder	Insg.	Bund	Länder
Max-Planck-Gesellschaft	79	50:50	935,2	467,6	467,6	963,2	481,6	481,6
Deutsche Forschungsgemeinschaft	–	58:42 (ab 2002)	1.177,6	683,0	494,6	1.287,5	746,8	540,7
Fraunhofer Gesellschaft	58	90:10	324,4[1)2)]	287,4	36,9	385,4[1)2)]	347,3	38,1
Akademienprogramm	7	50:50	41,4[3)]	20,7	20,7	43,0[3)]	21,5	21,5
Helmholtz-Zentren	15	90:10	1.607,6[1)]	1.446,8	160,8	1.656,0[1)]	1.490,4	165,6
Leibniz-Gemeinschaft	80	überwiegend 50:50	700,9	353,3	347,6	722,3	365,4	356,9
Deutsche Akademie Leopoldina, Halle/Saale	1	80:20	1,5[1)]	1,2	0,3	1,5[1)]	1,2	0,3
Insgesamt			4.788,5	3.260,1	1.528,4	5.058,9	3.454,2	1.604,7
Art. 91 a Hochschulbau ca.		50:50	2.120,0	1.060,0	1.060,0	1.850	925	925
Summe			**6.908,5**	**4.320,1**	**2.588,4**	**6.908,9**	**4.379,2**	**2.529,7**

[1)] Wird nicht im BLK-Verfahren beschlossen
[2)] Einschl. Übergangsfinanzierung für HHI und GMD. Steigerung der Zuwendung 2004 gegenüber Vorjahr unter Berücksichtigung einer Basisanpassung.
[3)] 2004: Steigerung gegenüber 2003 unter Berücksichtigung von Sondertatbeständen

Science

Increasingly, universities will be held responsible to act on their own economic initiative and have to develop closer links with industry. More variety in terms of their income structure will provide a greater extent of autonomy for them ultimately. This autonomy must also be conceded by the federal state however: universities must be able to keep and control their additional income and they must also be able to differentiate much more than now between each other and internally. Single institutes or faculties will then concentrate more on research and training young scientific experts, others on elementary teaching, further ones on industrial relations and services. Ultimately, obstacles of labour and salary agreements must be reduced that now deter from creating more flexibility in certain fields of employment and specific issues of central priority.

The Science Council has drawn up a statement in this respect, which aims to develop improved employment chances for qualified scientists after a qualification phase at universities and science institutions and establishing these permanently on the one hand, and on the other, to maintain the necessary flexibility in their use of human resources for universities. To this end it is intended that in future university legislation contains a modified right of giving notice to scientists that are employed on the basis of an indefinite contract period, which stipulates the permanent cessation of third party funds as basis for a redundancy for reasons of restructuring.

Moreover, a simplified system of payment intends to allow the honouring of excellent achievements at scientific institutions. If these recommendations were applied it should also become easier to establish specific industrial cooperation agreements with corresponding third party funded personnel and for scientists to change between public scientific institutions and industrial research. ■

Federal Project – Promotion of Research (Art. 91b) and Construction of Universities (Art. 91a) jointly by the federal government and state governments in millions of €

Source: BMBF

Art. 91 b Establishment	Number of Institutes	Financing key	2003 Actual Value			2004 Forecast		
			Total	State Govern.	Regional Govern.	Total	Federal Govern.	State Govern.
Max-Planck Society	79	50:50	935,2	467,6	467,6	963,2	481,6	481,6
German Research Association	–	58:42 (as of 2002)	1.177,6	683,0	494,6	1.287,5	746,8	540,7
Fraunhofer Society	58	90:10	324,4[1)2)]	287,4	36,9	385,4[1)2)]	347,3	38,1
Programme of Academics	7	50:50	41,4[3)]	20,7	20,7	43,0[3)]	21,5	21,5
Helmholtz Centres	15	90:10	1.607,6[1)]	1.446,8	160,8	1.656,0[1)]	1.490,4	165,6
Leibniz-Gemeinschaft	80	predominantly 50:50	700,9	353,3	347,6	722,3	365,4	356,9
Deutsche Akademie Leopoldina, Halle/Saale	1	80:20	1,5[1)]	1,2	0,3	1,5[1)]	1,2	0,3
Total			4.788,5	3.260,1	1.528,4	5.058,9	3.454,2	1.604,7
Art. 91 a Construction of Universities approxim.		50:50	2.120,0	1.060,0	1.060,0	1.850	925	925
Sum			6.908,5	4.320,1	2.588,4	6.908,9	4.379,2	2.529,7

[1)] Is not stipulated in federal/state government commision procedure

[2)] Incl. temporary financing for HHI and GMD. Increase of subsidies in 2004 against previous year considering a basic adjustment

[3)] 2004: Increase against 2003 considering special circumstances

Company Profile

Soforthilfe bei personellen Engpässen
Immediate help for shortage of personnel

Adecco Personaldienstleistungen GmbH

Gründungsjahr/Year of Foundation: 1962

Mitarbeiter insgesamt /Employees:
30.000,
6.000 Niederlassungen in mehr als 70 Ländern, in Deutschland allein 200 Niederlassungen und mehr als 10.000 Firmenkunden/
30,000,
6,000 branch offices in more than 70 countries, alone in Germany, 200 branch offices and more than 10,000 corporate clients

Geschäftstätigkeit/Business Activity:
Zeitarbeit, Personalvermittlung, Outsourcing, Outplacement, Engineering, Finance, Call Center, IT-Service
Temporary work, personnel placement, outsourcing, outplacement, engineering, finance, Call Center, IT-Service

Anschrift/Address:
Hauptverwaltung/Headquarters
Flemingstraße 20–22
D-36041 Fulda
Telefon   +49 (661) 93 98-0
          +49 (18 02) 900 900 (24 Std Hotline)
Telefax   +49 (661) 93 98-100
E-Mail   info@adecco.de
Internet www.adecco.de

Fotos: 200 Niederlassungen allein in Deutschland bringen täglich Arbeitskräfte und Firmenkunden zusammen.
Photographs: 200 branch offices in Germany alone bring together workforce and corporate clients each day.

Überall auf der Welt kann der Wandel von der Industrie- zur Dienstleistungsgesellschaft beobachtet werden. Wechselnde Anforderungen an den Arbeitsmarkt erfordern neue flexible Arbeitsmodelle – erfordern Spezialisten im Bereich Mensch und Arbeit. Adecco ist ein Forbes-500-Unternehmen und Weltmarktführer für Personaldienstleistungen. Über sein Netzwerk von 30.000 Mitarbeitern und 6.000 Niederlassungen in mehr als 70 Ländern in aller Welt bringt Adecco jeden Tag 700.000 Arbeitskräfte mit mehreren hunderttausend Firmenkunden zusammen. Jedes Jahr erhalten mehr als vier Millionen Menschen weltweit über Adecco neue berufliche Perspektiven.

In Deutschland stehen mehr als 200 Niederlassungen und Job-Center bundesweit zur Verfügung. Ihnen obliegt die Betreuung der rund 12.500 Mitarbeiter und mehr als 10.000 Firmenkunden. Neben den Kerndienstleistungen Zeitarbeit, Personalvermittlung und Outsourcing bietet Adecco mit seinen speziellen Geschäftsbereichen und Tochtergesellschaften Lösungen für jede Art des Personalbedarfs – ob kurzfristige Bewältigung einer Produktionsspitze, Vermittlung eines Managers auf Zeit, Outsourcen eines kompletten Bereiches oder Steuerung der gesamten Personalplanung. Als Personaldienstleister ist Adecco immer dann gefragt, wenn engagierte und motivierte Menschen gesucht werden, die sich optimal in bestehende Arbeitsstrukturen integrieren lassen – unabhängig von Qualifikation oder Berufsbild. Über 40 Jahre Erfahrung in Deutschland machen Adecco zum Experten in Sachen Mensch und Arbeit. ∎

Currently, the transition from an industrial to a service providing society is perceivable in the entire world. Changing demands required from the labour market make new flexible work concepts necessary – require specialists for the fields of human resources and labour. Adecco is one of the Forbes-500 listed companies and world market leader for personnel services. Through its network of 30,000 employees and 6,000 branches in more than 70 countries all over the world, each day Adecco joins together 700,000 staff members with several hundreds of thousands of corporate clients. Each year, more than four million people worldwide receive new professional perspectives through Adecco.
In Germany, there are more than 200 branch offices and job centres available nationwide. Their task is to support around 12,500 staff members and more than 10,000 corporate clients. Besides its core services rendered like temporary work, personnel placement and outsourcing, Adecco offers solutions for any kind of personnel requirement with its special business fields and subsidiaries, be it the short-term dealing with a production peak, placing a manager for a certain length of time, the outsourcing of a complete division or controlling the entire personnel planning. As a personnel service provider, Adecco is always sought after when committed and motivated people are at stake that can be integrated in existing working structures in an optimal way, independently of their qualifications or professional career. Over 40 years of experience in Germany have turned Adecco into an expert in terms of human resources and work. ∎

Company Profile

DB Zeitarbeit – Erfolg durch Flexibilität am Arbeitsmarkt

DB Zeitarbeit – innovative ideas in the labour market

Die Bahn DB

Die Zeitarbeitsbranche hat sich zu einem bedeutenden Wirtschaftsfaktor entwickelt. Unternehmen stehen heute vor der Herausforderung, ihr Personalmanagement in zentrale strategische Planungsprozesse einzubeziehen.

Die DB Zeitarbeit als 100%iges Tochterunternehmen der DB AG bietet als Personaldienstleister seit ihrer Gründung im Jahr 2001 Komplettlösungen in der Personalüberlassung und -vermittlung von Fachpersonal. Entsprechend dem Marktpotenzial bieten wir Zeitarbeit als strategisches Planungsinstrument für Personalmanagementprozesse. Im Markt für Verkehr und Logistik steht die DB Zeitarbeit mit wachsenden Mitarbeiterzahlen für hochqualifizierte Fachkräfte, erfahrene Projektleiter und Ingenieure. Die Spezialisierung unserer 1.300 Mitarbeiter umfasst folgende Qualifikationen und Tätigkeitsbereiche:

- verkehrsspezifische Tätigkeiten
- kaufmännische Tätigkeiten
- gewerbliche Tätigkeiten
- Ingenieure

Wir sind in der Vermittlung von Fachpersonal zur direkten Festanstellung in Kundenunternehmen bundesweit an 14 Standorten tätig.

Wir nehmen die Herausforderung gerne an, unserem Kunden in kürzester Zeit den Experten für sein Unternehmen zu präsentieren. Gemeinsam mit unseren Kooperationspartnern Randstad und Ferchau Engineering garantieren wir einen Full-Service in der Personalüberlassung und -vermittlung.

Innovative Ideen für den Arbeitsmarkt zeichnen uns aus:

In der vermittlungsorientierten Personalüberlassung von Beamten haben wir uns ein einmaliges Know-how erworben.

Gleichzeitig agiert die DB Zeitarbeit seit 2003 als Agentur für Berufsstarter. ∎

The branch of temporary work has developed into a significant economic factor. Today, companies are facing the challenge of having to include their management of human resources into central processes of strategic planning.

As wholly owned subsidiary of DB AG, DB Zeitarbeit offers personnel services since its foundation in the year 2001, providing comprehensive solutions in personnel leasing and the recruitment of expert personnel.

According to the potentials of the market, we offer temporary work as strategic instrument for the planning of human resources processes. In the market of transport and logistics, DB Zeitarbeit stands for highly-qualified experts, experienced project managers and engineers with a constantly growing number of employees. The areas of specialisation covered by our 1.300 staff members comprise the following qualifications and fields of activities:

- transport-specific activities
- administrative and commercial activities
- industrial activities
- Engineering.

We act as an agency providing expert personnel for direct permanent vacancies in our clients' companies nationwide in 14 locations. With pleasure we take on the challenge to present our client the right expert for his company in the shortest of time. Together with our cooperation partners Randstad and Ferchau Engineering we guarantee full service in personnel leasing and recruitment.

Our distinguishing features are innovative ideas for the labour market:

We have acquired a unique know-how in agency-oriented personnel leasing of civil servants.

At the same time, DB-Zeitarbeit acts as agency for new entrants to the job market. ∎

DB Zeitarbeit

Geschäftsführung/Managers:
Ursula Ebert,
Silvia Müller

Gründungsjahr/Year of Foundation: 2001

Geschäftstätigkeit/Business Activities:
Erbringen und Vermarkten von Personaldienstleistungen mit den Hauptgeschäftsfeldern Personalüberlassung und Arbeitsvermittlung, insbesondere in den Bereichen Verkehr und Logistik; die vermittlungsorientierte Personalüberlassung zur Beschäftigungssicherung von Beamten insbesondere in Eisenbahnverkehrs- und Infrastrukturunternehmen und Einrichtungen des öffentlichen Rechts
Rendering as well as sale and marketing of personnel services including the main business fields of temporary employment and recruitment agency, particularly in the areas of transport and logistics; recruitment-oriented staffing for securing employment of civil servants, particularly in companies of railway transport and infrastructure as well as in public institutions

Anschrift/Address:
Geschäftsführung:
Universitätsstraße 2–3a
D-10117 Berlin

Vertriebsregion Nord/Northern Region:
Caroline-Michaelis-Straße 5–11, D-10115 Berlin

Vertriebsregion Ost/Eastern Region:
Ernst-Kamieth-Straße 16, D-06112 Halle

Vertriebsregion West/Western Region:
Herrenstraße 3–5, D-30159 Hannover

Vertriebsregion Süd/Southern Region:
Richelstraße 3, D-80634 München

Kontakte/Contacts:
Info-Tel. +49 (30) 25 35 67 00
Fax   +49 (30) 25 35 67 20
E-Mail   DB.Zeitarbeit@bahn.de
Internet www.db.de/zeitarbeit

*Die Karte in der Mitte zeigt:
DB Zeitarbeit – immer nah am Kunden.
DB Zeitarbeit ist bundesweit in
4 Vertriebsregionen mit
14 Geschäftsstellen vertreten.*

*The map in the centre shows:
DB Zeitarbeit – always right next to its clients. DB Zeitarbeit has representative offices nationwide in 4 sales regions with 14 branches.*

Wachstumsmärkte

Wachstumsmarkt China – Chance für den Standort Deutschland?

Growth market China – a chance for the business location Germany?

Die wirtschaftliche Entwicklung der Volksrepublik China in den vergangenen 25 Jahren ist beispiellos. Bei einem durchschnittlichen jährlichen Bevölkerungswachstum von über einem Prozent – was bei rund 1,3 Milliarden Menschen ein Plus von ca. 15 Millionen Einwohnern p. a. ausmacht – gelang es, das Bruttoinlandsprodukt pro Kopf der Bevölkerung von 379 Yuan (ca. 45 US-Dollar) im Jahr 1978 auf gegenwärtig 8.184 Yuan (ca. 986 US-Dollar) zu steigern.

Dies gelang in einem Land, in dem nach wie vor die Hälfte der erwerbstätigen Bevölkerung in der Landwirtschaft arbeitet, 70 Prozent der Einwohner auf dem Lande wohnen und – je nach Zählmethode bzw. Quelle – 30 bis 100 Millionen Menschen unter der Armutsgrenze des 1-Dollar-Einkommens pro Tag leben. Aber auch in einem Land, dessen wachsender Wohlstand die absolute Binnennachfrage der USA bald übertroffen haben wird.

China ist schon jetzt die sechstgrößte Volkswirtschaft der Welt und auf dem Weg, die viertgrößte Welthandelsnation zu werden. Mit dem erfolgreichen bemannten Raumflug ist China 2003 zur dritten Raumfahrtnation der Welt aufgestiegen. Es ließen sich viele weitere Beispiele für den außerordentlichen Stellenwert nennen, den sich China in Industrie, Handel und technologischer Entwicklung erworben hat. China ist damit für die deutsche Wirtschaft Markt und Partner, gleichzeitig aber auch schon Konkurrent geworden. Vor dem Hintergrund ungebrochenen Wachstums- und Innovationsdenkens in China und fast entgegengesetzten Phänomenen in Deutschland muss man sich der Chancen, Herausforderungen und Risiken für die deutsche Wirtschaft in und mit China bewusst werden.

Das chinesische Wirtschaftswundermodell

Die 1978 eingeleitete Reform- und Öffnungspolitik des Landes entfaltete im Jahre 1992, nach der berühmt gewordenen Inspektionsreise des großen und einflussreichen elder Statesman Deng Xiaoping in den Süden, eine nachhaltige Dynamik. Dengs Message war kurz und knapp: Fortsetzung der Öffnung nach außen und der Wirtschaftsreform nach innen. Seinen Landsleuten rief er zu: „Werdet reich!"

Die Kommunistische Partei Chinas hat in den Jahren danach die Umsetzung der Deng'schen Gedanken in ihr Programm übernommen und auf staatlicher Ebene in der Verfassung verankert. Die Marktwirtschaft sozialistischer (chinesischer) Prägung ist heute verinnerlicht und geht so weit, dass Privatunternehmer, also Kapitalisten, Mitglieder der Kommunistischen Partei werden können – und schon sind. Auf Beschluss des Nationalen Volkskongresses im März 2004 wurde der Schutz des Privateigentums nun auch in die Verfassung aufgenommen. Vielleicht ist es gerade die pragmatische Verbindung von verschiedenen Systemen, die das Erfolgsrezept Chinas entscheidend mitbestimmt, zumindest in der Wirtschaft. „Ein Land – zwei Systeme" gilt auch in Bezug auf das Verhältnis zu dem 1997 wieder chinesisch gewordenen Hongkong. Der Umgang mit dieser Besonderheit zeigt den chinesischen Pragmatismus.

Wirtschaft im Wandel

Seit Mitte der 90er-Jahre lagen die Zuwachsquoten des Bruttoinlandsprodukts nie unter 7 Prozent – meist wurden deutlich höhere Werte bis hin zu 9,8 Prozent im Jahr 1996 erzielt. Nicht nur die Planungen der Zentralregierung, sondern auch internationale Beobachter gehen davon aus, dass noch bis zum Jahr 2020 hin Wachstumsquoten von mindestens 7 Prozent zu verzeichnen sein werden.

Wuhan Iron and Steel Corporation (WISCO) wird ausgestattet mit SIROLL Automatisierungstechnik geliefert von Siemens.

Wuhan Iron and Steel Corporation (WISCO) will be equipped with SIROLL automation technology provided by Siemens.

Joachim Broudré-Gröger

Der 1944 geborene Autor absolvierte nach einer Industrie- und EDV-Kaufmannslehre bei IBM ein Betriebswirtschaftsstudium an der FU Berlin mit dem Abschluss als Dipl.-Kfm; ein Studium an der Universität Madrid und eine Ausbildung am Deutschen Institut für Entwicklungspolitik Berlin folgten. Eintritt in das Auswärtige Amt 1971. Seitdem war er u. a.: Vize-Konsul in Hong Kong; Redenschreiber und persönlicher Assistent im Büro des Bundeskanzlers Willy Brandt; Leiter der Wirtschaftsabteilung der Deutschen Botschaft in Mexiko; Botschafter in der SR Vietnam; Botschafter in Algerien; Leiter der Wirtschaftsabteilung des Auswärtigen Amts. Von 2001 bis 2004 war Joachim Broudré-Gröger Botschafter der Bundesrepublik Deutschland in der VR China.

The author was born in 1944 and completed studies of business administration at the FU Berlin graduating as Diplom-Kaufmann (certified merchant) after qualifying from an apprenticeship as industrial clerk and computer merchant (Industrie- und EDV-Kaufmann). He completed further studies at the University of Madrid and training at the German Institute for Development Politics in Berlin. He joined the Foreign Office in 1971. Since then he has served, among other things, as Vice Consul in Hong Kong; speechwriter and personal assistant in the office of former Chancellor Willy Brandt; Head of the Economic Department of the German Embassy in Mexico; Ambassador to the SR Vietnam; Ambassador in Algeria; Head of the Economic Department of the Foreign Office. From 2001 until 2004 Joachim Broudré-Gröger was Ambassador of the Federal Republic of Germany in the PR of China.

Growth Markets

Produkte von Siemens PTD werden im Tian-Guang Projekt eingesetzt, einem der Schlüsselprojekte in China zur Hochspannungs-Gleichstrom-Übertragung.

Siemens PTD products are used in the Tian-Guang project, one of China's key HVDC power transmission projects.

In the past 25 years the economic development of the People's Republic of China has been unparalleled. It has been achieved to increase the per capita gross domestic product of the population from 379 Yuan (approx. 45 US dollars) in 1978 to presently 8,184 Yuan (approx. 986 US dollars) at an average annual population growth of over one per cent, which given about 1.3 billion people comes to a plus of approx. 15 million inhabitants p. a. This has been achieved in a country in which still half of the working population works in agriculture, 70 per cent of inhabitants live in the countryside and – according to the relevant counting method or source – 30 to 100 million people live below the poverty line of 1 dollar income per day. But this also occurred in a country, whose growing prosperity will soon have exceeded the absolute domestic demand of the USA.

Already today, China is the world's sixth-largest national economy and well on its way to becoming the world's fourth-largest trading nation. Following its successfully completed manned spaceflight, China rose to third rank among space nations of the world in 2003. One could mention many other examples of the extraordinary position that China has acquired in industry, trade and technological development. Consequently, China is a market and partner for the German economy, but at the same time it has already become a competitor.

Against the background of growth and innovation thinking in China and almost contrary phenomena in Germany, one has to be conscious of the chances, challenges and risks for the German economy in and with China.

The Chinese economic miracle

The country's policy of reform and openness initiated in 1978 developed in the year 1992 sustainable dynamism, after the now famous inspection journey to the South of the great and influential elder statesman Deng Xiaoping. Deng's message was clear and brief: continuing the opening up to the outside and economic reforms on the inside. He shouted out to his countrymen: "Be rich!"

In subsequent years, the Communist Party of China assumed the realisation of Deng's ideas in its programme and institutionalised it on state level in the constitution. A socialist-style (Chinese) market economy has been internalised completely today, to the extent that private entrepreneurs, capitalists in fact, can become members of the Communist Party – which already happens. By order of the National People's Congress in March 2004, the protection of private property has also been included in the constitution.

Maybe it is precisely the pragmatic linkage of different systems that plays a major role in China's recipe for success, at least in the economy. "One country – two systems" is also valid with respect to the relationship with Hong Kong, which became Chinese

Wachstumsmärkte

Dies entspricht zum einen der Notwendigkeit, Wohlstandszuwachs besonders auch in den derzeit noch unterdurchschnittlich von der Entwicklung profitierenden ländlichen Gebieten und westlichen sowie nordöstlichen Regionen des Landes zu erreichen und die jährlich rund 15 Millionen neu hinzukommenden Einwohner in den Wirtschaftskreislauf zu integrieren. Zum anderen bedingen der notwendige Ausbau der Infrastruktur, die z. T. überfällige Modernisierung der alten staatswirtschaftlichen Betriebe und Investitionen in modernste Technik ein quasi selbstinduziertes Wirtschaftswachstum.

Die Volksrepublik China wird bislang oft als „Werkbank der Industrienationen" angesehen. Es ist nicht von der Hand zu weisen, dass die niedrigen Lohnkosten die Verlagerung von Produktion auch bei geringerer Produktivität lohnend machen. Das Interesse Chinas, Investitionen ins Land zu holen, um in den Besitz von Technologie und Know-how zu gelangen und hochwertige Arbeitsplätze zu schaffen, deckt sich insoweit mit dem Interesse europäischer, US-amerikanischer und anderer westlicher Unternehmen, den komparativen Kostenvorteil Chinas zu nutzen.

Wenn man den Eindruck bekommt, dass in deutschen Kaufhäusern und Versandhandelskatalogen, also im Bereich der Konsumgüter wie z. B. Spielzeug, Textilien, Werkzeuge und einfachere Elektrogeräte, das „Made in China" schon fast überwiegt, ist dies zunächst kein Anlass zur Sorge: Es gibt im Prinzip kein Geschäft, das nicht für beide Seiten Vorteile bringt. Und letztlich kommt der Konsument in den Genuss günstiger Preise.

Betrachtet man die bilaterale Handelsbilanz zwischen Deutschland und China, muss man feststellen, dass geradezu traditionell ein chinesischer Überschuss zu verzeichnen ist. 1992 importierte Deutschland wertmäßig doppelt so viele Waren aus China wie aus unserem Land nach China geliefert wurden. Allerdings war das Handelsvolumen insgesamt noch von bescheidener Größe: Es betrug nur knapp 9 Milliarden Euro. Bis zum Jahr 2002 vervierfachte sich dieses Volumen auf knapp 36 Milliarden Euro, und das Verhältnis der deutschen Importe aus China zu den Exporten nach China lag bereits bei 21 zu 15. Aktuell erlebten wir einen Anstieg der deutschen Exporte nach China um knapp 30 Prozent, während die Importe aus China „nur" um knapp 20 Prozent zulegten. Die Schere beginnt sich also zu schließen.

Wenn in letzter Zeit der chinesische Außenhandel insgesamt einen deutlich sinkenden Überschuss aufweist, so liegt einer der Gründe dafür in der stark zunehmenden temporären Nachfrage nach hochwertigen Konsumartikeln und technologisch wertvollen Investitionsgütern. Hier liegen die Wachstumschancen.

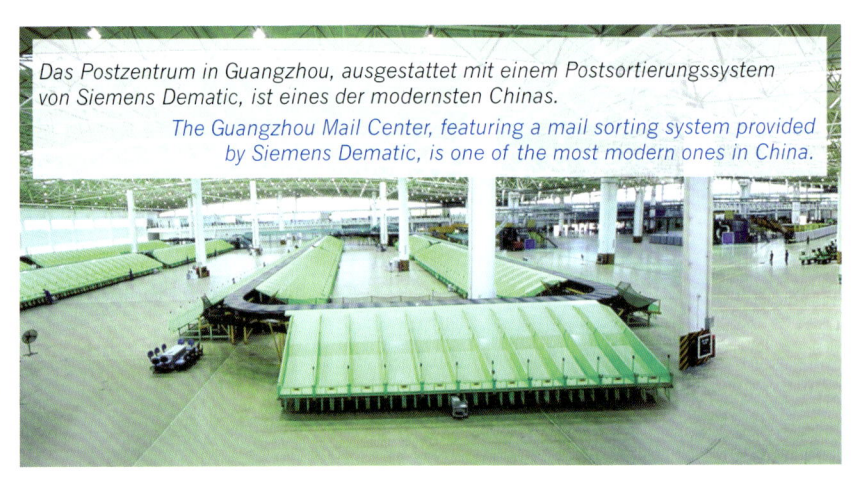

Das Postzentrum in Guangzhou, ausgestattet mit einem Postsortierungssystem von Siemens Dematic, ist eines der modernsten Chinas.
The Guangzhou Mail Center, featuring a mail sorting system provided by Siemens Dematic, is one of the most modern ones in China.

Das Beispiel der Automobilbranche verdeutlicht diesen Aspekt. Hersteller international renommierter Kraftfahrzeuge der Oberklasse nennen häufig die südchinesische Provinz Guangdong als besten Absatzmarkt weltweit. Aber die Nachfrage der sich ständig ausweitenden mittelständischen Käufergruppe (und auch eine in relativen Zahlen vielleicht gering erscheinende Zielgruppe ergibt absolut gesehen im 1,3-Milliarden-Land China eine enorm große Nachfrage) zielt nicht unbedingt auf die Oberklasse, sondern auf solide Fahrzeuge mit gutem Namen. Hier hat sich die VOLKSWAGEN AG frühzeitig und beispielhaft durch ihre Investitionen in Form eines Joint Ventures in Shanghai einen Spitzenplatz gesichert, der durch den ebenfalls zielstrebig vorangetriebenen Aufbau von Produktionskapazitäten durch AUDI in Changchun für die Gruppe ergänzt wurde.

Aber: Deutschland wird wie andere entwickelte Wirtschaften um größere Defizite in der Handelsbilanz nicht herumkommen, wenn China seine eigenen industriellen Kapazitäten weiter vehement ausweitet. Ein Beispiel: ein Fünftel des deutschen Exports nach China entfiel auf Autos und damit verbundene Zulieferungen. Die Investitionen gerade der deutschen Industrie in China, getätigt oder geplant, werden schon bald ein empfindliches Loch in diesen Export reißen.

Erhalt des Technologie- und Managementvorsprungs

Zu den deutschen Investitionen in China gibt es keine sinnvollen Alternativen, vor allem nicht durch Verzicht auf sie oder durch Technologie-Rückhalt. Sie dienen durchaus nicht nur der kostengünstigen Produktion für den lokalen, den heimischen und den Weltmarkt. Es gilt vielmehr, sich durch strategische Investitionen im chinesischen Markt selbst zu positionieren, um regionale wie globale Kompetenz und Marktposition anhaltend abzusichern.

Vor dem Besuch Bundeskanzler Schröders im Dezember 2003 in Peking, Guangzhou und Chengdu sagte der chinesische Außenminister Li Zhaoxing zu den bilateralen Wirtschaftsbeziehungen: „Die Deutschen sind in ihrem Vorgehen klüger als andere!" Nicht nur VOLKSWAGEN hat dies mit seinem Shanghaier Joint Venture, das seit Jahren auf Platz 1 der Bewertungsliste von Unternehmen in China mit ausländischer Beteiligung steht, unter Beweis gestellt. Praktisch alle großen Industrieunternehmen, seien es SIEMENS, THYSSEN-KRUPP, BAYER oder BASF, gehören heute zu den großen Investoren im Land. Hinzu kommen Banken und Versicherungen, Logistik-Unternehmen und Handelshäuser.

Was ist es nun, das deutsches Engagement aus chinesischer Sicht bislang „klüger" erscheinen lässt? Das Chinageschäft braucht langen Atem, die Überwindung kultureller Unterschiede und die Bereitschaft, die chinesischen Partner an Technologie und Know-how teilhaben zu lassen. Diesen Erfordernissen trägt die deutsche Wirtschaft in der Regel in überdurchschnittlicher Weise Rechnung. Die andere Seite des im internationalen Vergleich großzügigen deutschen Technologietransfers ist der wachsende Druck, sich in jeder Phase mit noch besserer Technologie gegen eine chronische „Technologie-Osmose", d. h. Nachahmer und Konkurrenzentwicklungen, zu behaupten. Hinzu kommt, dass China sehr schnell von sich aus eigene Standards, z. B. in der Telekommunikation, setzen und durchzusetzen versuchen wird. Hier muss die deutsche Industrie am Ball bleiben, um mitmachen und mithalten zu können. Dies setzt allerdings voraus, dass wir auch zu Hause „klüger" bleiben, dass der Standort Deutschland zu Spitzenqualität und Innovation nachhaltig fähig bleibt und sich nicht allmählich technologisch und fertigungsmäßig aufgibt mit einer Aussteigeoption, z. B. in China mithalten zu können – durch Verlagerung von Kernentwicklungen und Spitzenfertigungen dorthin. In diesem „worst case"-Szenario wären die Rollen und Gewichte auf beiden Seiten umgekehrt. Um dies zu vermeiden, gilt es, die Dynamik des chinesischen Marktes synergetisch zu

Growth Markets

again in 1997. The treatment of this peculiarity shows the quality of Chinese pragmatism.

Economy in transformation

Since the mid-nineties, growth rates of the GDP have never been below 7 per cent – mostly, markedly higher values were achieved: up to 9.8 per cent in 1996 for instance. Not only the plans of the central government, but also international observers assume that until the year 2020, growth rates of at least 7 per cent can be expected. This is on the one hand corresponding to the necessity that growth of prosperity must be achieved especially in rural areas, which are currently still benefiting below average from the development, and in western and northeastern regions of the country, thereby integrating annually around 15 million additional inhabitants into the economic cycle. On the other hand, the necessary expansion of infrastructure, the partly overdue modernisation of old state-economy enterprises and investments in modern technologies entail a quasi self-induced economic growth.

The People's Republic of China has often been seen as the "workbench of industrial nations" so far. It cannot be dismissed that low wage costs make a relocation of production worthwhile even in the event of lesser productivity. Chinas interest to bring investments into its country in order to acquire know-how and technology and create high-quality workplaces conforms to the interest of European, US-American and other Western companies insofar as they use the comparative cost advantage of China.

There is no cause for concern if one gets the impression that in German department stores and mail order catalogues, in fact in the sector of consumer goods like for instance toys, textiles, tools and simple electrical equipment, "Made in China" is almost in the majority. In principle there is no business that does not bear advantages for both sides. And ultimately the consumer can enjoy the favourable prizes.

If one looks at the bilateral trade balance between Germany and China one must note that it has been active almost traditionally on the Chinese side. In 1992, Germany imported goods worth double as much from China than were supplied from our country to China. However, the total trade volume still had a modest size: it amounted only to just under 9 billion euros. Until the year 2002, this volume quadrupled to just under 36 billion euros and the ratio of German imports from China against the exports to China was already at 21 to 15. We presently experienced an increase of German exports to China of just under 30 per cent, while imports from China "only" rose by just under 20 per cent. So the gap is actually closing.

If in recent times the Chinese export trade generally has shown a markedly declining balance, one of the reasons for this is the strongly increasing temporary demand for high-quality consumer articles and technologically valuable investment goods. This is where there are growth chances.

The example of the automobile branch can clarify this aspect. Producers of internationally re-nowned vehicles of the upper class frequently call the South Chinese province of Guangdong the best sales market worldwide. But the demand of the constantly expanding middle class purchase group (and also a seemingly small target group seen in relative figures results in an enormously great demand seen in absolute figures in a country of 1.3 billions like China) is not particularly geared toward the upper class, but on solid vehicles that have a good reputation. In this respect, the VOLKSWAGEN AG secured its top position early and in an exemplary way through its investments in form of a joint venture in Shanghai, which was subsequently expanded through the ambitiously pursued creation of production capacities for the group by AUDI in Changchung.

However: like other developed economies, Germany cannot avoid larger deficits in the trade balance if China continues to extend vehemently its own industrial capacities further. For example: one fifth of German exports to China can be allotted to automobiles and to pertinent supplies. Soon investments, especially of the German industry in China, planned or carried out already, will tear a serious hole in these exports.

Maintenance of technology and management advantage

There are no reasonable alternatives to Germany making investments in China, particularly not by refraining from doing so or by keeping back technology. They certainly not only serve to obtain inexpensive production for local, domestic and world markets. The issue is actually to position oneself through strategic investments in the Chinese market itself in order to secure sustainably regional as well as global competence and market position. Before Chancellor Schröder visited Peking, Guangzhou and Chengdu in December 2003, the Chinese Foreign Minister Li Zhaoxing said about bilateral trade relations: "The Germans are cleverer than others in their approach!" Not only VOLKSWAGEN has

Die Siemens Transportation Group hat für die Guangzhou U-Bahnlinie Nr. 1 Anlagen geliefert und das gesamte Projektmanagement übernommen.
Siemens Transportation Group provided equipments and total project management for Guangzhou Metro Line No. 1.

proven this with its Shanghai-based joint venture, which has been on rank 1 of the evaluation listing of companies in China with foreign participation for years now. Practically all large industrial corporations, be it SIEMENS, THYSSEN-KRUPP, BAYER or BASF, belong to the large-scale investors in the country today. In addition, there are banks and insurance companies, logistics enterprises and trading companies.

What is it that has made German commitment seemingly "cleverer" so far from a Chinese point of view? Business in China needs a lot of staying power, overcoming cultural differences and the readiness to let Chinese partners participate in technology and know-how. The German economic sector meets these requirements generally in an above-average way. The other coin of the on international comparison generously extensive German technology transfer is the growing pressure to stand one's ground against a chronic "technological osmosis", i.e. imitators and competitive developments, in every phase with even better technology. Additionally, it is obvious that China will try to establish and assert its own standards, e.g. in tele-communications, very quickly. This is where the German industry must keep pace, to be able to participate and to cope with new developments. However, this presumes that we stay "cleverer" also at home, that Germany as a business location keeps a sustainable capacity of producing top quality and innovations and does not gradually opt out by giving up technologically and in terms of production, for instance to keep pace in China – by relocating core developments and top productions to that country. In this "worst case scenario" the roles played and major influences would be inverted on both sides. In order to avoid this it is essential to use the dynamism of the Chinese market synergistically to gain momentum ourselves again. That is the only way we deserve being ascribed the quality, in the long run not only to be "cleverer" but also "faster" in future.

Acting economically – political accompaniment

If today the German TRANSRAPID is only running in Shanghai, the subways of Guangzhou and

Wirtschaftlich handeln – politisch begleiten

Wenn heute der deutsche TRANSRAPID einzig in Shanghai in Betrieb ist, die U-Bahnen von Guangzhou und Shanghai deutsche Technik nutzen und auf dem Pekinger Flughafen die einzige Wartungshalle Asiens steht, in der vier Boeing 747 Jumbos gleichzeitig Platz finden (ein Joint Venture der LUFTHANSA) – diese Reihe von Beispielen ließe sich fortsetzen –, dann beruht dies sowohl auf unternehmerischer Initiative wie auch auf politischer Prioritätensetzung und persönlichem Einsatz der Repräsentanten unseres Landes. Nicht zuletzt sei erwähnt, dass ein Teil der uns in China attestierten „Klugheit" auch in der zielgerichteten deutschen Entwicklungshilfe in China begründet ist. Zwar stehen Armutsbekämpfung und Umweltschutz im Vordergrund. Doch ergeben sich bei der Mehrzahl der Maßnahmen auch Anknüpfungspunkte für geschäftliches Engagement. Im Umweltschutz ist dies der Einsatz erneuerbarer Energieträger – ein Bereich, in dem deutsche Unternehmen führend sind. Beratungsprojekte für chinesische Institutionen bei Reformmaßnahmen der Wirtschaft, in der Berufsausbildung sowie in der Verkehrsplanung sind Beispiele für die Praxisnähe dieser Zusammenarbeit. Zum Beispiel haben bislang 3.000 ehrenamtliche Einsätze des „Senior Experten Service" chinesischen Firmen nicht nur in praktischer Weise mit Rat und Tat gedient; sie haben auch dazu beigetragen, das Verständnis füreinander auf menschlich-persönlicher Basis zu stärken. In diesem Sinne wirken auch Studenten und Wissenschaftler, die das jeweilige Partnerland auf Zeit besuchen und quasi als Spin-off-Effekt Kontakte herstellen, die in ihrer Bedeutung nicht zu unterschätzen sind. So gibt es viele Beispiele großer und mittelständischer deutscher Firmen, die ihren Geschäftserfolg in China früher in Deutschland studierenden Mitarbeitern verdanken.

Die Chancen nutzen – die Risiken sehen

Das wirtschaftliche Potenzial Chinas ist angesichts der prognostizierten 7-prozentigen Wachstumsraten bis zum Jahr 2020 fast unermesslich. Deutsche Unternehmen können diese Chancen nutzen, wenn die Rahmenbedingungen beachtet werden. Natürlich gibt es auf deutscher Seite auch Befürchtungen der einen oder anderen Art wie z. B. des Wegfalls von Investitionen und Forschung in Deutschland selbst, der Verlagerung von Arbeitsplätzen oder des damit verbundenen Ausfalls von Steuern. Dagegen sind die Vorteile für viele weniger sichtbar, aber bei genauerer Betrachtung bedeutend. Sie ergeben sich aus der „ecomomy of scale" und aus den strategischen Chancen, gemeinsam auf dem globalen Markt zu agieren.

Auch in dieser Hinsicht stellt das Wachstumsland China für uns eine Chance dar. Weder Handel noch Investitionen sind auf Dauer eine Einbahnstraße. Die deutsche Wirtschaft und die Bundesregierung haben China frühzeitig diejenige Aufmerksamkeit gewidmet, die diesem Land zusteht. Es sollte alles daran gesetzt werden, den erworbenen Startvorteil, das erarbeitete Vertrauen und die vorhandenen Strukturen im beiderseitigen Interesse weiter auszubauen und zu nutzen. Wie weitreichend die Auswirkungen der Reform- und Öffnungspolitik der Volksrepublik inzwischen sind, ist schließlich auch mit Blick auf den Investitionsstandort Deutschland zu erkennen. Erste Übernahmen deutscher Firmen durch chinesische Investoren haben stattgefunden: Prominent zu nennen ist das Elektronikunternehmen SCHNEIDER. Weitere Akquisitionen stehen an. Auch hier liegt die Chance für die deutsche Wirtschaft in der Kooperation, am Standort Deutschland. Mit einer weiteren Stabilisierung des chinesischen Bankensektors, aber auch mittels der Bereitschaft deutscher Finanzhäuser, in das Obligo zu treten, zeichnet sich das Interesse potenter chinesischer Firmen immer deutlicher ab, eine Positionierung auf dem europäischen Markt vorzunehmen. Die Nähe der Bundesrepublik zu den Ländern Ost- und Mitteleuropas ist hier eindeutig ein Vorteil. Punktuelle komparative Nachteile wie z. B. eine Vielzahl von Vorschriften und Verordnungen sowie der Lohnkosteneffekt, der nachteilig erscheinen könnte, werden mehr als ausgeglichen durch die Stärken unseres Landes, die aus chinesischer Sicht noch hoch geschätzt werden: Stabilität, Effizienz und Innovations- bzw. Reformfähigkeit.

Die Beschäftigung mit China erlaubt uns nicht zuletzt den notwendigen Blick über unseren eigenen Tellerrand hinaus. Die Dynamik und Innovationsfähigkeit in China setzen fordernde Maßstäbe, an denen sich künftig der Rest der Welt wird orientieren müssen. ∎

Die meisten großen deutschen Industrieunternehmen investieren in China.

Most large German industrial corporations invest in China.

Growth Markets

Der TRANSRAPID, hier auf der Versuchsstrecke im Emsland, wirbt in Shanghai für deutsche Qualitätsarbeit.

The TRANSRAPID, here on testing tracks in the Emsland region, advertises German quality work in Shanghai.

Shanghai use German technology and Asia's only hangar that has space for the maintenance of four Boeing 747 Jumbos at the same time is on Peking Airport (a joint venture of LUFTHANSA) – and one could continue this series of examples – then this is certainly due both to entrepreneurial initiative as well as to the setting of political priorities and personal commitment of the representatives of our country.

Last but not least it should be mentioned that we owe part of the "cleverness" attested by China also to the specifically targeted German development aid provided to China. It is true that fighting poverty and environmental protection are major issues. However, during the majority of programmes conducted also links for commercial engagements emerge. In the field of environmental protection, it is the use of renewable energy sources – a field, in which German companies are world leaders. Consulting projects for Chinese institutions carrying out reform measures for the economic sector, for vocational education and for transport planning are some examples of the practical application of this cooperation. For instance, 3,000 voluntary assignments of the "Senior Expert Service" have served Chinese firms not only in a practical way in word and deed; they have also played a major role in strengthening the mutual understand for each other on a humane and personal basis. In this sense also students and scientists are working who visit their relevant partner country for a limited period and establish contacts so to speak as spin-off effect, the significance of which should not be underestimated. In fact there are many examples of large and medium-size German companies that owe their business success in China to formerly in Germany studying employees.

Using the chances – seeing the risks

Given the forecast of 7 per cent growth rates until the year 2020, China's economic potential is almost unlimited. German companies can utilize these chances if frame conditions are observed. Of course there are fears on the German side of one or the other kind, like for instance the loss of investments and research in Germany itself, the relocation of workplaces or the loss of taxes linked with it. In contrast, the advantages are less visible for many, but on closer consideration they are significant. They result from an "economy of scale" and from the strategic chances of acting jointly on global markets. China, the growth country, presents a chance for us also in this respect. Neither trade nor investments are a one-way road in the long run. The German economy and the Federal Government have dedicated that kind of attention to China early in time which the country deserves. Every effort should be made to expand and to use the initial advantage gained, the confidence won and existing structures in reciprocal interest further.

Just how extensive the effects of the policy of reform and openness of the People's Republic are mean- while, can be seen also with view of Germany as investment location. The first takeovers of German firms by Chinese investors have taken place: the most prominent case worth mentioning is the electronics enterprise SCHNEIDER. Further acquisitions are imminent. Also in this case there is a chance for the German economy to be active in co-operation at the business location of Germany. The interest of potent Chinese firms to position themselves on the European market has become ever more noticeable. It is conveyed through the further stabilisation of the Chinese banking sector, but also by means of the preparedness of German finance companies to assume guarantees. The Federal Republic's proximity to the countries of East and Central Europe is a clear advantage in this respect. Comparative and selective disadvantages like for instance the great number of rules and regulations as well as the effect of wage costs, which could seem disadvantageous, will be more than balanced out because of the strengths our country has. Indeed, from a Chinese point of view they are still highly valued: stability, efficiency and capacity of innovation and reform.

Dealing with China ultimately allows us to have the necessary overview beyond our own limits. Dynamism and capacity of innovation in China set demanding standards to which the rest of the world will have to orient itself in future. ∎

Company Profile

Lösungen für alle Probleme des Haftklebens

Solutions for all problems of adhesive bonding

Lohmann GmbH & Co. KG

Geschäftsführer/Managing Directors:
Herr Jürgen Walda
Herr Manfred Meier

Gründungsjahr/Year of Foundation: 1851

Mitarbeiter weltweit/Employees worldwide: 1.000

Umsatz/Turnover: 175 Mio. €

Geschäftsfelder/Business Fields:
Klebebandsysteme für Hygiene-Produkte, Mobile Communication und Technische Produkte (insbesondere Automobilindustrie, Bauindustrie, Sport- und Elektronikindustrie, Papierherstellung und Papierweiterverarbeitung sowie flexographischer Verpackungsdruck)
Adhesive tapes systems for hygiene products, mobile communication and technical products (particularly for the automotive industry, building industry, sports and electronics industry, paper production and paper processing as well as flexographic printing for packaging)

Anschrift/Address:
Postfach 1454
56504 Neuwied

Irlicher Straße 55
56567 Neuwied

Telefon   +49 (2631) 34 – 0
Telefax   +49 (2631) 34 – 6661
E-Mail   Info@lohmann-tapes.com
Internet   www.lohmann-tapes.com

Die Lohmann GmbH & Co. KG – ein Unternehmen mit mehr als 150 Jahren Geschichte – ist ein moderner Hersteller von doppelseitigen Klebebändern für eine Vielzahl von Anwendungen. Gemeinsam mit den Unternehmen Metafol in Remscheid und Koester in Altendorf bildet Lohmann die Klebebandgruppe mit den Geschäftsfeldern Technische Produkte, Hygiene und Mobile Communication.

Zu den Kunden in den genannten Geschäftsfeldern zählen Unternehmen aus der Automobil-, Druck-, Möbel- oder Bauindustrie, Hersteller von Hygieneprodukten aller Art und eine Vielzahl von Herstellern aus der Mobiltelefonindustrie. Insbesondere der Geschäftsbereich Mobile Communication ist der bedeutende Technologieträger der Klebebandgruppe. Geometrisch genaue Stanzteile, die aus vielen Einzelteilen bestehen können, halten z. B. das Display am richtigen Platz oder schützen die empfindliche Elektronik.

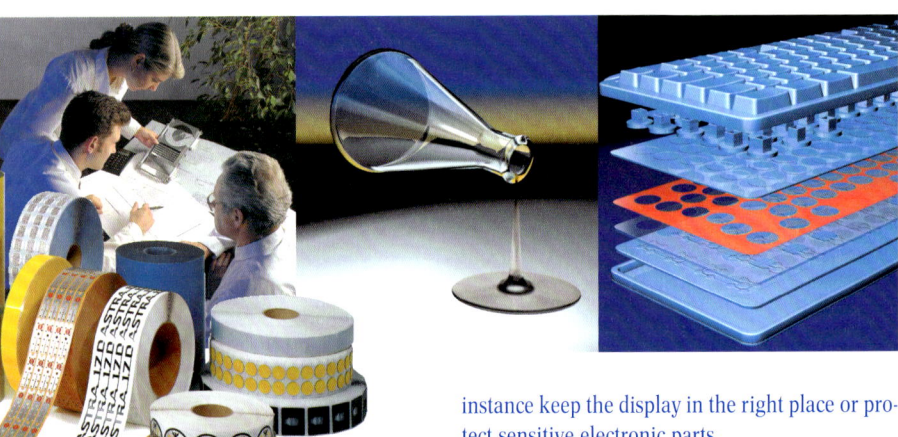

Mit Tochtergesellschaften in Europa, den USA und China sowie einem exklusiven Vertriebspartnernetz ist die Lohmann-Klebebandgruppe ein weltweit operierender Konzern, der seine Produkte in allen Märkten mit gleichbleibend hoher Qualität anbietet. Durch die Breite der eingesetzten Klebstoffsysteme (Kautschuk, Synthesekautschuk, Acrylat und Hotmelt) und die Tiefe der Verarbeitungsschritte (Polymerisation/Formulierung, Beschichtung, Konfektion und Stanzen) ist die Klebebandgruppe in der Lage, Lösungen für alle Probleme des Haftklebens anzubieten. ■

As a company with a longstanding history of more than 150 years, Lohmann GmbH & Co. KG is a modern producer of double-sided adhesive tapes for a great number of applications. Together with the companies Metafol of Remscheid and Koester of Altendorf, Lohmann is part of the Adhesive Tapes Group covering the business fields: technical products, hygiene and mobile communication.

Among the clients of the above mentioned business fields are companies from the automotive, printing, furniture or building industries as well as manufacturers of all kinds of hygiene products and a series of producers from the mobile phone industry.

Particularly the business field of mobile communication is a major technological pillar of the Adhesive Tapes Group. Precise geometric die cuts which can consist of many single components, for instance keep the display in the right place or protect sensitive electronic parts.

In cooperation with subsidiaries in Europe, the USA and China as well as with a network of exclusive sales partners the Lohmann Adhesive Tapes Group is a globally operating corporation that offers its products on all markets with a constantly high quality standard. Because of the wide range of application provided by its adhesive systems (rubber, synthetic rubber, acrylate and hotmelt glue) as well as the depth of its processing steps (polymerisation/formulation, coating, fabrication and pressing), the Adhesive Tapes Group is in a position to offer solutions for all problems of adhesive bonding. ■

Company Profile

Innovativer Partner der Automobilindustrie

BorgWarner Transmission Systems GmbH in Heidelberg – Spezialist für Komponenten und Systeme im weltweiten Getriebemarkt

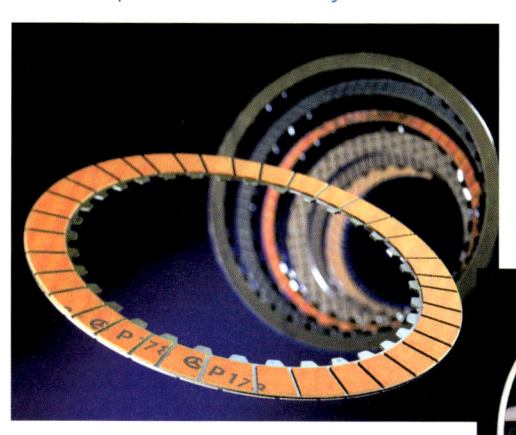

Links: Kupplungslamellen.
Unten: Freiläufe.

Wann immer in einem Fahrzeug die Getriebe-Automatik butterweich von einem Gang in den anderen schaltet, darf man sicher sein, dass Komponenten oder Systeme von BorgWarner Transmission Systems bei diesem Vorgang mitspielen. Der Antriebsspezialist gehört zum internationalen BorgWarner-Konzern und ist Weltmarktführer für die Produktion von Komponenten und Systemen für Automatikgetriebe. Kunden sind alle namhaften Hersteller – ob Automobilproduzent oder Getriebespezialist.

Stärke und Kompetenz bezieht das Werk in Heidelberg durch die Einbindung in die Transmission-Systems-Gruppe, eine der sechs Gruppen innerhalb des Konzerns. Die globale Vernetzung öffnet das Tor zum Weltmarkt und ermöglicht innovative Produkte durch schnellen Know-how-Transfer und unmittelbaren Zugriff auf Forschung und Entwicklung in konzerneigenen Technologiezentren.

Während im amerikanischen und japanischen Fahrzeugmarkt Automatikgetriebe dominieren, bietet Europa dem Unternehmen durch den noch relativ geringen Anteil an Automatikgetrieben hohe Wachstumspotenziale. BorgWarner Transmission Systems nutzt die Chancen in diesem wachstumsintensiven Bereich durch den strategischen Wandel vom klassischen Komponenten- zum kompetenten Systemhersteller, durch die Entwicklung innovativer Produkte und die Erschließung neuer Märkte. Beispiele:
- Neuartige Anfahrsysteme für noch wirtschaftlichere, kostengünstigere und komfortablere Automatikgetriebe. Zielgruppe: die traditionelle Klientel.
- Spezielle Systeme, die in herkömmlichen Handschaltgetrieben automatisches Schalten erlauben.

Diese Doppelkupplungsgetriebe sind kleiner, leichter und kostengünstiger als bisherige Automatikgetriebe. Zielgruppe: das in Europa starke Segment „handgeschalteter" Kompaktautos.

Innovation dient der Standort- und Arbeitsplatzsicherung und ist Basis des Erfolgs, verbunden mit hohem Qualitätsbewusstsein, Flexibilität, kontinuierlicher Produktverbesserung, Teamarbeit und optimaler Kundenbetreuung. Qualitätsmanagementsysteme nach TS 16949 (Qualitätsnorm der Deutschen Automobilindustrie) wurden vor Jahren etabliert und werden erfolgreich weitergeführt. Hohe Investitionen fließen in umweltschonende Produktionsabläufe.

Zukunftssicherung sieht das Unternehmen nicht nur in technischer Innovation, sondern auch in der Entwicklung der Mitarbeiter, insbesondere ihrer Weiterbildung im ständigen Verbesserungsprozess. Dazu gehört neben den umfangreichen Qualifikationsprogrammen ein weiterer Ausbau der Ausbildungsplätze.

Der Erfolg des Unternehmens spiegelt sich in signifikanten Umsatzsteigerungen der letzten Jahre, aber vor allem auch in der Schaffung neuer Arbeitsplätze. ∎

BorgWarner Transmission Systems

BorgWarner Transmission Systems GmbH

Geschäftsführer:
Dr. Bernd Matthes
Dan Paterra
Regis Trenda

Mitarbeiter:
- BorgWarner
  14.300 Mitarbeiter weltweit
  43 Produktionswerke in 14 Ländern
  6 Gruppen
- Transmission-Systems-Gruppe
  4.000 Mitarbeiter
  11 Produktionswerke in 4 Ländern
- Werke Heidelberg, Ketsch, Arnstadt
  600 Mitarbeiter

Kernprodukte:
- Reibelemente,
- Kupplungssysteme,
- Freiläufe,
- Freilaufsysteme,
- Wandlerüberbrückungskupplungen,
- Torsionsschwingungsdämpfer

Umsatz:
Konzern
3,1 Mrd. $

Anschrift:
Kurpfalzring
D-69123 Heidelberg
Telefon +49 (6221) 7 08-0
Telefax +49 (6221) 7 08-1 99
Internet www.bwauto.com

Energiewirtschaft

Mit Energie Zukunft gestalten

Shaping the future with power

Innovation ist zum Schlüsselbegriff der globalisierten Welt geworden. Nur durch das Beschreiten neuer Wege können Menschen und Unternehmen dem fundamentalen Strukturwandel weltweit und damit auch in Deutschland Rechnung tragen. Innovation ist auch immer mit Wagnis verbunden. In diesem Prozess müssen sowohl Gesellschaft als auch Unternehmen bereit sein, gewohnte Pfade zu verlassen und einen Schritt hin zur Nonkonformität zu riskieren.

Die Politik ist angehalten, durch die Bereitstellung der geeigneten Rahmenbedingungen Deutschland zu einem zukunftsfähigen, attraktiven Wirtschaftsstandort zu machen. Vergangenheitsorientierte Subventionen sollten in zukunftsweisende Investitionen überführt werden. Um Wohlstand und Beschäftigung in Deutschland zu erhalten, ist zudem eine offensive Erneuerungsdebatte unumgänglich, ja vielleicht der einzige Weg, um Deutschland aus seiner vermeintlichen „Krise" (auf hohem Niveau!) zu befreien.

Innovation geht vom Menschen aus. Die menschliche Kompetenz bildet einen entscheidenden Grundpfeiler, um Innovation erfolgreich zu gestalten und zu realisieren. Die Investition in Forschung und Entwicklung, die Förderung des menschlichen Potenzials ist daher notwendige Bedingung für einen effektiven Innovationsprozess. Erfolgversprechende Inventionen dürfen dabei nicht unerkannt bleiben, sondern müssen in innovative Produkte überführt werden.

Der Energiewirtschaft kommt in diesem Prozess eine Schlüsselrolle zu. Energie ist mehr als nur Strom aus der Steckdose – sie ist Voraussetzung für die Funktionsweise der essenziellen Bereiche unseres Lebens, sie ist Garant für die Erhaltung unseres Lebensstandards. Energie sichert Wohlstand und ermöglicht nachhaltiges Wirtschaften. Die wirtschaftliche und strukturelle Entwicklung unserer Volkswirtschaft ist in erheblichem Maße von Energiewirtschaft und Energiepolitik abhängig. Werden die Innovationspotenziale der Energiewirtschaft konsequent genutzt, kann dies einen großen positiven Einfluss auf die zukünftige Verfügbarkeit und Sicherheit von Energie, auf die wirtschaftliche Entwicklung des Landes und auf die Lebensqualität seiner Bewohner entfalten. Deutschland hat das Fachwissen, um auf diesem Sektor eine Vorreiterrolle in Europa, ja sogar weltweit einzunehmen.

Die spezifischen Rahmenbedingungen Deutschlands vergrößern die Notwendigkeit einer innovativen Energiewirtschaft. Mit rund 25 Prozent des europäischen Stromverbrauchs weisen wir einen hohen absoluten Energieverbrauch auf und nehmen damit eine bedeutsame wirtschaftliche Rolle in Europa ein. Ferner ist Deutschland zu einem hohen Grad exportabhängig, verzeichnet jedoch parallel dazu einen wachsenden Energie- und Rohstoffimport.

Erneuerung und Umstrukturierung kennzeichnen heute die Energielandschaft Deutschlands. Schnelle Veränderungsprozesse führten die Energiebranche in kürzester Zeit zu gewaltigen Herausforderungen. Herausforderungen, die neue Wege öffnen: Sie müssen entdeckt und mit einem tiefgreifenden Erneuerungs- und Innovationsschub bewältigt werden. Sinnvoll kann eine Diskussion über Innovation und Zukunft von Energie jedoch nur im gesellschaftlichen Kontext geführt werden. Um eine bestmögliche Ausschöpfung des innovatorischen Potenzials zu erreichen, ist eine anhaltende, vertiefte Kooperation von Wissenschaft, Wirtschaft, Politik und Medien unumgänglich. Gefordert ist ein leistungsfähiges Innovationssystem auf kooperativer Basis, frei von Partikularinteressen und einseitigen Ideologien. Sein Profil und seine Stärke kann ein derartiges Innovationssystem erst in einem länger bemessenen Zeitraum entfalten. In diesem Zeitraum müssen jedoch sowohl unmittelbare als auch mittel- sowie langfristig orientierte Innovationsvorhaben vorgeschlagen, geplant und durchgeführt werden.

Für die Implementierung einer offensiven Innovationspolitik sind die nächsten Jahre günstig. Wir als Energieversorgungsunternehmen sind gefordert, Deutschland sicher, nachhaltig und kostengünstig mit Energie zu versorgen. Neben den drei Grundparametern für die Zukunft der Energie – Versorgungssicherheit, Wirtschaftlichkeit sowie Nachhaltigkeit – hat sich die EnBW Energie Baden-Württemberg AG die Erhöhung ihrer Innovationsfähigkeit auf verschiedenen Feldern zum Ziel gesetzt. Dabei stehen wir vor der zentralen Aufgabe,

Prof. Dr. Utz Claassen

Der Autor, geboren 1963 in Hannover, ist seit 2003 Vorsitzender des Vorstandes EnBW Energie Baden-Württemberg AG, Karlsruhe. 1985 Abschluss als Diplom-Ökonom an der Universität Hannover, 1985–1987 Michael Wills Scholar am Magdalen College, University of Oxford; Forschungstätigkeit am Templeton College, The Oxford Centre for Management Studies, 1987–1989 McKinsey & Co., Düsseldorf, 1989 Promotion an der Universität Hannover, 1989–1992 Ford Europa, verschiedene leitende Positionen, 1992–1994 Volkswagen AG, zuletzt als Bereichsleiter Controlling Produktlinien, 1994–1997 SEAT S.A., Barcelona, Finanzvorstand und Vertreter des Präsidenten, 1997–2003 Sartorius AG, Göttingen. 2001 Bestellung zum Honorarprofessor an der Universität Hannover

The author was born in Hanover in 1963 and is chairman of the executive board of EnBW Energie Baden-Württemberg AG, Karlsruhe. He graduated as certified economist from the University of Hanover; from 1985–87 he was scholar of Michael Will at Magdalen College, University of Oxford; research assignments at Templeton College, The Oxford Centre for Management Studies followed; he joined McKinsey & Co., Düsseldorf from 1987–89; attained his PhD from the Univ. of Hanover in 1989; worked for Ford Europe in several management positions from 1989–92; for Volkswagen AG from 1992–94 his last position being head of the Division of Controlling – Product lines; from 1994–97 he served as Vice President and Corporate Treasurer for SEAT S.A., Barcelona; worked for Sartorius AG, Göttingen from 1997 – 2003. In 2001 he was appointed honorary professor at Univ. of Hanover.

Energy Industry

Innovation has become a keyword in a globalised world. Only by treading new paths can people and companies meet the fundamental structural change taking place worldwide and therefore also in Germany. Innovation is always linked with risks, too. In this process, both society and enterprises must be prepared to leave the usual paths and risk a step forward towards non-conformity.

Political circles are obliged to make Germany into an attractive, promising business location by providing appropriate frame conditions. Subsidies informed by the past should be turned into future-oriented investments. In order to maintain prosperity and employment in Germany, it is moreover indispensable to start an offensive debate about a new orientation, indeed it may be the only way to liberate Germany from its supposed "crisis" (on high level!).

Innovations come from people. Human competence constitutes a significant cornerstone to create and realise innovations successfully. Investment in research and development and the promotion of human potentials are therefore necessary requirements for an effective process of innovation. Promising inventions must not be left unnoticed, but must be converted into innovative products.

In this process the energy industry plays a major role. Energy is more than power coming out of the socket, it is a prerequisite for the functionality of essential areas of our life, and it is a guarantee for the maintenance of our living standards. Energy ensures prosperity and enables sustainable economic operation. The economic and structural development of our national economy depends to a considerable extent on energy industry and energy politics. If innovation potentials in energy industry are consistently utilised this can have a tremendously positive effect on the future availability and safety of energy, on the country's economic development and on the quality of life of its population. Germany possesses the expert knowledge to play a leading role in this sector in Europe, in fact even globally.

Germany's specific frame conditions increase the necessity of an innovative energy industry. With about 25 per cent of overall European electricity consumption, we have extremely high absolute energy consumption and therefore occupy a significant economic role in Europe. Furthermore, Germany depends on exports to a high degree, but in parallel it registers growth in energy and raw material import.

New orientation and restructuring distinguish the energy landscape in Germany today. Fast processes of change confronted the energy branch with enormous challenges in the shortest of time. Challenges that open up new ways: they need to be discovered and dealt with in a deep and dynamic impulse of new orientation and innovation. A sensible discussion about innovation and the future of energy can however only take place in a social context. For the best possible exploitation of innovatory potentials a lasting, profound cooperation of science, industry and commerce, politics and the media is crucial. What is required is an efficient system of innovation on collaborative basis, free of particular interests and one-sided ideologies. Such a system of innovations can only display its profile and strengths within a prolonged period. However, within this period both direct as well as mid- and long-term oriented innovation projects must be proposed, planned and executed.

The coming years are favourable for implementing an offensive innovation policy. We, as energy supply company, are required to supply Germany in a safe, sustainable and inexpensive way with energy. Besides the three basic parameters for the future of energy: supply safety, economic efficiency as well as sustainability, EnBW Energie Baden-Württemberg AG aims at increasing its capacity of innovation in several fields. In this respect we are faced with the central task to bring in line political demands with at first partly contrary expectations and wishes of clients. A task that requires a lot of creativity and flexibility, but is not impossible to achieve. Overcoming (seeming) contradictions will be one of our major tasks in future. To turn polarisation into integrative approaches may therefore be an important innovative achievement per se.

The liberalisation of the energy market demands the creation of new frame conditions, in order to strengthen the investment location Germany also in the long run. Industry and the jobs that depend on it rely to a great extent on safe, inexpensive energy supply. Their competitiveness rises and falls along with the costs of energy, overpriced energy costs may lead to relocating production into foreign countries and therefore to loss of workplaces. It is therefore vital to increase energy efficiency. It affects investment decisions directly.

There is also an acute need for action because the German power station park is facing a complete renovation. As agreed by the federal government and energy suppliers, phasing out of nuclear energy demands a drastic redistribution of existing energy mixes. In this connection, is also intended to reduce the presently high dependency on fossil fuels and to increase the percentage rate of regenerative energy sources. But also in this respect questions of availability and economic efficiency and ecological sustainability arise. The fact is that ecology and economy do not necessarily contradict each other, and indeed they should not. The coordination of future energy mixes is one of the significant issues for the coming decades. It is imperative to build a bridge between conventional energy production on the one hand and the use of regenerative energy sources on the other. EnBW is already playing a pioneering role in the field of renewable energies today. Primarily it is relying on the regional strengths of Baden-Württemberg: its "enormous waterpower", the use of biomass energy and also on geothermal energy in the long run. Technologies that are also extremely suitable for use in the base load range.

The global development of climate and the foreseeable enormous economic development in countries like China demonstrate clearly the pressure that exists for action in terms of creating an effective climate protection. Successful climate protection goes along with efficient and sustainable energy supply. The emission trading guideline of the EU is a clear directive, and its application is closely connected with significant effects on the structure of power stations and energy sources. Transferring the generation of energy away from large power stations to smaller power stations operated in a decentred way is partly regarded as a measure to reduce the

Die Konzernzentrale der EnBW Energie Baden-Württemberg AG in Karlsruhe.

Headquarters of the group EnBW Energie Baden-Württemberg AG in Karlsruhe.

Energiewirtschaft

politische Vorgaben mit den zunächst teilweise konträren Erwartungen und Wünschen der Kunden in Einklang zu bringen. Ein Auftrag, der viel Kreativität und Flexibilität erfordert, jedoch nicht unmöglich ist. Die Überwindung von (scheinbaren) Widersprüchen wird eine unserer wichtigsten Zukunftsaufgaben sein. Die Überführung von Polarisierung in integrative Ansätze kann dabei an sich schon eine wichtige innovatorische Leistung sein.

Die Liberalisierung des Energiemarktes verlangt die Schaffung neuer Rahmenbedingungen, um den Investitionsstandort Deutschland auch langfristig zu stärken. Die Industrie und die davon abhängigen Arbeitsplätze sind in hohem Maße auf eine sichere, günstige Energieversorgung angewiesen. Ihre Wettbewerbsfähigkeit steht und fällt mit den Energiekosten – zu hohe Energiekosten führen unter Umständen zur Verlagerung der Produktion ins Ausland und somit zu Arbeitsplatzverlusten. Eine Erhöhung der Energieeffizienz ist daher unerlässlich. Sie wirkt sich unmittelbar auf Investitionsentscheidungen aus.

Akuter Handlungsbedarf besteht auch, weil der deutsche Kraftwerkspark vor einer umfassenden Erneuerung steht. Der von Bundesregierung und Energieversorgern beschlossene Ausstieg aus der Atomenergie erfordert eine dramatische Umverteilung des bisherigen Energiemixes. Dabei soll auch die derzeit hohe Abhängigkeit von fossilen Brennstoffen reduziert und der prozentuale Anteil an regenerativen Energiequellen erhöht werden. Doch auch hier entstehen Fragen nach Verfügbarkeit, Wirtschaftlichkeit und Umweltverträglichkeit. Fakt ist, dass Ökologie und Ökonomie nicht im Widerspruch zueinander stehen müssen, ja nicht einmal dürfen. Die Gestaltung des zukünftigen Energiemixes ist eine der wesentlichen Fragen der nächsten Jahrzehnte. Es gilt, eine Brücke zu schlagen zwischen konventioneller Energieerzeugung einerseits und dem Einsatz von regenerativen Energiequellen andererseits. Schon heute nimmt die EnBW auf dem Gebiet der erneuerbaren Energien eine Vorreiterrolle ein. Sie setzt vor allem auf die regionalen Stärken Baden-Württembergs: die „große Wasserkraft", die Biomassenutzung und langfristig auch auf die Geothermie. Techniken, die sich auch für den Einsatz im Grundlastbereich sehr gut eignen.

Die weltweite klimatische Entwicklung und die absehbare gewaltige wirtschaftliche Entwicklung in Ländern wie China verdeutlichen den Handlungsdruck, Klimaschutz effektiv zu gestalten. Erfolgreicher Klimaschutz geht einher mit effizienter und nachhaltiger Energieversorgung. Die EU-Emissionshandelsrichtlinie ist eine klare Direktive, und ihre Umsetzung ist mit deutlichen Auswirkungen auf die Struktur von Kraftwerken und Energieträgern verbunden. Die Verlagerung der Energiegewinnung weg von Großkraftwerken hin zu kleineren dezentral betriebenen Kraftwerken wird teilweise als ein Schritt gesehen, um den Verbrauch fossiler Energiequellen und somit den CO_2-Ausstoß zu verringern. Hohe Priorität hat die Effizienzsteigerung von bewährten Kraftwerkstechnologien. Klar ist, dass die Umsetzung nationaler Klimaschutzprogramme nur im internationalen Kontext sinnvoll zu verwirklichen ist.

Vor diesem Hintergrund zeichnet sich eine drastische Veränderung der Energieversorgungslage in den nächsten Jahren ab. In Vorbereitung auf dieses Szenario – die Energiepreise werden sich womöglich deutlich erhöhen – ist es notwendig, auch Energieeinsparungspotenziale auszuschöpfen. Um die Energieeffizienz zu steigern, sind neue Instrumente erforderlich. Innovative Prozesse, Technologien, Strukturen und Dienstleistungen wirken sich dabei positiv aus – sowohl auf die Wettbewerbsfähigkeit der Unternehmen, als auch auf die Exportfähigkeit unserer Volkswirtschaft und den ökologischen Zustand unserer Erde. Ein deutliches Engagement in diesem Bereich wird aber auch schon kurzfristig positive Effekte aufzeigen.

Gerade auf dem Gebiet der Gebäudemodernisierung bieten sich schnell realisierbare, immense Einsparpotenziale. Derzeit werden in Deutschland ca. 30 Prozent des Primärenergieverbrauchs für die Gebäudeenergieversorgung (Wärme/Kälte, Strom) genutzt. Intelligenter Wärmeschutz und moderne Heiztechniken bei Neubau und Sanierung können perspektivisch ca. 80 Prozent des entsprechenden Energiebedarfes einsparen. Zudem versprechen die Komponenten und Systemlösungen eine hohe Rentabilität der Ersatzinvestitionen und ein sehr gutes Exportpotenzial.

Mittelfristig ergeben sich vor allem zwei Aufgaben: Zum einen geht es darum, relevante dezentrale Stromerzeugungstechnologien optimal zu steuern und die bisher ungenutzten Effizienz- und Speichermöglichkeiten strom- und wärmeseitig im Bereich dieser verteilten Energieerzeugung zu realisieren. Der Aufbau eines Leitsystems für das Systemmanagement ist dabei zentral für eine effiziente und umweltfreundliche Energieanwendung. Zudem versprechen seine Komponenten – innovative Leistungselektronik, Kommunikations- und Regelungstechnik sowie dynamische Netze – und das bei ihrer Entwicklung und Implementierung aufgebaute Know-how hohes Exportpotenzial.

Zum anderen müssen im bestehenden Kraftwerksbestand alle Möglichkeiten zur Steigerung der Effizienz, Zuverlässigkeit und Wirtschaftlichkeit ausgeschöpft werden. Es geht dabei um die Entwicklung und Errichtung der „Kraftwerksgeneration von morgen" in Deutschland. Und damit verbunden auch um die weitere Steigerung der Exportfähigkeit deutscher Energietechnologien und die Stärkung des Industriestandorts insgesamt. Zudem ist mit der Effizienzsteigerung im Kraftwerkspark eine starke und sofortige CO_2-Minderung realisierbar.

Deutschland hat eine sehr leistungsfähige Energiewirtschaft und eine ebenso starke Branche der verschiedenen Kraftwerkstechnologien und verwandten Industrien. Zudem hat Deutschland konstruktiv-kritische Kunden und Verbraucher, verschiedene moderne Politikansätze sowie eine exzellente wirtschaftliche Basis. Wenn die entsprechende Vernetzung gelingt, muss es möglich sein, mit Energie Zukunft so zu gestalten, dass Kunden und Aktionäre, Bürger und Politiker, Wirtschaftsforscher und Umweltschützer gleichermaßen Freude haben. ■

Die EnBW setzt vor allem auf die regionalen Stärken Baden-Württembergs: die „große Wasserkraft", die Biomassenutzung und langfristig auch auf die Geothermie. Foto: das Wasserkraftwerk in Iffezheim.

Energy Industry

Hohe Priorität hat die Effizienzsteigerung von bewährten Kraftwerkstechnologien, hier das Kraftwerk Altbach (Kohle, Gas).

To increase the efficiency of proven power station technologies is of high priority, here the Altbach power station (coal, gas).

EnBW relies above all on the regional strengths of Baden-Württemberg: its "enormous waterpower", the use of biomass energy and also on geothermal energy in the long run. Photo: Hydroelectric power station in Iffezheim.

consumption of fossil energy sources and therefore to reduce CO_2 emission. It is of high priority to increase the efficiency of proven power station technologies. It is obvious that the realisation of national climate protection programmes can only be accomplished reasonably within an international context.

Against this background, a dramatic change of the energy supply situation becomes apparent for the coming years. To prepare for this scenario, energy prices will probably increase significantly, it is also necessary to exploit all possible energy saving potentials. A positive effect will have innovative processes, technologies, structure and services in this respect, both on the competitiveness of enterprises and on the export capacity of our national economy and the ecological condition of our earth. A clear commitment in this field will however show positive effects also in the short term.

Particularly in the area of modernising buildings, immense savings potentials are available that can be realised rapidly. Presently, approx. 30 per cent of primary energy consumption in Germany is used for supplying energy to buildings (heat/cooling, electricity). Intelligent heat protection and modern heating technologies for new buildings and renovations prospectively can save approx. 80 per cent of the relevant energy requirement. Moreover, components and system solutions promise high profitability of replacement investment and excellent export potentials.

Primarily, in the mid-term two tasks arise: on the one hand, the issue is to control relevant decentred electricity generation technologies in an ideal way and to realise hitherto unused alternatives of efficiency and storing electricity and heating in the field of this distributed energy production. Creating an overall conduction system for system management is crucial in this regard to ensure the efficient and environmentally safe application of energy. Its components – innovative power electronics, communications and control technologies as well as dynamic networks – and the know-how built up during their development and implementation also promise a high export potential.

On the other hand, in the existing stock of power stations all possibilities of increasing efficiency, reliability and profitability must be exploited. Priority is given here to developing and establishing "tomorrow's power station generation" in Germany. And connected with it is also the further increase of the export capacity of German energy technologies and strengthening the industrial business location on the whole. Moreover, by increasing the efficiency in the park of power stations, a strong and immediate reduction of CO_2 becomes realisable.

Germany possesses an extremely efficient energy industry and an equally strong branch of different power station technologies and related industries. Furthermore, Germany has constructive-critical clients and consumers, several modern political approaches as well as an excellent economic basis. If it is succeeded to accomplish the corresponding networking, it must be possible to shape the future with energy in such way that customers and shareholders, citizens and politicians, economic researchers and environmentalists are equally satisfied.

Company Profile

EECH – European Energy Consult Holding AG

Vorstand/Executive Board:
Ing.(grad.) Tarik Ersin Yoleri
(Vorstandsvorsitzender/
Chairman of the Executive Board)
Dipl.-Kfm. Björn Hörner, Michael Bode

Gründungsjahr/Year of Foundation:
2001

Mitarbeiter/Employees:
131

Geschäftstätigkeit/Business Activity:
Akquisition, Entwicklung, Finanzierung und Vermarktung im Bereich der Erneuerbaren Energien; Beteiligungsprodukte
Acquisition, development, financing and sales and marketing of renewable energies, shareholding products

Anschrift/Address:
Pöseldorfer Weg 36
D-20149 Hamburg
Telefon +49 (040) 4 45 06 09-0
Telefax +49 (040) 4 45 06 09-80
E-Mail info@eech.de
Internet www.eech.de

Wir leben in einer Welt voller Energie. Wind, Sonne, Erdwärme, Biomasse – all diese Energiequellen stehen für uns bereit. Umweltfreundlich. Ressourcenschonend. Emissionsfrei. Zukunftsorientiert.

We live in a world full of energy. Wind, sun, natural heat of the earth, biomass – all these energy sources are naturally available for us. Ecofriendly. Sparing natural resources. Free of emissions. Future-oriented.

Europas Spezialist für Erneuerbare Energien

Europe's Specialist for Renewable Energies

Wir leben in einer Zeit des Wandels. Perspektiven verändern sich und Ansprüche wachsen permanent mit neuen, ungeahnten Möglichkeiten. Wer in solchen Zeiten keine klaren Ziele hat, ist morgen ganz schnell von gestern.

Die EECH – European Energy Consult Holding AG hat klare Ziele. Als innovatives Emissionshaus für Erneuerbare Energien aktiviert die EECH AG die enormen Emissionspotenziale eines faszinierenden, lukrativen Marktes und nutzt diese professionell – mit maßgeschneiderten Lösungen für Menschen, die in die Energie der Zukunft investieren wollen. Visionen werden zu profitablen Realitäten.

Akquisition, Entwicklung, Finanzierung und Vermarktung im Bereich der regenerativen Energien – mit dieser Kernkompetenz ist die EECH AG bereits im Jahr 2001 auf dem europäischen Markt angetreten. International tätig, bietet sie sowohl Projekt-Planern als auch expandierenden Energieversorgern lukrative Möglichkeiten der Zusammenarbeit – von der Projekt-Finanzierung bis zum Erschließen neuer Märkte.

Dabei profitiert das Unternehmen von seinem erfahrenen Expertenteam aus den Bereichen Betriebswirtschaft, Rechtswissenschaft, Ingenieurwissenschaft, Marketing und Vertrieb sowie internationalen Repräsentanzen in Spanien, Italien, Österreich und Frankreich.

Die EECH AG steht ihren Partnern und Kunden langfristig mit umfassendem Know-how zur Seite. So arbeitet jeder Mitarbeiter des Unternehmens täglich mit ganzer Kraft an dem wertvollsten Produkt, das es in unserer heutigen Zeit gibt: unserer gemeinsamen Zukunft. ∎

We're living in a time of constant change. Perspectives are transforming and demands are growing permanently with new, undreamed of opportunities. Whoever does not have clearly defined aims in such times, will be of yesterday very quickly tomorrow.

EECH European Energy Consult Holding AG has clearly defined aims. Being an innovative emission house for renewable energies, EECH activates the enormous emission potentials of a fascinating, lucrative market and uses these professionally with tailor-made solutions for people that want to invest in the energy of the future. Visions become profitable realities.

Acquisition, development, financing and marketing in the field of regenerative energies – with this core competence EECH AG entered the European market already in the year 2001. On international level, it offers both project planners and expanding energy suppliers lucrative possibilities for cooperation starting from project financing through to developing new markets.

The company benefits in this respect from its experienced team of experts in the fields of business administration, law, engineering, sales & marketing as well as international representative offices in Spain, Italy, Austria and France.

EECH AG supports its partners and customers with its extensive know-how on long-term prospect. Each company staff member therefore works daily on the most valuable product that exists in our present times with his or her entire commitment: our mutual future. ∎

Company Profile

Spezialist zum Antreiben, Steuern und Bewegen

Rexroth: The spezialist for Drive, Control and Motion

Rexroth bietet ein einzigartiges, komplettes und technologieübergreifendes Leistungsangebot – stark in der weltweiten Präsenz, mit innovativen Produkten, einem umfassenden Technologie-Portfolio und hoher Systemkompetenz. Rexroth-Kunden profitieren von hochwertigen Einzeltechnologien mit einem breiten Spektrum aus Komponenten, Modulen, Systemen sowie Service- und Dienstleistungen (best in class). Diese Technologien bündelt Rexroth auch zu Leistungspaketen – mit Best-in-class-Komponenten, weltweitem Service, technologie-übergreifender Branchenkompetenz und der zielgerichteten Auswahl der optimierten Technologie für seine Kunden (best as company). Darüber hinaus bietet Rexroth kundenspezifische Systeme und Komplettlösungen aus einer Hand, basierend auf einem ganzheitlichen Beratungs- und Projektierungs-Know-how (best in systems). ■

Rexroth offers a unique, complete range of goods and services, even beyond the bounds of technology – with a strong worldwide presence, innovative products, an extensive technology portfolio and a high level of system competence. Rexroth customers benefit from high quality individual technologies with a broad spectrum of components, modules and systems as well as services (best in class). Rexroth combines these technologies into complete packages for its customers (best as company) – with best-in-class components, worldwide service, branch competence reaching beyond the bounds of technology, as well as a targeted selection of optimized technology. In addition to this Rexroth offers customized systems and complete solutions from a single source, based on overall system know-how and competence in project design (best in systems). ■

Rexroth
Bosch Group

Bosch Rexroth AG

Vorstand/Board of Directors:
Manfred Grundke; (Vorsitzender/Chairman)
Dr. Georg Hanen;
Reiner Leipold-Büttner

Produkte/Products:
Produkte und Dienstleistungen
aller Antriebs- und Steuerungstechnologien:
Hydraulik, elektrische Antriebe und Steuerungen,
Linear- und Montagetechnik sowie Pneumatik
Products and services
cover all drive and control technologies:
hydraulics, electric drives and controls,
linear motion and assembly technologies
and pneumatics

Mitarbeiter/Employees:
26.400

Anschrift/Address:
Maria-Theresien-Straße 23
D-97816 Lohr am Main
Telefon   +49 (800) 99 33 222
Telefax   +49 (800) 99 33 111
E-Mail   info@boschrexroth.de
Internet http://www.boschrexroth.com

Company Profile

Aktuelle Lösungen für jedes Verpackungsproblem

Your business in focus
Up-to-date solutions to any packaging problem

Smurfit Deutschland

Geschäftsführer/Managers:
Edwin Goffard,
Alain Gaudré

Gründungsjahr/Year of Foundation: 1955

Mitarbeiter/Employees: 2.949

Umsatz/Turnover: 870 Mio. €

Geschäftstätigkeit/Business Activity:
Wellpappe, Verpackungen aus Wellpappe, Papier, Karton, Entsorgung
Corrugated cardboard, packaging made of corrugated cardboard, paper, carton; waste disposal

Anschrift/Address:
Tilsiter Str. 144
D-22047 Hamburg
Telefon +49 (40) 6 94 43-272
Telefax +49 (40) 6 94 43-157
E-Mail info@de.smurfitgroup.com
Internet www.smurfit.de

Smurfit Deutschland trägt mit 12 Wellpappenwerken, einem Gefachewerk, vier Papiermaschinen, einer Pappenmaschine und 7 Recyclingzentren dazu bei, die weltweit agierende Smurfit Group zu einem der größten Anbieter von Papier und auf Papier basierenden Verpackungen zu machen.
In Deutschland haben viele der früheren Europa Carton Werke, jetzt Teil der Smurfit-Organisation, in diesem Jahr das 50-jährige Bestehen zu feiern. 50 Jahre innovative Arbeit – darauf sind wir stolz! Smurfit Deutschland beschäftigt sich mit allen Verfahrensprozessen von der Aufbereitung des Rohstoffes Altpapier über die Produktion von Papier bis hin zur Fertigung von Transport- und Verkaufsverpackungen aus Wellpappe. So können wir unseren Kunden die beste Leistung zum besten Preis anbieten.
In der Gruppe bestehen alle denkbaren Möglichkeiten der Herstellung Ihrer Wellpappenverpackungen. Von der Faltkiste bis zur mehrfachgeklebten Stanzverpackung, vom einfachen Flexodirektdruck, High-Quality-Postprint, Preprint oder Offset-Druck, von der kleinen Displayverpackung bis zum Container aus Schwerwellpappe bleiben keine Wünsche offen. Wir verpacken Ihnen alles.
Besonders schätzen unsere Kunden die Vielfalt unserer Serviceangebote, die in jedem Werk zur Verfügung stehen.
- **Smurfit Verpackungsmaschinensysteme:** Maschinen- und Verpackungsberatung durch Ingenieure, die auf das reibungslose Zusammenspiel von Maschine und Verpackung spezialisiert sind.
- **Money Saver:** Optimierung von Verpackungen und Verpackungsprozessen in Ihrem Hause, mit dem Ziel, Ihnen zu Einsparungen zu verhelfen.
- **SMI:** Wir vereinfachen die Kommunikation und die Bestellvorgänge zwischen Ihnen und uns und übernehmen Ihre Lagerplanung.
- **Fulfilment:** Konfektionierung und Kommissionierung von Verpackungen
- **Smurfit Tools:** Datenbanken, in denen das Wissen der kreativen Designer unserer 169 Wellpappenwerke zusammengetragen ist. Damit kann an jedem Standort an der jeweils aktuellsten Lösung weitergearbeitet werden.

Damit schafft es Smurfit, als global agierender Konzern immer vor Ort bei seinen Kunden zu sein, mit Ihren Anforderungen im Fokus.

Smurfit – Your business in focus. ■

With a network of 12 corrugated plants, 1 partition plant, 4 containerboard machines, 1 boxboard machine and 7 recycling centres, Smurfit Germany is strengthening the position of the Smurfit Group as one of the leading global players in the area of paper and paper-based packaging material. Many of the former Europa Carton plants in Germany will celebrate their 50th anniversary in 2005. 50 years of innovation – that's an achievement we are proud of. Smurfit Germany is engaged in all operating processes from waste paper recycling to the production of paper and the manufacture of transport and retail packages, enabling our group to provide its customers with optimum and cost-effective packaging solutions.
Thanks to our comprehensive capabilities, our group is in a position to supply any type of corrugated package. From folding boxes to multiple-glued die-cut packages, from simple flexo printing to highgrade post print, preprint, or offset-print, from small display packages to high performance corrugated containers, there is nothing we cannot supply. We package everything for you.
A multitude of services offered by all of our plants are highly appreciated by our customers:
- **Smurfit Packaging Machinery Systems:** Consulting by our packaging engineers related to packaging machinery and packaging solutions to coordinate the smooth performance of machines and packages.
- **Money Saver:** Optimization of packages and packaging processes at your plant in order to help you achieve cost savings.
- **SMI (supplier-managed inventory):** Simplification of communication and purchasing processes including inventory management.
- **Fulfilment:** set-up/filling of boxes and order commissioning
- **Smurfit Tools:** Data bases comprising the expertise of the creative packaging designers of our 169 corrugated plants, giving all plant locations access to the most up-to-date packaging solutions.

All this is enabling Smurfit – a global player – to be close to its customers with their packaging needs in focus.

Smurfit – Your business in focus. ■

Company Profile

Der Global Player aus dem Schwarzwald

Global Player from the Black Forest

Das Duschen wurde zwar nicht im Schwarzwald erfunden, aber die Innovationen der Hansgrohe AG mit Sitz in Schiltach/Schwarzwald wie etwa die Brausenstange, verstellbare Strahlarten oder jüngst die AIR-Technologie haben das tägliche Brausebad immer wieder revolutioniert. Seit Jahren gilt das Unternehmen als Marktführer im Brausen-Segment und als Innovationsführer der internationalen Sanitärindustrie.

Mit neun Produktionsstätten auf drei Kontinenten, mit Vertriebsgesellschaften und kundennahen Beratungsstützpunkten in 24 Ländern rund um die Welt zählt die Hansgrohe AG heute zu den wenigen Global Playern der Sanitärbranche. Unter den Marken Hansgrohe, Axor, Pharo und Pontos bietet die Unternehmung weltweit innovative sanitärtechnische Produkte und moderne, designorientierte Badlösungen an. Ihre Brausen und Armaturen finden sich dabei unter anderem in den VIP-Lounges der Lufthansa in Frankfurt, im weltgrößten Kreuzfahrtschiff, der Queen Mary II, und im Bulgari Hotel in Mailand. Mit ihren knapp 2.700 Mitarbeiterinnen und Mitarbeitern, von denen ein Drittel im Ausland beschäftigt ist, erwirtschaftete die Hansgrohe Gruppe im Geschäftsjahr 2004 einen Gesamtumsatz von 428 Mio. Euro, davon 74 % außerhalb Deutschlands – im Vergleich zum Vorjahr ein Plus von 16 %. Seit Betriebsgründung vor mehr als 100 Jahren ist die Familie Grohe an führender Stelle im Konzern aktiv. Heute leitet Klaus Grohe, jüngster Sohn des Firmengründers, als Vorstandsvorsitzender das Unternehmen.

Immer wieder hat die Hansgrohe AG mit zukunftweisenden Innovationen der internationalen Badbranche wichtige Impulse gegeben. Dabei hat sich das Unternehmen den Ruf als Innovationsführer der Branche nicht nur in Technologie, sondern auch in Design erworben. Tatsächlich gehört das Bemühen um Perfektion auch in der Gestaltung, ausgezeichnet mit mehr als 200 Design-Preisen, zum Selbstverständnis des Unternehmens. Ihm zugrunde liegt die ebenso produktive wie ambitionierte Kooperation mit international renommierten Design-Größen wie Philippe Starck, Antonio Citterio und Phoenix Design. Die Erkenntnis, dass gutes Design als Synonym für Kreativität und Qualität in der Arbeit honoriert wird, befähigt die Hansgrohe AG dazu, immer wieder Trends im Markt zu setzen und den Markterfolg weiter auszubauen.

Although showering was not invented in the Black Forest, the innovations by Hansgrohe AG based in Schiltach in Germany's Black Forest, such as the shower wallbar, adjustable shower jets and most recently AIR technology, have consistently revolutionized the daily shower. The company has for years been the market leader in showers and leader in innovation in the international sanitation industry.

With nine production sites on three continents, marketing companies and advisory centers close to the customers in 24 countries around the world, Hansgrohe AG is today one of only a few global players in the sanitation industry. The company offers innovative technical sanitaryware products and modern design-based bathroom solutions under the brand names Hansgrohe, Axor, Pharo and Pontos. Its showers and faucets are to be found in Lufthansa's VIP lounges in Frankfurt, on the world's largest cruise liner, the Queen Mary II, in the Bulgari Hotel in Milan, and in the "Colosseo" in the Europa-Park. With a workforce of slightly under 2,700, one-third of whom are abroad, in 2004 the Hansgrohe Group had a total turnover of 428 million euros, 74 % of which came from outside Germany – an increase of 16 % over the previous year. The Grohe family has been at the helm ever since the company was founded more than 100 years ago. Today Klaus Grohe, youngest son of the company founder, is company CEO.

Hansgrohe AG has always provided significant impulses for the international bathroom industry with its future-oriented innovations. The company has won itself the reputation of industry leader in innovation in both technology and design. In fact, the company regards its endeavors to achieve perfection in design – which have been rewarded with more than 200 design prizes – as a matter of course. They are based on its productive and ambitious co-operation with the internationally renowned design greats such as Philippe Starck, Antonio Citterio and Phoenix Design. The recognition that good design as a synonym for creativity and quality in work is honored and acknowledged is what encourages Hansgrohe AG to keep on setting new trends on the market and develop its success.

---

hansgrohe
AXOR | PHARO

Hansgrohe AG

Firmensitz/Company base:
Schiltach/Schwarzwald

Gründungsjahr/Founded in: 1901

Konzernumsatz/Group turnover:
428,1 Mio. Euro (2004)

Mitarbeiter/Workforce:
2.672, davon 1.744 in Deutschland
(Stand: 31. Dezember 2004)
*2,672 in total, of which 1,744 in Germany
(as at 31 December 2004)*

Marken/Brands:
Hansgrohe (Ablauftechnik, Brausen, Armaturen, Thermostate, Badausstattung, Küchenarmaturen), Axor (komplette Designprogramme für das individuelle Bad), Pharo (Dusch- und Hydromassagesysteme, Whirlpools und Dampfduschen) und Pontos (intelligente Wasserrecycling-Anlagen)
Hansgrohe (discharge technology, showers, faucets, thermostats, bathroom interiors, kitchen faucets), Axor (complete design programs for the individual bathroom), Pharo (shower and hydro massage systems, whirlpools and steam showers) and Pontos (intelligent water-recycling systems)

Produktionsstandorte/Production sites:
Schiltach (zwei Werke), Offenburg (zwei Werke), Alpirsbach, Wasselonne (Frankreich), Westknollendam (Niederlande), Alpharetta (USA) und Shanghai (China)
Schiltach (two works), Offenburg (two works), Alpirsbach, Wasselonne (France), Westknollendam (Netherlands), Alpharetta (USA) and Shanghai (China)

Weitere Informationen/Further information:
Hansgrohe AG
Telefon +49 (7836) 51-0
Telefax +49 (7836) 51-1300
E-Mail info@hansgrohe.com
Internet www.hansgrohe.com

Hohes Innovationstempo sichert Marktanteile

High pace of innovation secures market shares

Wir schreiben das Jahr 2000: Mit den drei Geschäftsbereichen Naval Systems, Land- und Flug- sowie Simulationssysteme gehört die Bremer STN Atlas Elektronik GmbH zu den weltweit führenden Anbietern von Ortungs- und Elektroniksystemen für zivile und militärische Anwendungen. Voraussetzung für erfolgreiches Wirtschaften in dieser Branche sind nach dem Ende des Kalten Krieges und fundamentalen Verschiebungen in den globalen Bedrohungsszenarien mehr denn je innovative Produkte, die höchsten Anforderungen gerecht werden. Gerade die Wehrtechnik gilt als eine der wissensintensivsten Branchen, in der Wohl und Wehe eines Anbieters vor allem davon abhängen, wie schnell und wie effizient er neue, immer ausgefeiltere Systeme auf den Markt bringen kann.

An Erfindergeist hat es den mehr als 1.500 Experten, die Atlas zu dieser Zeit allein in den Bereichen Design, Fertigung und Produktion beschäftigte, nie gemangelt. Und doch war irgendwann deutlich geworden, dass sich viele Synergieeffekte, die sich das Management aus der Fusion von Elektronikbereichen von AEG, Krupp und MBB erhofft hatte, noch nicht in zufriedenstellendem Umfang eingestellt hatten. Das Weiterleben früherer Unternehmenskulturen und damit einhergehender mangelnder Wissensaustausch führten vielfach zu Doppelarbeiten und unnötig langen und aufwändigen Entwicklungszeiten. Bald war allen klar: Atlas kann mehr! Und: Der Schlüssel dazu liegt in den Köpfen der Mitarbeiter. Ihr Wissen, vor allem aber die gegenseitige Nutzung und Weiterentwicklung ihres Wissens, ist das Erfolgsrezept für die Zukunft.

Allerdings schien uns eine gewisse Vorsicht geboten: Zu dieser Zeit war der Begriff des Wissensmanagements in aller Munde. Viele verstanden darunter die Einführung einer entsprechenden Softwarelösung, getrieben durch die EDV-Fachabteilungen. Was folgte, war oft ernüchternd. Die Pflege und Nutzung der neuen Systeme wurde von den Beschäftigten vieler Unternehmen als lästige Pflicht angesehen, die ihnen keinen Vorteil brachte.

In der Geschäftsführung von Atlas Elektronik herrschte dagegen Einigkeit: Das Thema Wissen war zu wichtig, um als „Modetrend" abgehandelt zu werden. Ganz im Gegenteil: Für ein Unterneh-

Hans-Georg Morawitz

Der Autor, 1955 in Neunkirchen/Saar geboren, ist diplomierter Wirtschaftsingenieur. Seit 2003 ist Morawitz Geschäftsführer der RHEIN METALL DEFENCE ELECTRONICS GMBH, Bremen.
The author, born in Neunkirchen/Saar in 1955, is a graduated industrial engineer. Since 2003, he has been managing director of RHEINMETALL DEFENCE ELECTRONICS GMBH in Bremen.

Dr. Hanno Brandes

Der Co-Autor, 1956 in Erfurt geboren, hat acht Jahre Erfahrung in der Industrie gesammelt. Bei MANAGEMENT ENGINEERS berät der habilitierte Maschinenbauer seit 14 Jahren vor allem Unternehmen der Elektronik- und Prozessindustrie. Er ist Teilhaber und Direktor des Düsseldorfer Beratungshauses.
The co-author, born in Erfurt in 1956, gained his professional experience in eight years' work in the industrial sector. The PhD graduate in mechanical engineering has been a consultant with MANAGEMENT ENGINEERS for 14 years and supports above all companies of the electronics and process industry. He is a partner and director of the Düsseldorf-based consulting enterprise.

Knowledge Management

It was in the year 2000: with its three business divisions Naval Systems, Landing, Flight and Simulation Systems, the Bremen-based STN Atlas Eletronik GmbH is one of the global market leaders of locating and positioning as well as electronics systems for civil and military application. After the demise of the Cold War, now more than ever before innovative products that meet the highest standards of technological requirement are a prerequisite for successful management in this branch. Especially defence technology is regarded as one of the most knowledge-driven branches, in which the weal and woe of a contractor depends above all on how fast and how efficiently he can launch ever more sophisticated systems on the market.

The more than 1,500 experts, which Atlas employed at that time in the fields of design and production alone, never lacked the necessary spirit of inventiveness. But at some point it became clear that many of the expected synergy effects that the management had hoped to emerge from the fusion of the electronics divisions of AEG, Krupp and MBB, had not materialized to a satisfactory extent yet. The further existence of previous company cultures and the pertinent lack of knowledge exchange often lead to work being duplicated and unnecessarily long and expensive periods of development work. Soon it became clear to all parties involved:
Atlas is capable of doing more! And the key to achieve this is in the heads of its staff members. Their knowledge, but primarily the mutual use and continuous development of their knowledge, is the concept of success for the future.

However, it seemed that we had to be careful to a certain extent: at this time the term of knowledge management was very popular. Many understood it to be the introduction of a corresponding software solution operated by relevant computer departments. The consequence was frequently somewhat sobering. Use and maintenance of the new systems was regarded by staff in many companies as a nuisance and obligation that brought no advantage.

The management of Atlas Elektronik, however, was completely convinced: the subject of "knowledge" was much too important to be dealt with as mere "trendy fashion". On the contrary: for an enterprise with such innovation and technology-driven products knowledge is the central aspect for success and must therefore be treated as such with utmost priority and on top level. But: our idea of securing long-term and sustainable competitiveness through the knowledge factor could not be realised with the aid of a more or less complex software solution.

We were convinced that the solution first of all was in solving the following questions:
- What kind of knowledge will secure the company success of Atlas Elektronik and where can it be found (contents)?
- How can this knowledge be archived, made accessible in general and constantly updated (processes)?
- How can giving knowledge and taking knowledge be promoted through changes in leadership and organisation (culture)?
- What must computer tools consist of that would support all these issues effectively (tools)?

The answers formed the basis for a knowledge management concept that integrated all four elements – contents, processes, culture and tools, which was mutually developed by Atlas staff and experts from Management Engineers and tailor-made to serve the specific requirements of the company.

We were pursuing the following aims:
- securing the company's expertise and improving its power of innovation by archiving the existing knowledge
- fast and global accessibility (also) of locally developed expert knowledge
- fast and efficient localisation of knowledge providers and networking of the same
- exhaustion of synergy effects instead of duplicated work and mistakes through systematic exchange of knowledge
- more flexibility in the employment of staff and more efficient knowledge transfer and
- last, but not least: fusion of the different company cultures through a common platform of communication that would be used by all and useful to all.

For the project, which involved overall more than 150 staff members during a total running period of two years, we first dealt with the core processes at Atlas and defined contents for the fields of market development/sales, contract processing and business development, and set up processes, responsibilities and rules. Focussing on the most important business divisions played a major role in firmly establishing the newly won understanding about the value of knowledge in the minds of colleagues. Today it can be said with hindsight that this introduction has reached such an extent of success, because we started with especially suited pilot projects and only afterwards carried the application systematically into the entire company and thus were able to notice the first concrete successes only after some few months, for instance:

- **in sales:** greater success in market development, because we were able to deal with customer wishes faster and better, were able to present offers faster and to plan target costs more precisely,
- **when processing contracts:** shorter delivery times, lower stocks, faster reaction to customer wishes and generally a higher customer satisfaction,

Wissensmanagement

men mit derart innovations- und technikgetriebenen Produkten ist Wissen der zentrale Erfolgsfaktor – und muss als solcher mit oberster Priorität, als „Chefsache", behandelt werden. Aber: Mit Hilfe einer mehr oder weniger komplexen Softwarelösung waren unsere Vorstellung von einer langfristigen und nachhaltigen Sicherung der Wettbewerbsfähigkeit über den Faktor Wissen nicht zu realisieren.

Die Lösung lag nach unserer Überzeugung zunächst in der Klärung folgender Fragen:
- Welches Wissen sichert den Unternehmenserfolg von Atlas Elektronik und wo befindet es sich (Inhalte)?
- Wie wird das Wissen gespeichert, allgemein nutzbar gemacht und ständig aktuell gehalten (Prozesse)?
- Wie können Wissengeben und Wissennehmen durch Veränderungen in Führung und Organisation gefördert werden (Kultur)?
- Wie muss ein EDV-Werkzeug beschaffen sein, das dieses alles wirksam unterstützt (Tools)?

Die Antworten bildeten die Grundlage für ein gemeinsam von Atlas-Mitarbeitern und Experten von Management Engineers entwickeltes, ganz auf die speziellen Bedürfnisse des Unternehmens zugeschnittenes Wissensmanagementkonzept, das alle vier Elemente berücksichtigte – Inhalte, Prozesse, Kultur und Tools.

Folgende Ziele wollten wir damit erreichen:
- Sicherung des Unternehmens-Know-hows und Verbesserung der Innovationskraft durch Archivierung des vorhandenen Wissens,
- schnelle und globale Verfügbarkeit (auch) von lokal aufgebautem Spezialwissen,
- schnelle und effiziente Lokalisierung von Know-how-Trägern und ihre Vernetzung,
- Ausschöpfen von Synergieeffekten statt Doppelarbeiten und Fehlern durch systematischen Wissensaustausch,
- mehr Flexibilität beim Mitarbeitereinsatz und effizienter Wissenstransfer,
- und nicht zuletzt: Zusammenführung der verschiedenen Unternehmenskulturen durch eine einheitliche Kommunikationsplattform, die von allen genutzt wird und allen nützt.

In einem Projekt, in dem über eine Gesamtlaufzeit von zwei Jahren insgesamt mehr als 150 Mitarbeiter involviert waren, haben wir uns zunächst die Kernprozesse von Atlas vorgenommen und für die Bereiche Marktbearbeitung/Vertrieb, Auftragsabwicklung und Entwicklung Inhalte definiert, Prozesse, Verantwortlichkeiten und Regeln entwickelt. Gerade die Fokussierung auf die wichtigsten Unternehmensbereiche hat maßgeblich dazu beigetragen, das neu gewonnene Verständnis vom Wert des Wissens in den Köpfen der Kollegen zu verankern. Die Einführung war aus heutiger Sicht aber auch deswegen so erfolgreich, weil wir mit besonders geeigneten Pilotprojekten begonnen und die Anwendung erst dann systematisch in das ganze Unternehmen getragen haben – und damit schon nach wenigen Monaten die ersten greifbaren Erfolge verzeichnen konnten, beispielsweise: 
- **im Vertrieb:** mehr Erfolg bei der Marktbearbeitung, weil wir schneller und besser auf die Wünsche der Kunden eingehen konnten, schneller Angebote vorlegen und die Zielkosten präziser planen konnten,
- **in der Auftragsabwicklung:** kürzere Lieferzeiten, geringere Bestände, schnellere Reaktion auf Kundenwünsche und insgesamt eine höhere Kundenzufriedenheit,
- **in der Entwicklung:** kürzere Entwicklungszeiten und Innovationszyklen, bessere Produkte und hohe Einsparungen durch Vermeiden von Doppelarbeiten.

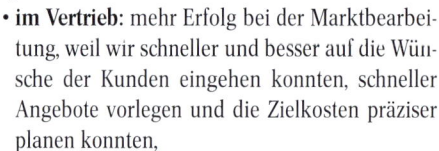

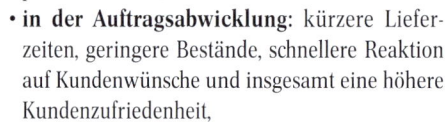

Nichts überzeugt so sehr wie der Vorteil, den man selbst aus einer Veränderung zieht. In dem Projekt bei Atlas Elektronik haben alle Mitarbeiter in vergleichsweise kurzer Zeit die konkrete Erfahrung gemacht, wie stark sie vom Wissen der anderen profitieren können. Trotzdem kommt sicher kein gelungenes Wissensmanagementprojekt ohne die systematische Betrachtung des Faktors Unternehmenskultur aus. Dazu gehört ein von der Führung kompromisslos vorgelebtes Leitbild ebenso wie ein Belohnungskonzept, das den vorbildlichen Umgang mit der Kernressource Wissen nicht nur ideell, sondern auch finanziell angemessen honoriert – und dabei ganz bewusst auf eine starke Signalwirkung nach innen setzt. Umso mehr hat es uns gefreut, dass wir für unser Projekt durch die Auszeichnung als „Wissensmanager des Jahres" nur wenige Zeit später auch öffentlich höchste Anerkennung erfahren haben. Bei der Verleihung der von Commerzbank, Financial Times Deutschland und Impulse ausgelobten Auszeichnung am 21. Dezember 2003 in Berlin hat der Vertreter des Bundesministeriums für Wirtschaft und Arbeit die Ganzheitlichkeit und Vorbildlichkeit des Konzepts als besonders preiswürdig herausgestellt. Wie es in der Begründung der renommiert besetzten Jury hieß, habe Atlas Elektronik die persönlichen Fachkompetenzen der Mitarbeiter zum Wohle des Unternehmens erfolgreich zu Kernkompetenzen vernetzt – trotz komplexester Materie und unter Wahrung strengster Geheimhaltungspflichten.

Inzwischen gibt es die „alte" STN Atlas nicht mehr. Mitte 2003 wurde sie zwischen ihren beiden Gesellschaftern Rheinmetall und BAE Systems aufgeteilt. Die „neue" Atlas Elektronik hat den gesamten Bereich der Marineelektronik übernommen: Rund 1.600 Mitarbeiter entwickeln und produzieren hier elektronische Ortungs- und Lenksysteme für U-Boote und Schiffe, aber auch nicht-militärische Produkte wie zum Beispiel Schiffsverkehrssysteme oder Anlagen für Vermessung und Hydrografie. Daneben gibt es als Tochter der Rheinmetall DeTec AG die jetzige Rheinmetall Defence Electronics. Ihr Kerngeschäft sind die Bereiche Land- und Flugsysteme, also beispielsweise Geräte für die elektronische Aufklärung und Kommunikationssysteme, aber auch alle Arten von Simulationssystemen – vom Flugsimulator bis zum Übungssystem für Fahrschüler. Beide Unternehmen genießen – genauso wie früher STN Atlas, und sicherlich auch aufgrund des hier beschriebenen Projekts – bei ihren Kunden in aller Welt einen ausgezeichneten Ruf.

Deswegen sind wir heute der Überzeugung: Atlas Elektronik und Rheinmetall DeTec ist die schwierige Aufgabe gelungen, Wissensmanagement als zentralen Teil des Tagesgeschäfts in den Köpfen der Mitarbeiter zu etablieren. Und wir haben es geschafft, den virtuellen Faktor Wissen zu einem messbaren Profitabilitätsfaktor weiterzuentwickeln. ■

Knowledge Management

Inhalte/Contents

Fähigkeiten/Capacities
Wissensdaten/Knowledge Data
Wissensdomänen/Knowledge Domains

Prozesse/Processes

Prozesskette/Process Chain

- Erwerben/Acquisition
- Entwickeln/Development
- Lokalisieren/Localisation
- Sammeln/Collection
- Identifizieren/Identification
- (Ver-)Teilen/Distribution
- Bewahren/Preservation
- Nutzen/Usage

Pflege und Controlling/Maintenance and Controlling

Wissensmanagement / Knowledge Management

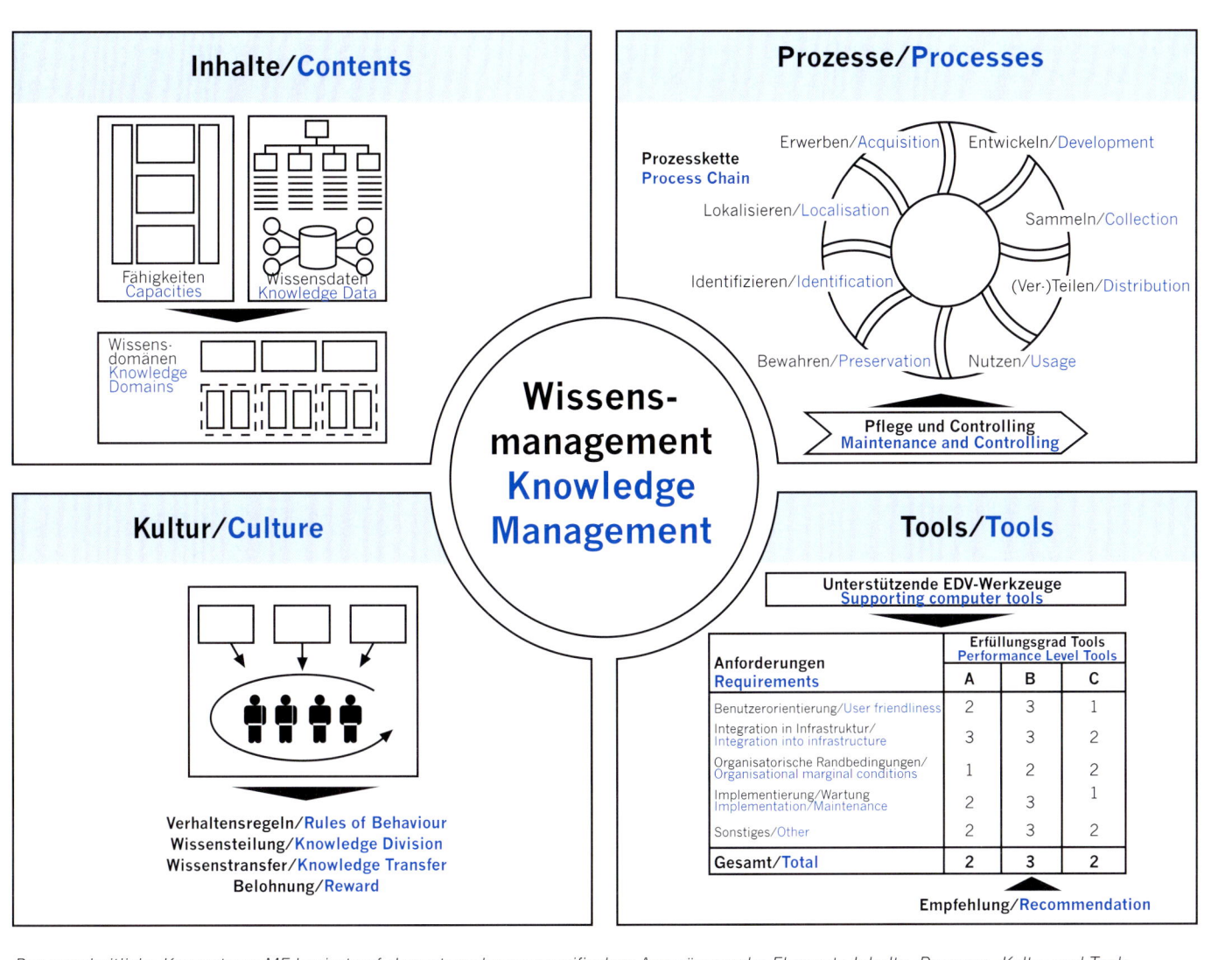

Kultur/Culture

Verhaltensregeln/Rules of Behaviour
Wissensteilung/Knowledge Division
Wissenstransfer/Knowledge Transfer
Belohnung/Reward

Tools/Tools

Unterstützende EDV-Werkzeuge / Supporting computer tools

Anforderungen Requirements	Erfüllungsgrad Tools Performance Level Tools		
	A	B	C
Benutzerorientierung/User friendliness	2	3	1
Integration in Infrastruktur/Integration into infrastructure	3	3	2
Organisatorische Randbedingungen/Organisational marginal conditions	1	2	2
Implementierung/Wartung Implementation/Maintenance	2	3	1
Sonstiges/Other	2	3	2
Gesamt/Total	2	3	2

Empfehlung/Recommendation

Das ganzheitliche Konzept von ME basiert auf der unternehmensspezifischen Ausprägung der Elemente Inhalte, Prozesse, Kultur und Tools.
The integral concept of ME is based on the characteristic nature of the company-specific elements of contents, processes, culture and tools.

- **in development:** shorter development periods and cycles of innovation, better products and higher savings by avoiding duplicated work.

Nothing is as convincing as the advantage that one draws oneself from any changes. During the project carried out at Atlas Elektronik all staff members experienced concretely in a comparably short time just how much they can benefit from other people's knowledge. However, surely no successful knowledge management project can do without systematically considering the factor of company culture. This includes setting an uncompromising example by the management as well as the existence of a reward concept that honours an exemplary handling of knowledge as a core resource not only by non-material recognition, but also financially in an appropriate way, thereby consciously seeking to give strong signals within the company. All the more we were glad that we received with the award of "Knowledge Manager of the Year" shortly after also the highest public recognition for our project.

When the award offered by Commerzbank, Financial Times Germany and Impulse was handed over on 21st December 2003 in Berlin, the representative of the Federal Ministry of Economy and Labour emphasized the integral aspects and the exemplary nature of the concept as particularly praiseworthy. The reasons for the renowned jury's choice explained that Atlas Elektronik had successfully networked personal expert competence fields of staff members to the benefit of the entire company despite an extremely complex subject matter, while it observed the strictest obligation to maintain secrecy.

Meanwhile, the "old" STN Atlas does not exist any more. In the middle of 2003 it was divided up between its two shareholders Rheinmetall and BAE Systems. The "new" Atlas Elektronik has taken over the complete division of marine electronics: around 1,600 employees develop and produce electronic location and positioning equipment and steering systems for submarines and ships here, and also non-military products such as shipping transport systems for instance or equipment for surveying and hydrographs. Furthermore, Rheinmetall Defence Electronics has been founded as a subsidiary of Rheinmetall DeTec AG. Its core business is in the area of land and flight systems, in devices for electronic reconnaissance and communication systems for instance, and covers also all types of simulation systems starting from flight simulators through to training systems for student drivers. Both companies enjoy- just as STN Atlas in former times, and certainly also because of the project described above – an excellent reputation with their clients in the entire world.

For this reason we are convinced today: Atlas Elektronik and Rheinmetall DeTec have succeeded in the difficult task to establish knowledge management firmly in the minds of their staff members as central part of their daily business. And we have managed to continue developing the virtual factor of knowledge into a measurable factor of profitability. ■

Company Profile

Ticona – mit Hightech-Kunststoffen Brücke zur Zukunft schlagen

Ticona – building bridges to the future with high-tech plastics

Hochleistungskunststoffe von Ticona erlauben Innovationen in jedem Format: Mal werden sie zur 26 Meter langen Tragflächenkante im neuen Super-Airbus A 380 verarbeitet, mal in Spritzen, deren Öffnung gerade 0,17 Millimeter klein ist. Um diese Bandbreite zu ermöglichen, sind leistungsstarke Werkstoffe und umfangreiches Produkt-Know-how notwendig. Beides hat Ticona durch mehr als 40 Jahre intensive Forschungsarbeit erworben.

Markterfolg sichern
Inzwischen beschäftigt sich etwa jeder elfte Mitarbeiter des weltweit tätigen Unternehmens mit Forschungs- und Entwicklungsfragen. Erfolg am Markt sichern gute Marktkenntnis, Produkt- und Verarbeitungs-Know-how sowie vorausschauendes Handeln. So gelingt es Ticona, von der Konzernzentrale in Kelsterbach bei Frankfurt am Main die Brücke zielorientiert in die Zukunft zu schlagen. Schon heute führt der Kunststoffspezialist durch kontinuierliche Weiterentwicklung der Produkte gleich mit zwei seiner Polymere, Hostaform und GUR, den Weltmarkt an. Insgesamt betrug der Umsatz des Unternehmens 2003 675 Millionen Euro.

Große Nachfrage bei Schlüsselindustrien
Automobilbau und Luftfahrt, Telekommunikation und Medizintechnik – nahezu alle Schlüsselindustrien nutzen für ihre Produkte Ticona-Werkstoffe. Die Gründe dafür liegen nah: Durch ihre besonderen physikalischen und chemischen Eigenschaften ersetzen Hochleistungspolymere herkömmliche Materialien wie Metall oder Glas, weil sie im Vergleich deutlich belastbarer und leistungsfähiger sind. Außerdem lassen sie sich oft einfacher verarbeiten. Dies spart nicht nur Herstellungszeit und -kosten, sondern sichert auch entscheidende Wettbewerbsvorteile.

Saubere Energie für morgen: Brennstoffzelle
Ein Beispiel: Als Energiequelle der Zukunft gilt die Brennstoffzelle. Nahezu alle Autobauer arbeiten mit Hochdruck an dieser Schlüsseltechnologie des 21. Jahrhunderts und testen bereits Prototypen. Wem es zuerst gelingt, Fahrzeuge mit dem alternativen Antrieb in Serie anzubieten, hätte einen enormen Vorsprung gegenüber der Konkurrenz. Ticona beschleunigt jetzt dieses Wettrennen. Ende 2004 präsentierte das Unternehmen erstmals eine funktionstüchtige Brennstoffzelle, die aus hauseigenen Hightech-Polymeren hergestellt ist. Zur Produktion von Brennstoffzellen eignen sich zwei Werkstoffe – Vectra, LCP und Fortron, PPS. In Bipolarplatten ersetzen sie goldbeschichteten Edelstahl, Aluminium, Graphit oder Duroplast-Graphit-Mischungen. Drei Kardinalprobleme der zukunftsweisenden Technologie löst Ticona damit: Brennstoffzellen können fortan günstiger produziert werden, verlieren deutlich an Gewicht und sind dauerhaft leistungsstärker.

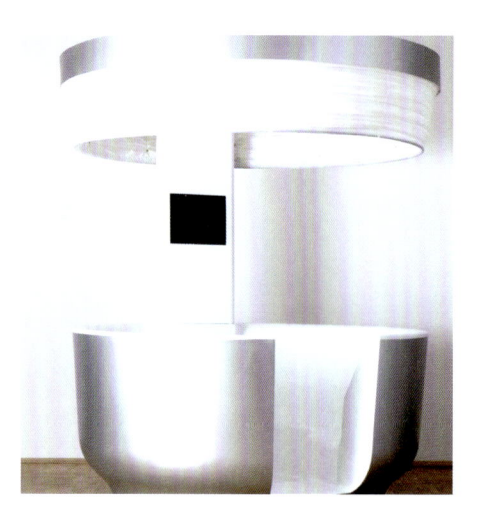

Visionäre Strategien und Produktinnovationen
Nur Rohstofflieferant zu sein, ist Ticona zu wenig. Deshalb wird neben der Weiterentwicklung der Brennstoffzelle an zahlreichen zukunftsweisenden Projekten gearbeitet. Und die dürfen gerne auch mal etwas visionärer sein, um Impulse zu geben oder rechtzeitig dem gesellschaftlichen Wandel Rechnung zu tragen. So präsentierte Ticona im Oktober 2004 zwei Konzeptstudien, den TiconaMat, eine Waschmaschine mit drei Trommeln, sowie eine Badekapsel als Wellness-Oase für zu Hause.
Ein wichtiger Ideengeber für neue Anwendungen ist die hoch spezialisierte Kelsterbacher Abteilung „Technologies & Services". Rund 40 Mitarbeiter, größtenteils Kunststofftechniker, Ingenieure und Laborfachkräfte, spüren Markttrends auf und setzen diese in enger Kooperation mit Kunden in neue Produkte um. Beispiel Luftfahrt- und Automobilindustrie: Hier schwören die Ingenieure und Entwickler auf konsequente Leichtbaustrukturen. Beim neuen Airbus der Superlative, dem A 380, substituieren deshalb technische Kunststoffe herkömmliche Materialien wie Metall oder Leichtmetall und ermöglichen so Gewichtseinsparungen von bis zu 40 Prozent.

Konzeptstudien von Ticona: TiconaMat, eine Waschmaschine mit drei Trommeln, und eine Badekapsel als Wellness-Oase für zu Hause.
Conceptual studies by Ticona: TiconaMat, a washing machine with three drums and a bathing capsule as wellness oasis to be used at home.

Auch in Bodennähe leisten Hightechpolymere unermüdliche Dienste. In nahezu jedem Fahrzeug – unter der Motorhaube, im Innenraum oder am Fahrzeugäußeren – sind sie zu finden und garantieren auf den Straßen mehr Sicherheit und Fahrspaß. Dass dies auch auf Know-how aus Kelsterbach zurückgeht, ist den BMW-, Mercedes-, Opel- oder VW-Fahrern meist nicht bewusst, wohl aber der Industrie. Kundennähe und exzellenter Service machen Ticona hier zu einem idealen Partner, schließlich verbessern technische Kompetenz und Systemexpertise die eigene Wettbewerbssituation.

Herausforderung: Hochkonjunktur für Hochleistungspolymere
Hersteller von technischen Kunststoffen stehen vor großen Herausforderungen. Einerseits verlangen die Kunden immer leistungsstärkere und günstigere Produkte, andererseits formuliert der Gesetzgeber immer höhere Ansprüche an die Umweltverträglichkeit. Ticona stellt sich den Herausforderungen. Der Standort Kelsterbach nimmt mit seinen 1.000 Mitarbeitern dabei eine Schlüsselstellung ein. So wird das Werk gerade um eine weitere Produktionsstraße ausgebaut. Dadurch sollen das Tempo des Entwicklungsprozesses hochgehalten und noch mehr Produkte zur Marktreife geführt werden. Fest steht dabei schon heute: Qualitätskunststoffe von Ticona haben Hochkonjunktur. Verarbeitet in Autos, elektrischen Zahnbürsten, Kaffeemaschinen, Laptops, Handys und vielem anderen mehr sind sie unsere täglichen Begleiter – auch auf dem Weg in die Zukunft. ■

Company Profile

High-performance plastics made by Ticona allow innovations in every conceivable format: sometime they may be processed into a 26-metre long wing edge in the new Super Airbus A 380, another time in syringes, which have such small openings that only measure 0.17 millimetres. In order to achieve this bandwidth highly efficient materials and an extensive product know-how is necessary. Ticona has acquired both in more than 40 years of intensive research work.

Securing success on the market
Meanwhile, each eleventh employee that works in this global enterprise is engaged with research and development issues. Success on the market is ensured through a good knowledge of local markets, product and processing know-how as well as foresighted action. Thus, Ticona has succeeded to build a bridge to the future in a target-oriented way from its headquarters in Kelsterbach near Frankfurt/Main. Today, the plastics specialist is already leading the world market through a continuous development of its products with two of its polymers, namely Hostaform and GUR. The company generated an overall turnover in 2003 amounting to 675 mio. euros.

Great demand from key industries
Automobile construction and aviation, telecommunications and medicine engineering, almost all key industries use Ticona-materials for their products. The reasons for this are obvious: because of the special physical and chemical characteristics, high-performance polymers replace common materials like metal or glass, since they are markedly more resistant and more efficient. Moreover, often they can be processed much easier. This does not only save production time and costs, but also secures decisive competition advantages.

Clean energy for tomorrow: fuel cells
An example: the fuel cell is regarded as energy source of the future. Almost all automobile producers are working at full stretch on this key technology of the 21st century and are already testing prototypes. Whoever is the first to offer vehicles with this alternative drive in series would have an enormous advantage against competitors. Ticona is now accelerating this race. At the end of 2004, the company presented a functioning fuel cell for the first time, which was produced from high-tech polymers made in-house. For the production of fuels cells two materials are suitable – Vectra, LCP and Fortron, PPS. In bi-polar plates they replace materials like gold-coated stainless steel, aluminium, graphite or Duroplast-Graphite mixtures. Thus, Ticona is solving three cardinal problems of this pioneering technology: from now on, fuel cells can be produced cheaper, will loose weight markedly and will be lastingly more efficient.

Visionary strategies and product innovations
It is not sufficient for Ticona to be a mere supplier of raw materials. Therefore, besides continuing to develop the fuel cell, work is underway on numerous future-oriented projects. These may well be of a more visionary nature in order to give impulses or to take account of social changes early in time. For instance in October 2004, Ticona presented two conceptual studies, the TiconaMat, a washing machine with three drums, as well as a bathing capsule to be used as wellness oasis at home.

One major provider of ideas for new applications is the highly-specialised department based in Kelsterbach "Technologies & Services". Around 40 employees, mainly plastics technicians, engineers and laboratory technicians, detect market trends and convert these in close cooperation with clients into new products. For example in the aviation and automobile industries: engineers and developers here swear by consistently lightweight constructions. For the new superlative among Airbuses, the A 380, therefore technical plastic materials have substituted common materials like metal or light metal and thus allow savings in weight of up to 40 per cent.

But also on the ground, high-tech polymers render invaluable services. They can be found in almost every vehicle – under the bonnet, in the vehicle's interior or exterior parts – and are sure to guarantee more safety and driving enjoyment on the roads. Usually, BMW, Mercedes, Opel or VW drivers are not aware that the know-how for this partly goes back to Kelsterbach, but the industry knows. Closeness to customers and excellent service have turned Ticona into an ideal partner, finally technical competence and system expertise improve one's own competitive situation.

Challenge: boom for high-performance polymers
Producers of technical plastics are presently facing great challenges. On the one hand, customers are demanding ever more efficient and inexpensive products, on the other legal regulations require ever higher demands towards environmental safety. Ticona is facing these challenges. With 1,000 employees, the business location based in Kelsterbach occupies a key role in this respect. The works is being expanded by another production line right now. Thus, the speed of development processes is to be maintained at a high level and even more products are to be finished into marketable commodities. One thing is certain already today: quality plastics made by Ticona are experiencing a boom at present. Being processed in cars, electrical toothbrushes, coffee machines, laptops, mobile phones and much more they accompany us every day – also on our way into the future.

Ticona

Ticona GmbH

Geschäftsführung/Management:
Lyndon Cole (President),
Neil Robertson
(Vice President Global Finance),
Thomas L. Hensel
(Vice President Global Demand Management),
Lisa Ryan
(Vice President Global Strategy Innovation),
John Wardzel (Vice President Global Supply & Asset Management)

Eigentümer/Proprietor:
Celanese Corporation

Gründungsjahr/Year of Foundation: 1961

Mitarbeiter/Employees: 2.000

Branche/Branch:
Technische Kunststoffe/
Technical plastics

Märkte/Markets:
Alternate, Automobilindustrie,
Elektro-/Elektronikindustrie, Flugzeugindustrie,
Haushaltsgeräte, Konsumgüter, Medizintechnik,
Verpackungsindustrie
Alternate, automobile industry,
Electrical/electronics industry, aviation,
Household goods, consumer goods,
Medicine engineering, packaging industry

Hauptsitz/Headquarters:
Kelsterbach/Deutschland;
Florence,
Kentucky/USA

Anschrift/Address:
Professor-Staudinger-Straße
D-65451 Kelsterbach
Information Service
Telefon +49 (0) 180 5 84 26 62 (Germany)
 +49 (0) 69 30 51 62 99 (Europe)
Telefax +49 (0) 180 2 02 12 02
E-Mail infoservice@ticona.de
Internet http://www.ticona.com

Global Player

Loyalität, Engagement und Liebe zum Produkt – Basis wirtschaftlichen Erfolgs

Loyalty, engagement and love of the product – the basis of economic success

Die J. J. Darboven GmbH & Co. KG in Hamburg ist bereits seit mehr als 135 Jahren das, was heute als Global Player bezeichnet wird. Seit dem 19. Jahrhundert importieren wir weltweit unseren Rohkaffee, und in dieser Zeit sind viele zuverlässige Geschäftsverbindungen bis hin zu freundschaftlichen, ja, in meinem Fall sogar verwandtschaftlichen Beziehungen entstanden, die bis auf den heutigen Tag eine hohe Wertigkeit haben.

Wer mit einem so hochspekulativen Rohstoff wie Kaffee überall auf der Welt, ob in Fernost, Südost oder Mittel- und Südamerika, handelt, der wird, ob er will oder nicht, stark kosmopolitisch geprägt. Und diese Fähigkeit, global zu denken und zu handeln, ist heute nicht nur in meiner Branche wichtig. Ohne kosmopolitische Bildung, möchte ich behaupten, ist in der Zeit der Globalisierung wirtschaftlicher Erfolg nicht möglich.

Übereifriger nationaler Patriotismus hat leider, wie wir alle wissen, in den vergangenen Jahrzehnten zu erschreckendem Übermut geführt. Dagegen sehe ich im Wirken unserer Rohkaffeezunft einen wertvollen Faktor der Verständigung der Völker. Rohkaffee steht als Handelsgut nach dem Erdöl an zweiter Stelle, aber Kriege um Kaffee hat es noch nie gegeben.

Ein Global Player muss die Fähigkeit haben, sich immer wieder auf die landestypischen Individualitäten einzustellen. Das dürfte einem Kosmopoliten sicher nicht schwer fallen, wenn er im Jugendalter schon rechtzeitig an unterschiedliche Gewohnheiten, Eigenarten und Sprachen herangeführt wurde, wenn er begriffen hat, dass sich die Welt nicht um ihn selbst dreht.

Für mich persönlich ist es ein großes Erlebnis, immer neue Kulturen kennen zu lernen. Und ich habe sehr viel Freude daran, dass der Rohkaffee aus vielen Erdteilen dieser Welt – mit unserem Namen versehen – wieder in viele Länder als Röstkaffee exportiert wird.

Nun einige Gedanken zum Mittelstand.
Dieser bildet überall, wo freie soziale Marktwirtschaft herrscht, das Rückgrat einer Volkswirtschaft. Gäbe es den Mittelstand nicht, würden wir hilflos in eine Monopol-Wirtschaft geraten, die sich von einer Kommando-Wirtschaft nicht mehr unterscheidet – auf einem anderen Niveau zwar, aber mit demselben Resultat.

Wenn ein Mittelständler die ersten, oft schwierigen Jahre gut überstanden hat und allmählich eine Firmen-Kultur mit eigener Philosophie entsteht, wird diese zu seinem Leitbild, und eine innere Stimme sagt ihm dann immer wieder, was der richtige Weg ist. Eine gerechte, leistungsbezogene und soziale Menschenführung hilft gerade in einem Inhaber- oder Familienbetrieb, diesen Weg erfolgreich zu gehen.

Es ist Unsinnn, zu glauben, dass ein mittelständischer Unternehmer jeden Tag mit der Steuertabelle unter dem Arm herumläuft, um Steuern zu sparen. Nein, ein Mittelständler denkt vor allem daran, ein gutes wirtschaftliches, operatives Unternehmen aufzubauen, für das er dann eben auch im Interesse der Allgemeinheit Steuern zu zahlen hat. Denn er weiß: Von einem Beitrag zur Allgemeinheit kann sich keiner ausschließen, wenn er nicht auch selbst von der Allgemeinheit ausgeschlossen werden möchte.

Der Mittelstand ist besonders gekennzeichnet durch seine Liebe zu seinen Mitarbeitern und die verständnisvolle Zusammenarbeit mit ihnen. Angestellte werden oft über Jahre hinaus gefördert, um einmal leitende Positionen zu übernehmen. Dabei wird ihnen gleichzeitig der loyale und engagierte Einsatz für das Unternehmen und die Liebe zum entsprechenden Produkt vermittelt.
Wenn man diese drei Momente beherzigt, die Loyalität, das Engagement und die Liebe zu dem Produkt, steht ein Unternehmen auf einem gesunden Fundament.

In der heutigen Zeit wird leider sehr viel Pessimismus verbreitet, von den Medien ebenso wie von einigen Unternehmern und Verbänden. Manchmal gibt es Gründe dafür, oft aber auch nicht. Ich bin der Auffassung, dass man sich durch Selbstdisziplin zur Gelassenheit erziehen und seiner Umwelt mit Optimismus und Fröhlichkeit darstellen kann. Sorgen, die jeder mal hat, sollte man mit sich selbst ausmachen.

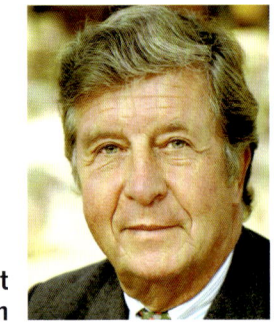

Albert Darboven

Der 1936 in Darmstadt geborene Autor ist geschäftsführender Gesellschafter der J. J. Darboven GmbH & Co. KG, Hamburg.
Nach einer kaufmännischen Ausbildung baute Albert Darboven von 1956 bis 1960 die Einkaufs-Agenturen für die Firma Rothfos in El Salvador und Costa Rica auf und war für diese Firma in Nicaragua sowie bei der Firma Truxo Ltd. in England tätig.
The author was born in Darmstadt in 1936 and is managing partner of J. J. Darboven GmbH & Co. KG, Hamburg.
After completing training in business management, Albert Darboven built up several buying agencies for Messrs. Rothfos in El Salvador and Costa Rica from 1956 to 1960; he also worked for this company in Nicaragua as well as with Truxo Ltd. in England.

Global Player

AM ANFANG WAR DIE IDEE

Als Johann Joachim Darboven im Jahr 1866 begann, Kaffee zu vertreiben, hatte dies vor allem einen Grund: Er wollte den Hamburger Hausfrauen, die bisher den Rohkaffee selbst in der Pfanne geröstet hatten, die Arbeit erleichtern. Deswegen verkaufte er als erster Anbieter bereits gerösteten Kaffee, der, in Tüten verpackt, auch noch den Vorteil längerer Haltbarkeit hatte. Durch den Versand des Kaffees profitierten bald auch viele Menschen außerhalb der Stadtgrenzen von dieser wegweisenden Idee.

Es war wiederum der Nutzen des Verbrauchers, der bei einem weiteren Meilenstein in der Entwicklung des Unternehmens im Vordergrund stand: Unter dem Namen „IDEE" wurde 1927 ein Kaffee eingeführt, der aufgrund eines neuen Herstellungsverfahrens zum ersten Mal Bekömmlichkeit mit dem Genuss des vollen Aromas verband und damit schon damals einer gesunden Lebensweise Rechnung [trug]. Der magenfreundliche Kaffee wurde ein [Erfolg]; die Expansion der Firma nahm ihren [Lauf].

Heute beliefert J.J. Darboven nicht nur den Lebensmittelhandel mit ausgesuchten Qualitätskaffees, sondern auch renommierte Hotels, Restaurants und Cafés im In- und Ausland. Über den IDEE Office Coffee Service werden bundesweit kleine bis mittlere Büros und Betriebe mit den Spitzenkaffees beliefert. Qualitätskaffee am Arbeitsplatz, verbunden mit einem professionellen Service, garantieren ein gutes Betriebsklima.

Zur Unternehmensgruppe gehören 11 Tochterfirmen in 6 europäischen Ländern. Rund 900 Mitarbeiter erwirtschafteten 2003 einen Umsatz von ca. 210 Mio. €. Dennoch ist J.J. Darboven ein Familienbetrieb geblieben. Albert Darboven und Arthur Darboven leiten heute das Unternehmen – und dass die Firma auch in der sechsten Generation von Mitgliedern der Familie geführt wird, ist jetzt bereits gesichert.

Aus Freude am Leben
J. J. DARBOVEN • HAMBURG

Global Player

Ich empfinde jedes Mal großes Bedauern, wenn ich erfahre, dass ein Betrieb stillgelegt ist oder sich ins Ausland verlagert hat. Und ich frage mich dann: Mussten wirklich eine intakte Infrastruktur und gewachsene Kulturen aufgelöst werden? Und ist dem Unternehmer klar, welche Anstrengungen und wieviel Investitionen es kostet, in einem fremden Land und in einer kaum bekannten Kultur eine neue Firma zu errichten? Vom Heimweh ganz zu schweigen …

Ich weiß auch, dass unsere Steuersätze, wie sie zur Zeit bestehen, uns natürlich außerordentlich belasten. Wir müssen noch mehr tun, damit wir unsere Regierung überzeugen, dass solch wirtschaftlicher Unsinn nicht weitergehen kann. Wir müssen versuchen, eine sinnvolle und akzeptable Lösung für alle zu finden.

Ich als Mittelständler denke stets darüber nach, wie unser Unternehmen wettbewerbsfähig bleibt und Investitionen am Wirtschaftsstandort Deutschland getätigt werden können. Ich denke jedoch nicht an eine Verlagerung in ein Steuerparadies. Das wäre ein Beispiel, das ich anderen nicht geben möchte.

Unser Unternehmen ist 1866 gegründet worden. In diesen 139 Jahren hat unser Familienunternehmen drei Kriege überlebt und zwei Inflationen überstanden und existiert heute in der vierten Generation.

Mein Sohn Arthur E. Darboven hat schon einen Großteil des Unternehmens übernommen, er vertritt nun die fünfte Generation. Wir sind klare Verfechter des gesunden Mittelstandes, auch in Zeiten wirtschaftlicher Krisen. Sofern der Nachwuchs sich richtig einbringt, dürfte einer erfolgreichen Zukunft nichts mehr im Wege stehen.

Und das alles unter unserem Motto „Aus Freude am Leben". ∎

Global Player

For more than 135 years J. J. Darboven GmbH & Co. KG of Hamburg has been what today is described by the term of "global player". Since the 19th century we have imported our raw coffee worldwide and within this time many reliable business relationships have emerged as well as friendly ones, in my own case even close family ties that remain to be of great value up to today.

Whoever deals with such a highly speculative raw material as coffee anywhere in the world, whether in the Far East, Southeast or Central and South America, will – take it or not – be influenced strongly by cosmopolitan traits. And this capacity to be able to think and act globally is not only important in my own branch today. Without cosmopolitan training, I would like to say, economic success is not possible in this time of globalisation.

As we all know, over-ambitious national patriotism has led to a dreadful arrogance in past decades. Instead, through the activities in our raw coffee guild I can recognise the valuable factor of understanding between the peoples. As a commodity, raw coffee ranks on second place after mineral oil, but there have never been wars about coffee.

A global player must have the ability to adjust himself to country-specific individualities again and again. Surely this is not difficult for a cosmopolitan person if he was introduced to different customs, peculiarities and languages early in his youth and has understood that the world does not only revolve around his own person.

For me personally, it is a great adventure to become familiar with new cultures again and again. I enjoy the fact very much that raw coffee from many parts of the world is exported again – bearing our name – into many countries as roasted coffee afterwards.

Some thoughts about the medium-size business sector. Everywhere, where there is a free and social market economy, it forms the backbone of a national economy. If it was not for the medium-size business sector, we would helplessly encounter ourselves in an economy of monopolies that would not be different from an economy of under command – maybe at another level, but definitely with the same end results.

When a medium-sized business has overcome its first, often difficult years well and slowly a company culture harbouring its own philosophy emerges, the latter becomes its guideline and an inner voice keeps repeating that he it on the right path. The just, performance-related and social management of personnel helps especially owner or family-managed companies to pursue this way successfully.

Believing that a medium-sized company businessman is running around with a tax table in his hand every day is complete nonsense. No, a medium-sized company businessman primarily thinks of building up a well-functioning, economically efficient enterprise for which he eventually has to pay tax also in the interest of the general public. Because he knows: no-one can exclude himself from rendering his contribution to society, if he himself does not want to be excluded from society.

The medium-sized business sector is particularly characterised by the love towards its employees and its sympathetic collaboration with them. Frequently, employees receive support for many years so that they can take over a management position one day. At the same time they are trained to acquire loyal commitment and engagement for the company and the love of the corresponding products. If one gives consideration to these three elements, loyalty, engagement and love of the product, a company is grounded on a sound foundation.

Unfortunately, much pessimism is spread by the media as well as by some companies and associations today. Sometimes there are certainly reasons for this, but often there are none. I am of the opinion that through self-discipline one can train oneself to acquire composure and present oneself to one's environment with optimism and happiness. Worries, which everyone has to face one day, one should deal with by oneself.

Every time I learn that a company has been closed down or has relocated to a foreign country I feel great regret. And then I question myself: was it really necessary to dissolve an integral infrastructure and a locally grown culture? And is the businessman aware of the efforts and how much investments it takes to establish a new firm in a foreign country and in a hardly familiar culture? All this does not take into account the nostalgia.

I also know that our present tax rates are an extreme burden on us, of course. We have to do much more to convince our government that such economic nonsense cannot continue any longer. We must endeavour to find a sensible and acceptable solution for all.

As a medium-sized company businessman myself I am constantly pondering about the question how our company can remain competitive and investments can be made within the business location of Germany. But I am not thinking to relocate into a tax haven. That would be an example I do not wish to give to others.

Our company was founded in 1866. During these 139 years our family enterprise has survived three wars and overcome two inflations, and today it exists in its fourth generation.

My son Arthur E. Darboven has already taken over a large part of the company and he now represents the fifth generation. We are clear supporters of a healthy medium-sized company sector, also in times of economic crises. If the upcoming young professionals can show the right commitment there should be nothing in the way of a prosperous future.
And we follow the slogan: "For the love of it". ■

Company Profile

Personalkonzept und Branchenfokussierung

Concept of human resources and sector focus

MANAGEMENT ENGINEERS (ME) sind eine Unternehmensberatung, die nachweisbar überdurchschnittlichen Nutzen bringt. An diesem Anspruch lassen wir uns messen. Unsere Klienten schätzen an uns vor allem unsere strikte Orientierung an ihrem Unternehmensergebnis und unsere Fähigkeit, konkrete Veränderungen zu bewirken. Diese Stärken schöpfen wir aus zwei Quellen: unserem Personalkonzept und unserer Branchenfokussierung. Wir arbeiten grundsätzlich nur mit berufserfahrenen Beratern – Ingenieuren, Naturwissenschaftlern und Kaufleuten. Unsere Berater wissen aus der Praxis, wovon sie reden. Deshalb sind sie auch für die Mitarbeiter unserer Klientenunternehmen kompetente Coaches und Innovationsgeneratoren.

Unsere Arbeitsgebiete sind die Strategie- und Prozessberatung sowie vor allem auch die aktive Realisierungsbegleitung. Unser Ziel ist, die Wettbewerbsfähigkeit unserer Klienten zu stärken. Was uns dabei von anderen unterscheidet, ist die Befähigung, innovative Konzepte nicht nur zu entwickeln, sondern auch zu implementieren. In unserem Beraterteam finden sich sowohl herausragende Konzeptentwickler als auch langjährig erfahrene Praktiker. Diese besondere Mischung hat sich als äußerst effektiv und erfolgreich erwiesen: So bescheinigen uns die Manager deutscher Unternehmen z. B. in einer Studie von Prof. Dietmar Fink unter anderem den ersten Platz in der Kategorie Umsetzungs- und Realisierungsberatung (Die „Hidden Champions" des Beratungsmarkts, Bonn 2003).

Als Strategieberater unterstützen wir Unternehmen dabei, ihre Strategie zu definieren, auf den Prüfstand zu stellen, zu verändern und nicht zuletzt: umzusetzen.

Wir
- entwickeln Geschäftsfeld- und Wachstumsstrategien,
- untersuchen Märkte und Wettbewerbssituationen,
- definieren Kernkompetenzen und Produktportfolios,
- erstellen und auditieren Bussinesspläne,
- erarbeiten Standort- und Wertschöpfungsstrategien,
- bereiten Mergers und Spin-offs vor und führen sie zum Erfolg.

Als Prozessberater verbessern wir Unternehmensprozesse – sei es im umfassenden Reengineering von Abläufen und Strukturen des ganzen Unternehmens, sei es bei einzelnen Unternehmensfunktionen.

Wir auditieren und optimieren
- den Innovationsprozess,
- die Beschaffung und das Supply-Chain-Management,
- die Wertschöpfung und die Instandhaltung,
- den Vertrieb und den Kundendienst,
- die Unternehmensplanung und das Controlling.

In besonderem Maße beherrschen wir die ganzheitliche Reduzierung der Kosten von Produkten und Dienstleistungen entlang der kompletten Wertschöpfungskette.

Unsere Klienten kommen aus dem Maschinen- und Fahrzeugbau, aus der Automobil- und ihrer Zulieferindustrie, aus Elektronik, Chemie, Pharma, Energieversorgung und Wehrtechnik, aus Holzverarbeitung und technischen Dienstleistungen, kurz: aus allen Branchen mit hohem Anspruch an die Technologie ihrer Produkte und Prozesse. In den letzten Jahren haben auch Finanzdienstleister, Logistik- und Handelsunternehmen unser Prozess- und Organisations-Know-how in Anspruch genommen.

Mit mehr als 115 vollzeitig tätigen Beratern und einem Umsatz von 46 Mio. € (2004) sind wir seit 1978 zu einer der größten Strategieberatung in deutscher Hand herangewachsen. Wir sind im ausschließlichen Besitz von derzeit 13 aktiv als Berater tätigen Partnern. ■

Bilder: Unsere Berater arbeiten in den Branchen, die sie kennen: Einstellungsvoraussetzung ist eine mehrjährige Berufserfahrung in der Industrie. Deswegen können wir nicht nur innovative Konzepte entwickeln, sondern diese auch erfolgreich in den Unternehmen umsetzen.

Pictures: Our consultants work in the sectors they know: prerequisite for employment is several years of professional experience in industry. We are therefore not only able to develop innovative concepts but also to implement them successfully within the companies.

Company Profile

Management Engineers (ME) is a management consulting firm with a proven record of generating above-average benefits for our clients. We invite you to measure us against this claim. Above all, our clients value us for always making their performance our strict objective and for our ability to effect tangible change. We derive these strengths from two sources: our own concept of human resources and our focus on specific sectors. As a matter of principle, we work only with professionally experienced consultants – engineers, scientists, and businessmen. Our consultants know what they are talking about from practical experience. For this reason, they also become competent coaches and can even foster innovation by the employees of our client companies.

We are strategy and process consultants with an additional emphasis on the active support of project realization. It is our declared objective to strengthen the competitiveness of our clients. In this regard, we distinguish ourselves from others by our ability not only to develop innovative concepts but also to implement them. In fact, every one of our project teams includes outstanding concept developers as well as practitioners with many years of experience. This combination has proven to be extremely effective, with documented success. For example, in a study conducted by Prof. Dietmar Fink, managers of German companies confirm, that we rank first in the category of implementation and realization consulting (The Hidden Champions of the Consulting Market, Bonn 2003).

As strategy consultants, we help companies to define strategies, put them to the test, modify them, and, not in the least, to implement them.

We:
• develop business and growth strategies,
• conduct market research and competitive analysis,
• define core competencies and product portfolios,
• compile and audit business plans,
• prepare location and value-adding strategies,
• plan mergers and spin-offs and lead them to success.

As process consultants, we improve company processes – with projects ranging in scope from the comprehensive re-engineering of processes and structures throughout an entire company, down to the individual company functions.

We audit and optimize:
• the innovation process,
• procurement and supply-chain management,
• value-adding and maintenance processes and structures,
• sales, marketing, and customer service,
• company planning and control.

We are particularly regarded for the strength of our ability to reduce the cost of products and services along the entire value-added chain.

Our clients come from the fields of mechanical engineering and vehicle construction; from the automotive industry and its suppliers; from the electronics, chemicals, and pharmaceutical industries; from energy supply and defense industries, from wood-processing and technical services – in short, from all sectors that demand high standards of technology for their products and processes. In recent years, financial service providers, logistics firms, and trade companies have also called upon our process and organizational know-how.

With 115 full-time consultants and sales of € 46 mill. (2004), we have grown since 1978 to become one of the largest German-owned strategy consulting company. We are wholly owned by 13 partners who also work as consultants. ∎

MANAGEMENT ENGINEERS

MANAGEMENT ENGINEERS GmbH + Co. KG

Geschäftsführer/Managing Directors:
Bodo F. Holz, Vorsitzender der Geschäftsführung/
Chairman of the Board of Management
Dieter W. Kaiser
Hans-Ulrich Stamer

Gründungsjahr/Year of Foundation:
1978 als/as Ingersoll Manufacturing Consultants

Mitarbeiter (2004)/Employees (2004):
140 Mitarbeiter,
davon 115 festangestellte Berater
140 employees,
of these 115 permanent consultants.

Umsatz (2004)/Sales (2004):
46 Mio. €

Geschäftsfelder/Business Fields:
Automobil- und Zulieferindustrie
Chemie/Pharma
Elektronik- und Elektrotechnikindustrie
Energieversorgung
Finanzdienstleistungen
Maschinen- und Anlagenbau
Automobile industries and its suppliers
Chemical and pharmaceutical industries
Electronics and electrical engineering industries
Financial services
Mechanical and plant engineering
Utilities

Geschäftstätigkeit/Business Activities:
Das Leistungsspektrum reicht vom ganzheitlichen Reengineering bis zur Optimierung einzelner Unternehmensfunktionen –
von der Konzeption bis zur Umsetzung
Our services range from comprehensive reengineering to the optimisation of individual operative functions within a company – from concept planning through to its realisation

Anschrift/Address:
Am Seestern 8
D-40547 Düsseldorf
Telefon   +49 (211) 53 000
Telefax   +49 (211) 5 300 300
E-Mail   info@Management-Engineers.com
Internet www.Management-Engineers.com

Innovationen im Handwerk erschließen neue Märkte

Innovations in skilled trade open up new markets

Die Wirtschafts- und Gesellschaftsgruppe Handwerk befindet sich – wie der Mittelstand insgesamt – mitten in einem Prozess des Wandels und des Umbruchs, der in seiner Dimension, seiner Vielschichtigkeit und seinem Tempo wohl einzigartig in der langen Geschichte des Handwerks und seiner Organisationen ist. Fest steht, dass neue Strategien der Anpassung entwickelt werden müssen. Jeder Betrieb ist gezwungen, seine Stärken und Schwächen zu analysieren und seine Geschäftsstrategie zu überprüfen. Das gilt angesichts der katastrophalen Konjunktur im Binnenmarkt, das gilt erst recht angesichts der zweiten Erweiterungsrunde der Europäischen Union mit ihren Risiken und Chancen. Die vom Handwerk nachhaltig geforderten Übergangsfristen helfen auch bei dieser Erweiterungsrunde der EU, den Anpassungsdruck zu mindern und zu strecken. Doch wir machen uns nichts vor: Seit dem 1. Mai 2004 agiert die osteuropäische Konkurrenz vor der eigenen Haustür – zu völlig anderen Konditionen. Aber: Wir werden uns trotz der derzeitigen schwierigen wirtschaftlichen und politischen Rahmenbedingungen nicht entmutigen lassen. Eine gesunde Portion Optimismus gepaart mit Tatkraft gehört ja gerade zur Mentalität des Handwerks. Unternehmer und Arbeitnehmer im Handwerk mit ihrer ausgezeichneten Qualifikation können sich offen den Herausforderungen stellen.

Innovationen erschließen neue Märkte

Das Handwerk hat in seiner langen Geschichte schon viele Krisen gemeistert, weil es stets flexibel, anpassungsfähig und innovativ war. Personenunternehmer im Handwerk sichern nämlich ihren betrieblichen Erfolg und ihre Zukunft vor allem aus eigener Kraft. Ein wichtiger Erfolgsfaktor ist die Fähigkeit, den Herausforderungen der täglichen Arbeit mit innovativen Ideen zu begegnen. Und diese müssen sich nicht notwendigerweise nur auf den Hightech-Bereich beziehen. Sie sind in allen Gewerken möglich und auch notwendig.
Aus dem Blickwinkel der Öffentlichkeit erscheinen handwerkliche Erfindungen und Verbesserungen von Produkten und Dienstleistungsangeboten oft weniger spektakulär als etwa Erfindungen in der Industrie. Aber die mit Abstand größte Zahl von Innovationen kommt aus dem Mittelstand! Dabei ist klar: Nicht bei jeder Neuerung muss es sich gleich um ein völlig neues Produkt oder eine so genannte „Durchbruchs-Innovation" handeln. Auch neuartige Dienstleistungen, Komplett-Angebote durch Kooperationen, ja selbst altbekannte Leistungen wie etwa Autoreparaturen haben innovativen Charakter, wenn sie z. B. als Express-Dienstleistung über Nacht erledigt werden. Solche Innovationen sind nicht weniger wegweisend und sie stärken die Leistungsfähigkeit der Betriebe. Denn die Innovationen tragen dazu bei, Märkte zu sichern und auch neue Märkte für das Handwerk zu erschließen.

Ich denke hier etwa an den Markt für Umweltschutztechnik oder an regenerative Energien, die dank des Wertewandels der Gesellschaft neue Betätigungsfelder eröffnen. Im Bereich der Medizintechnik können die Gesundheitshandwerke von Entwicklungen in der Mikrosystemtechnik profitieren, wenn sie die Ergebnisse aus den Laboren der Forschungseinrichtungen konsequent für sich nutzen. Nicht zuletzt hat auch die Anwendung neuer Technologien wie Laser-, CAD-, Roboter- und Kommunikationstechniken zu einem Innovationsschub im Handwerk geführt. Prozess- und Herstellungskosten konnten in erheblichem Maße reduziert werden.

Durch die kreative Nutzung neuer Technologien und Fertigungsverfahren kann sich das Handwerk auch über die Grenzen hinweg auf internationalem Parkett Märkte erschließen – ob als leistungsstarker Zulieferer für die Automobilindustrie oder als Systemanbieter für Umweltschutz- und Heiztechnik.

Der große Vorteil des Handwerks in Deutschland ist dabei – noch – das Qualifikationsniveau; individuelle Problemlösungen auf hohem qualitativen Niveau, das ist der Markt, auf dem unsere Betriebe punkten können.

Kundennähe fördert Kreativität

Der Anstoß zu innovativen Leistungen entsteht häufig aus dem direkten Kontakt der Handwerker zu ihren Kunden. Das Bedürfnis der Kunden nach individuellen Gütern und Dienstleistungen ist der zentrale Auslöser für die Entwicklung innovativer

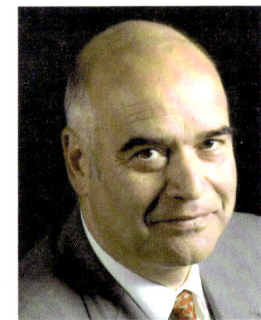

Otto Kentzler

Der Autor ist seit Januar 2005 Präsident des Zentralverbandes des Deutschen Handwerks (ZDH). 1941 in Dortmund geboren, absolvierte er zunächst eine Lehre zum Gas-Wasser-Installateur und Klempner und nahm dann ein Studium des Allgemeinen Maschinenbaus an der Technischen Universität Hannover auf, das er als Diplom-Ingenieur abschloss. Otto Kentzler ist Geschäftsführender Gesellschafter der Firma Kentzler GmbH & Co. KG in Dortmund und übt weitere Ehrenämter aus, u. a. als Präsident der Handwerkskammer Dortmund und als Vorsitzender des Arbeitsausschusses für Wirtschafts-, Finanz- und Kreditpolitik beim Nordrhein-Westfälischen Handwerkstag (NWHT).

The author has been President of Zentralverband des Deutschen Handwerks (ZDH) since January 2005. He was born in Dortmund in 1941 and first completed training as a gas-water fitter and plumber, then took up studies of general machine construction at the Technical University of Hanover graduating as certified engineer. He is Managing Associate of Messrs. Kentzler GmbH & Co. KG in Dortmund and occupies several honorary posts, including President of the Chamber of Handicrafts Dortmund and Chairman of the Working Committee for Economic, Finance and Credit Policy at the Assembly of Handicrafts for North Rhine-Westphalia.

Logistik-, Produktions- und Kommunikationstechnologien im Handwerk. Insofern spiegelt jede Neuerung im Handwerk das wider, was der Kunde wünscht. Und die Kunden – das ist ihr gutes

Skilled Trade

The social and economic sector of handicrafts or skilled trade currently is – just as the medium-size business sector overall – in the midst of undergoing a major transitional process and change, which in its dimension, diversified facets and speed is probably unique in the long history of skilled trade and its organisations. One thing is certain, namely that new strategies of adjustment must be developed. Each company is forced to analyse its strengths and weaknesses and to examine its business strategy. This applies given the catastrophic economic situation of the domestic market, and applies much more so, given the second round of Enlargement of the European Union with all its risks and chances. The transition period forcefully demanded by the skilled trade sector also helps in this round of EU Enlargement to reduce the pressure of adjustment and to extend it. But we don't want to fool ourselves: since 1st May 2004, the East European competition has been active in front of our own doorstep – but at completely different conditions. However, we are not going to loose courage, despite the present difficult economic and political frame conditions. A fair amount of optimism coupled with drive is essentially part of the skilled trade mentality. Entrepreneurs and employees in handicrafts with their excellent qualifications can confront the challenges openly.

Innovations open up new markets

The skilled trade sector has mastered already many a crisis during its long history, because it has always been flexible, capable of adjusting and innovative. In fact, independent entrepreneurs in handicrafts secure the success of their companies and their future above all by their own effort. One major factor of success is the capacity to meet the challenges of daily work with innovative ideas. And these must not necessarily be limited to the field of high-tech. Indeed, they are possible and also necessary in all trades.

From the public's point of view, inventions and improvements of products and service provisions in skilled trade frequently seem less spectacular than inventions in industry. But by far the greatest number of innovations emerge from medium-size businesses! It is clearly evident: not every invention must be a completely new product or a so-called "pioneering innovation". Also newly created services, comprehensive provisions through cooperation agreements, even well-established services like car repairs can have an innovative character, if they are carried out as Express Service over night for instance. Such innovations are not less ground-breaking and they strengthen the efficiency of companies. In effect, innovations play a major role in securing markets and also in developing new markets for the skilled trade sector.

I am thinking here of the market for environmental engineering or regenerative energies, which, owing to the change of values in society, open up new fields of activities. In the field of medicine engineering, trades belonging to the health care sector can benefit from developments in micro system engineering, if they consistently utilize the results from the laboratories in research institutions for themselves. Ultimately, the application of new technologies like laser, CAD, robotics and communications technologies, have led to a surge of innovations in skilled trade. Process and production costs have been reduced to a considerable extent. Through the creative use of new technologies and production methods the skilled trade sector can also develop markets beyond its regional borders on an international level, be it as efficient supplier to the automobile industry or as system provider for environmental engineering or heating technologies.

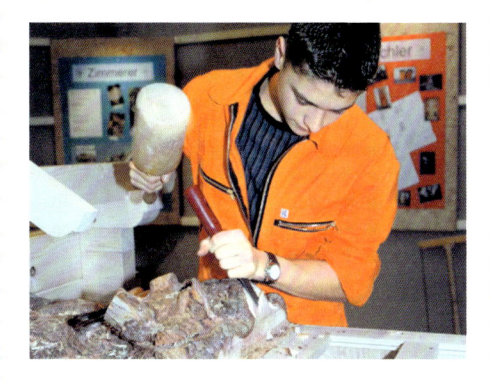

The great advantage for skilled trade in Germany is still the level of qualification; individual problem solutions of a high quality standard, that is the market on which our companies can score points.

Closeness to customers promotes creativity

The first initiative to create innovative products or services often emerges from the direct contact of skilled tradesmen with their clients. The need of clients to have individually produced goods and services is the main cause to trigger off the development of innovative logistics, production and communications technologies in handicrafts. In this respect, each innovation in skilled trade reflects exactly the wishes of customers. Moreover, customers are becoming ever more demanding, and they have every right to do so: they expect extensive and at the same time special services tailored exactly to meet their requirements at a reasonable cost-effectiveness. This frequently also includes solutions that convince through originality and power of innovation in detail, that continue developing and perfecting already existing technicalities. This refers particularly to the building and interior decoration sector, but generally is necessary and expected of all skilled trade services.

Besides products and services, also information and customer service are increasingly becoming a basis for a client deciding to purchase. Therefore, the Internet is turning into an ever more important marketing instrument. A great part of companies uses the Internet for operational matters but above all also to maintain their clientele.

Cooperation creates synergies

Another possibility that serves to secure future prospects of the economic sector is the cooperation between skilled trade enterprises. Through cooperation, mid-sized tradesmen compensate their disadvantages caused by size, and this did not just start today, but increasingly more often since on the other hand the economic sector is characterised by a process of concentration. Indeed, in skilled trade one has recognised long ago that through collaboration and cooperation with other partners it is frequently possible to set more things into motion than alone.

Examples of successful cooperation can be found easily. One example that is particularly doing well is the "Competence Association for Monument Protection", which offers its clients a comprehensive restoration of historic buildings. To ensure a smooth teamwork, this partnership consisting of seven companies based in the Osnabrücker Land has found a practical approach for the organisation of work. Already during the planning phase, different trades like joiners, carpenters, painters or landscape artists find the best possible agreements so that the execution can take place without delays. These efforts of time saving lead to noticeable cost reductions, which in turn can be passed down to the customers.

Handwerk

Recht – werden immer anspruchsvoller: Sie erwarten umfassende und gleichzeitig speziell auf ihre Bedürfnisse zugeschnittene Dienstleistungen zu einem angemessenen Preis-Leistungs-Verhältnis. Dabei sind oft auch Lösungen gefragt, die durch Originalität und Innovationskraft im Detail bestechen, die Bestehendes technisch weiterentwickeln und vervollkommen. Das gilt im Besonderen für den Bau- und Ausbausektor, ist aber prinzipiell für alle handwerklichen Leistungen notwendig und gefordert.

Neben dem Produkt und der Dienstleistung werden auch die Information und der Service immer mehr zur Grundlage für die Kaufentscheidung eines Kunden. Deshalb wird das Internet zu einem immer wichtigeren Marketing-Instrument. Ein Großteil aller Betriebe setzt das Internet für seine betrieblichen Zwecke und vor allem auch zur Kundenpflege ein.

Kooperationen: Synergien schaffen

Kooperationen handwerklicher Betriebe sind eine weitere Möglichkeit, die der Zukunftssicherung des Wirtschaftsbereichs dient. Mit Kooperationen gleichen mittelständische Handwerker ihre größenbedingten Nachteile aus – nicht erst heute, sondern sukzessive immer mehr, je mehr auf der anderen Seite die Welt der Wirtschaft durch Konzentrationsprozesse geprägt wird. Im Handwerk ist nämlich längst die Erkenntnis angekommen, dass man durch Zusammenarbeit und Kooperation mit Partnern oft noch mehr bewegen kann als allein.

Beispiele für erfolgreiche Kooperationen lassen sich viele finden. Ein besonders gelungenes ist das des „Kompetenzverbunds Denkmalschutz", der seinen Kunden die Komplett-Restaurierung historischer Gebäude anbietet. Für ein reibungsloses Zusammenspiel hat diese Kooperation aus sieben Betrieben aus dem Osnabrücker Land einen praxisnahen arbeitsorganisatorischen Ansatz gefunden. Schon in der Planungsphase stimmen sich die verschiedenen Gewerbe wie Tischler, Zimmerer, Maler oder Gartengestalter bestmöglich untereinander ab, so dass die Durchführung ohne Verzögerung stattfinden kann. Zeiteinsparungen führen zu spürbar verringerten Kosten, die wiederum an die Kunden weitergegeben werden.

Handwerksbetriebe sind seit langen Jahren auch mit grenzüberschreitenden Kooperationen aktiv. In den bisherigen europäischen Grenzregionen funktioniert das nahezu ohne Reibungsverluste. Kooperationen mit den neuen Beitrittsländern spielen zunehmend eine Rolle. Dabei gibt es eine Reihe von Problemen, vor allem aufgrund erheblicher bürokratischer Belastungen, die die Kooperationen mit Betrieben in den neuen Beitrittsländern noch komplizieren. Dennoch: Langfristig betrachtet wird der erweiterte Binnenmarkt Deutschland nutzen und auch das Handwerk wird davon profitieren, denn wer heute sein Geschäft in den Mitgliedsstaaten aufbaut, verbessert seine Chancen in den wachsenden Märkten.

Basis: Qualifikation

Die vielfältigen Neuerungen und kreativen Leistungen im Handwerk wären undenkbar ohne die hochwertige Ausbildung und die kontinuierliche Weiterbildung von Betriebsinhabern und Mitarbeitern. Qualifizierung ist Voraussetzung, um in der Wissensgesellschaft bestehen zu können. Qualifizierung ist ein klarer Standortvorteil auf regionalen und europäischen Märkten.

Um auch künftig eine breite Grundlage herzustellen, auf der sich kreative Potenziale entfalten können, modernisiert das Handwerk die Aus- und Weiterbildung. Dabei bleibt der Meisterbrief die Spitzenqualifikation. Er stellt auch in Zukunft ein effizientes Instrument der Qualifikation und des Verbraucherschutzes dar. Kunden haben dadurch die Gewähr, dass ihr Auftragnehmer sein Handwerk versteht. Für die Mitarbeiter, Geschäftspartner und Kreditgeber ist der Meisterbrief Ausweis dafür, dass ein Handwerker auch in unternehmerischer Hinsicht für seine Tätigkeit qualifiziert ist. Die Zahlen sprechen für sich: In keinem anderen Wirtschaftsbereich ist die Gründerquote so hoch wie im Handwerk – eben durch den Meisterbrief, die einzige Ausbildung für die Selbständigkeit, die zugleich für die hohe wirtschaftliche Stabilität der Existenzgründungen und Innovationskraft im Handwerk sorgt.

Das Handwerk muss auch künftig daran arbeiten, das hohe Qualifikationsniveau seiner Mitarbeiter zu halten. Dazu gehört, die Anstrengungen zur Modernisierung der Aus- und Weiterbildung auf nationaler Ebene in den europäischen Kontext einzubetten. Die handwerkliche Aus- und Weiterbildung kann in Zukunft nur attraktiv bleiben, wenn sie auch genügend Angebote für eine europäische Bildungs- und Beschäftigungs-Karriere vorhält. Welche Rolle der Wirtschaftsbereich Handwerk in Zukunft im internationalen Wettbewerb spielt, das hängt maßgeblich von der Leistungsfähigkeit der Bildungs- und Berufsbildungssysteme und damit vom Reservoir gut ausgebildeter Fachkräfte ab. ■

Prozentuale Verteilung der Betriebsbestände auf die Anlagen A, AeT einf. Tätigkeiten, B1 und B2 im 1. Halbjahr 2004
Percentage distribution of companies based on A, AeT simple activities, B1 and B2 in the first half of 2004

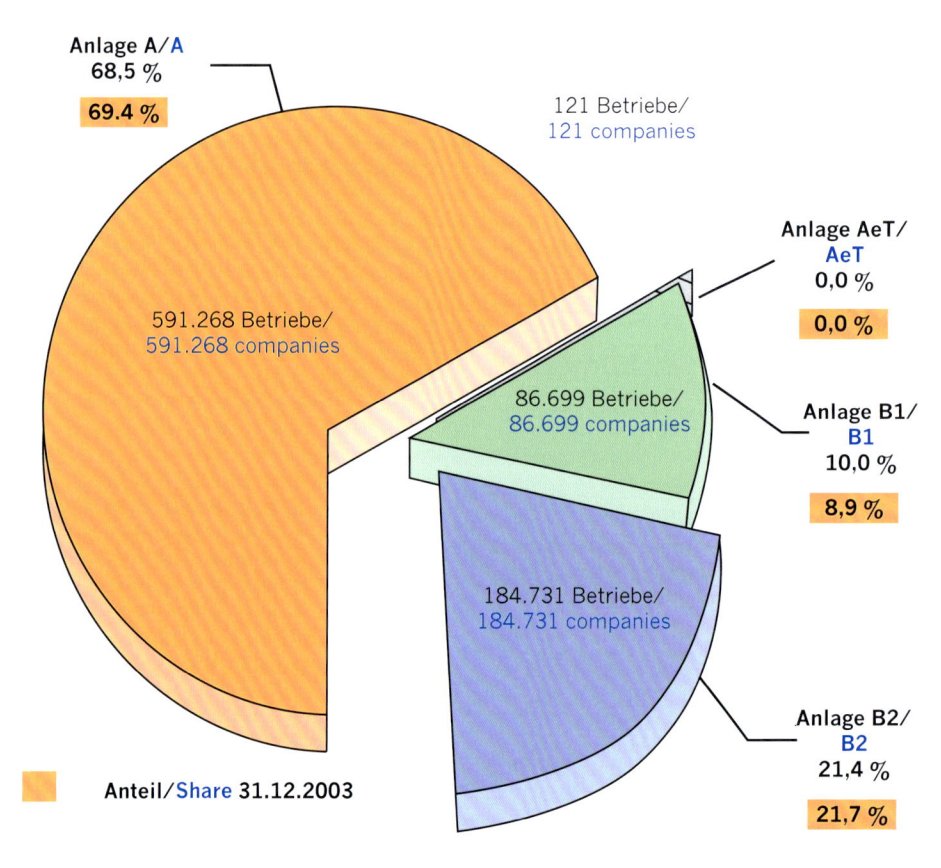

Anlage	Betriebe/companies	Anteil 31.12.2003	Anteil 1. Halbjahr 2004
Anlage A / A	591.268	68,5 %	69,4 %
Anlage AeT / AeT	121	0,0 %	0,0 %
Anlage B1 / B1	86.699	10,0 %	8,9 %
Anlage B2 / B2	184.731	21,4 %	21,7 %

Handwerksbetriebe insgesamt/Total handicrafts enterprises: 862.819

Quelle/Source: zdh

Skilled Trade

Entwicklung der Betriebsbestände im Handwerk in Deutschland 1996 – 1. Halbjahr 2004
(Anlagen A, A einf. Tätigkeiten, B1 und B2)

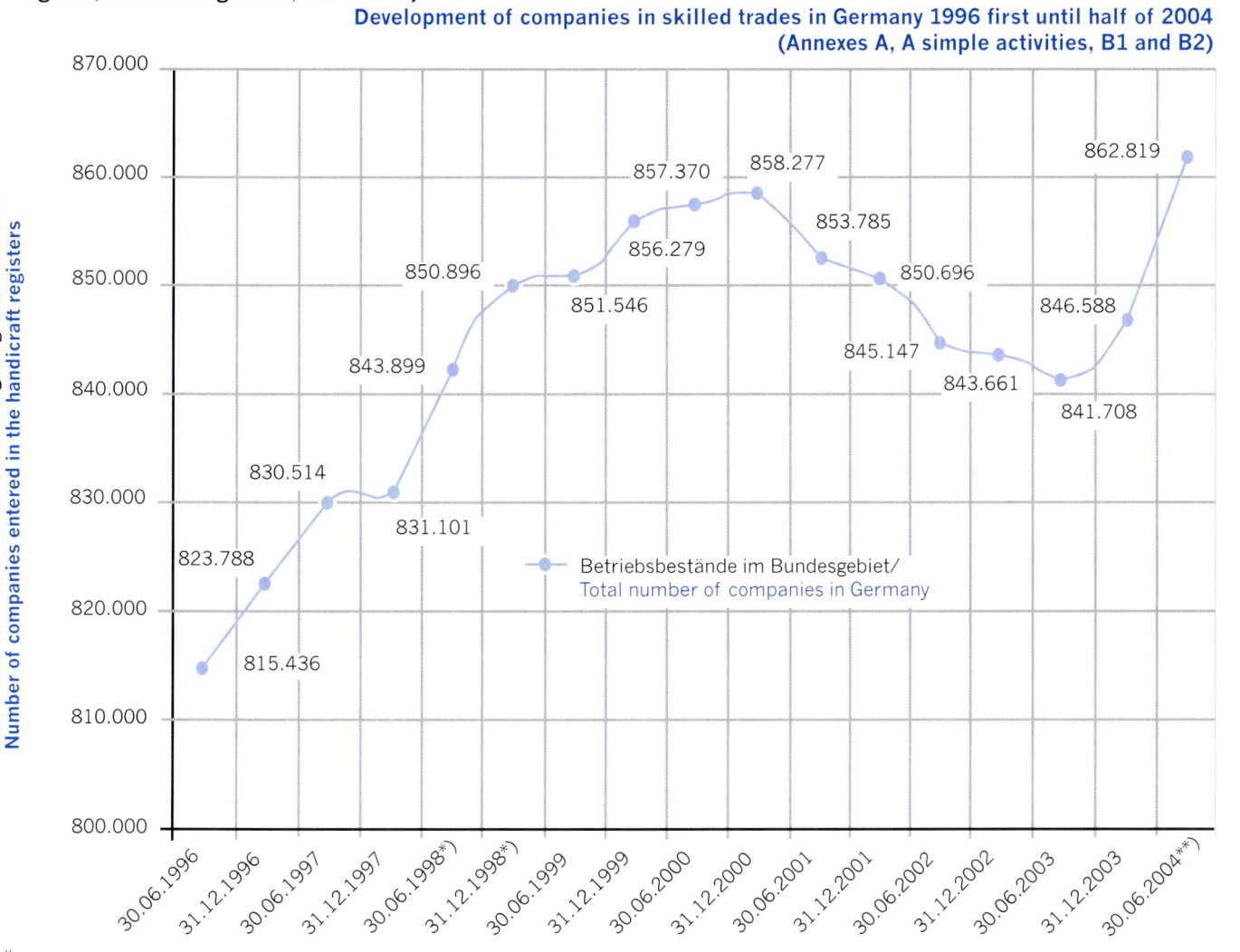

Development of companies in skilled trades in Germany 1996 first until half of 2004
(Annexes A, A simple activities, B1 and B2)

Anzahl der in den Handwerksrollen eingetragenen Betriebe/
Number of companies entered in the handicraft registers

Date	Total number of companies in Germany
30.06.1996	815.436
31.12.1996	823.788
30.06.1997	830.514
31.12.1997	831.101
30.06.1998*)	843.899
31.12.1998*)	850.896
30.06.1999	851.546
31.12.1999	857.370
30.06.2000	856.279
31.12.2000	858.277
30.06.2001	853.785
31.12.2001	850.696
30.06.2002	845.147
31.12.2002	843.661
30.06.2003	841.708
31.12.2003	846.588
30.06.2004**)	862.819

*) Änderung der HwO/Modification of the Handicrafts Code   **) Novellierung der HwO/Amendment of the Handicrafts Code

Quelle/Source: zdh

For many years now, handicraft enterprises have also been active in cooperation agreements across the borders. Within the previous European border regions this functions almost without any frictional losses. Cooperation agreements with new accession countries are gaining a major role gradually. There are a number of problems, primarily because of considerable bureaucratic difficulties, which still complicate the cooperation with firms in new accession countries. However: Viewed from a long-term perspective, the enlarged European market will be useful for Germany, and also the skilled trade sector will benefit from this fact, because, whoever builds up his business in one of the member countries, certainly improves his chances in the growing markets.

Fundamental basis: qualification

Numerous innovations and creative achievements in handicrafts would be unthinkable without the high level of training and continuous qualification of company owners and employees. Qualification is a precondition to stand one's ground in the knowledge society.

Qualification is a clear location advantage on regional and European markets.

In order to create a broad basis also in future on which creative potentials can be developed, the skilled trade sector is modernising training and further education facilities. The Master Craftsman Certificate will remain a top qualification in this respect. It represents also in future an efficient instrument of qualification and for consumer protection. Customers thus have the guarantee that their contractor really knows his trade. For employees, business partners and creditors, the Master Craftsman Certificate is a proof that a tradesman is also qualified in terms of entrepreneurship to perform his craft. In fact the figures speak for themselves: no other economic sector shows such a high rate of company foundations as the skilled trades – precisely through the Master Craftsman Certificate, which is the only training providing a direct way into self-employment, which at the same time ensures a high economic stability of independent firms and provides power of innovation in handicrafts.

The skilled trade sector must continue working on maintaining the high level of qualification of staff members also in future. This includes integrating efforts of modernising training and further education on national level into the European context. Training and further education in skilled trades can only continue to be attractive in future if it provides sufficient offers for a European educational and employment career. The role that the economic sector of skilled trade will play in international competition in future depends to a great extent on the efficiency of education and vocational education systems and therefore on the reservoir of well-trained specialists available. ■

Company Profile

Simon Hegele
Ideen bewegen

Simon Hegele Gesellschaft
für Logistik und Service mbH

Geschäftsführer/Managing Directors:
Dieter Hegele,
Siegfried Kiefer

Gründungsjahr/Year of Foundation: 1920

Mitarbeiter/Employees:
ca. 1.200 insgesamt (2004)/
approx. 1,200 altogether (2004)

Umsatz/Turnover: 120 Mio. Euro (in der Gruppe)

Geschäftstätigkeit/Business Activity:
- Umzug Logistik & Service
- Medizin Logistik & Service
- IT/Industrie Logistik & Service
- Procurement Solutions
- Ersatzteile Logistik & Service
- Clinical Logistik & Service
- Aktenservice
- Moving logistics & services
- Medical logistics & services
- IT/Industry logistics & services
- Procurement solutions
- Spare parts logistics & services
- Clinical logistics & services
- Archives services

Anschrift/Address:
Hardeckstraße 5
D-76185 Karlsruhe
Telefon   +49 (721) 5 70 09
Telefax   +49 (721) 5 70 09 130
E-Mail   info@hegele.de
Internet www.hegele.de

Das Logistikunternehmen mit Tradition

Logistics Enterprise of long-standing Tradition

Simon Hegele ist ein moderner, flexibler Dienstleister, der sich mit kundennahen Logistikdienstleistungen erfolgreich im Markt positioniert und mit innovativen Ideen neue Märkte eröffnet. Über die historischen Wurzeln einer Möbelspedition längst hinausgewachsen, ist sich das Karlsruher Traditionsunternehmen seiner Stärken bewusst und entwickelt daraus zukunftsorientierte Businessstrategien im Bereich logistischer Komplettlösungen.

Logistik als Full-Service-Philosophie
Die Bandbreite reicht hierbei von professionellem Einkauf mit webbasierter eProcurement-Plattform, über die produktionssynchrone Beschaffung und die Fertigungsversorgung, bis hin zur weltweiten Distributionslogistik. Simon Hegele kümmert sich um Beschaffung und Einkauf, organisiert die Warenströme vom Lieferanten bis zum Produktionsort und übernimmt die Qualitätsprüfung und Lagerhaltung in modernen Logistik Centern. Die hierfür vorhandenen Logistik- und Lagerflächen belaufen sich auf rund 320.000 m² (das entspricht etwa 50 Fußballfeldern) an 16 Standorten im Bundesgebiet und im Ausland. Geschulte Mitarbeiter kommissionieren, konfektionieren und montieren Produkte vor, mit denen sie die Fertigungslinien der Kunden just-in-time versorgen. Dabei bedient sich das Unternehmen hauseigener Konzepte und Entwicklungen wie spezieller Datenverarbeitungssysteme und Barcode-Steuerungen. ■

Simon Hegele is a modern, flexible service provider that is successfully positioned in the market with customer-oriented logistics services and is developing new markets with innovative ideas. Having outgrown its historical roots of a removal firm, the traditional Karlsruhe-based company knows its strengths and develops thereby future-oriented business strategies in the field of comprehensive logistics solutions.

Logistics as full service philosophy
The service spectrum extends from professional purchase with web-based e-procurement platform across the procurement synchronised for production and supply for manufacture through to a worldwide system of distribution logistics. Simon Hegele deals with procurement and purchasing, organises the flow of goods from supplier to production location and takes over quality testing and storage in modern logistics centres. To this end, logistics and storage areas amounting to about 320,000 m² are available (corresponding to around 50 football pitches) at 16 locations domestically and abroad. Well-trained employees carry out order picking, assemble and mount products in advance, in order to supply the production lines of customers just-in-time. The firm uses in-house concepts and developments like special computer processing systems and barcode controls. ■

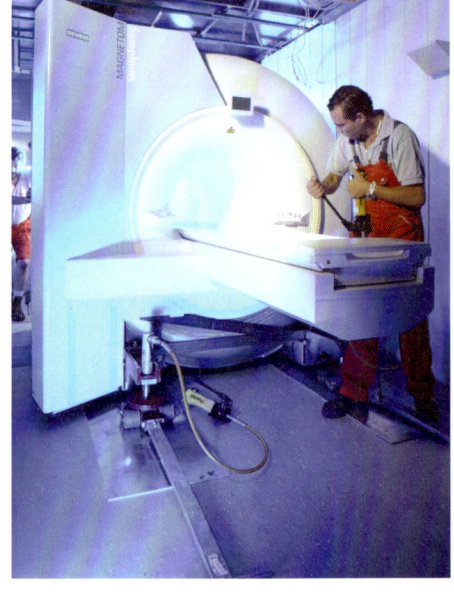

Company Profile

Immobilien für die mobile Gesellschaft

Immovable property for a mobile society

Die ARWOBAU Apartment- und Wohnungsbaugesellschaft mbH mit Sitz in Berlin ist eines der großen Dienstleistungsunternehmen der Immobilienbranche. Als technischer und kaufmännischer Facility-Manager mit den Schwerpunkten Vermietung, Verwaltung und Revitalisierung erbringt sie Dienstleistungen für private Auftraggeber und Fondsgesellschaften. Die ganzheitliche Betreuung von Objekten als Asset Manager zählt ebenfalls zur Kernkompetenz des Unternehmens. Die ARWOBAU wurde 1964 als städtische Gesellschaft mit dem Ziel gegründet, die Wirtschaft des isolierten West-Berlin mit der Bereitstellung von möbliertem Wohnraum für zuziehende Arbeitskräfte zu unterstützen. Nach der Privatisierung im Jahre 1996 entwickelte sich die ARWOBAU zu einem bundesweit tätigen Immobiliendienstleister. Mit rund 8.000 möblierten Apartments ist sie heute Marktführer und der größte Anbieter für temporäres Wohnen in Berlin. Dazu zählen auch 12 exklusive Apartmenthäuser, die unter der Marke „CentralHome® – First Choice Berlin" geführt werden. Zusätzlich vermietet und verwaltet das Unternehmen ca. 20.000 Wohnungen und 2 Mio. m^2 Gewerbeflächen in ganz Deutschland.

Die ARWOBAU dient als kompetenter Ansprechpartner für Firmen und Institutionen, die ihren Sitz nach Berlin verlegen oder zeitweilig hier tätig sind. Die individuelle Betreuung und Beratung der Mitarbeiter bei der Apartmentwahl bzw. Wohnungssuche wird von den Unternehmen gerne als Dienstleistung angenommen. Mit ihrer Dienstleistungskompetenz hat sie u. a. den Regierungsumzug von Bonn nach Berlin und zahlreiche weitere Standortverlegungen begleitet und ist Partner für viele Unternehmen in Deutschland. ∎

ARWOBAU Apartment- und Wohnungsbaugesellschaft mbH with seat in Berlin is one of the major service providing companies in the real estate branch. Being a technical and commercial Facility Manager focussing on lease, administration and revitalisation, it renders services to private contractors and fund management companies. Also included in our competencies is the comprehensive management of objects as Asset Managers.

ARWOBAU was founded in 1964 as municipal company, with the aim to support West-Berlin's isolated economy by providing furnished housing for an arriving workforce. After privatisation in the year 1996, ARWOBAU developed into a nationwide active real estate service provider. With around 8,000 furnished apartments, today it is market leader and the largest provider of temporary accommodation in Berlin. This also includes 12 exclusive apartment houses, which run under the brand name "CentralHome® – First Choice Berlin". Additionally, the company lets and manages approx. 20,000 apartments and 2 million m^2 of industrial areas all over Germany.

ARWOBAU serves as competent contact partner for firms and institutions that want to relocate their company seat to Berlin or be active here for a short period. Companies appreciate that they receive individual service and consulting when looking for housing or selecting an apartment. With their service competence it has accompanied for instance the relocation of the Federal Government from Bonn to Berlin and numerous other relocations. It is partner of many companies in Germany. ∎

ARWOBAU Apartment- und Wohnungsbaugesellschaft mbH

Geschäftsführer/Managers:
Gert Sielaff (Sprecher/Speaker)
Dr. Elmar Müller

Gründungsjahr/Year of Foundation: 1964

Mitarbeiter/Employees: 330

Geschäftstätigkeit/Business Activity:
Bundesweit tätiger technischer und kaufmännischer Facility-Manager mit den Schwerpunkten Vermietung, Verwaltung und Revitalisierung für private Auftraggeber und Fondsgesellschaften.
Technical and commercial Facility Manager focussing on lease, administration and revitalisation for private contractors and fund management companies nationwide.

Anschrift/Address:
Hallesches Ufer 74–76
D-10963 Berlin
Telefon   +49 (030) 25441-0
Telefax   +49 (030) 25441-162
Internet   www.arwobau.de

Company Profile

Die Vivanco Gruppe AG – Technologie für Lifestyle

The Vivanco Group AG – technology for lifestyle

Vivanco Gruppe AG

Vorstand/Executive Board:
Paul Jähn
(Vorstandsvorsitzender/ CEO)
Frank Bussalb

Gründungsjahr/Year of Foundation:
1920 als de Vivanco & Co.
Heute: Vivanco Gruppe AG,
börsennotiert, amtlicher Handel
1920 as de Vivanco & Co.
Today: Vivanco Group AG,
listed on the stock exchange, official trading

Mitarbeiter/Employees:
Deutschland 250/250 in Germany
Weltweit 550/550 worldwide

Geschäftstätigkeit/Business Activity:
Entwicklung, Herstellung und Vertrieb von Zubehörprodukten in den Bereichen Unterhaltungselektronik, Informationstechnologie, Telekommunikation und Verbindungstechnologie.
Development, production and sale of accessory products in the fields of Consumer Electronics, Information Technology, Telecommunications and Access Technology.

Anschrift/Address:
Ewige Weide 15
D-22926 Ahrensburg
Telefon   +49 (4102) 231-0
Telefax   +49 (4102) 231-160
E-Mail   info@vivanco.de
Internet www.vivanco.de

Vivanco-Vorstandsvorsitzender Paul Jähn.
Vivanco Chairman Paul Jähn.

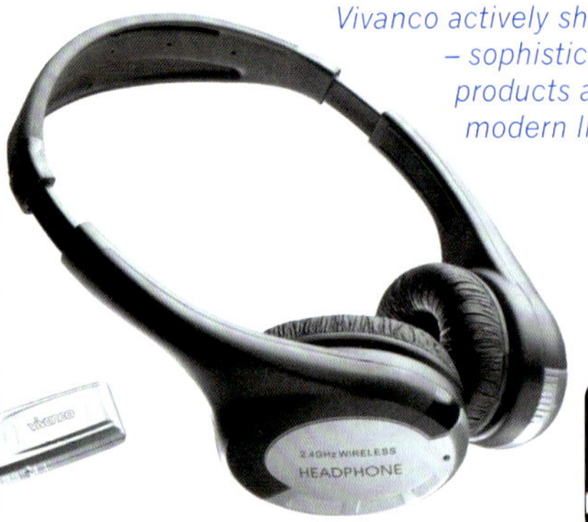

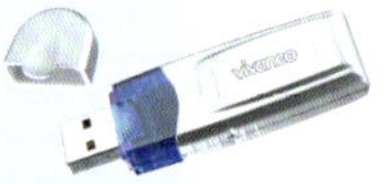

Vivanco gestaltet Markttrends – anspruchsvolle technologische Produkte werden mit Lifestyle Elementen verbunden.
Vivanco actively shapes market trends – sophisticated technological products are combined with modern lifestyle elements.

Die Vivanco Gruppe AG mit Stammsitz in Ahrensburg bei Hamburg ist einer der europaweit führenden Zubehörspezialisten in den Bereichen Unterhaltungselektronik, Informationstechnologie, Telekommunikation und Verbindungstechnologie. Die starke Marke Vivanco wird flankiert von den Technologie Marken Teccus und Prowire sowie von den Lifestyle Marken bazoo und Babyfon. Die Produkte werden erfolgreich in Deutschland, in Europa über acht Tochtergesellschaften und weltweit über mehr als 20 Distributeure vertrieben.

With headquarters in Ahrensburg near Hamburg, Vivanco Group AG is one of the European-wide leading accessories specialists in the fields of Consumer Electronics, Information Technology, Telecommunications and Access Technology. The strong Vivanco brand is supported by the Technology brands Teccus and Prowire as well as by the Lifestyle brands bazoo and Babyfon. Products are succesfully sold in Germany, by eight subsidiaries in Europe and by more than 20 distributors worldwide.

Vivanco – der Spezialist für technisches Zubehör in Europa

Durch die Kombination anspruchsvoller technologischer Produkte mit Lifestyle Elementen ist Vivanco ein Gestalter von Markttrends. Die Produkte sind anders in Form, Farbe und Design und bestechen durch eine Top-Qualität und ein Top-Preis-Leistungsverhältnis.

Darüber hinaus ist Vivanco ein routinierter Akteur auf dem Beschaffungsmarkt Fernost, der die gesamte Wertschöpfungskette von der Innovation bis zum Kunden abdeckt. Mit über sechs Millionen China Importkartons bewältigt Vivanco die erhöhten Logistikanforderungen von Fernost bis an den Point of Sales in Europa.
Über das hochtechnisierte Logistikzentrum in Ahrensburg werden jährlich ca. 20 Millionen Produkte versendet. Um diese Anforderungen zu bewältigen sind weltweit 550 Mitarbeiter für die Vivanco Gruppe AG tätig. ■

Vivanco – Specialist for technical accessories in Europe

Through the combination of sophisticated technological products containing lifestyle elements, Vivanco actively shapes current market trends. Products are different in shape, colour and design and captivate one's attention through top-quality and excellent cost-effectiveness.

Furthermore, Vivanco is an experienced player on the procurement market in the Far East, which covers the complete value-added chain from innovation through to the customer. With over six million imported cartons from China Vivanco successfully deals with increased logistics demands from the Far East right through to points of sale in Europe.
Via the highly mechanised logistics centre in Ahrensburg, each year approx. 20 million products are dispatched. In order to manage this request for delivery successfully, Vivanco Group AG employs worldwide 550 staff members. ■

Company Profile

Faszination für den Sportfan

Fascination for sport fans

betandwin e. K.

Geschäftsführer/Managing Director:
Dr. Steffen Pfennigwerth

Gründungsjahr/Year of Foundation: 1990

Mitarbeiter/Employees:
rund/around 40

Geschäftsfeld/Business field:
Sportwetten/Sporting bets

Anschrift/Address:
betandwin e.K.
Breitscheidstraße 20
D-02727 Neugersdorf
Telefon   +49 (35 86) 77 17 17
Telefax   +49 (35 86) 77 17 88
E-Mail   management@betandwin.de
Internet www.betandwin.de

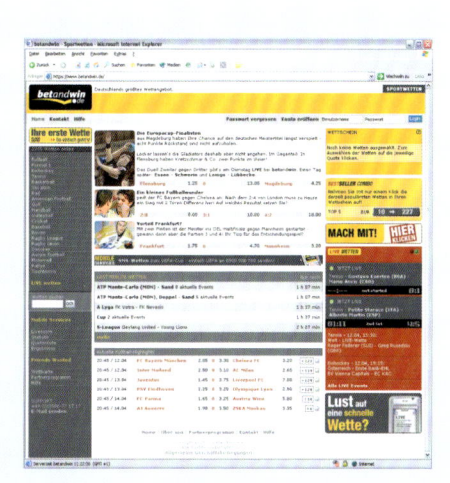

Spannung, Herausforderung und die Chance auf lukrative Gewinne – www.betandwin.de bietet das umfangreichste Online-Sportwettenangebot im deutschen Markt. Egal ob Fußball, Formel 1, Eishockey, Tennis oder amerikanische Sportligen – zu über 40 verschiedenen Sportarten finden Sportfans bei www.betandwin.de ein Angebot von bis zu 4.000 Wetten.

Der Eigentümer der **bet**and**win** e. K., Dr. Steffen Pfennigwerth, gründete das Unternehmen im April 1990 und verfügt seitdem über eine Lizenz zum Anbieten von Sportwetten. 2002 erwarb die österreichische BETandWIN.com Interactive Entertainment AG, der größte Sportwettenanbieter Kontinentaleuropas mit Sitz in Wien, eine 50 %ige atypisch stille Beteiligung an der **bet**and**win** e. K. Als einer von vier privaten lizenzierten Wettbietern in Deutschland ist betandwin einer der wichtigen Sponsoren des deutschen Sports. Mit einem Marketingbudget von über 20 Millionen Euro sponsert **bet**and**win** unter anderem die Ausstattung von über 7.000 Amateur-Fußballvereinen mit über einer Million Euro.

Ein wichtiges Ziel von **bet**and**win** ist die Förderung des fairen sportlichen Wettbewerbs und die Bereitstellung eines sicheren Wettangebotes. Mit der vorhandenen Expertise in Sachen Sicherheit ist **bet**and**win** daher ein wichtiger Partner von Verbänden und Politik bei der Diskussion um sichere Standards für Sportwetten. ∎

The thrill, the challenge and the chance to make lucrative winnings – www.**bet**and**win**.de offers the most extensive online sporting bets on the German market. Be it football, Formula 1, ice hockey, tennis or American sports leagues – sport fans can find offers covering over 40 different types of sports at www.**bet**and**win**.de for up to 4,000 bets.

The proprietor of **bet**and**win** e. K., Dr. Steffen Pfennigwerth founded the company in April 1990 and since that time has a licence to offer sporting bets. In 2002, the Austrian-based BETandWIN.com Interactive Entertainment AG, the largest sporting bets provider of continental Europe with seat in Vienna, atypically acquired 50 % a silent share in **bet**and**win** e. K.

Being one of four private licensed sporting bets providers in Germany, betandwin is one of the major sponsors of German sports. With a marketing budget of over 20 million Euros, **bet**and**win** sponsors, among others, equipments of over 7,000 amateur football clubs providing over one million Euros.

One important aim of **bet**and**win** is the promotion of fair and sportive competition and providing safe sporting bets. The existing experience in terms of safety therefore enables **bet**and**win** to act as important partner to associations and political circles in discussions about safety standards for sporting bets. ∎

Massenmedien

Wie attraktiv ist die Darstellung des Standorts Deutschland in den Medien?

How attractive is the presentation of Germany as a business location in the media?

Zwischen Krise und Zuversicht

Wer möchte investieren in einem Land, das sich in Zeiten der Krise „voller Schwäche, Weichheit und Angst" präsentiert, als „kranker Mann Europas" bezeichnet wird (Welt am Sonntag, 11.5.2003, S. 12), bei dem „fast alle Indizes der Wettbewerbsfähigkeit und wirtschaftlichen Freiheit nach unten zeigen" (FAZ, 16. 9. 2003, S. 16), und das „aus einem Teufelskreis von Reformstau, dramatischen Arbeitslosenzahlen und sinkender Wirtschaftskraft" (SZ, 10.3.2003, S. 2) nicht herauskommt?

Besser wäre es wohl, ein Land zum Standort zu wählen, in dem der Werkzeugmaschinenbau „eine Weltrangliste anführt", dessen Biotechnologie „im europäischen Vergleich durchaus gut" dasteht (FAZ, 20. 1. 2004, S. 12), dessen Ausbildungsstand und Infrastruktur von ausländischen Unternehmen gelobt werden (FAZ, 17. 9. 2003, S. 17) und das derzeit Exportweltmeister ist (FTD, 8. 4. 2004, S. 18).

In beiden Fällen handelt es sich um Aussagen über denselben Standort Deutschland. Wie so häufig im Leben, fallen die Urteile und Meinungen dazu in den Medien eben unterschiedlich aus. Dabei konnte man in den letzten Jahren durchaus den Eindruck gewinnen, als werde der Standort Deutschland pauschal schlecht geredet. Welche Rolle spielen dabei die Medien?

Akteure und Instrumente

Medien sind – in der Wirtschaft ebenso wie in der Politik – Akteure und Instrumente gleichermaßen. Sie lassen sich nicht auf eine Rolle festlegen, und das ist vielleicht auch gut so. Als eigenständige Akteure, Interpreten, Kommentatoren gestalten sie Haltungen und Überzeugungen in der Öffentlichkeit mit. Medien können überzeugen, anstoßen und abstoßen.

Ihre Berichte erzeugen Druck und führen oft genug zu Veränderungen in Politik und Wirtschaft. Sie können helfen, den Standort Deutschland zu „verkaufen", ja sogar für ihn zu werben; sie können ihn aber auch unattraktiv machen und Investoren von ihm fernhalten. Dabei kann ihre Berichterstattung für unterschiedlichste Interessen instrumentalisiert werden. Gleichzeitig befinden sich Redakteure und Redaktionen im Meinungs- und Konkurrenzstreit miteinander. Auch dies ist Ursache dafür, dass es eine einheitliche Haltung – etwa in der Einschätzung des Wirtschaftsstandorts – in den Medien nicht gibt. Im Gegenteil, Meinungsvielfalt herrscht vor. Diese Qualität zeichnet die facettenreiche deutsche Medienlandschaft aus. Jedenfalls sind die Medien – ob Zeitungen, Rundfunk und Fernsehen oder Internet – auch und gerade im Hinblick auf die Attraktivität des Standorts außerordentlich wichtig. In unseren Medien werden wirtschaftliche, regionale, kulturelle, soziale und andere Besonderheiten erörtert, die für Unternehmensentscheidungen, gerade hier und nirgendwo anders zu investieren, von großer Bedeutung sind.

Medien schildern die Vor- und Nachteile einer Region und ihrer Wirtschaft; sie analysieren die Lage und zeigen Entwicklungslinien auf. Sie vermitteln also wichtige Informationen, die in- und ausländische Investoren beeinflussen. Gleichzeitig wirken Medien auch auf den Standort selbst ein. Indem sie politische und wirtschaftliche Entscheidungsprozesse thematisieren und auf den Prüfstand heben, helfen sie mit, Veränderungen herbeizuführen, überkommene Traditionen aufzubrechen und das Bewusstsein für dringend notwendige Reformen zu schärfen.

Das öffentliche Gespräch als Standortfaktor

Um den Wirtschaftsstandort Deutschland attraktiv zu erhalten und zu stärken, ist es eine vordringliche Aufgabe der Politik, günstige Rahmenbedingungen zu schaffen und dringend notwendige Reformen wie etwa die Agenda 2010 durchzusetzen. Dabei muss die Regierung viel Überzeugungskraft entwickeln, um das Vertrauen der Bürger und Bürgerinnen, aber auch der Wirtschaft und besonders von Investoren zu gewinnen. Ohne die Medien ist dies nicht zu leisten. Gerade die Politik ist deshalb auf sie angewiesen. Keine demokratische Regierung wird indes erwarten, dass unabhängige Medien lediglich das nacherzählen, was die Politik gern möchte.

Umgekehrt wird vorausgesetzt, dass Medien nicht nur um der reinen Opposition willen von

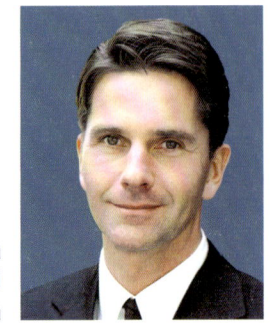

Béla Nikolai Anda

Der Autor ist Sprecher der Bundesregierung und Chef des Presseamtes. Geboren 1963 in Bonn, studierte Béla Nikolai Anda nach einem Volontariat bei der „Welt am Sonntag" Politikwissenschaft am Otto-Suhr-Institut (OSI) an der FU Berlin und an der London School of Economics (LSE). 1991 schloss er das Studium als Diplom-Politologe ab. 1992 wurde er Bild-Redakteur (Politik) und 1994 Chefreporter von „Bild". 1996 erschien sein Buch „Gerhard Schröder. Eine Biographie" (mit Rolf Kleine).
Von Februar 1999 bis Oktober 2002 war Anda stellvertretender Sprecher der Bundesregierung, seit Oktober 2002 ist er Chef des Presse- und Informationsamtes der Bundesregierung sowie Regierungssprecher im Rang eines Staatssekretärs.

The author is Speaker of the Federal Government and Head of the Press Office. Born in Bonn in 1963, Béla Nikolai Anda studied political sciences at the Otto Suhr Institute (OSI) of FU Berlin and at the London School of Economics (LSE) after completing practical training at the newspaper "Welt am Sonntag". In 1991, he graduated as certified political scientist. In 1992, he joined "Bild Zeitung" as editor (politics) and became chief correspondent in 1994. In 1996, his book "Gerhard Schröder. A Biography" was published (together with Rolf Kleine).
From February 1999 until October 2002, Anda served as substitute Speaker of the Federal Government, since October 2002, he has been Head of the Press and Information Office of the Federal Government and Spokesman of the Government having the rank of State Secretary.

Mass Media

Between crisis and confidence

Who wants to invest in a country that presents itself in times of crisis "full of weaknesses, failings and fear", is called "the ill man of Europe" (Newspaper: Welt am Sonntag, 11.05.2003, p. 12), in which "almost all indices about competitiveness and economic freedom are revealing downward trends" (FAZ, 16.09.2003, p. 16) and which does not seem to be able to pull itself out of the "vicious circle of reform barriers, dramatic unemployment figures and declining economic power" (SZ, 10.03.2003, p. 2).

It would certainly be better to chose a country as business location that is "leading the world ranking" in machine tool manufacture, with a bio-technology sector that is "in quite a good position at European level" (FAZ, 20.01.2004, p. 12), whose training standards and infrastructure are praised by foreign companies (FAZ, 17.09.2003, p. 17) and that presently is world champion in exports (FTD, 08.04.2004, p. 18).

Both statements are about the same business location, namely Germany. As frequently in life, opinions and attitudes about it vary in the media. In recent years, one could actually get the impression that Germany as a business location was categorically denigrated. What role do the media play in this?

Players and instruments

In the economic sector as well as in politics, the media are both players and instruments. They cannot be restricted to playing a specific role and that is probably good as it is. Being independent players, interpreters and commentators, they participate in shaping attitudes and convictions in the public. The media can have a convincing, an encouraging and a repulsive effect.

Their reports create pressure and often lead to changes in politics and economics. They can help to "sell" the business location of Germany, and even advertise it; but they can also make it unattractive and keep investors away from it. The way of reporting can be exploited as instrument for the most different interest lobbies. At the same time, reporters and editorial offices are in constant battle of opinions and competition with each other. This is another reason for the non-existence of a unified attitude – like the assessment of the business location – in the media. On the contrary, there exists a diversity of opinions. This is a quality that distinguishes the multifaceted German media landscape. Indeed, the media – whether newspapers, radio and television or the Internet – are extremely important, especially with regard to the attrac-

Was lesen und was glauben? Der deutsche Leser hat eine Riesenauswahl.
What shall one read and what believe? The German reader has a huge choice.

tiveness of the business location. Economic, regional, cultural, social and other peculiarities are discussed in our media that are of great significance for decision-making in companies to invest precisely here and not in any other place.

The media describe the advantages and disadvantages of a region and its economy; they analyse its situation and explain the course of its development. They therefore convey important information, which influences domestic and foreign investors. At the same time, the media also have an effect on the business location itself. The media also help to bring about changes, to break up handed down traditions and to sharpen the consciousness for necessary reforms by focussing on the topics of political and economic decision-making processes and subjecting them to an examination.

Public discussions as a location factor

It is an imperative task of the political sector to create favourable conditions and implement the urgently necessary reforms like the Agenda 2010 for instance, in order to maintain and strengthen the attractiveness of Germany as a business location. In this respect, the government must develop great power of conviction to gain the trust of citizens and also of economic sectors, particularly of investors. This cannot be realized without the media. Because of this, especially the political sector depends on them. No democratic government will of course expect that independent media only repeat what politicians would like to be told.

In turn, it is assumed that the media do not take a stance against the activities of the Federal Government from the outset for mere reasons of opposition. It is important that in and through the different media a public dialogue between political, economic and social circles takes place. And in this very dynamic discussion, the advantages and disadvantages of Germany as a business location will emerge. The media act as mediator, as is their task, they participate in discussions and are vital instruments for all those taking part in the discussions.

Positive or negative presentation?

The opinion expressed from time to time that Germany as a business location is virtually denigrated falls short. For instance an assessment carried out between January 2003 and April 2004 in my own department of articles published in major daily newspapers and financial papers about Germany as a business location showed that the tendency of statements made actually balanced one another: of 107 articles, 44 assessed the location more positively, 36 more negatively and 27 positively and negatively. So whoever had the impression that the press of the business location of Germany was mainly negative, had to be taught otherwise by this not very representative example. On the contrary: a quite differentiated picture emerged, and declarations and assessments were of a positive point of view in the majority, if only slightly. However, it must be questioned how the impression of "denigrating" could have emerged.

Massenmedien

Linke Abbildung: Mehr als fünf Tonnen Zeitungen werden von der FAZ-Druckerei werktags als Luftfracht transportiert, an den Wochenenden sind es mehr als elf Tonnen.

Left: More than five tons of newspapers are transported by the FAZ printing office as air cargo on weekdays, on weekends it is more than eleven tons.

Rechte Abbildung: In der Frankfurter Societäts-Druckerei in Mörfelden-Walldorf wird die F.A.Z. gedruckt.

Right: The F.A.Z. is printed in the Frankfurter Societäts-Druckerei in Mörfelden-Walldorf.

vorneherein gegen das Handeln der Bundesregierung eingestellt sind. Meinungsvielfalt ist gefragt. Entscheidend ist, dass in und durch verschiedene Medien ein öffentlicher Dialog zwischen Politik, Wirtschaft und Gesellschaft stattfindet. Und in diesem – sehr dynamischen – Gespräch miteinander kristallisieren sich die Vor- und Nachteile des Standorts Deutschlands heraus. Medien vermitteln dabei, wie es ihre Aufgabe ist, sie sprechen mit und sie sind wichtige Instrumente aller an dem Gespräch Beteiligten.

Positive oder negative Darstellung?

Die bisweilen geäußerte Ansicht, der Standort Deutschland werde geradezu schlecht geredet, greift zu kurz. So zeigte etwa eine in meinem Haus vorgenommene Auswertung von Artikeln großer Tageszeitungen und Wirtschaftsblätter zum Standort Deutschland zwischen Januar 2003 und April 2004, dass sich die Aussagen in ihrer Tendenz durchaus die Waage hielten: Von 107 Artikeln beurteilten 44 den Standort eher positiv, 36 eher negativ und 27 positiv und negativ. Wer also den Eindruck hatte, die Presse des Standorts Deutschland sei überwiegend negativ, musste sich durch dieses – allerdings nicht repräsentative – Beispiel eines Besseren belehren lassen. Im Gegenteil: Es ergab sich ein differenziertes Bild, und bei den Aussagen und Bewertungen überwog sogar die positive Sicht, wenn auch nur leicht. Dennoch ist zu fragen, wie der Eindruck des „Schlechtredens" entstehen kann. Mir scheint, wir neigen in Deutschland zu einer gleichsam dialektischen Sichtweise: Indem die Nachteile, die kritikwürdigen und verbesserungsbedürftigen Aspekte des Standorts drastisch in den Vordergrund geschoben, analysiert und betont werden, verhelfen sie den Vorteilen zum Durchbruch. Das mag für Außenstehende bisweilen befremdlich erscheinen; aber vielleicht ist gerade dies eine Eigen-art unserer Kultur und Geschichte, über die es sich lohnt nachzudenken. Natürlich ist nicht zu übersehen, dass es in Deutschland den einen oder anderen Manager gibt, der gerade gegenüber der Presse oder auch auf Auslandsreisen ein besonders negatives Bild seines Landes entwirft. Dieses Phänomen hat Jürgen Weber, Aufsichtsratchef der Deutschen Lufthansa und neben Klaus Mangold (DaimlerChrysler) und Heinrich von Pierer (Siemens) einer der drei Beauftragten der Bundesregierung bei „Invest in Germany", erst vor kurzem ausdrücklich bedauert (Financial Times Deutschland, 23. April 2004, S. 16). Weber entwickelte ein Bündel von Argumenten für den Standort Deutschland, mit denen er ausländische Unternehmen anziehen möchte. Dazu gehört u. a., dass Deutschland Europas führende Volkswirtschaft und der derzeitige Exportweltmeister ist. Unser Land liegt im Herzen Europas und wird von der EU-Erweiterung erheblich profitieren. Deutschland hat eine herausragende Infrastruktur und konnte in den vergangenen Jahren seine Produktivität um über 30 Prozent steigern. Es ist darüber hinaus das innovativste Land in Europa mit den meisten Patentanmeldungen und gehört zu den Volkswirtschaften mit den geringsten Hindernissen für Auslandsbeteiligungen. Außerdem verfügt Deutschland über einen fortschrittlichen Kapitalmarkt und ist für die „New Economy" der aufregendste Markt in Europa, denn neue und traditionelle Industrien ergänzen sich perfekt. Viele dieser Argumente finden sich auch in der Berichterstattung der Medien, die sich immer wieder an dem Vorwurf reiben, Deutschland sei als Standort unattraktiv. Der Vorwurf, es werde alles schwarz gesehen, gejammert und schlecht geredet, trifft denn auch nur die eine Seite. Auf der anderen Seite stehen zahlreiche Gegenargumente, die gerade wegen des Überdrusses am Jammern sich viel kräftiger artikulieren als wir annehmen.

Perspektiven von außen

„Wer wissen will, wie es um Deutschland steht, bekommt nüchterne Urteile womöglich aus dem Ausland", hieß es vor einigen Wochen in der Financial Times Deutschland (Thomas Fricke, „Deutscher Weltmeistertitel kommt manchem ungelegen", FTD, 8. April 2004, S. 18). Ohne Zweifel ist die ausländische Berichterstattung über den Standort nicht nur für ausländische Unternehmen, die hier investieren wollen, von Bedeutung, sondern auch zur Urteilsbildung in unserem eigenen Land. Kulturelle Unterschiede und andere Sichtweisen rücken so manches Wehgeschrei zurecht und relativieren allzu pessimistische Einschätzungen.

Eine Auswertung verschiedener Quellen von „Invest in Germany" (März 2004) über die Wahrnehmung des Wirtschaftsstandortes Deutschland im Ausland fördert ein differenziertes Bild zutage: Trotz einiger Verbesserungswünsche wissen ausländische Firmen um die Vorteile des Wirtschaftsstandorts Deutschland. Als Plus werden neben dem großen Absatzmarkt und der Nähe zu Osteuropa stets auch das Potenzial gut ausgebildeter Fachkräfte und die Forschungs- und Entwicklungseinrichtungen genannt. Die sehr gute Infrastruktur, die Rechtssicherheit und die Nähe zu den interessanten, wachstumsstarken osteuropäischen Märkten stehen ebenfalls in der Wahrnehmung Deutschlands von außen ganz oben. Fest steht, Deutschland gehört für internationale Investoren zu den wichtigsten Anlageländern. Ein Maßstab für die Attraktivität des Standortes Deutschland ist die vorhandene Anzahl ausländischer Firmen, die weiterhin im Wachstum begriffen ist. Schätzungsweise 22.000 ausländische Unternehmen sind bereits am Standort Deutschland, darunter auch die 500 größten Unternehmen der Welt. Sie alle beschäftigen in Deutschland mehr als 2,7 Millionen Menschen. Die Umsätze haben inzwischen die 1.000-Milliarden-Euro-Grenze überschritten.

Wenn wir dies alles berücksichtigen, können wir mit der Frage, wie attraktiv die Darstellung des Standorts in den Medien sei, gelassener umgehen. Gewiss, die Darstellung in unseren inländischen Medien schwankt; insgesamt ist sie aber differenziert. Zu Alarmismus besteht daher kein Anlass, weder für die Wirtschaft noch für die Politik. Auch wenn ich mir wünschen würde, dass der Prozess notwendiger Reformen bisweilen konstruktiver begleitet würde. ∎

Mass Media

Die Medien zeichnen ein sehr differenziertes Bild des Wirtschaftsstandortes Deutschland.
The media draw a very differentiated picture of Germany as a business location.

I think that in Germany we tend to pick a so to speak dialectic point of view: since the disadvantages, the location's aspects worthy of criticism and those that need improvement are dramatically pushed into the limelight, analysed and emphasised they help the advantages to achieve a breakthrough. This may seem strange now and then to outsiders; but maybe this is precisely one feature of our culture and history worth thinking about. Of course, it cannot be overlooked that in Germany there is one or the other manager that especially in front of the press or also on journeys abroad draws a particularly negative image of his country. This phenomenon was expressly regretted recently by Jürgen Weber, head of the supervisory council of Deutsche Lufthansa and besides Klaus Mangold (DaimlerChrysler) and Heinrich von Pierer (Siemens) one of three representatives of the Federal Government at "Invest in Germany" (Financial Times Deutschland, 23rd April 2004, p. 16). Weber developed a package of arguments that he uses to attract foreign companies to the business location of Germany. They include for instance that Germany is Europe's leading macro economy and present world champion in exports. Our country is situated in the heart of Europe and will benefit considerably fro the Enlargement of the EU. Germany has an excellent infrastructure and has been able to increase its productivity in recent years by over 30 per cent. Furthermore, it is the most innovative country in Europe boasting the majority of patent registrations and is among the macro economies holding the least obstacles for foreign investments. Moreover, Germany has a progressive capital market and is the most exciting market for the "New Economy" in Europe, because new and traditional industries complement each other perfectly. Many of these arguments can also be found in reports by the media, which time and again cause friction with the accusation that Germany is unattractive as a business location. The criticism that everything is painted black, moaned about and put down, therefore only affects one side. On the other side, numerous counter arguments are being articulated much stronger than we actually assume especially because of excessive weariness of moaning.

Perspectives seen from outside

Some weeks ago, the Financial Times Germany wrote (Thomas Fricke, "World Champion title for Germany inconvenient for some", FTD, 08.04.2004, p. 18): "Whoever wants to know in what position Germany is at present, can get objective opinions maybe from abroad". Undoubtedly, reports from abroad about the business location are not only important for foreign companies that want to invest here, but also to reach conclusions here in our own country. Cultural differences and other points of view straighten out a lot of wailing and help extremely pessimistic assessments to become relative.

An evaluation of different sources by "Invest in Germany" (March 2004) about the perception of Germany as a business location abroad revealed a differentiated picture: despite the desire for some improvements foreign companies know about the advantages Germany holds as a business location. As a point in favour is always mentioned the potential of well-trained experts and its research and development institutions besides the large sales market and its vicinity to Eastern Europe. Top on the list of the perception of Germany as it is seen from outside is also its excellent infrastructure, legal security and the proximity to the interesting growth markets of East Europe. The fact is, Germany is one of the most important investment countries for international investors. One benchmark for the attractiveness of Germany as a business location is the existing number of foreign firms, which is still growing. An estimated 22,000 foreign companies have settled already at the business location of Germany, including also the major 500 global corporations. All together they provide jobs for more than 2.7 million people in Germany. Turnover sales meanwhile exceed beyond the 1,000 billion euro limit.

If we consider all these facts, we can be more relaxed about the question of how attractive the business location is presented in the media. Indeed, there is uncertainty about its presentation in our domestic media; but on the whole it is differentiated. There is no need therefore to be alarmed, neither for the economic nor for the political sector. Even if I would like that the process of necessary reform be accompanied more constructively at times.

Company Profile

Die Kraft der Farbe
Drucker, Verlage, Agenturen und Markenartikler in aller Welt vertrauen auf Epple

*The Power of Colour –
Printers, publishers, agencies and branded companies worldwide rely on Epple*

Erste Adresse für Bogenoffset-Kunden in aller Welt: die Epple Druckfarben AG in Neusäß bei Augsburg.

First-class address for sheet offset customers in the entire world: Epple Druckfarben AG in Neusäß near Augsburg.

Die Epple Druckfarben AG ist heute der führende Druckfarbenhersteller für hochwertigen Bogenoffset in Europa und vielen weiteren Regionen auf der ganzen Welt. Seit 1889 steht Epple für Vielfalt, Innovationskraft und höchste Qualitätsansprüche im Bereich Bogenoffset-Druckfarben.

Die hochwertigen Produkte der Epple Druckfarben AG, wie Öko-Farben, Hybridfarben oder das aniva®plus-Farbsystem sind Resultate permanenter Forschung und Weiterentwicklung. Die Fachkompetenz der gut eingespielten, kundenorientierten Epple -Teams in Verkauf und Anwendungstechnik ist Garant für Qualität, Flexibilität und Lieferschnelligkeit. Beste Voraussetzungen, um den Vorsprung im Markt täglich aufs Neue zu bestätigen.

Umfassende Produktpalette
Das Produktspektrum von Epple deckt nahezu alle Anwendungsgebiete des modernen Bogen-Offsetdrucks ab. Es umfasst ausgereifte und innovative Farbserien für alle gängigen Druckaufträge, sowie Spezialserien für besondere Anforderungen.
Mit der Entwicklung der Öko-Farben, und hier im speziellen mit den Klassikern **Öko Plus** und **Öko Speed**, setzte Epple schon ab Anfang der 90er Jahre neue Maßstäbe. Für die stetig steigenden Anforderungen in der Druckerei hat Epple aktuell die zwei neuen „Alleskönner" **Print Power** und **Top Sprint** entwickelt. Die Top Sprint Skala ermöglicht durch sehr schnelles Wegschlagen ein sehr schnelles Umschlagen und eine sehr schnelle Weiterverarbeitung. Die Print Power zeichnet sich als hochwertige Allroundskala durch hohe Farbintensität, sehr gute Scheuerfestigkeit und sehr guten Glanz aus.

Mit der **Low Ghost** Serie ist eine Minimierung der papierabhängigen Kontakt- und Geistereffekte gelungen.

Die **Starbrite Serie** ermöglicht Inline UV Lackierung für höchste Glanzwerte in einem einzigen Arbeitsschritt, was sich wirtschaftlich sehr vorteilhaft auswirkt. Ergänzt wurde die Serie durch eine innovative gerucharme Variante.

Die von Epple entwickelten **BrightSign-Farben** besitzen neben den Merkmalen normaler Bogenoffsetfarben zusätzliche Fluoreszenzeigenschaften. BrightSign Druckprodukte zeigen in dunkler Umgebung unter Schwarzlicht eine ähnliche Brillanz wie herkömmliche Drucke unter Tageslicht.

Die umfassende Palette an **Schwarzfarben** deckt sämtliche Aufgabengebiete ab, und die zahlreichen verschiedenen Drucklacke erfüllen von einfachen Schutzfunktionen über Glanz- und Matt-Oberflächen bis hin zu Perlglanz-Effekten punktgenau alle Wünsche.

Die umfassende Auswahl an **Pantone®** und individuell hergestellten **Schmuckfarben** macht Epple ebenso zum Experten für Spezialitäten wie die innovativen Metalleffektfarben.
Feuchtmittelzusätze, **Druckhilfsmittel** und **Dispersionslacke** runden das Angebotsspektrum ab.

aniva®plus-Farbsystem
Mit dem revolutionären Farbsystem aniva®plus schließt Epple Druckfarben die qualitative Lücke zwischen Photographie und Druck. Basierend auf den Erkenntnissen der Bildwahrnehmung wurde das patentierte aniva®plus-Farbsystem konzipiert. Es besteht aus aniva®-Farben und einem speziellen ICC-Profil, das den Farbraum der Farben voll erschließt. Besonderer Vorteil für den Kunden ist, dass diese Farbraumerweiterung mit nur vier aniva®-Farben zu erreichen ist, die zudem der internationalen Norm ISO 2846-1 genügen.

Markenschutz
Nach einer Untersuchung des OECD entsteht durch Markenpiraterie weltweit ein wirtschaftlicher Schaden von 250 Milliarden Euro im Jahr. Die Epple Druckfarben AG hat ein breites Produktspektrum entwickelt, um Druckprodukte und Verpackungen sicherer zu machen. Neben einfachen Sicherheitsmerkmalen wie Kopierschutz und thermochromen Farben bietet Epple als einziger Offsetfarbenhersteller die zur Umsetzung der Hochsicherheitstechnologie CIT (Concealed Image Technology) benötigten Farben und Lacke.

Epple Druckfarben AG ist zertifiziert nach der Qualitätsnorm ISO 9001:2000 und der Umweltnorm ISO 14001. ∎

Company Profile

Today Epple Druckfarben AG is one of the leading printing ink manufacturer for high-quality sheet-fed offset inks in Europe and in many other regions worldwide. Since 1889, Epple stands for variety, innovation and highest quality in the field of sheet-fed offset printing inks.

The high-quality products made by Epple Druckfarben AG, like eco-ink, hybrid ink or the aniva®plus colour system are the results of permanent research and continuous development. The professional competence of the customer-oriented Epple-Team in sale and application technology, working well together, is a guarantee for quality, flexibility and fast delivery. These are the best prerequisite to confirm Epple's lead within the market daily anew.

Wide product range

Epple's product spectrum covers almost all fields of application of modern sheet-fed offset printing. It comprises mature and innovative ink series for all common print jobs as well as special series for special requirements.

With the development of the eco inks and here in particular with the classic products **Eco Plus** and **Eco Speed**, Epple has set new standards since the beginning of the nineties. For continuously increasing demands in printing Epple has lately developed the two new "universal series" **Print Power** and **Top Sprint**. Through very fast settings, the Top Sprint series allows a fast work and turn and very fast further processing. The Print Power series distinguishes itself as high-quality "universal series" through high intensity, excellent rub resistance and outstanding brilliance.

With the **Low Ghost** series Epple succeeded in the development of a series optimised in view of contact and ghost effects.

The **Starbrite Series** allows an Inline UV lacquering for the highest brilliance values in only one single printing step, which is of great economic advantage. The series has been supplemented by an innovative scent reduced alternative.

The **BrightSign inks**, developed by Epple, possess besides the characteristics of normal sheet-fed offset inks additional fluorescence properties. BrightSign printing products show in dark environment under black light a similar brilliance as common prints in daylight.

An extensive spectrum of **black inks** covers the complete field of possible applications and the numerous different varnishes are fulfilling all requirements, from simple protective functions up to glossy and matt surfaces as well as pearlescent effects.

The wide range of **Pantone®** and individually produced spot colours makes Epple an expert for specialities as well as the innovative metal effect inks.

Fountain solution, **printing additives** and **dispersion varnishes** complete the product spectrum.

aniva®plus colour system

With its revolutionary colour system aniva®plus, Epple Druckfarben is closing the quality gap between photography and printing. The patented aniva®plus colour system was conceived based on the perception of image cognition. It consists of aniva® inks and a special ICC profile, which fully opens the colour space of the inks. For the customer it is of particular advantage that this colour space expansion can be achieved with only four aniva®-inks, which moreover fulfil the requirements of the international norm ISO 2846-1.

Protection of trademarks

According to a survey of the OECD, an economic damage of 250 billion Euros a year is created through brand piracy worldwide. Epple Druckfarben AG has developed a wide range of products, making safer printing products and packaging. Besides the simple safety characteristics like copy protection and thermo-chromic inks, Epple, as sole manufacturer of offset inks is offering varnishes and inks necessary for implementing the high-security technology CIT (Concealed Image Technology).

Epple Druckfarben AG has passed third party certification tests according to ISO 9001:2000 and ISO 14001.

Epple Druckfarben AG

Vorstand/Executive Board:
Joachim Erlach (Sprecher/Spokesman),
Edgar Buck,
Dr. Klaus-Dieter Schröter
Aufsichtsratsvorsitzender/
Chairman of the Supervisory Board:
Kilian Berz

Gründungsjahr/Year of Foundation: 1889

Geschäftstätigkeit/Business Activity:
Entwicklung, Herstellung und Vertrieb von Druckfarben für nahezu alle Anwendungsgebiete modernen Bogen-Offsetdrucks./
Development, production and sale of printing inks for almost all fields of application of modern sheet-fed offset printing.

Anschrift/Address:
Gutenbergstraße 5
D-86356 Neusäß/Augsburg
Telefon +49 (821) 46 03-0
Telefax +49 (821) 46 03-200
E-Mail info@epple-druckfarben.de
Internet www.epple-druckfarben.de
www.aniva.info

Filmindustrie

Der deutsche Film – immer wieder ein Fall für ein Happy End

German cinema – always a good case for a happy end

Dass der amerikanische Film Hollywood schon in seiner Frühzeit als *den* Standort gewählt hat, den er bis heute behalten hat, soll auch damit zu tun gehabt haben, dass in dieser Gegend der Welt besonders viele Sonnentage gezählt wurden. Es gab mithin reichlich von dem Licht, das der Film viele Jahrzehnte brauchte, bis das künstliche Licht nach und nach sogar die kalifornische Sonne ersetzen konnte.

Der deutsche Film war in diesem natürlichen Sinne nie von der Sonne verwöhnt. Zwar hat es Zeiten gegeben, in denen auch er in einer gewissen Hinsicht im hellen Licht der Sonne lag. Babelsberg war in den 20er-Jahren und bis zu jenem Exodus der Kreativen, für den die Nazis gesorgt hatten, ein Ort, der es mit Hollywood durchaus aufnehmen konnte. Vielleicht nicht wirtschaftlich – der amerikanische Markt war nun einmal schon immer der weitaus größere. Wohl aber, was die künstlerische Seite betraf. Viele von denen, die Deutschland verlassen mussten – Regisseure wie Ernst Lubitsch, Billy Wilder, Douglas Sirk, Fritz Lang oder Curtis Bernhardt –, haben es später in Hollywood zu Glanz und Ehren gebracht.

Keine Frage, sie haben dem deutschen Film nach dem Zweiten Weltkrieg gefehlt. Ob sie allerdings die amerikanische Vorherrschaft beim Kinofilm hätten gefährden können, wird man schon deshalb bezweifeln dürfen, weil diese Vorherrschaft sich überwiegend auf ökonomische Faktoren gründete, die viel mit dem *large of scale* zu tun haben. Nicht zuletzt Verleih und Vertrieb, Schlüsselbranchen für den *blockbuster*, den an der Kasse erfolgreichen Film, kamen und blieben zu großen Teilen in der Hand von amerikanischen *companies*. Bis heute. Und allen Versuchen, etwa an diesem Umstand etwas Substanzielles zu ändern, war am Ende kein Erfolg beschieden.

Man kann die amerikanischen Studios wie Universal, Paramount oder Disney auch nicht mit den deutschen Studios wie Studio Hamburg, Bavaria oder Babelsberg vergleichen, eher mit so bekannten Plätzen wie der Cinecittà in Rom oder den Pinewood Studios in London, die Alfred Hitchcock gerne benutzte. Aber auch sie haben als Produzenten nur eine kurzfristige Bedeutung erlangt. In den deutschen Studios sind 85 Prozent der Produktionen solche für das Fernsehen. Und auch die jüngsten technologischen Entwicklungen wie etwa das Internet haben dafür gesorgt, dass die starken amerikanischen Filme noch stärker wurden, indem sie schon Monate vor ihrem Kinostart gewissermaßen im eigenen Hause beworben werden konnten, weil die Studios auch über mächtige, weltweit tätige Internetportale verfügen.

Hat man dies alles einmal zur Kenntnis genommen und sich dazu verstanden, keine großen Klagegesänge anzustimmen, sondern jenseits dieser amerikanischen Dominanz nach eigenen Möglichkeiten zu suchen, dann bleibt am Ende Platz genug für einen auch wirtschaftlich erfolgreichen deutschen Film – im Rahmen seiner Möglichkeiten, versteht sich. Und dies umso mehr dann, wenn in Englisch gedreht wird.

Im Rahmen seiner Möglichkeiten – das heißt: Deutsche Kinofilm-Produzenten haben in aller Regel Budgets zur Verfügung, die etwa ein Drittel der Gage eines US-amerikanischen Hauptdarstellers betragen. Doch auch das führt nicht dazu, dass wir die Hände verdrossen in den Schoß legen. Vielmehr meldet sich der deutsche Film, weniger kontinuierlich (was besser wäre) als in Wellenbewegungen (was auch noch gut ist), immer wieder international zu Wort. Denn bis auf die heute nicht mehr ganz so dringend benötigte Sonne ist in Deutschland, vor allem in den Zentren wie Berlin und München, Hamburg und Köln, alles zur Hand, was man für einen guten und professionell gemachten Film braucht. Dazu gibt es hervorragende Autoren, Komponisten, Architekten, Kameraleute und vor allem auch Regisseure, die mit den ältesten Regeln des Handwerks und neuesten Techniken erfolgreich arbeiten. Kurz: Alles ist je für sich reichlich vorhanden. Sogar ein A-Festival, die Berlinale unter Dieter Kosslick, das sich in den letzten Jahren neue Geltung verschafft hat. Was dem deutschen Film nach wie vor fehlt, ist der eigene große nationale Markt (für den zum Beispiel in Frankreich von Seiten des Staates einfach schon immer besser gesorgt wurde, weil der Film in Frankreich ein Stück akzeptierter und erwünschter Kultur ist). Und was ihm auch fehlt, sind genügend große Produzenten, die nach amerikanischem

Prof. Regina Ziegler

Die Autorin, 1944 in Quedlinburg geboren, entschloss sich 1973 ihre eigene Produktionsfirma – Regina Ziegler Filmproduktion – zu gründen. Ihre erste Produktion *Ich dachte, ich wäre tot* wurde mit dem Bundesfilmpreis ausgezeichnet. Von den bis heute nahezu 300 Filmen, die sie produziert hat, wurden viele mit nationalen und internationalen Preisen geehrt. Regina Ziegler wurde 1998 das *Bundesverdienstkreuz* verliehen, 1999 erhielt sie den *Adolf Grimme Preis* und den *American Cinema Foundation Freedom Award*, 2001 den *Verdienstorden des Landes Berlin*. Die Internationalen Filmfestspiele Berlin zeichneten Regina Ziegler 2004 mit der *Berlinale Kamera* aus.

The author was born in Quedlinburg in 1944 and decided to start her own production company – Regina Ziegler Filmproduktion – in 1973. For her first production "Ich dachte, ich wäre tot" (I thought I had died) she received the German film award "Bundesfilmpreis". Of almost 300 films that she has produced until today, many obtained national and international awards. Regina Ziegler received the *Order of the Federal Republic of Germany* in 1998, the *Adolf Grimme Award* and the *American Cinema Foundation Freedom Award* in 1999 and the *Order of Merit of the Federal State of Berlin*. Regina Ziegler was awarded the "*Camera of The Berlinale*" at the Berlin International Film Festival in 2004.

Vorbild agieren, also die eigentlichen „Bestimmer" sind. Beides lässt sich zum Besseren verbessern. Was schwer zu erreichen ist, sind Budgets, die

Film Industry

The fact that the American film industry chose Hollywood in its early days as *the* location, which it has kept until today, is said to be also due to that in that part of the world there is an abundance of sunny days. Thus, there was plenty of light, which the film industry needed for decades until artificial light by and by replaced the Californian sun.

The German film industry of course has never been spoilt naturally by the sun like that. Indeed there have been times in which to a certain degree it also enjoyed the bright light of the sun. In the twenties and up to that exodus of creative people that the Nazis were responsible for, Babelsberg had been a place that was absolutely able to compete with Hollywood. Maybe not in economic terms – the American market has by far always been by far the greater one. But certainly with respect to the artistic aspect. Many of those that had to leave Germany – directors like Ernst Lubitsch, Billy Wilder, Douglas Sirk, Fritz Lang or Curtis Bernhardt – achieved fame and glory later on in Hollywood.

No doubt, they were missed by the German film industry after the Second World War. But one may doubt whether they could have really endangered the American predominance in cinema, especially because this predominance was mainly based on economic factors that had much to do with the large of scale. Ultimately, the sectors rental and distribution, key branches for the *blockbuster*, the film that is successful at cash points, by and large remained in the hands of American companies. Until today. And all endeavours to change anything substantial in this situation would be unsuccessful in the end anyway.

Indeed, one cannot compare American studios like Universal, Paramount or Disney to German studios like Studio Hamburg, Bavaria or Babelsberg, but rather to famous locations like Cinecittà in Rome or the Pinewood Studios in London, which Alfred Hitchcock liked to use. But even these only achieved a short-lived significance as producers. In German studios, 85 per cent of productions are made for television. And also the latest technological developments, like for instance the Internet, have ensured that the strong American films have become even stronger, by advertising the same months before their start in the cinemas practically at home, because the studios also possess powerful, worldwide accessible Internet portals.

If one takes notice of all these facts and agrees not to indulge in great lamentations, but instead to search for one's own possibilities beyond this American dominance, then in the end there will be enough space for an also economically successful German film industry – within the scope of its possibilities, of course. And this will be much more the case, if shooting is done in English.

Within the scope of one's possibilities – that means: German cinema producers on the whole have budgets available that amount to about one third of the fee paid for US-American lead actors. However, we do not intend to twiddle our thumbs reluctantly now. On the contrary, German cinema is piping up, albeit less continuously (which would be better) than in wave motions (which is still good), internationally again and again. In fact, apart from the sun, which is actually not that necessary today, there is everything available at hand that one needs for a good professionally made film in Germany, above all in centres like Berlin and Munich, Hamburg and Cologne. There are excellent writers, composers, architects, camera people and especially also directors, who work with the oldest rules of the trade and the latest state-of-the-art. In short: every single thing is abundantly available. There is even an A-Festival, the Berlinale under Dieter Kosslick, which has achieved new renown in recent years. The thing still missing in German cinema is its own large scale national market (which for example in France has always been better provided for by the state). And anoth-

Von oben nach unten: Im Schatten der Macht, Matthias Brandt und Michael Mendl – Solo für Klarinette, Corinna Harfouch und Götz George – Korczak, Wojtek Pszonial.

From above to below: In the Shadow of Might, Matthias Brandt and Michael Mendl – Solo for Clarinet, Corinna Harfouch and Götz George – Korczak, Wojtek Pszonial.

Filmindustrie

einen international verkäuflichen Film ausmachen. Es gibt viele – manche meinen: viel zu viele – kleine Filme in Deutschland, die meistens aus wirtschaftlichen Gründen zu früh produziert werden. Der Produzent hat nicht genug Kapital zur Verfügung, um den Stoff, die Besetzung bis zu einem Punkt reifen zu lassen und einen Zustand zu erlangen, der zu einem Erfolg führen kann. Es gibt zu selten die wirklich großen Stoffe, die immer auch ein großes Risiko bedeuten – Stoffe in den Dimensionen eines amerikanischen *blockbuster*, der so viel einspielt, dass sich der Produzent zur Not eine paar Flops leisten kann. Regisseure und/oder Kameraleute, wie etwa Wolfgang Petersen, Roland Emmerich, Michael Ballhaus oder Jost Vacano, aber auch Schauspieler(innen) wie Til Schweiger, Franka Potente, Armin Müller-Stahl oder Ralf Möller, die derartige Filme im Auge haben, gehen nach Amerika und arbeiten dort erfolgreich.

Doch auch die kleineren Filme, die in Deutschland der Normalfall sind, geben keine Veranlassung, sie fortgesetzt klein zu reden. Sie können sich durchaus sehen lassen und wurden zuletzt auch gut gesehen. Es muss nicht immer das große Geld sein. Manchmal reicht einfach die große Kunst wie etwa bei Rainer Werner Fassbinder, der mit eher kleinen Budgets gearbeitet hat und von dem in Amerika noch heute, Jahre nach seinem Tod, die Leute schwärmen. Oder die fabelhaften und fabelhaft inszenierten Ideen wie bei *Goodbye Lenin*, *Bella Martha* oder *Rosenstraße*.

Diese und andere Beispiele ermutigen immer wieder dazu, das Risiko eines Spielfilmes einzugehen. Denn ein Risiko ist ein solches Vorhaben immer, sogar für solche, die eine recht gute Nase haben wie etwa Bernd Eichinger, der so schöne Filme wie *Der Name der Rose* oder *Das Geisterhaus* produziert hat und derzeit *Das Parfum* vorbereitet.

Weil der Erfolg nicht berechenbar ist und weil man sich in Deutschland anders als in den USA einen Flop nicht leisten kann, da man im Zweifel nur eine einzige Chance hat, braucht es, anders als in anderen „Industrien" eine Unterstützung, die weder mit Almosen noch gar mit unerlaubten Beihilfen verwechselt werden sollte. Eine beträchtliche Hilfe sind und leisten die Filmförderungen, auch wenn es im Einzelfall ein bürokratisches Hindernisrennen sein kann, auf das man sich einlässt, wenn man Geld von ihnen haben will. Aber wo bekommt man schon Geld umsonst? Eine Förderung wie die Filmstiftung NRW vergibt pro Jahr immerhin fast 35 Millionen Euro – auch übrigens für Fernsehproduktionen, die ihrerseits den Film beflügeln können, was sich an Arbeiten von Regisseuren wie Dominik Graf oder Andreas Dresen, Max Färberböck oder Christian Paetzold zeigen ließe. Die Verbindung von Film und Fernsehen, wie sie sich in Deutschland zuletzt entwickelt hat, keineswegs nur zur Freude der klassischen Filmemacher, für die Fernsehen immer nur das zweitbeste Medium war und ist, ist maßgeblich dafür in Anspruch zu nehmen und zu loben, dass es der deutsche Film immer wieder geschafft hat, seine Krisen zu überleben.

Es macht also keinen Sinn, wie das Kaninchen auf die amerikanische Schlange zu starren und davon zu träumen, dass der deutsche Film eines schönen Tages von irgendeinem Ölprinzen wach geküsst und in amerikanische Dimensionen aufgeblasen wird. Es ist unsinnig, das Unvergleichbare fortgesetzt zu vergleichen und aus der Differenz einen Dauerschmerz zu ziehen, der allenfalls lähmt, jedenfalls nicht beflügelt. Sinn macht es, die deutschen Gegebenheiten nicht nur zur Kenntnis, sondern auch in Anspruch zu nehmen. Dass dabei manches noch verbesserungswürdig ist, kann niemanden überraschen. Dass etwa die Banken nach Basel II noch zugeknöpfter auf diesem Feld in Erscheinung treten, bzw. eben nicht, ein Feld, auf dem viel Geld umgesetzt wird, ist ein Handicap, das so leicht nicht auszugleichen ist. Dass sich auf dem Gebiet der Filmfonds die Spreu nur langsam vom Weizen trennt und die Amerikaner viel *stupid money* aus Deutschland dankend in Empfang genommen haben, hat ebenfalls nicht gerade förderlich gewirkt. Dass die Außenvertretung des deutschen Films zuzeiten etwas geschwächelt hat, wird man nicht als einen Pluspunkt verbuchen wollen. Dafür hat zum Beispiel das Fernsehen, vor allem das öffentlich-rechtliche, schon seit Jahren an einem Filmförderungsabkommen mitgewirkt, das mit dafür sorgt, dass der deutsche Film auch in schwächeren Phasen überlebt. Dafür wird an deutschen Filmschulen nicht nur für den deutschen Bedarf exzellent ausgebildet. Dafür zeigen die Absolventen dieser Schulen auch *best practice* im internationalen Maßstab, etwa der Ludwigsburger Schule, die konsequent eine technologische Lücke besetzt und beseitigt hat.

Ist es also so wie auch sonst im Leben? Dass Licht und Schatten sich ablösen? Es scheint so. Die kalkulierte Abfolge von Licht und Schatten gehört gewiss zu den besonders erfolgreichen Instrumenten, mit denen man einen Film groß machen kann. Die unkalkulierbare Abfolge von Licht und Schatten dagegen gehört zu den Erlebnissen, die man auf der Seite der Produzierenden hat. Das macht die Dinge jederzeit spannend, riskant, jederzeit gut für Überraschungen. Wer Hitze nicht ertragen kann, sollte die Küche meiden. Wer diese produktive Ungewissheit liebt und wer sie aushalten kann, wird keinen schöneren Beruf finden als den des Filmemachers, des Filmproduzenten, bei dem auch Scheitern in aller Regel wenigstens auf hohem Niveau stattfindet.

Auch und gerade in Deutschland.

Film Industry

Beide Seiten, von links nach rechts:
Kamikaze 1989, Rainer Werner Fassbinder – Wellen, Monica Bleibtreu, Sunnyi Melles – Fabian, Hans-Peter Hallwachs.

Both pages, from left to right:
Kamikaze 1989, Rainer Werner Fassbinder – Waves, Monica Bleibtreu, Sunnyi Melles – Fabian, Hans-Peter Hallwachs.

er thing missing is sufficient great producers that act after their American examples, which means that they are the real "decision-makers". Both aspects can be changed to the better. But what will be difficult to achieve are budgets that determine if a film is easy to sell internationally.

There are many – some think: much too many – small films made in Germany, which mostly are produced far too early for economic reasons. The producer does not dispose of enough capital to let the material, the casting develop to the point that it is able to lead to success. There are very seldom those really great materials, which always also bear great risks – materials with the scope of an American *blockbuster* that brings in such huge amounts that the producer can afford to have a few flops. Directors and/or camera men like for instance Wolfgang Petersen, Roland Emmerich, Michael Ballhaus or Jost Vacano, but also actors and actresses like Til Schweiger, Franka Potente, Armin Müller-Stahl or Ralf Möller, who keep an eye on this kind of films, go to America and work there successfully.

But also the smaller movies, which are the normal scenario in Germany, are no cause for making them look small continuously. One can definitely be proud of them and lately they have also received a good amount of recognition. It does not always have to be the big money. Sometimes, just the artistic value is enough, like with Rainer Werner Fassbinder for example, who worked with rather small budgets, and people still rave about him in America even years after his death. Or the fabulous and fabulously staged ideas like with *Goodbye Lenin*, *Bella Martha* or *Rosenstraße*.

These and other examples continue to motivate one to take the risk of making a movie. For in fact, such a project bears always a risk, even for such people that have a real good nose for these things, like Bernd Eichinger, for instance, who produced such beautiful films like *The Name of the Rose* or *The House of the Spirits* and is presently preparing the movie *The Perfume*.

Because success is incalculable and because in Germany, contrary to the USA, one cannot afford to have a flop, since in doubt one has only one chance, conversely to other "industries", some kind of support is necessary, which cannot be mistaken for charity or even for illegal funding. Considerable assistance is rendered by the state film subsidy, even if at times it can be a bureaucratic steeplechase, which one has to deal with if one wants to receive a grant from them. But where can you get money for nothing? Funding of the kind that the Filmstiftung NRW (Film Foundation of the State of North Rhine-Westphalia) provides per year comprises almost 35 million Euros – by the way also for television productions, which on their part can inspire filmmaking, an aspect that can be pointed out by the works of directors like Dominik Graf or Andreas Dresen, Max Färberböck or Christian Paetzold. The link between film and television in the way that it has developed lately in Germany, which by no means filmmakers only derive pleasure from since television has always only been second best for them as a medium, has played a substantial role and must be praised for it that the German film industry has managed again and again to survive its crises.

It therefore makes no sense to be staring at like a rabbit on the American snake and dreaming of the German film industry one day being saved by some rich oil prince and blown into American proportions. It is nonsense to continuously try to compare the incomparable and derive permanent pain from the difference, which at most may stifle, but not inspire. It would make sense though to acknowledge the German circumstances and moreover make use of them. It can not be surprising that thereby one will find many a thing that is worthy of improvement. The fact that banks after the Basel II Agreement (Guideline of the "Basle Committee for Banking Regulation") are even more reserved in this field than ever, or do not want to get involved at all, a field in which a lot of money is turned over, is a handicap that cannot be compensated for that easily. The fact that in the sector of film funds the wheat is only separated very slowly from the chaff and Americans have thankfully accepted a lot of *stupid money* from Germany has also not had a supporting effect. The fact that foreign representations for the German film industry have been a little weak at times cannot be regarded as an advantage either. Instead television for instance, above all state broadcasting stations, participated in a film subsidy agreement, which is partly ensuring that the German film industry keeps surviving also during a weak phase. And to make up, German film schools provide excellent training not only to cover the German demand. And graduates of these schools also show *best practice* by international standards, as for example the Ludwigsburg School that consistently covers a technological niche.

Does that mean things are the same as everywhere else in life? That light and shadow take turn with one another? It actually seems so. A calculated sequence of light and shadow certainly is one of the particularly successful instruments that serve to make a great film. However, the incalculable sequence of light and shadow is one of the experiences that one makes on the part of the producing staff. This makes things always thrilling, risky, and always good for a surprise. Whoever cannot bear the heat should avoid the kitchen. But whoever loves this productive uncertainty and can stand it will not find a more beautiful profession than that of filmmaker, film producer, who generally at least experiences failures on a high level.

Definitely also and especially in Germany. ■

Company Profile

Mehr als Sie erwarten ...

More than you expect ...

Marketing MetropolRegion Nürnberg e. V.
www.metropolregion-nuernberg.org

Geschäftsführer/Managers:
Dr. Jörg Hahn
Gabriele Engel

Gründungsjahr/Year of Foundation:
Sommer/summer 1996

Geschäftstätigkeit/Business Activity:
Die Kompetenzfelder der Metropolregion Nürnberg sowohl nach innen als auch nach außen zu kommunizieren und der Metropolregion noch höheres internationales Ansehen zu verleihen.
To communicate competence fields of the Metropolitan Region Nuremberg both inland and to the outside and to give the region an even higher international standing.

Anschrift/Address:
Michael-Vogel-Straße 3
D-91052 Erlangen
Telefon +49 (9131) 72 76 77
Telefax +49 (9131) 72 76 55
E-Mail   info@metropolregion-nuernberg.org
Internet www.metropolregion-nuernberg.org
         www.highqualityoflife.com
         www.existenzgruenderpool.de

Bild oben:
Nürnberger Altstadtrennen.
Unten:
Gabriele Engel, Geschäftsführerin und Dr. Jörg Hahn, Hauptgeschäftsführer des Vereins „MetropolRegion Nürnberg e. V."
Picture above:
Rally in Nuremberg's Old City Centre.
Below:
Gabriele Engel, Managing Director and Dr. Jörg Hahn, General Director of the association "MetropolRegion Nürnberg e. V."

...bietet die Region rund um die Metropole Nürnberg. Wer bei ihr nur an Lebkuchen, Christkindlesmarkt, Bratwürste und Albrecht Dürer denkt, übersieht dabei, dass sich das wirtschaftliche Kraftzentrum Nordbayerns mit seinen 100.000 Unternehmen in den letzten Jahren innerhalb Europas deutlich nach vorne gearbeitet hat. Die Metropolregion Nürnberg ist in das geographische Zentrum des wiedervereinigten Europas getreten und mit einer Fläche von 13.000 km² sowie fast 2,5 Millionen Einwohnern Deutschlands sechstgrößte Wirtschaftsregion. Eine optimale Infrastruktur, gesichert durch den internationalen Flughafen, ein dichtes Autobahnnetz und das Güterhafenzentrum, sorgt für kurze Wege, schnelle Verbindungen und eine ideale Erreichbarkeit. Da ist es nicht verwunderlich, dass Nürnberg zu einem der größten Messestandorte und Handelszentren Europas gehört.

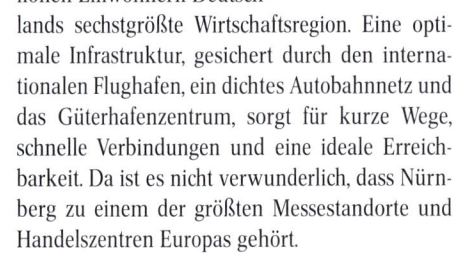

Besonders stolz ist die weltoffene Metropolregion auf ihre hohe Lebensqualität, die ihr bereits in zahlreichen europa- und weltweiten Umfragen bestätigt wurde. Einzigartige landschaftliche Höhepunkte wie die Fränkische Schweiz und das Fränkische Seenland, ein vielfältiges Sport- und Kulturangebot sowie viele Feste und Festivals prägen das Bild dieser Region.

Der Regionalmarketingverein „MetropolRegion Nürnberg e. V." hat sich unter anderem zum Ziel gesetzt, die Kompetenzfelder der Metropolregion Nürnberg sowohl nach innen als auch nach außen zu kommunizieren und somit der Region noch höheres, internationales Ansehen zu verleihen.
Zu ihren Kernkompetenzen zählen „Energie & Umwelt", „Informations- und Kommunikationstechnologie", „Verkehr & Logistik" sowie „Neue Materialien". Sehr kompetenzstark ist die Region auch im Bereich „Medizin, Pharma & Gesundheit" und ist dabei, sich als „Medical Valley" international zu profilieren. ■

...the region around the Nuremberg Metropolis has much more to offer. Whoever is only reminded of the Christmas gingerbread called Lebkuchen, the famous Christmas Market, fried sausages and Albrecht Dürer certainly overlooks that in the recent years the economic power centre of North Bavaria has advanced tremendously with its 100,000 companies within Europe. The Metropolitan Region of Nuremberg has entered the geographic centre of a reunited Europe and forms the sixth largest economic region in Germany with an area of 13,000 km² as well as a total of almost 2.5 million inhabitants. An optimal infrastructure, which is secured through an international airport, a dense network of motorways and the freight traffic centre, provides short transport routes, fast connections and ideal accessibility. It is therefore not surprising that Nuremberg is one of the largest locations for exhibitions and a major trade centre in Europe.

The open-minded metropolitan region is particularly proud of its high quality of life, which has been attested already in numerous European and worldwide surveys. Unique highlights of landscapes like the "Fränkische Schweiz" (Franconian Switzerland) and the Franconian Lakeland district, a variety of sports and cultural offers as well as many events and festivals illustrate the character of this region.

Some of the aims of the region's marketing association "MetropolRegion Nürnberg e.V." are for instance to communicate competence fields of the Nuremberg Region both inland and to the outside and to give the metropolitan region an even higher international standing.
Among its core competence areas are "Energy & Environment", "Information and Communications Technology", "Transport and Logistics" as well as "New Materials". The region possesses also strong competency in the field of "Medicine, Pharmaceutics and Health" and is about to distinguish itself as "Medical Valley". ■

Company Profile

Maschinentechnik in Welt-Spitzenposition

Global top position in machine engineering

Seit dem Gründungsjahr 1968 beschäftigte sich die Edgar Georg GmbH & Co. KG in Neitersen unter anderem mit Maschinenbau. Im Februar 2002 wurde der Geschäftsbereich Maschinenbau verselbstständigt und firmiert seit 1. Februar als Georg Maschinentechnik GmbH & Co. KG.

Hier werden mit hohem technischen Know-how mechanische und hydraulische Pressen bis 50.000 kN Presskraft gefertigt sowie vollautomatische Anlagen für die spanlose Formgebung.

Mit Sondermaschinen zur Herstellung von speziellen Komponenten für den Antrieb von PKWs nimmt Georg auf dem Weltmarkt eine führende Position ein. Im Segment Kugelkäfigstanzen ist das Unternehmen aus Neitersen Weltmarktführer. Durch die Aufnahme von Kunststoffblasmaschinen für große Hohlbehälter und Transferanlagen für die Herstellung von Stahlfelgen wurde das Fertigungsprogramm um zwei wesentliche Bestandteile ausgebaut.

Neben der Entwicklung und Herstellung der genannten Produkte zählt auch die Entwicklung und Anwendung technischer Software zum Leistungsspektrum von Georg.

Das Unternehmen beliefert die Branchen der Automobilzulieferindustrie, Automobilindustrie, Umformtechnik, Maschinentechnik und Kunststofftechnik.

Leistungsfähige Einrichtungen, 65 motivierte Mitarbeiter und ein breites Ingenieurwissen sichern den Erfolg in Qualität, Zuverlässigkeit und hoher Flexibilität. ■

Since the year of its establishment in 1968, one of the activities at Edgar Georg GmbH & Co. KG of Neitersen covers the field of machine construction. In February 2002, the business field of machine construction became independent and acquired the name of Georg Maschinentechnik GmbH & Co. KG on 1st February.

With high-quality technical expertise mechanical and hydraulic stamping machines with a force of pressure of up to 50.000 kN are manufactured here as well as fully automatic plants for forming without cutting.

Georg occupies the position of world market leader for special machines for the production of specific components for the drive units of motorcars. In the segment of pressing ball bearing cages the Neitersen-based company is world market leader. The product range was extended by two major components, namely through the additional production of plastic blowing machines for large hollow mould casting and transfer plants for the production of steel wheel rims. Besides development and manufacture of the above mentioned products, also the development and application of technical software forms part of Georg's service range. The company supplies the branches of automobile supplier industry, automotive industry, forging industry, machine engineering and plastics technology.

Efficient facilities, 65 motivated staff members and far-reaching engineering expertise ensure success in quality, reliability and a high level of flexibility. ■

MASCHINENTECHNIK GEORG

Georg Maschinentechnik GmbH & Co. KG

Geschäftsführer/Manager:
Guido Brassart

Gründungsjahr/Year of Foundation: 1968

Mitarbeiter/Employees: 65

Geschäftsfelder/Business areas:
Maschinentechnik:
- Entwicklung und Herstellung von mechanischen und hydraulischen Pressen
- Entwicklung und Anwendung technischer Software
- Entwicklung und Herstellung von Automatisierungslinien für die Automobilindustrie

Machine engineering:
- Development and production of mechanical and hydraulic stamping machines
- Development and application of technical software
- Development and production of automation lines for the automobile industry.

Produkte:
- mechanische und hydraulische Pressen
- Kugelkäfigstanzen
- Automatisierungslinien für PKW- und LKW-Räder
- Stauköpfe für die Kunststoffindustrie
- Werkzeuge

Products:
- Mechanical and hydraulic stamping machines
- Stamping machines for ball bearing cages
- Automation lines for motorcar and lorry wheels
- Hold-up heads for the plastics industry
- Tools.

Anschrift/Address:
Rheinstraße 18
D-57638 Neitersen
Telefon +49 (26 81) 804-0
Telefax +49 (26 81) 804-210
E-Mail info@georg-gruppe.de
Internet www.georg-gruppe.de

Foto oben:
Georg Kugelkäfigstanze PED 100 SD.

Photo above:
Georg stamping machine for ball bearing cages – PED 100 SD.

Foto unten:
Georg Hydraulische Doppelständerpresse PHD 800/1050.

Photo below:
Georg hydraulic double stand press PHD 800/1050.

Die Zukunft einer gerechten Gesundheitsversorgung

The future of just health care

Sichere Gesundheitsversorgung als Stütze und Sinn des Staates

In der bisherigen Geschichte in nahezu allen ethisch hoch stehenden Kulturen und Religionen hatte das Prinzip der Sorge aller um das Wohl der einzelnen Kranken und Schwachen in der Gesellschaft eine tragende gemeinschaftsbildende und stabilisierende Rolle. Dies sollte unabhängig von der Position in der Gesellschaft und der eigenen Schuld an dem hilfsbedürftigen Zustand geschehen. Verknappung von Ressourcen und die daraus resultierende Rationierung der Mittel haben aber auch zu allen Zeiten die Diskussion um die Möglichkeit der Entsolidarisierung in der Gesellschaft aufkommen lassen. Die potenziell zumindest teilweise vorhandene Schuld des Einzelnen an seiner Krankheit durch leichtsinniges oder ungesundes Verhalten lässt dabei auch die Frage aufkommen, warum dafür die Allgemeinheit eigentlich finanziell aufkommen soll. Müsste nicht vielmehr gesundes und damit gesundheitsökonomisch vernünftiges Verhalten belohnt und/oder potenziell selbstschädigendes Tun bestraft werden, da es ja auch indirekt die Allgemeinheit schädigt? Solche Überlegungen kurzerhand mit „sozialem Eiszeit-Denken" vom Tisch zu wischen, greift zu kurz. Wir brauchen vielmehr zunächst eine tiefer gehende ausführliche Diskussion über die Vor- und Nachteile eines schuldunabhängigen Solidarprinzips und die gerechte Finanzierung dieses Systems in unserem Staat. Welche Auswirkungen hätte eine Entsolidarisierung in der Gesellschaft auch auf die Gesunden, Jungen und Starken? Wie kann überhaupt die Schuld an einer Erkrankung zuverlässig festgestellt werden? Ist es gerecht, wenn nur die Arbeitnehmer und die Arbeitgeber in den Solidartopf einzahlen und andere Einkommensquellen und Gruppen unberücksichtigt bleiben? Gibt es andere Gesundheitssicherungssysteme, die zum Beispiel die Eigenverantwortung und Selbstbeteiligung stärker betonen und gleichzeitig effektiver für den Einzelnen und die Allgemeinheit sind?

Derzeit stehen nach dem Solidarprinzip grundsätzlich allen Versicherten die gleichen Leistungen zu, unabhängig von dem jeweiligen Beitrag, persönlichem gesundheitlichen Risiko, Verhalten, Eintrittsalter und Familienstand. Dieses Solidarprinzip ist der Grundpfeiler der gesetzlichen Krankenversicherung. Hierdurch unterscheidet sich die gesetzliche Krankenversicherung wesentlich von der privaten. Es fehlen zuverlässige Untersuchungen in und außerhalb Deutschlands zum Vergleich dieser beiden Gesundheitsversicherungsformen. Sind etwa freiwillig privat Versicherte wirklich medizinisch besser versorgt und ist dies wirtschaftlicher als in der gesetzlichen Versicherung? Von welchem System profitieren der Einzelne und die Allgemeinheit am stärksten? Hier benötigen wir keine ideologischen Ansichten, sondern aussagekräftige Erhebungen, Studien und zuverlässige

Prof. Dr. med. Peter T. Sawicki

Der Autor, geboren 1957 in Warschau, studierte Humanmedizin in Bonn und Düsseldorf, 1984 Approbation als Arzt. Anschließend klinische Ausbildung zum Facharzt für Innere Medizin. Seit 1991 Facharzt für Innere Medizin. Seit 1991 Diabetologe nach den Richtlinien der Deutschen Diabetes Gesellschaft. 1984 bis 2000 klinisch-wissenschaftliche Tätigkeit an der Klinik für Stoffwechselkrankheiten der Universität Düsseldorf, 1991 bis 2000 Leiter der Ambulanz für Diabeteskomplikationen. Ab 2000 Direktor der Abteilung für Innere Medizin des St. Franziskus Hospitals in Köln. 2002 Gründer des Institutes für evidenzbasierte Medizin (DIeM) in Köln. Seit 2004 Leiter des Institutes für Qualität und Wirtschaftlichkeit im Gesundheitswesen.

The author was born in 1957 in Warsaw and studied human medicine in Bonn and Düsseldorf; in 1984 he received his doctor's licence. In the following, he completed clinical training as specialist for interior medicine. Since 1991, he has been a specialist for interior medicine. Since 1991, he has been a certified diabetes specialist according to the guidelines of the German Diabetes Society. From 1984 to 2000 he carried out clinical-scientific activities at the Clinic of Metabolism Diseases at the University of Düsseldorf; from 1991 to 2000, he served as head of the Ambulance for Diabetes Complications. As of 2000, he worked as Director of the Department of Interior Medicine of St. Franziskus Hospital in Cologne. In 2002, he founded the Institute of evidence-based Medicine in Cologne. Since 2004, he has been head of the Institute of Quality and Efficiency in Health Care.

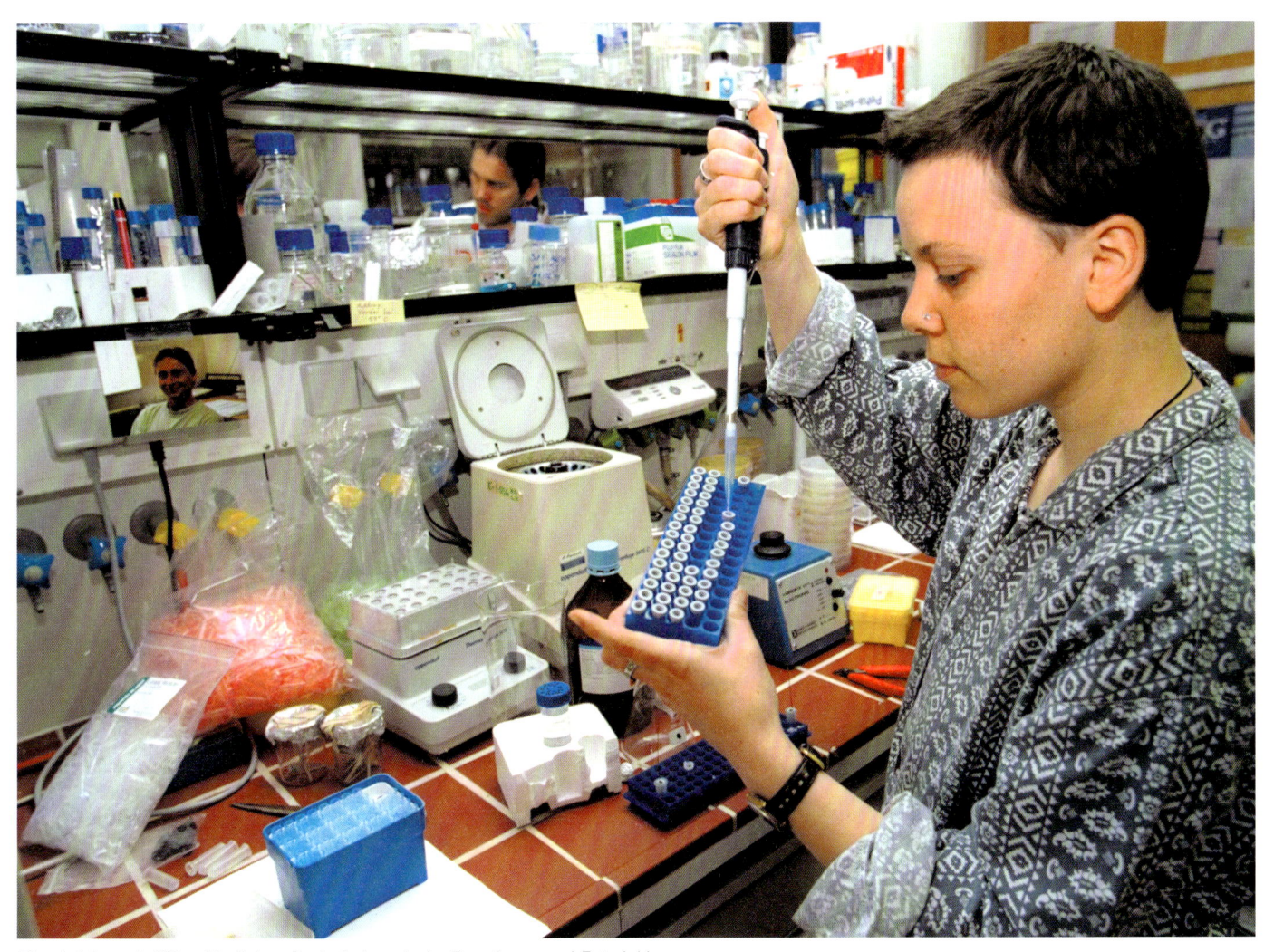

Eine leistungskräftige Medizin erfordert eine starke Forschung und Entwicklung.

Powerful medicine requires a strong research and development sector.

Secure health care provision as pillar and mission of the state

Throughout history so far, the principle of everyone caring for the welfare of ill and weak individuals in society has had an important community-building and stabilising role in almost all ethically high standing cultures and religions. This should occur independently of one's position in society and one's own guilt with respect to the needy condition prevailing. However, the lack of resources and the rationing of means resulting from it have provoked discussions about the possibility of not showing solidarity in society at all times. At least the partly potentially existing blame of the individual for his own illness because of thoughtless or unhealthy behaviour poses the question, why in fact everybody has to bear the costs for this. Indeed, should healthy and therefore economically healthy and sensible behaviour not rather be rewarded and/or potentially self-damaging action be punished, since it also damages the general public indirectly? It would certainly fall short to do away with such thoughts as being merely "social ice-age ideas". We definitely need now a deeper and more extended discussion about the advantages and disadvantages of the blame-independent solidarity principle and a just financing of this system in our country. How would not showing solidarity in society affect healthy, young and strong people? How can one's blame for contracting an illness be reliably determined at all? Is it fair that only employers and employees have to lump everything together in solidarity and other sources of income and other groups are not considered? Are there other health care securing systems that give more emphasis to personal responsibility and cost-sharing for instance and are more effective for the individual and the general public at the same time?

According to the principle of solidarity, all insured persons are entitled to the same benefits at present, independently of their relevant contributions, personal health risk, behaviour, age at entry and marital status. This principle of solidarity is the cornerstone of compulsory health insurance. This is what differentiates compulsory health insurance substantially from the private one. There is a lack of reliable investigations in and outside of Germany to compare these two forms of health insurances. Is it true that persons who have a private insurance on a voluntary basis receive better medical care and is this more economical than the compulsory health insurance? Which system benefits the individual and the general public the best? We do not need ideological views here, but meaningful surveys, studies and reliable data on the basis of which a constructive, factual dialogue can take place before we make any decisions that lead to an early dismantling of well-established structures.

But the basic idea of the solidarity principle is also that the general public only has to bear the necessary costs of health care provision for the individual. What is necessary and economical can be assessed reliably and objectively through modern

Gesundheitspolitik

Daten, auf deren Basis ein konstruktiver, sachlicher Dialog geführt werden kann, und dies, bevor wir Entscheidungen treffen, durch die bewährte Strukturen vorschnell abgebaut werden.

Die Grundidee des Solidarprinzips ist aber auch, dass die Allgemeinheit nur die notwendigen Kosten für die gesundheitliche Versorgung des Einzelnen trägt. Was medizinisch notwendig und wirtschaftlich ist, kann durch moderne wissenschaftliche Methoden zuverlässig und objektiv beurteilt werden. Die Definition dessen, was medizinisch erforderlich ist, wurde jahrhundertelang aber der alleinigen ärztlichen Entscheidung überlassen, die auf der Erfahrung der einzelnen Ärzte beruhte. Die schnelle Entwicklung der Medizin und die Notwendigkeit, Entscheidungen zu treffen, die sich aufgrund der Komplexität der Beurteilung durch die ärztliche Erfahrung entziehen, verlangt zunehmend nach anderen, moderneren Methoden der Entscheidungsfindung. Darüber hinaus ist eine Beteiligung der Allgemeinheit an diesen Entscheidungen notwendig. Dies erfordert eine bessere Gesundheitsbildung der Bevölkerung, die schon in den Schulen anfangen müsste. Eine solche Gesundheitsbildung sollte auch die wissenschaftlichen Methoden der Beurteilung von Risiken und der Einschätzung der Risikoänderung beinhalten.

Die Definition des Notwendigen durch die evidenzbasierte Medizin

Auf welchen Denkstilen basieren medizinische Entscheidungen, und welchen Aufwand soll die Allgemeinheit für den Kranken oder Gefährdeten tragen und welchen nicht? Schon immer bestand hier der Wunsch nach der Reduktion der Entscheidungsbeliebigkeit und dem Aufbau einer belastbaren wissenschaftlichen Struktur. Im ersten mittelalterlichen Versuch einer staatlichen Kodifizierung der Rechtsordnung, der Liber Augustalis, schrieb im Jahr 1231 Kaiser Friedrich II.: „Da die Medizin niemals erfolgreich sein kann … ohne die Kenntnis der Logik, befehlen wir, dass keiner Medizin studiere, der nicht vorher mindestens drei Jahre Logik betrieben habe."

Im Grunde basieren die unterschiedlichen medizinischen Entscheidungsmodelle der verschiedenen Staaten heutzutage auf folgenden Grundgedanken: der Abwägung zwischen dem potenziellen Nutzen und dem Schaden medizinischer Maßnahmen und dem Grad der Irrtumswahrscheinlichkeit dieser Aussagen. Diese Möglichkeit bietet die so genannte „evidenzbasierte Medizin", die sowohl konkrete, für die Patienten wichtige Ergebnisse vorstellbar darstellt und als auch gleichzeitig die Qualität des zugrunde liegenden Wissens festlegt, also die mögliche Effektstärke und die Wahrscheinlichkeit des Irrtums der Aussagen beschreibt. Dieser wissenschaftliche Denkstil müsste in alle gesundheitspolitischen Diskussionen verpflichtend Eingang finden. Dies würde nicht nur die Ergebnisse verbessern, sondern auch zur Versachlichung und damit zur Beruhigung der häufig emotional überladenen Kontroversen in diesem Sektor führen.

Jede konkrete medizinische Entscheidung macht aber auch das Abwägen zwischen der Unsicherheit der Aussage, der Art und Schwere der Erkrankung, der Größe des Therapieeffektes und dem Vorhandensein einer Alternative notwendig. Existiert keine gut belegte Alternative, ist die Erkrankung ggf. tödlich und der potenzielle Effekt der Maßnahme groß, wird eine größere wissenschaftliche Unsicherheit in Kauf genommen werden müssen und umgekehrt. So erfordern zum Beispiel so genannte „Vorsorgemaßnahmen", deren Therapieeffekt häufig

Die Wirkung einer Behandlung kann von vielen kaum vorherzusehenden Faktoren abhängen. So ist das Ergebnis einer bestimmten Operationsart auch von der Erfahrung der Chirurgen, Güte der Narkose, Organisation der Pflege, der psychologischen Betreuung vor und nach der Operation und vielem mehr abhängig. Die Fotos entstanden während einer Operation im Universitätsklinikum Frankfurt am Main.

The effect of a treatment can depend on many hardly foreseeable factors. For instance the result of a certain type of operation can indeed depend also on the experience of the surgeons, quality of the anaesthesia, organisation of after care, psychological support before and after the operation and much more. The photographs were made during surgery at the University Hospital Frankfurt am Main.

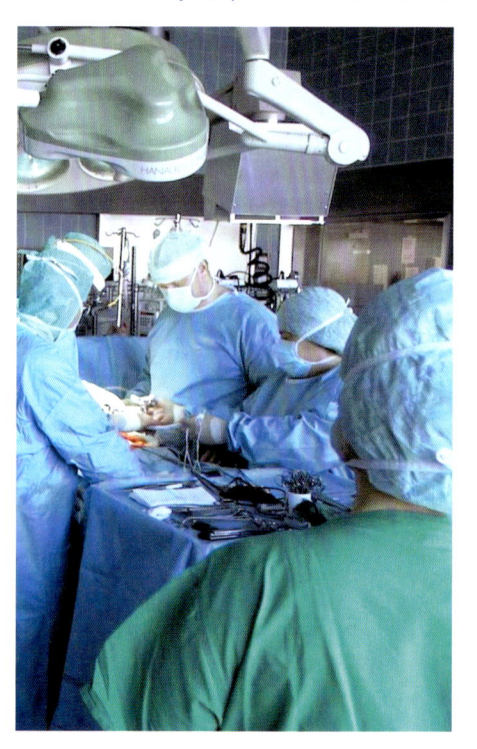

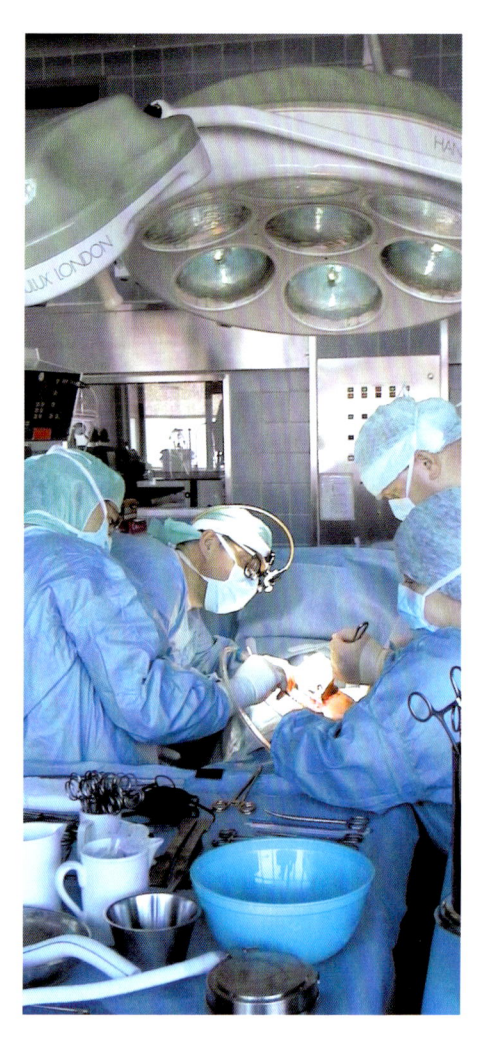

klein ist und die sich in den meisten Fällen an Gesunde wenden, eine sehr belastbare wissenschaftliche Absicherung. Dieses Entscheidungsmodell der evidenzbasierten Medizin beruht vor allem auf wissenschaftlichen Untersuchungen, berücksichtigt aber auch die Erfahrung der Ärzte und die individuelle Situation der Patienten.

Die Individualität der Entscheidung erhalten

Medizinische Entscheidungen werden nach individuellen ärztlichen Beratungen von den Patienten getroffen. Sie sind abhängig vom Wissen der Patienten und der Ärzte. Das medizinische Handeln wird dabei nur zu einem Teil geleitet durch ärztliches Können und Erfahrung, die abhängig von Übung und Zeit sind. Immer mehr wird diese Entscheidung durch das vorhandene abstrakte Regelwissen bestimmt, das sich aus der notwendigerweise künstlichen medizinischen Forschung ergibt. Nur durch die Betonung dieser beiden Seiten, also der praktischen Erfahrung und des theoretischen Regelwissens in der individuellen medizinischen Entscheidung wird ein optimales Ergebnis erzielt. Die Beurteilung des Wissens erfolgt dabei in drei Stufen:

Health Policy

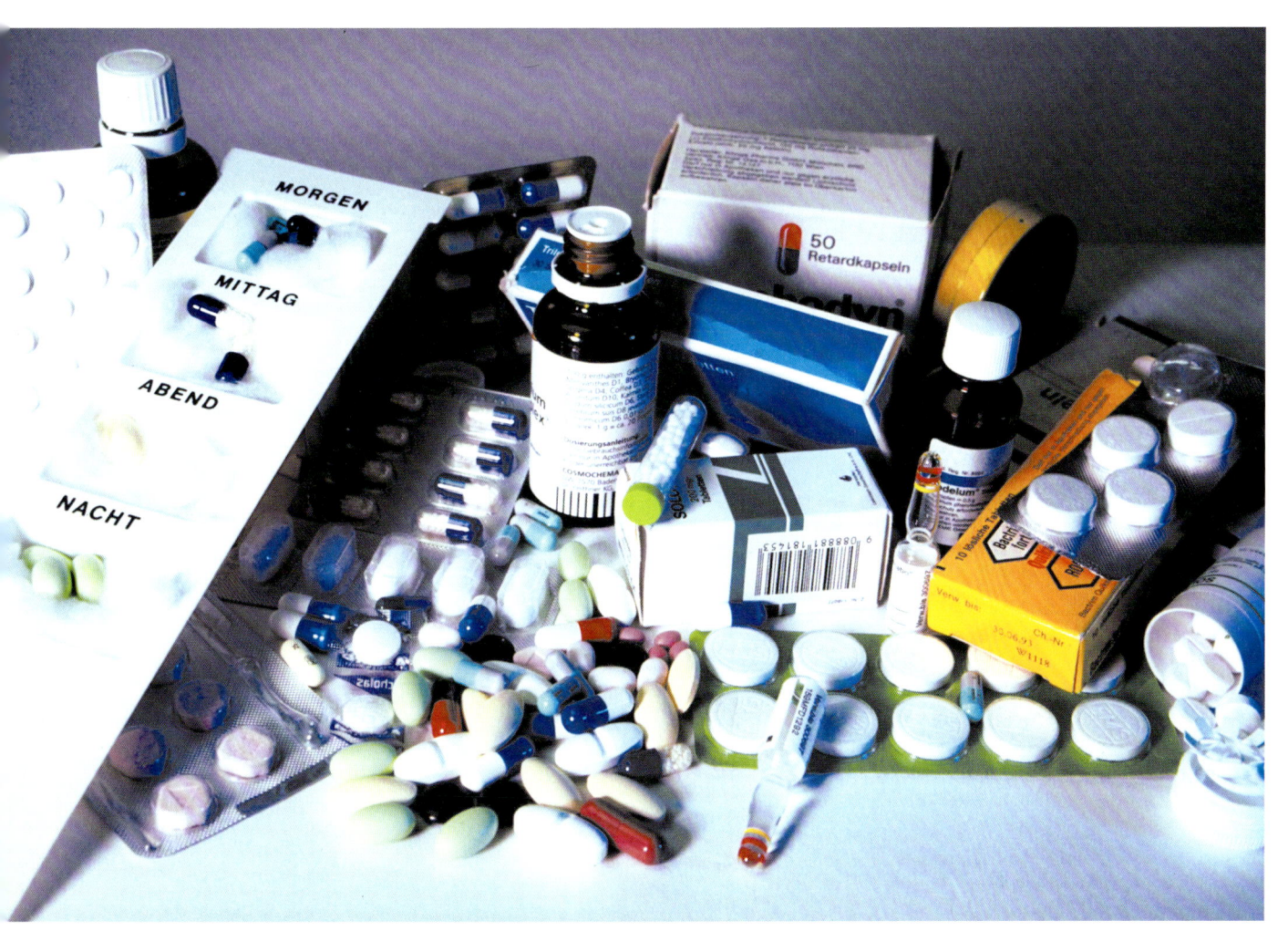

scientific methods. However, the definition of what is actually necessary from a medical point of view has for centuries been left solely to the doctor's decision, which in turn was based on the experience of individual doctors. Fast developments in medicine and the necessity to make decisions, whereby assessments drawn from doctoral experience are eluded because of their complexity, require increasingly other, more modern methods of decision making. Moreover, participation of the general public is necessary for these decisions. This requires a better health education of the population that should start already in schools. Such health education should also include the scientific methods of assessing risks and evaluation of changed risks.

The definition of the precedent conditions through evidence-based medicine

On what systems of thought are medical decisions based and which costs should the general public bear for the ill or endangered and which not? There has always been the desire to reduce the randomness of decision making and to build up a steadfast scientific structure. In the first intent of a codification of the legal system by the state, the Liber Augustalis, Emperor Frederick II wrote in the year 1231: "Since medicine can never be successful without the knowledge of logic, we command that no one study medicine, who has not previously taken at least three years of logic."

In essence, the different medical decision-making models of various states are based today on the following basic ideas: weighing up the potential benefit and the damage of medical provisions and the degree of probable errors these statements may contain. The so-called "evidence-based medicine" offers this alternative as it illustrates vividly concrete results that are important to patients and at the same time determines the quality of the knowledge they are based on, i.e. the possible strength of the effect and the probability of error in the statements. It should be compulsory to integrate this scientific thought system in all health policy debates. This would not only improve results, but also lead to a more objective debate and thus to calming the controversies frequently excessively influenced by emotions in this sector.

Each concrete medical decision however, also makes it necessary to weigh up between an insecure statement, the type and seriousness of the illness, the size of therapy effect and the existence of an alternative. If a well-founded alternative does not exist, the illness may be fatal and the potential effect of the provision is large, greater scientific insecurity will have to be accepted and vice versa. For instance so-called "preventive measures", the therapeutic effects of which are often small and which in most cases are oriented towards healthy persons, require a very reliable scientific reassurance. Above all, this decision making model of evidence-based medicine rests on scientific investigations, but it also considers the experience of doctors and the individual situation of patients.

Maintaining the individuality of decision

After individual medical consultation the patients make medical decisions. These therefore depend on the knowledge of patients and doctors. Therapeutic action in this respect is only partly guided by medical expertise and experience, which

Gesundheitspolitik

- 1. Validität: Stimmt die Information?
- 2. Wichtigkeit: Ist die Information versorgungsrelevant?
- 3. Fallbezug: Ist die Information auf den konkreten Fall anwendbar?

Evidenzbasierte Medizin ist also in keinem Fall eine Keule oder Zwangsjacke, die den praktisch tätigen Arzt und den Patienten bedroht oder einengt – im Gegenteil. Sie bietet eine ehrliche, objektive Übersicht über das fallbezogene Wissen und seine Qualität und überlässt dem Arzt und dem Patienten die Entscheidung darüber, ob und wie sie sich gemeinsam für eine bestimmte medizinische Maßnahme entscheiden. Evidenzbasierte Medizin schafft also die Grundlage für eine freie diagnostische und therapeutische Entscheidung. Sie kann nur individuell in einem interaktiven Prozess zwischen Arzt und Patient getroffen werden. Dies erfordert bei beiden das notwendige objektive Faktenwissen, um den für den Einzelfall bestmöglichen Weg einzuschlagen. Die unbedingte Voraussetzung dafür ist eine inhaltlich hervorragende und unabhängige Information von Ärzten und Patienten. Viele Patienten würden auf manche medizinischen Leistungen verzichten, wenn sie genau darüber informiert wären, wie gering der potenzielle individuelle Nutzen der Maßnahme und wie unsicher der wissenschaftliche Beleg ihrer Wirksamkeit sind. Der bewusste persönliche Verzicht auf unsichere Leistungen hätte nicht nur eine Zunahme der Qualität in der medizinischen Versorgung zur Folge, sondern würde ganz sicher gleichzeitig auch zu einer massiven Kostensenkung führen.

Förderung echter Innovationen für eine bessere Medizin

Eine auch zukünftig leistungskräftige Medizin erfordert eine starke Forschung und Entwicklung. Dies setzt sowohl eine Förderung der patientenorientierten universitären Forschung und Lehre voraus als auch Anreize für die forschende pharmazeutischen Industrie, Besseres zu entwickeln. In diesem Punkt sind Anpassungen notwendig. Die medizinische Wissenschaft ist in Deutschland sehr stark grundlagenorientiert und nur wenige unabhängige Mittel fließen in praxisrelevante und unabhängige medizinische Forschung. Für die pharmazeutischen Unternehmen ist die Forschung und Entwicklung wirklich neuer therapeutischer Verfahren teuer und risikobehaftet. Dagegen ist die Produktion so genannter Nachahmer-Präparate zunächst billiger und risikoärmer, weil diese Präparate in einer ähnlichen Form bereits wissenschaftlich von anderen getestet wurden. Der Patentschutz und die Kostenerstattung durch die gesetzliche Krankenversicherung unterscheiden aber nicht zwischen einer echten Innovation, die einen Fortschritt für den Patienten bedeutet, und so genannten „Scheininnovationen", die häufig unzureichend untersucht und deshalb nicht ausreichend sicher sind. Diese Situation fördert die Produktion unnötiger Kopien echter Neuerungen, die die Therapie unsicherer und teuerer machen. Hier braucht die pharmazeutische Industrie bessere Bedingungen für eine finanzielle Sicherheit wirklicher Innovationen und Ermunterung neue Wege zu gehen. Dies würde sich für alle lohnen. Denn wirklich neue und fortschrittliche Medikamente, die Erkrankungen wirksam bekämpfen, reduzieren die Kosten im Gesundheitswesen. Hingegen sind Entwicklungs- und Produktionskosten für „Scheininnovationen" verlorenes Geld. Zudem können Wirkstoffe, auch wenn sie nur auf einer geringen Moleküländerung eines gut untersuchten Medikamentes beruhen, durchaus unkalkulierbare Risiken bergen, die Haftungsrisiken für die Industrie mit sich bringen können.

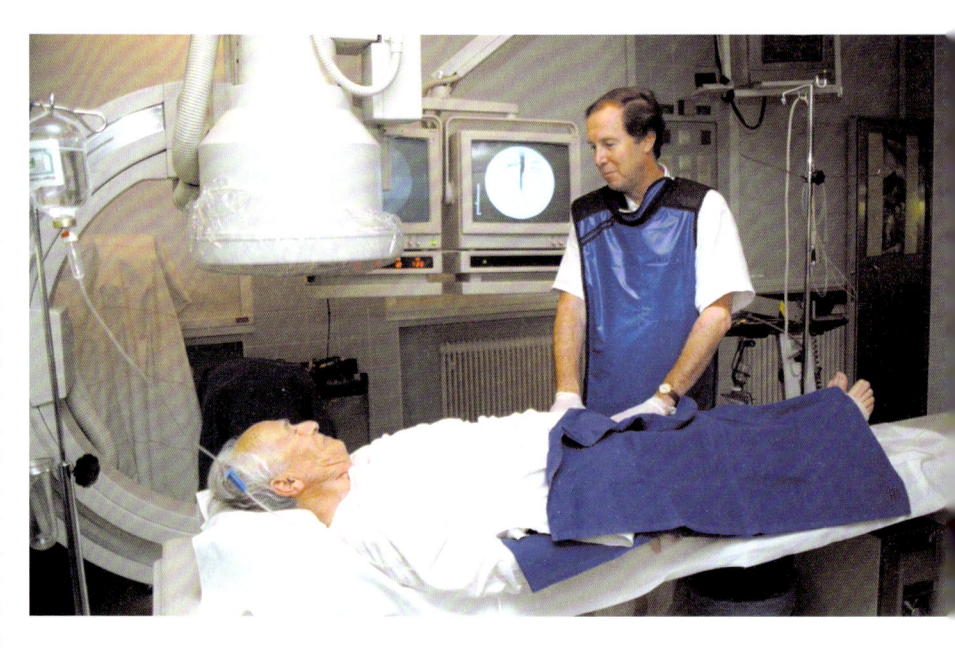

Qualität im Gesundheitswesen

Die Wirksamkeit einer medizinischen Maßnahme darf nicht mit ihrer Wirkung gleichgesetzt werden. Die Wirksamkeit ergibt sich meist aus entsprechenden wissenschaftlichen Studien, die notwendigerweise in einer künstlichen Umgebung durchgeführt werden. Die Wirkung dieser Maßnahme kann in einem bestimmten Krankenhaus oder Fall ganz anders sein. Dies kann von vielen kaum vorherzusehenden Faktoren abhängen. So ist das Ergebnis einer bestimmten Operationsart durchaus auch von der Erfahrung der Chirurgen, Güte der Narkose, Organisation der Pflege, der psychologischen Betreuung vor und nach der Operation und vielem mehr abhängig. Alle diese

Viele Patienten würden auf manche medizinischen Leistungen verzichten, wenn sie wüssten, wie gering der potenzielle individuelle Nutzen der Maßnahme und wie unsicher der wissenschaftliche Beleg ihrer Wirksamkeit ist.

Many patients would turn down certain medical provisions if they had precise information about how small the potential individual benefit of the provision is and how insecure the scientific prove of its effectiveness.

Aspekte werden meist bei der wissenschaftlichen Beurteilung der Wirksamkeit einer Maßnahme nicht berücksichtigt. Daher ist es erforderlich, die Qualität in allen Bereichen der medizinischen Leistungen anhand patientenrelevanter Ergebnisse zu erheben, die Richtigkeit und Vollständigkeit der Daten zu prüfen, sie in einem Benchmarkverfahren mit den Ergebnissen anderer zu vergleichen und zwar so, dass die Unterschiede deutlich werden. Dies genügt aber allein nicht. Es muss im Weiteren eine strukturierte Ergebnisanalyse und ggf. Fehleranalyse erfolgen, aus der sich konkrete individuelle Interventionen einschließlich Fehlermanagement ergeben. Dabei wird zunächst untersucht, ob überhaupt Fehler für ein „schlechteres" Ergebnis verantwortlich sind, falls ja, wie diese Fehler behoben werden können, gefolgt von der praktischen Umsetzung der gefundenen Verbesserungsvorschläge. Danach folgt eine erneute Ergebnisanalyse, die im Stande ist darzustellen, ob diese Intervention erfolgreich war. Die Leistungsfähigkeit und die Qualität des deutschen Gesundheitssystems sind gut. Damit dies auch so in Zukunft bleibt, benötigen wir auf allen beteiligten Ebenen der Gesundheitsversorgung eine wissenschaftsgeleitete Änderung der Denkstile, die eine fortwährende Verbesserung des jetzigen Zustands zum Ziel haben. ∎

Health Policy

depend on practice and time. Increasingly, this decision is determined by an existing abstract regular knowledge, which results from the necessarily artificial medical research. Only by emphasizing these two aspects, i.e. the practical experience and the theoretical regular knowledge, in individual therapeutic decisions an optimal result can be achieved. Assessment of this knowledge is carried out in three stages:
• 1. Validity: is the information correct?
• 2. Importance: is the information relevant to the provision?
• 3. Case-driven approach: is the information applicable to this concrete case?

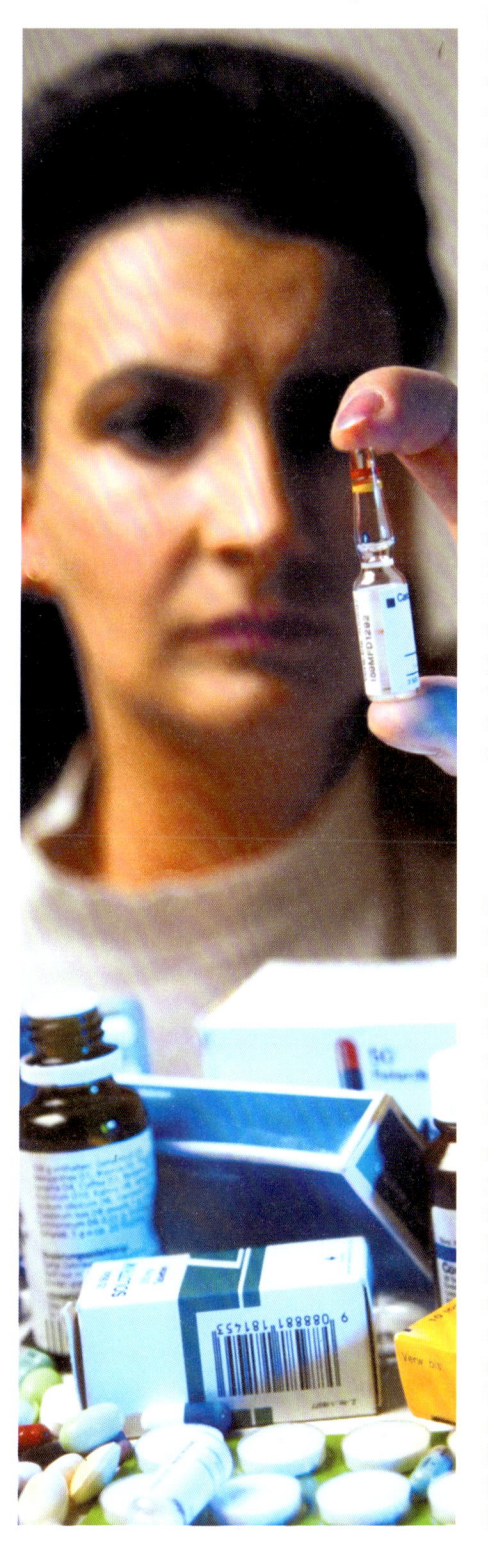

By no means is evidence based medicine therefore a hit with a club or a straitjacket that threatens or limits the practically working doctor and the patient, on the contrary. It offers an honest and objective overview about case-driven knowledge and its quality, and leaves the decision about whether and how they mutually decide on a certain medical provision to the doctor and the patient. Evidencebased medicine therefore creates the basis for a free diagnostic and therapeutic decision. It can only be made individually within an interactive process that takes place between the doctor and the patient. It requires that both have the necessary objective factual knowledge to find the best possible practice for each individual case. To this end, it is an indispensable prerequisite that doctors and patients receive excellent and independent information in terms of contents. Many patients would turn down certain medical provisions if they had precise information about how small the potential individual benefit of the provision is and how insecure the scientific prove of its effectiveness. Conscious personal relinquishment of insecure provisions would not only lead to an increased quality in medical care, but would surely also result in a massive cost reduction.

Supporting real innovations for better medicine

If the medical sector wants to be powerful also in future it needs a strong research and development sector. This implies both the support of patient-oriented university research and teaching as well as incentives for research in the pharmaceutical industry to develop improvements. At this point adjustment will be necessary. Medical science in Germany is very much oriented towards pure research and only little independent funds flow into practically relevant and independent medical research. Research and development of truly new therapeutic procedures are expensive and risky for pharmaceutical companies. However, the production of so-called generic drugs is at first cheaper and bears less risks, because these drugs have already been tested scientifically in similar form by others. Patent rights and reimbursement of costs by compulsory health insurance do not differentiate between a real innovation, which signifies progress for patients, and so-called "pseudo-innovations", which often did not receive sufficient investigation and are therefore not sufficiently safe. This situation supports the production of unnecessary copies of real innovations, which make therapy more unsafe and more expensive. This is where the pharmaceutical industry requires better conditions for the financial security of real innovations and stimulation to break new ground. Certainly, everyone would benefit from this. Indeed, truly new and progressive medicines that fight ailments effectively will reduce costs in the health care system. On the other hand, development and production costs for "pseudo-innovations" are lost capital. Moreover, substances, even if they only rest on the tiny molecule change of an investigated medicine, can bear incalculable risks, which can lead to the risk of industry being made liable.

Quality in health care

The effectiveness of medical provision must not be equalled with its effect. The effectiveness results mainly from corresponding scientific studies, which inevitably must be conducted within an artificial environment. The effect of such provision can be quite different in a specific hospital or case. This can depend on many hardly foreseeable factors. For instance the result of a certain type of operation can indeed depend also on the experience of the surgeons, quality of the anaesthesia, organisation of after care, psychological support before and after the operation and of much more. All these aspects mostly are not considered when scientific assessments of the effectiveness of a provision are given. Therefore it is necessary to raise the quality in all sectors of medical services by means of patient-relevant results, to test the correctness and completeness of data, to compare the same within a benchmark process with the results of others and this must be carried out in such a way that differences become clearly visible. But this alone is not enough. In the following, a structured result analysis and eventually an error analysis must follow from which concrete individual interventions including error management will result. First, it will be investigated if there were errors responsible for a "worse" result at all and if so, how these errors can be rectified, followed y the practical application of proposals for improvement found. Subsequently, there will be a renewed result analysis, which is capable of illustrating whether this intervention was successful.

The efficiency and quality of the German health care system are of first-class value. In order to maintain these standards also in future we need a science-oriented change of thought systems that aim to continuously improve present conditions

Company Profile

Moderne Therapien – gut versorgte Patienten

Modern therapies – well attended patients

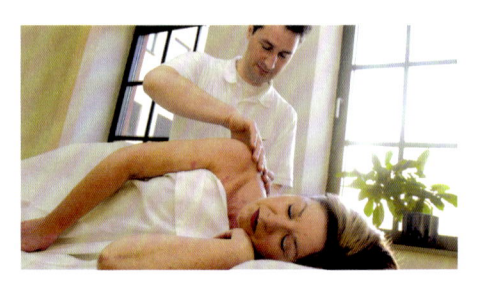

PARACELSUS KLINIKEN DEUTSCHLAND GmbH

Paracelsus-Kliniken Deutschland GmbH

Gesellschafter/Shareholder:
Dr. med. Manfred Georg Krukemeyer

Aufsichtsratsvorsitzender/Chairman of the Managing Board:
Ass. jur. Klaus Schenke

Geschäftsführer/Managing Directors:
Ass. jur. Joachim Bovelet
Ass. jur. Peter Clausing

Gründungsjahr/Year of Foundation:
1968

Mitarbeiter/Employees:
ca. 5.000

Fachgebiete/Specialist Fields:
Abhängigkeitserkrankungen, Anästhesie, Atemwegserkrankungen, Augenheilkunde, Chirurgie, Dermatologie, Gynäkologie und Geburtshilfe, HNO, Innere Medizin, Intensivmedizin, Mund-, Kiefer-, Gesichtschirurgie, Neurochirurgie, Neurologie, Nuklearmedizin, Oralchirurgie, Orthopädie, Phlebologie, Polytoxikomanie, Psychosomatik, Radiologie, Strahlentherapie, Unfallchirurgie, Urologie

Anschrift/Address:
Sedanstraße 109
D-49076 Osnabrück
Telefon   +49 (541) 66 92 0
Telefax   +49 (541) 66 92 189
E-Mail   info@pk-mx.de
Internet   paracelsus-kliniken.de

Die Konzernzentrale der Paracelsus-Kliniken in Osnabrück.
Headquarters of the Paracelsus-Kliniken Group is in Osnabrück.

Entspannung und gezielte Therapien unterstützen den Genesungsprozess in den Paracelsus-Kliniken.
Relaxation and specific therapies support the healing process at Paracelsus-Kliniken.

Ganzheitliche Betreuung, qualitätsgesicherte und aufeinander abgestimmte Therapieabläufe, hervorragende Beratung und Unterstützung – das sind einige der Vorteile, die die Paracelsus-Kliniken Deutschland GmbH ihren Patienten durch die systematische Entwicklung neuer Versorgungsformen bietet. So konnte im Frühjahr 2005 der erste Vertrag zur integrierten Versorgung von Patienten mit psychischen und psychosomatischen Erkrankungen abgeschlossen werden.

Bei dieser neuen Form der Versorgung werden stationäre Therapie und ambulante Versorgung optimal vernetzt. Zusätzlich wird der Patient während der gesamten Behandlung von einem persönlichen Fallbetreuer auf dem Weg durch die Versorgungsbereiche unterstützt.

Mit dieser Entwicklung setzen die Paracelsus-Kliniken eine Tradition fort. Denn schon die erste Paracelsus-Klink, die 1970 in Osnabrück eröffnet wurde, stellte eine Innovation dar: Diese Praxisklinik war mit der Verbindung von ambulanter und stationärer medizinischer Versorgung unter einem Praxisklinikdach bereits damals ein außerordentlich modernes Konzept.

Heute gehört die Paracelsus-Kliniken Deutschland GmbH mit insgesamt 34 Einrichtungen, darunter 19 Akutkrankenhäuser, elf Rehakliniken und vier ambulante Einrichtungen, zu den großen privaten Klinikträgern Deutschlands. In diesen Einrichtungen werden knapp 4.300 Betten vorgehalten. Im Jahre 2004 wurden in den Paracelsus-Kliniken rund 100.000 stationäre Patienten behandelt. Insgesamt beschäftigt die Gruppe knapp 5.000 Mitarbeiter.

Die Kliniken verstehen sich als Dienstleistungsunternehmen, die sich an den Wünschen und Bedürfnissen ihrer Patienten orientieren. Überdurchschnittlich qualifizierte und motivierte Mitarbeiter, attraktive Standorte, anspruchsvolles Ambiente und patientenorientierte Pflege und Behandlung sind wichtige Bestandteile dieses Qualitätsanspruchs. Die Paracelsus-Kliniken wollen durch eine qualitativ hochwertige und innovative Medizin den anvertrauten Patienten helfen, gesund zu werden. Gleichzeitig bleibt der Anspruch, in Zusammenarbeit mit den Patienten die wiedererlangte Gesundheit auf Dauer zu bewahren. ■

An integral care, quality assured and coordinated therapy processes, excellent consulting services and support – these are some of the advantages that Paracelsus-Kliniken Deutschland GmbH offers its patients through the systematic development of new forms of health care. In spring of the year 2005 for instance, the first agreement for integrated care of patients with psychic and psycho-somatic diseases was closed.

In this new form of health care, stationary therapy and out-patient health care are linked together in an optimal way. In addition, the patient receives support during the entire treatment of personal case attendants on his way through the different care sectors.

Paracelsus-Kliniken is continuing a long-standing tradition with this development. In fact the first Paracelsus-Klinik, which was opened in Osnabrück in 1970, represented an innovation: this clinical surgery was even in those days an extraordinarily modern concept with its combination of out-patient and stationary medical care. Today, with a total of 34 institutions, including 19 hospitals for acute cases, eleven rehabilitation hospitals and four out-patient institutions, Paracelsus-Kliniken Deutschland GmbH is one of the major private hospital operators in Germany. These facilities provide just about 4,300 beds. Around 100,000 stationary patients were treated in Paracelsus-Kliniken in the year 2004. In total, the group has a staff of about 5,000 employees. The hospitals see themselves as service enterprises that are oriented towards the wishes and needs of their patients. Above average qualified and motivated employees, attractive locations, sophisticated ambience and patient-oriented care and treatment are important components of this claim in quality standard. Paracelsus-Kliniken intends to help entrusted patients to become healthy again through high quality standard and innovative medicine. At the same time, the call to maintain once regained health lastingly, in cooperation with patients, remains. ■

Company Profile

Innovative Produkte für die Augenchirurgie

Innovative products for ophthalmic surgery

Die *Acri.Tec Gesellschaft für ophthalmologische Produkte mbH ist die innovative Entwicklungs- und Produktionsfirma für ophthalmologische Medizinprodukte mit Sitz in Brandenburg. Die von *Acri.Tec hergestellten Produkte werden in der Mikrochirurgie am Auge eingesetzt (Ophthalmologie, Ophthalmochirurgie). Das Leistungsspektrum umfasst Forschung, Entwicklung, Produktion und Vertrieb von qualitativ hochwertigen Medizinprodukten für Ophthalmochirurgen und Augenärzte – Made in Germany. Laufende Marktanalyse und gemeinsame Entwicklung mit den ärztlichen Anwendern sichern *Acri.Tec eine vollständige und anwendungsorientierte Produktpalette.

Die wichtigsten Produkte der Firma sind Intraokularlinsen (IOL), also hochpräzise Ersatzlinsen für die bei grauem Star eingetrübten natürlichen Augenlinsen. Daneben stellt *Acri.Tec andere Augen-Implantate und sterile Spezialflüssigkeiten sowie Produkte für die vitreoretinale Chirurgie her, die bei jeder Augenoperation gebraucht werden. Die Firma liefert augenchirurgische Diamantmesser aus eigener Werkstatt, augenchirurgische Instrumente und andere innovative Spezialprodukte.

Die strategische Ausrichtung der Firma basiert auf der hohen Qualität ihrer Produkte, auf innovativen Designs, auf eigener Fertigung der jeweils modernsten Produkte und auf der Anfertigung von Spezialtypen und Individualmodellen. Die Produktion der Standardprodukte wird zunehmend ausgelagert. Die Firma verfügt über modernste, computergesteuerte Präzisionsmaschinen sowie über Reinräume der höchsten Anforderungsklasse. Die gesamte Firma ist nach ISO 9001 und DIN EN ISO 13485 zertifiziert. ∎

The *Acri. Tec Gesellschaft für ophthalmologische Produkte GmbH is an innovative development and production enterprise for ophthalmic medicinal products resident in Brandenburg. Products manufactured by *Acri.Tech are used in microsurgery for the eyes (ophthalmology, ophthalmic surgery). The product range comprises research, development, production and sales of qualitative high-ranking medicinal products for ophthalmic surgeons and eye specialists – made in Germany. Constant market analyses and mutual developments together with medical practitioners ensure that *Acri.Tec maintains a complete and application-oriented product spectrum.

The company's most important products are intraocular lenses (IOL), i.e. high-precision replacement lenses for natural eye lenses suffering from opacity through cataract. Furthermore, *AcriTec produces other eye implants and special sterile solutions as well as products for vitreous-retinal surgery, which are used for any ophthalmic surgery. The company also supplies ophthalmic surgery diamond knives made in in-house workshops, ophthalmic surgery instruments and other innovative specialist products.

The company's strategic orientation is based on the high quality of its products, on innovative designs, on in-house production of the latest state-of-the-art and on manufacturing special types and individual models. Production of standard products is increasingly outsourced. The company disposes of the most sophisticated, computer-aided precision machines as well as of clean rooms complying with the highest standards required. The entire firm is certified after passing qualification audits according to ISO 9001 and DIN EN ISO 13485. ∎

---

*Acri.Tec

*Acri.Tec Gesellschaft für ophthalmologische Produkte mbH

Geschäftsführer/Management:
Dr. Christine F. Kreiner
Dr. Dagmar Hebendanz
Dr. Rainer Schuhmann

Leitung Auftragsabwicklung/Order Processing Manager: Edeltraud Rother

Gebietsleiter/Area Manager:
Dr. Andreas Fischer
Dr. Roger Regler
Dr. Marie-Theres Sudhoff
Dr. Kerstin Neubauer
Dr. Stefan Lenz
Dr. Nina Link

Export/Export: Alexander Paraker

Gründungsjahr/Year of Foundation: 1997

Mitarbeiter/Employees: 98

Geschäftstätigkeit/Business Activity:
Entwicklung, Herstellung und Vertrieb von Produkten für die Ophthalmochirurgie: Sterile Medizinprodukte in Form von festen und flüssigen Implantaten, Instrumenten und Diamantmessern
Development, manufacture and sales of products for ophthalmological surgery: Sterile medical products in the form of solid and liquid implants and diamond knives

Anschrift/Address:

Firmensitz, Produktion/
Head Office and Production Facility:
Neuendorfstraße 20a
D-16761 Hennigsdorf b. Berlin
Telefon   +49 (3302) 202 6000
Telefax   +49 (3302) 202 6060
E-Mail   info@acritec.de
Internet   www.acritec.de

Vertriebsbüro/Sales Office:
Schatzbogen 52
D-81829 München
Telefon   +49 (89) 42 71 84-0
Telefax   +49 (89) 42 71 84-40
E-Mail   vertrieb@acritec.de

Service:
0800-470 50 30
Service-Fax:
0800-4 70 50 00

Fußball-WM 2006

Die WM 2006 in Deutschland – was bringt sie der deutschen Wirtschaft?

The Football World Championship 2006 in Germany – what benefit will it bring to the German economy?

Der Autor mit Bundesinnenminister Otto Schily.
The author together with Federal Minister of the Interior Otto Schily.

Schon in der Phase der Bewerbung, Ende der 90er-Jahre, hatten wir ein sozio-ökonomisches Gutachten in Auftrag gegeben, um die Auswirkungen einer Fußball-Weltmeisterschaft zu erfassen. Die damalige Prognose der Universität Paderborn: Es werde ein Nettogegenstandswert von 4,6 Milliarden Mark entstehen, berechnet auf einen Zeitraum von 15 Jahren und einbezogen auch alle Aktivitäten, die nicht unmittelbar mit der WM zu tun haben, beispielsweise Maßnahmen im Straßenbau und zur Verkehrslenkung. Ob sich diese Zahlen so bewahrheiten, können wir im Organisationskomitee nur vermuten, keineswegs verbindlich bestätigen, wobei aber die konkret vorliegenden Daten ein gutes Gefühl für die Gesamtlandschaft vermitteln.

So werden in den Neu-, Aus- und Umbau der zwölf Stadien insgesamt 1,5 Milliarden Euro investiert, schon längst abgeschlossene Projekte wie die Arena AufSchalke und Hamburg eingeschlossen. Nur das teuerste Vorhaben, die mit 250 Millionen Euro taxierte Total-Renovierung des Berliner Olympiastadions, wird komplett von der öffentlichen Hand finanziert. Ansonsten kommt es fast überall zum Public-Private-Partnership. Noch bei der WM 1974 wurden die damals neun Stadien komplett von Steuergeldern gebaut. Wichtig damals wie jetzt: Es ist keine Investition für die Dauer eines Turniers, sondern für die nächsten Jahrzehnte und hier vor allem für die Fußball-Bundesliga, die mit zehn Millionen Zuschauern pro Saison das größte Freizeitunternehmen hierzulande darstellt.

Nur der Vollständigkeit halber sei erwähnt, dass im WM-Sog auch in Städten gebaut wird, an denen das Turnier der besten Balltreter ansonsten vorbeiläuft: Düsseldorf glänzt ab Herbst 2005 mit einer neuen Rheinarena, ebenso Mönchengladbach, dazu Bremen mit einem wiederum modernisierten Weserstadion. Rostock und Wolfsburg haben schon sehr beachtlich aufgerüstet, nun folgt auch Duisburg und nach der WM wohl auch Leverkusen. Die Bauwirtschaft gehört somit fraglos zu den Gewinnern – um so mehr, wenn man das Stadionumfeld hinzurechnet, wo neue An- und Abfahrten, S- und U-Bahnhöfe und Parkleitsysteme entstehen.

Zweiter großer Gewinner dürfte die Hotellerie und Gastronomie werden. Denn wir erwarten 3,2 Millionen Besucher bei den 64 Spielen, davon eine Million aus dem Ausland. Nun wird diese Million nicht permanent einen Monat lang in Deutschland verweilen, weil aus dem benachbarten Ausland bequem zu einzelnen WM-Begegnungen angereist werden kann, per Bus, Bahn und PKW sowieso, theoretisch sogar mit dem Fahrrad. Aber viele, vor allem die Fans aus Übersee, bleiben einige Wochen. Für die sowie für alle Mannschaften und Offiziellen, besonders auch für die Medien, ist vorgesorgt, indem sehr frühzeitig etwa 35.000 Hotelbetten geblockt wurden. Die werden verwaltet von einem eigens für die WM 2006 gebildeten Joint Venture, das ein Angebot für alle Hotelkategorien machen kann, von der Pension bis zur Suite in einer Fünf-Sterne-Herberge. Der Durchschnittspreis liegt bei „nur" 190 Euro, damit erheblich unter Messe-Standards, was beabsichtigt war, um so zu verhindern, dass wegen einer Hochpreis-Politik ein Negativ-Image entsteht.

Wolfgang Niersbach

Der 1950 geborene Autor ist seit 2001 Vizepräsident des Organisationskomitees für die Fußball-Weltmeisterschaft 2006 in Deutschland. Er kennt beide Seiten des Mediengeschäfts. Als Redakteur der Nachrichtenagentur Sport-Informations-Dienst arbeitete er mit den Fachgebieten Fußball und Eishockey mehr als ein Jahrzehnt lang bei zahlreichen Welt- und Europameisterschaften sowie bei Olympischen Spielen. Als Pressechef der EURO88 in Deutschland sammelte Niersbach erste Erfahrungen in der Organisation von Medienarbeit, die er ab 1988 als Pressechef und Mediendirektor des Deutschen Fußball-Bundes umsetzte.

The author was born in 1950 and has been Vice President of the Organisational Committee of the Football World Championship 2006 in Germany since 2001. He knows both sides of the media business. As editorial journalist for the news agency Sport Information Service he worked in the special fields of football and ice hockey for more than a decade at numerous world and European championships and at Olympic Games. As chief press officer of EURO-88 in Germany, Niersbach gained his first experiences in organising media work, which he was able to put into practice as chief press officer and media director of the German Football Association as of 1988.

Hier involviert als Kooperationspartner ist die Deutsche Zentrale für Tourismus (DZT), die wiederum in einer eigens gegründeten Tourismus AG vertreten ist, deren Ziel es wiederum ist, mit dem PR-Vehikel der Weltmeisterschaft das Reiseland Deutschland auch über 2006 hinaus zu beleben. Dazu gehört eine Offensive der Freundlichkeit.

Football World Championship 2006

Already during the candidature acceptance procedure, at the end of the nineties, we had commissioned a socio-economic expertise to establish the effects of a football World Championship. The forecast of the University of Paderborn at the time showed: a net value of objects amounting to 4.6 billion marks would be created, calculated for a period of 15 years and also including all activities that are not directly connected with the World Championship, for instance road construction projects and traffic guidance systems. In the Organisational Committee we can only assume that these figures are actually correct, but cannot confirm them officially, whereby the concrete available data have given us a good feeling for the overall situation.

A total of 1.5 billion Euros are being invested in the new construction, expansion and conversion of twelve stadiums, including already completed projects like the Arena AufSchalke and Hamburg. Only the most expensive project, the 250 million Euros worth total renovation of the Berlin Olympic Stadium, will be completely financed by the state. Otherwise, almost everywhere public-private partnership agreements have been established. For the 1974 World Championship the nine stadiums at the time were completely built with tax monies. Most importantly, then as it is now: investments are not only made for the duration of one tournament, but for the next decades and especially for the Federal Football League, which represents the largest leisure enterprise in this country with ten million spectators attending per season.

To complete the picture it may be mentioned that in the maelstrom of the World Championship construction work is also underway in cities that are normally not affected by the tournament of the best ball-artists: Düsseldorf will be able to boast a new Rhine Arena as of the autumn 2005, also Mönchengladbach and in addition Bremen will have a re-modernised Weser Stadium. Rostock and Wolfsburg have upgraded their cities considerably already, and now Duisburg is following and probably also Leverkusen will follow after the World Championship.

Therefore, the building industry is doubtlessly among the winners, much more so if one adds the stadium environments to this, where new access and exit roads, regional train stops and subway stops as well as parking guidance systems are being created.

The second largest winners will certainly be the hotel and restaurant businesses. Because we are expecting 3.2 million visitors for the 64 games, of which one million come from abroad. Now, this million will not be staying permanently for one month in Germany, because it is easy to travel from neighbouring countries to individual World Championship matches, per bus, train and car anyway, but theoretically even by bicycle. But many, particularly the fans from overseas, will stay on for several weeks. Provisions have been made for these in any case, for all teams and accompanying officers and especially for the media by blocking very early about 35,000 hotel beds. Administration of this reservation is carried out by an especially formed joint venture for the World Championship 2006, which can make offers for all hotel categories, starting from a pension through to a suite in a five-star accommodation. The average price is "only" at 190 Euros and therefore considerably below exhibition level, which was purposely fixed in order to avoid a negative image because of a high price policy.

The German centre for tourism, Deutsche Zentrale für Tourismus (DZT), which in turn is represented in the specifically founded Tourismus AG, is involved here as cooperation partner and aims to revive Germany as a tourism destination also for the times after 2006 through the PR vehicle of the World Championship. This includes a campaign for friendliness. Taxi drivers, waiters, hostesses, the about 15,000 voluntary helpers, policemen and generally all people are to internalize the World Championship slogan "The world is visiting friends".

One special issue is the entrance tickets. Starting with the 1st February 2005, they on offer as, and this is not a daring prophecy, probably the most valuable asset, which will not be sufficient to cover the demand despite the firstly impressing sounding figure of 3.2 million tickets. Here is the example of the European Championship 1988: when the Dutch national team conquered the title at that time, up to 50,000 "Oranje" fans walked in their footsteps. This time there will only be 5,000 to 6,000 per game, because more than eight per

Um diesen Pokal geht es!
Von rechts:
der Präsident des Organisationskomitees Franz Beckenbauer,
Fußball-Legende Pele,
FIFA-Präsident Joseph Blatter,
Formel-1-Weltmeister Michael Schumacher
und DFB-Präsident Gerhard Meyer-Vorfelder.

It's all about this Cup!
From right:
the President of the Organisational Committee Franz Beckenbauer,
football legend Pele,
FIFA President Joseph Blatter,
Formula 1 World Champion Michael Schumacher
and DFB President Gerhard Meyer-Vorfelder.

Fußball-WM 2006

Taxifahrer, Kellner, Hostessen, die etwa 15.000 freiwilligen Helfer, Polizisten und überhaupt alle sollen den WM-Slogan „Die Welt zu Gast bei Freunden" verinnerlichen.

Ein besonderes Kapitel sind die Eintrittskarten. Seit dem 1. Februar 2005 werden sie angeboten als – dies ist keine gewagte Prophezeiung – wohl kostbarstes Gut, das trotz der zunächst imposant klingenden Zahl von 3,2 Millionen Tickets nicht ausreichen wird, um die Nachfrage zu decken. Beispiel von der Europameisterschaft 1988: Als damals die holländische Nationalmannschaft den Titel eroberte, wandelten bis zu 50.000 „Oranje"-Besucher auf ihren Spuren. Diesmal werden es pro Spiel nur 5.000 oder 6.000 sein können, weil mehr als acht Prozent der vorhandenen Kapazität für jede am Spiel beteiligte Mannschaft zur Verfügung gestellt werden kann. Das italienische Kontingent könnte leicht über in Deutschland lebende Italiener abgesetzt werden, ebenso der türkische oder kroatische Anteil. Summa summarum verdeutlichen diese Beispiele, dass im Gegensatz zur Expo in Hannover der Zustrom aus dem Ausland limitiert bleiben muss. Es sei denn, viele Fans reisen auch ohne Karte an und begnügen sich mit dem ganz speziellen WM-Feeling im Land, das in Städten und Gemeinden zu spüren sein wird – so jedenfalls die jetzt schon formulierte Zielsetzung für WM-Feiern mit öffentlichen TV-Übertragungen („Public Viewing") auf öffentlichen Plätzen.

Die Medien: 15.000 bis 20.000 Berichterstatter, Techniker eingeschlossen, werden akkreditiert sein und Deutschland ins Schaufenster der Weltöffentlichkeit rücken. In 215 Länder flimmerten Bilder der letzten WM 2002 in Korea und Japan – Steigerung kaum möglich, weil es nicht mehr Länder gibt. 30 Milliarden Menschen, die fünffache Zahl der Erdbevölkerung, waren via Bildschirm live dabei – Steigerung möglich und sogar wahrscheinlich, weil die Anstoßzeiten für den Kernmarkt Europa viel günstiger sind mit 15, 18 und 21 Uhr. Bei jedem Spiel, und es sei eine vergleichsweise unattraktive Paarung wie Kanada gegen Norwegen, werden durchschnittlich 500 Millionen Fernsehzuschauer präsent sein, bedient übrigens erstmals mit Bildern im HDTV-Format, das nun einen ähnlichen Siegeszug antreten soll wie seinerzeit das Farbfernsehen. Jedes Spiel wird mit bis zu 30 Kameras abgedeckt, die Bilder laufen zusammen im Fernsehzentrum München, wo auf dem Messe-Gelände eine ultramoderne TV-Landschaft auf einer Gesamtfläche von 40.000 Quadratmetern entsteht, und werden von dort in die ganze Welt verschickt.

Weitere astronomisch anmutende Zahlen wären hier anzufügen, etwa im Bereich Hospitality. Wo bei der Weltmeisterschaft 1974 eine Tasse Kaffee und ein Stück Kuchen ausreichten, werden beim WM-Finale im Berliner Olympiastadion 15.000 Gäste zu bewirten sein, was logistisch nur auf dem benachbarten Maifeld zu bewältigen ist. Summa summarum haben wir einen Etat von 430 Millionen Euro darzustellen, wobei der Fußball-Weltverband (FIFA) als Veranstalter und der Deutsche Fußball-Bund (DFB) mit dem von ihm eingesetzten Organisationskomitee (OK) als Ausrichter fungiert. Aus dieser jurstischen Position heraus erklärt sich auch, dass die FIFA sämtliche Verträge für Fernsehen und Werbung (im Marketing-Bereich gibt es 15 globale Topsponsoren und sechs nationale Förderer) abgeschlossen hat. Wichtigste Einnahmequelle für das OK sind die Eintrittskarten. Hier kalkulieren wir mit 200 Millionen Euro. Ein FIFA-Zuschuss über 170 Millionen Euro und 60 Millionen Euro als Lizenzsumme von den sechs nationalen Förderern stehen außerdem auf unserer kakulierten Habenseite.

Aus tiefer Überzeugung, die sich auf ungezählte Begebenheiten stützt, stelle ich fest, dass kein anderes Ereignis, ja überhaupt kein anderes Thema in und für Deutschland so positiv besetzt ist wie diese FIFA-Fußball-Weltmeisterschaft 2006. Sie ist ein Geschenk, wie Franz Beckenbauer spontan nach dem Zuschlag am 6. Juli 2000 meinte, und gerade in der aktuell oft lethargisch anmutenden Gesamtsituation eine Art Fixstern. Gemeinsam müssen wir etwas daraus machen – für den Fußball, für den Sport, aber ganz besonders auch für unser Land. Eine bessere Chance gibt es nicht. ∎

Football World Championship 2006

cent of existing capacities for each game can be provided to each participating team. The Italian contingent could easily be sold over Italian people living in Germany, the same goes for the Turkish or Croatian share. All in all the examples show that contrary to the Expo in Hannover, crowds of people from abroad must be limited. Unless many fans decide to travel without tickets and be happy to enjoy the special World Championship feeling in the country that will be experienced throughout the cities and communities, as it is already aimed for World Championship celebrations with public TV broadcasts (public viewing) on public squares.

The media: 15,000 to 20,000 reporters, including technicians, will be accredited and move Germany into the centre of the world's attention. The images of the last World Championship 2002 in Korea and Japan were on TV in 215 countries, which can hardly be surpassed, because there are no more countries. 30 billion people, five times the number of the world's population, participated live via TV screens, a figure that can be and probably will be surpassed, because kick-off times are more favourable for the core market of Europe being set at 15, 18 and 21 hours. For each match, and even if it should be a comparatively unattractive pairing like Canada against Norway, an average of 500 million TV viewers will be present, and by the way will be served with images in HDTV format, which is now designed to have a similar triumph as colour television in its time. Each match will be covered with up to 30 cameras, pictures will be gathered in the television centre of Munich, where an ultramodern TV landscape is being created on the grounds of the exhibition centre covering a total area of 40,000 square metres, and will be sent into the entire world from there. Further astronomically seeming figures could be added here for instance for the field of hospitality.

If at the World Championship 1974 a cup of coffee and a piece of cake were enough, at the finals of this World Championship 15,000 guests will require hosting at Berlin's Olympic Stadium, a task that can only be managed on the neighbouring grounds of Maifeld. All in all, we are responsible for a budget of 430 million Euros, whereby the Football World Association (FIFA) as promoter and which German Football Association (DFB) together have implemented an Organisational Committee (OC) that acts as organizer. These legal positions also clarify why it was FIFA that made all the contracts for television and advertising (in the field of marketing there are 15 global top sponsors and six national supporters). The OC's most significant source of income is entrance tickets. We are calculating here 200 million Euros. Furthermore, our calculated credit side shows a FIFA subsidy of 170 million Euros and 60 million Euros as license sum coming from the six national supporters.

It is my deepest conviction, which is founded on countless circumstances, that no other event or even any other subject has such a positive publicity as this FIFA Football World Championship 2006 in and for Germany. It is a gift, as Franz Beckenbauer called it spontaneously after acceptance as host country on 6th July 2000, and especially in the currently often lethargic general situation it is a kind of fixed star. Together, we have to make it a great event for football, for sports, but particularly for our country. There will be no better opportunity.

Linke Seite:
Kein anderes Ereignis ist so positiv besetzt wie die WM 2006 – die Organisatoren sind überall gefragte Gesprächspartner.

Left page:
No other event has such positive publicity as the World Championship 2006; organisers are sought after as talk partners everywhere.

Zwei, die sich um den deutschen Fußball verdient gemacht haben: Franz Beckenbauer und Rudi Völler.
Two people that have rendered outstanding services to German football: Franz Beckenbauer and Rudi Völler.

Company Profile

Weltweit Marktführer für Unternehmenssoftware

Worldwide Leader in Business Software

SAP Deutschland AG & Co. KG

Vorstand/Executive Board:
Henning Kagermann

Gründungsjahr/Year of Foundation:
1972

Mitarbeiter/Employees:
weltweit: rund 31.500/worldwide: about 31,500

Geschäftstätigkeit/Business Activity:
Unternehmenssoftware, Integrationstechnologie, Mittelstandssoftware, IT-Lösungen, Implementierungsberatung, Business Consulting, Schulung
Business Software, Integration technology, Software for small and medium-size businesses, IT-solutions, Implementation Consulting, Business Consulting, Training

Umsatz/Turnover:
7,0 Mrd. Euro (2003)

Anschrift/Address:
Neurottstraße 15a
D-69190 Walldorf
Telefon +49 (800) 5343424
Telefax +49 (800) 5343420
E-Mail info.germany@sap.com
Internet www.sap.de

SAP auf der CeBit 2004.
SAP at the CeBit 2004.

Oben:
SAP-Unternehmenszentrale in Walldorf
Unten:
Vorstandssprecher Dr. Henning Kagermann
Above:
SAP Headquarters in Walldorf
Below:
Dr. Henning Kagermann, Executive Board

Die SAP AG, mit Hauptsitz in Walldorf, ist der weltweit führende Anbieter von Unternehmenssoftware. Das Portfolio der SAP umfasst die Geschäftsanwendungen der mySAP™ Business Suite sowie Softwarelösungen für den Mittelstand, die auf der Technologieplattform SAP NetWeaver™ aufbauen. Für kleine und mittelständische Firmen werden außerdem leistungsfähige Standardlösungen angeboten. Darüber hinaus unterstützt SAP mit mehr als 25 branchenspezifischen Lösungsportfolios industriespezifische Kernprozesse von Automobil bis Versorgung sowie öffentliche Verwaltung. Damit sind Organisationen in der Lage, ihre Geschäftsprozesse intern sowie mit Kunden, Partnern und Lieferanten erfolgreich zu organisieren und die betriebliche Wertschöpfung maßgeblich zu verbessern. Mehr als 13 Millionen Anwender bei 24.450 Kunden setzen SAP-Lösungen in mehr als 120 Ländern ein. SAP wurde 1972 gegründet und ist heute der weltweit drittgrößte unabhängige Softwareanbieter mit Niederlassungen in über 50 Ländern. Im Geschäftsjahr 2003 erzielte das Unternehmen einen Umsatz von 7,0 Mrd. Euro. Derzeit beschäftigt SAP über 31.500 Mitarbeiter, davon mehr als 13.350 in Deutschland. SAP Deutschland AG & Co. KG mit Hauptsitz in Walldorf, Baden, wurde am 1. Januar 2001 als rechtlich selbstständige Tochter der SAP AG gegründet. Der unternehmerische Fokus der SAP Deutschland AG & Co. KG liegt auf den Geschäftsfeldern Vertrieb, Beratung, Schulung und Marketing rund um das Produktportfolio der SAP AG in Deutschland. Neben dem Hauptsitz in Walldorf unterhält die SAP Deutschland AG & Co. KG weitere Standorte in Berlin, Düsseldorf, Hamburg, Hannover, Mannheim, München, St. Ingbert und Stuttgart. Weitere Informationen unter: www.sap.de oder www.sap.com ∎

SAP is the world's leading provider of business software solutions. Today, more than 24,450 customers in over 120 countries run more than 84,000 installations of SAP® software from distinct solutions addressing the needs of small and mid-size businesses to enterprise-scale suite solutions for global organizations. Powered by the SAP NetWeaver™ platform to drive innovation and enable business change, mySAP™ Business Suite solutions are helping enterprises around the world improve customer relationships, enhance partner collaboration and create efficiencies across their supply chains and business operations. SAP industry solutions support the unique business processes of more than 25 industry segments, including high tech, retail, public sector and financial services. With subsidiaries in more than 50 countries, the company is listed on several exchanges, including the Frankfurt stock exchange and NYSE under the symbol "SAP." Additional information at www.sap.com ∎

Company Profile

Innovative Technik für Beruf, zu Hause und unterwegs

Innovative technology at work, at home and on the road

Motorola ist ein international führendes Technologieunternehmen mit den Schwerpunkten Mobilkommunikation, Breitband und Kfz-Telematik, das innovative technologische Lösungen gestaltet, von denen Menschen zu Hause, im Beruf und unterwegs profitieren. Im Bereich Mobiltelefone ist Motorola der zweitgrößte Anbieter weltweit. In Deutschland ist das Unternehmen durch die Motorola GmbH präsent. Zu ihr zählen die Bereiche Funk, TK-Lösungen, Mobiltelefone, Computersysteme, Breitbandkommunikation sowie Automotive. Mit dem Engagement und der Innovationskraft der deutschen GmbH wurden wichtige Impulse in allen Bereichen der Entwicklung gegeben. Heute zählt Motorola in Deutschland zu den Top-100 sowie zu den größten US-amerikanischen Hightech-Unternehmen und Arbeitgebern.

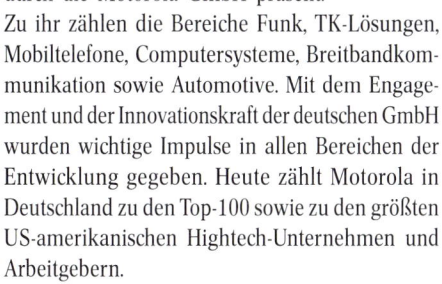

Deutschland ist für Motorola nicht nur ein großer Absatzmarkt, sondern auch wichtiger Standort für Fertigung, Forschung und Entwicklung. Rund 2.500 Mitarbeiter engagieren sich in Produktentwicklung, Produktion, Marketing, Vertrieb und Verwaltung. Auch beim Sprung in die dritte Mobilfunkgeneration machte Motorola den Anfang: Mit dem A830 stellte das Unternehmen das weltweit erste UMTS-Handy vor, das in Flensburg produziert wird. Ebenfalls führend ist Motorola in der Automobilelektronik: Die Motorsteuerung und das Global Positioning System (GPS) basieren auf Produkten und Lösungen von Motorola. ∎

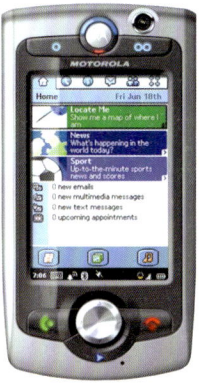

Motorola is an internationally leading technology company focussing on mobile communication, broadband and car telematics that designs innovative technological solutions, which are beneficial for people at home, at work and on the road. In the field of mobile telephones, Motorola is the second-largest provider worldwide. In Germany, the company is represented by the firm Motorola GmbH. It covers the fields of wireless solutions, telecommunications solutions, two-way-radios, computer systems, broadband communication and as well as automotive solutions. The engagement and power of innovation of the German subsidary played a major role in providing important impulses to developments in all above areas. Today, Motorola is among the Top 100 German as well as the largest US-American high-tech companies and employers.

Germany is for Motorola not only a large sales market, but also a significant business location for production, research and development. Around 2,500 employees are enthusiastically engaged in product development, manufacture, marketing, sales and administration. Motorola has also taken the initiative in the giant leap to develop the third generation of mobile phones: the company introduced the first UMTS mobile phone named A830, which is produced in Flensburg. Furthermore, Motorola is also leading in the branch of automobile electronics: engine steering and the Global Positioning System (GPS) are based on products and solutions made by Motorola. ∎

MOTOROLA

Motorola GmbH

Geschäftsführung/Board of Management:
Roland Dürr,
Dr. Christoph Hollemann,
Heinrich Korte,
Norbert Quinkert
(Vorsitzender der Geschäftsführung/
Chairman of the Board of Management)

Gründungsjahr/Year of Foundation: 1968

Mitarbeiter/Employees: 2.500

Umsatz 2004/Turnover 2004: 4,3 Mio €

Geschäftstätigkeiten/Business Activities:
Mobiltelefone/Personal Devices,
Mobilfunkausrüstung/Networks,
Regierungs- und Geschäftskunden/
Government and Enterprise,
Breitband/Connected Home

Anschrift/Address:
Heinrich-Hertz-Straße 1
D-65232 Taunusstein
Telefon +49 (6128) 70 700
Telefax +49 (6128) 70 4900
Internet www.motorola.de

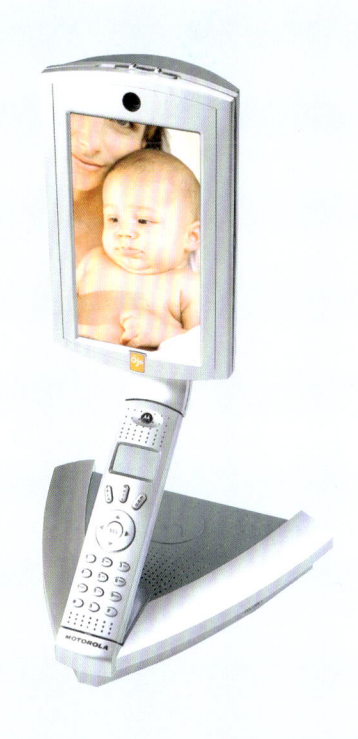

Wirtschaftsgeschichte

Ein vorübergehendes Formtief – zur Wirtschaftsgeschichte der BRD

A momentary loss of form – about the economic history of the Federal Republic of Germany

Die Wirtschaftsgeschichte der Bundesrepublik Deutschland begann nicht erst mit der Gründung der Bundesrepublik als einem von zwei deutschen Teilstaaten im Jahre 1949. Entscheidende Grundlagen für das „Wirtschaftswunder" wurden vielmehr bereits vorher gelegt. Man denke an die Währungsreform oder an den Marshallplan. Aber auch die erneute Etablierung preisgesteuerter Märkte, die Abwehr von Sozialisierungsplänen, die bis weit in die CDU hinein verfolgt wurden, die Errichtung einer politisch unabhängigen Zentralbank und das Kartellverbot gehören zu diesen Grundlagen der bundesdeutschen Wirtschaft, die im Prinzip bis heute unangetastet geblieben sind.

Mit der Währungsreform vom 20. Juni 1948, einem Oktroi der westalliierten Besatzer, wurde die Deutsche Mark anstelle der Reichsmark als neues Zahlungsmittel eingeführt. Viel wichtiger war jedoch die damit einhergehende radikale Verringerung der Geldmenge in den drei westlichen Besatzungszonen Deutschlands um mehr als 90 Prozent. Diese gigantische Enteignungsmaßnahme, die damals von vielen auch so empfunden worden ist, beseitigte den durch die Kriegsfinanzierung des NS-Regimes angestauten Geldüberhang, der zuvor sämtliche von Geld normalerweise ausgeübten Funktionen, die Tausch-, Rechen- und Wertaufbewahrungsfunktion, paralysiert hatte, wodurch die westdeutsche Wirtschaft an dem in Europa allenthalben einsetzenden Nachkriegsaufschwung bis dahin kaum teilnehmen konnte. Da gleichzeitig mit der Währungsreform durch das von Ludwig Erhard, damals Direktor der bizonalen Verwaltung für Wirtschaft, konzipierte so genannte Leitsätzegesetz die behördliche Bewirtschaftung und Preiskontrolle in einem großen Teil der gewerblichen Wirtschaft aufgehoben wurde, konnte das nun wieder funktionsfähige neue Geld seine positiven Wirkungen auf erneut entstandenen Märkten entfalten. Es setzte sofort ein hohes Wirtschaftswachstum ein, zumal eine wesentliche Voraussetzung dafür, nämlich in Privateigentum befindliche Unternehmen, infolge des amerikanischen Vetos gegen jegliche Sozialisierungsabsichten erhalten geblieben war.

Im Wesentlichen der amerikanischen Besatzungsmacht war auch die Unabhängigkeit der Bank deutscher Länder, Vorläufer der deutschen Bundesbank (bis 1957), zu danken, hatte diese sich doch mit ihren diesbezüglichen Vorstellungen sowohl gegen deutsche Politiker und Ökonomen als auch ihr britisches Pendant durchgesetzt. Infolge dessen gelang es der Bank in der Tat rasch, international, aber vor allem auch beim doppelt inflationsgeschädigten deutschen Publikum Vertrauen in die Stabilität der D-Mark zu erzeugen und diese zu einer der härtesten Währungen der Welt zu machen. Das Modell war so erfolgreich, dass es in den 1990er Jahren schließlich sogar auf die Europäische Zentralbank und den Euro übertragen wurde.

Das vom Alliierten Kontrollrat 1947 verhängte Kartellverbot – dem Prinzip nach 1957 durch das Gesetz gegen Wettbewerbsbeschränkungen (GWB) in deutsches Recht übernommen – brach mit einer alten Tradition Deutschlands, das seit dem Kaiserreich als das Land der Kartelle anzusehen war. Von jetzt an sollte der Wettbewerb eine wichtigere Rolle in (West-) Deutschland spielen, dessen effektive Überwachung und Förderung heute Angelegenheit des Bundeskartellamts, aber auch der Europäischen Kommission ist, die in dieser Hinsicht manche für die Gesamtwirtschaft positive, wenn auch für einzelne deutsche Unternehmen recht schmerzhafte Entscheidungen gefällt hat.

Schließlich brachte der Marshallplan für Westdeutschland nicht nur eine Fortsetzung der seinerzeit unverzichtbaren Dollarhilfe zur Finanzierung unbedingt erforderlicher Importe. Er ermöglichte darüber hinaus die Bildung eines Investitionsfonds aus den DM-Erlösen dieser Importe, der, damals für dringende Investitionen in Engpassbereichen verwendet, bis heute zur Speisung verschiedener Kreditprogramme der KfW eingesetzt wird. Der wichtigste Beitrag des Marshallplans zur Nachkriegsentwicklung war jedoch, dass die zur Verteilung seiner Mittel gegründete „Organization of European Economic Cooperation" (OEEC; heute: OECD) auf Drängen der USA bald zu einem entscheidenden Promotor der Liberalisierung des innereuropäischen und weltweiten Handels und Zahlungsverkehrs wurde. Nur dadurch war es nämlich möglich, dass die Exporte bereits im Lauf der fünfziger Jahre zum bedeutendsten Wachstumsmotor Westeuropas und ganz besonders der

Prof. Dr. Christoph Buchheim

Der Autor hat Volkswirtschaftslehre und Neuere Geschichte an den Universitäten München und Oxford studiert. 1982 promoviert und 1989 habilitiert, ist er seit 1991 Inhaber des Lehrstuhls für Wirtschaftsgeschichte an der Fakultät für Volkswirtschaftslehre der Universität Mannheim. Er ist Fachgutachter der DFG sowie Vorsitzender des Wirtschaftshistorischen Ausschusses des Vereins für Socialpolitik. Seine Forschungsschwerpunkte sind die Industrielle Revolution sowie die Wirtschaftsgeschichte Deutschlands und Europas im 20. Jahrhundert.

The author studied political economy and modern history at the Universities of Munich and Oxford. He earned his doctorate in 1982 and qualified as university lecturer in 1989. Since 1991, he has occupied the chair of economic history at the faculty of political economy at the University of Mannheim. He is specialist for expert opinions at the German Research Society as well as chairman of the economic history committee of the Association for Social Politics. Focal points of his research field are the industrial revolution as well as the economic history of Germany and Europe in the 20th century.

Bundesrepublik wurden, indem sie immer erneut Investitionen generierten und so die Durchsetzung produktivitätssteigernden technischen Fortschritts förderten.

Implizit wurden im Vorangehenden bereits die wesentlichen Charakteristika der Ordnung der sozialen Marktwirtschaft aufgezählt, so wie diese von ihren zeitgenössischen Protagonisten, etwa Walter Eucken oder Wilhelm Röpke, verstanden

Economic History

The economic history of the Federal Republic of Germany did not only start when the Federal Republic was founded as one of two German states in the year 1949. In fact, a significant basis for the "economic miracle" was laid much earlier. One could mention the monetary reform or the Marshall Plan in this respect. But also the renewed establishment of price-controlled markets, the rejection of plans for socialisation, which were pursued right into the conservative party CDU, the creation of a politically independent central bank and the ban of cartels are part of the foundations on which the German economy is based, which in principle have remained unchallenged until today.

The Deutsche Mark was introduced instead of the Reichsmark as new currency with the monetary reform of 20th June 1948, which was imposed by the occupation forces of the Western allies. But much more important was the radical reduction of money supply it involved in the three Western occupation zones by more than 90 per cent. This enormous measure of expropriation, which indeed was felt by many in that way at the time, removed the surplus of money accumulated by the NS-regime for financing the war. Before, it had paralysed all functions that money normally carries out, like for instance exchange, accounting and value depositing functions, which resulted in that the West-German economy until then hardly had been able to participate in the gradually emerging post-war economic upswing in Europe. Since parallel to the monetary reform, through the so-called "Law of Basic Principles", created by Ludwig Erhard, former director of the two-zone administration of economy, the official management and price control was dispensed with in the major part of the industrial sector, the new money that became functional again was able to exert its positive influence on newly created markets. Immediately, tremendous economic growth set in, since an important prerequisite for this, namely companies that were private property, had remained preserved because of the American veto against any intentions of socialisation.

It was thanks to the American occupation forces primarily that the Bank of German States, predecessor of the German Federal Bank (until 1957), remained independent. In fact, the former had asserted itself with its relevant ideas against German politicians and economists as well as against its British counterpart. As a result, the bank succeeded in fact quite rapidly to win international confidence, but above all with the because of the inflation double disenchanted German public, in the stability of the D-Mark and to make it one of the hardest currencies in the world. The concept was that successful that it was even transferred to the European Central Bank and the Euro finally in the nineties.

The law against cartels passed by the Control Council of the Allied Forces in 1947 – which was taken over in principle by the Law against Restraint of Trade in 1957 by German Law – broke with one of the old traditions in Germany, which had been considered since Imperial times as the land of cartels. From now on, competition was to play a more important role in (West-) Germany, the effective supervision and development of which today is the task of the Federal Cartel Office, but also that of the European Commission. The latter has made in this respect many a painful decision for individual German enterprises, which are of positive nature for the overall economy.

Ultimately, the Marshall Plan did not only result in a continuation of at the time indispensable dollar aids for West Germany, which were urgently necessary to finance imports. Moreover, it enabled the creation of an investment fund from the DM revenues of these imports, which, then used for urgent investments in restricted or difficult areas, until today serves to supply the different credit program-mes of the banking institute Kreditanstalt für Wiederaufbau (KfW). The most significant contribution of the Marshall Plan to post-war developments was however that the organisation founded to distribute its funds "Organization of European Economic Cooperation" (OEEC; today: OECD) on urging of the USA soon became a decisive impetus for the liberalisation of inner-European and global trade and payment transactions. Actually, only thereby it became possible that exports rose to be the major growth engine of Western Europe in the fifties already and especially in Germany, because they continuously generated new investments and therefore enhanced the consolidation of productivity increasing technical progress. The above elaborations already implicate the major characteristics of the structure social market economy has, as it was understood by its contemporary protagonists like Walter Eucken or Wilhelm Röpke for instance. Indeed, it is a widespread error to believe social market economy is market economy garnished with extensive social benefits. In fact, market economy as such was already seen as a highly social economic structure, which it doubtlessly is compared to the NS-system or socialism. Indeed through it is possible to generate the best possible overall economic product with actually existing relevant resources and with it the material basis for the general social wellbeing can be maximised. Moreover, it is the economic system in which the individual is capable of developing most freely his economic opportunities and his spirit of entrepreneurship and in which the demand has the greatest influence on the composition of production. However, for a functioning market economy certain prerequisites are required, which above all include the possibility of free entrepreneurial initiative, the safety of private property as well as untainted competition, whereby the state has to play an important role. In effect, it not only should refrain from touching these prerequisites, but should actually also ensure their effective implementation, often against the resistance of individual employer lobbies, by providing as much as possible inflation-free money through an independent central bank and by ensuring the complete up-keep of competition by hindering the formation of monopolies and cartels as well as through a liberal import policy.

It was such a market economy, so-to-speak armoured by the state that its defenders had in mind then, when they spoke of social market economy. And as we have seen, the foundation for this was laid very early already by the occupation forces, above all by the Americans.
While the currency reform and the Law of Basic Principles, in a way acting as catalysts of the boom of reconstruction already long underway in the rest of Europe, now also affected West Germany, the vitalisation of the economy involving the liberalisation of export trade opened up completely new scope for growth in terms of

Straßenbahn in Ludwigshafen, Abfahrt Schumacherbrücke, 1972.

Tram stop "Schumacher Bridge" in Ludwigshafen 1972.

Wirtschaftsgeschichte

wurde. Denn es ist ein weit verbreiteter Irrtum zu glauben, soziale Marktwirtschaft sei Marktwirtschaft garniert mit umfangreichen Sozialleistungen. Vielmehr wurde die Marktwirtschaft als solche bereits als eine höchst soziale Wirtschaftsordnung verstanden, was sie im Vergleich zum NS-System oder dem Sozialismus zweifellos auch ist. Denn durch sie kann mit den jeweils vorhandenen Ressourcen das größtmögliche gesamtwirtschaftliche Produkt erwirtschaftet und damit die materielle Grundlage der gesamtgesellschaftlichen Wohlfahrt maximiert werden. Zudem ist sie die Wirtschaftsordnung, in der der Einzelne seine wirtschaftlichen Möglichkeiten und seinen Unternehmergeist am freiesten entfalten kann und in der die Nachfrage den größten Einfluss auf die Zusammensetzung der Produktion hat. Allerdings bedarf es für eine funktionierende Marktwirtschaft bestimmter Voraussetzungen, zu denen vor allem die Möglichkeit freier unternehmerischer Initiative, die Sicherung des Privateigentums sowie unverfälschter Wettbewerb gehören, wobei der Staat eine wichtige Rolle zu spielen hat. Denn er darf nicht nur diese Voraussetzungen selbst nicht antasten, sondern muss auch für ihre effektive Durchsetzung, oft genug gegen den Widerstand einzelner Unternehmenslobbys, sorgen, indem er ein weitgehend inflationsfreies Geld durch eine unabhängige Zentralbank bereitstellt und durch Verhinderung von Monopolen und Kartellen sowie eine liberale Importpolitik für die volle Aufrechterhaltung des Wettbewerbs sorgt. Eine solche, gewissermaßen vom Staat armierte Marktwirtschaft war es, was deren Verfechter damals im Sinn hatten, wenn sie von sozialer Marktwirtschaft sprachen. Und hierfür wurden, wie wir gesehen haben, die Grundlagen bereits sehr früh von den Besatzungsmächten, vor allem der amerikanischen, gelegt.

Während Währungsreform und Leitsätzegesetz gewissermaßen als Katalysatoren des im übrigen Europa längst im Gang befindlichen Rekonstruktionsaufschwungs auch in Westdeutschland wirkten, eröffnete die mit der Liberalisierung der Außenwirtschaft einhergehende Dynamisierung der Wirtschaft ganz neue Wachstumsspielräume im Zeichen der Konvergenz in Richtung des amerikanischen Produktivitätsniveaus. Denn in den USA angewandte Technologien und Organisationsmodelle waren den deutschen und europäischen bereits vor dem Ersten Weltkrieg überlegen gewesen, ein Abstand, der sich seitdem noch vergrößert hatte, da die Investitionstätigkeit in den europäischen Volkswirtschaften infolge des Hochprotektionismus der Zeit zwischen den Kriegen und des damit verbundenen Stotterns des Exportmotors stark gelitten hatte. Erst jetzt konnten diese produktivitätssteigernden Rezepte in Westeuropa rasch imitiert werden, da der allgemeine Exportboom die Investitionsneigung der Unternehmen massiv ansteigen ließ. Und so kam es, dass in der Bundesrepublik bis in die siebziger Jahre hinein weit überdurchschnittliche Wachstumsraten registriert wurden und der Lebensstand breitester Schichten der Bevölkerung in nie zuvor erreichtem Ausmaß anstieg, ein Phänomen, das als „Wirtschaftswunder" in die Geschichte eingegangen ist. Aber nicht nur die Bundesrepublik erlebte damals ein Wachstum sondergleichen, vielmehr war es recht eigentlich ein westeuropäischer Wachstumsboom. Nicht umsonst spricht man von dieser Periode in Westeuropa als „golden age of growth", das „export-led" gewesen sei, wobei die deutsche Wirtschaft durch ihre besondere Stärke im Maschinenbau und in der Investitionsgüterausfuhr eine nicht unwesentliche materielle Voraussetzung dafür bereitgestellt hat.

Noch schneller als die wirtschaftliche Produktion stiegen damals jedoch die sozialen Leistungen an, und der deutsche und westeuropäische Wohlfahrtsstaat erreichte seine volle Blüte. Die Paradoxie, die darin lag, dass in einer Zeit nie zuvor erlebter Realeinkommenssteigerungen und dadurch enorm vergrößerter Möglichkeiten der Eigenvorsorge die Sozialleistungen anstatt zu sinken sich noch überproportional ausdehnten, wurde von Anhängern des Konzepts der sozialen Marktwirtschaft durchaus notiert und gegeißelt. Dies konnte jedoch nichts an dem Faktum ändern, ließ sich doch die Finanzierung immer neuer sozial motivierter Ausgaben infolge des anhaltend hohen Wachstums relativ leicht bewerkstelligen und war dies doch ein probates Mittel im politischen Parteienwettbewerb um die Wählergunst. Letzteres macht auch plausibel, warum ein Großteil der Sozialleistungen gar nicht den ärmsten Mitgliedern der Gesellschaft besonders zugute kam, sondern vor allem die breiten Mittelschichten begünstigte. Man denke in diesem Zusammenhang etwa nur an die dynamische Rente, die Eigenheimzulage und die Sparförderung, alle noch aus den fünfziger Jahres stammend. Allerdings ist, zumindest in der Rückschau, auch klar, dass das den permanenten Ausbau des Wohlfahrtsstaates ermöglichende hohe Wachstum nicht von Dauer sein konnte. Denn der Aufholprozess gegenüber den USA, der das im Vergleich zu diesen raschere Wachstum ja ermöglicht hatte, musste irgendwann zu einem Abschluss kommen, und dadurch mussten die Wachstumsraten wieder auf ihr langfristiges, für entwickelte kapitalistische Volkswirtschaften typisches Normalniveau zurückfallen. Das war im Verlauf der siebziger Jahre tatsächlich der Fall. Da jedoch die diesbezüglichen gesellschaftlichen Erwartungen nicht sofort ebenfalls nach unten korrigiert wurden, ja im Gegenteil, mit dem 1967 gerade erst verabschiedeten Stabilitäts- und Wachstumsgesetz die Vorstellung um sich gegriffen hatte, Wirtschaftswachstum und Konjunktur seien prinzipiell politisch beherrschbar, änderte sich zunächst weder an dem massiven Aufwärtstrend der Löhne etwas, noch an der mit immer neuen staatlich veranlassten Ausgaben verknüpften Reformorientierung des politischen Systems. Alles zusammen war jedoch infolge des niedrigeren Wachstums nicht mehr finanzierbar, was die siebziger Jahre zum Jahrzehnt der Verteilungskämpfe und, dadurch bedingt, der Inflation werden ließ. Zu den innerdeutschen Verteilungskämpfen kamen noch internationale, nämlich als die in den Vietnamkrieg verstrickten USA den Umlauf der Leitwährung Dollar ungehemmt vermehrten, was im damit verbundenen Zugriff auf fremde Ressourcen zu der berüchtigten ‚Dollarschwemme' und schließlich 1973 zum endgültigen Zusammenbruch des Systems fester Wechselkurse führte, sowie der Verteilungskampf zwischen Industrie- und ölproduzierenden Entwicklungsländern, der in den siebziger Jahren in wiederholte Ölpreisschocks mündete.

Im Zeichen des keynesianischen Stabilitäts- und Wachstumsgesetzes versuchte die Regierung der sozial-liberalen Koalition unter Bundeskanzler Helmut Schmidt durch wiederholte expansive Konjunkturprogramme der vielfältigen Krisen Herr zu werden. Angesichts der andauernden „Stagflation" – wie man den Zustand relativ hoher Inflation kombiniert mit vergleichsweise niedrigen durchschnittlichen Wachstumsraten nannte – wurde der Staatshaushalt jedoch überhaupt nicht mehr konsolidiert, und die staatliche Verschuldung stieg

convergence towards the American level of productivity. In effect, technologies and concepts of organisation applied in the USA were already superior to the German and European ones even before World War I; a gap that had even increased since then, because the activities of investment in European national economies had suffered tremendously as a result of the extreme protectionism in the times between the wars and the stuttering of the export motor linked with it. It was only now possible to imitate these productivity increasing methods in Western Europe quickly, since the general export boom prompted the inclination of companies to invest drastically. It therefore occurred that until well into the seventies far above average growth rates were registered in the Federal Republic and the standard of living increased to never before reached extent in the most widespread classes of society; a phenomenon that entered history as the "economic miracle".

But not only the Federal Republic experienced an unparalleled growth at that time, actually it was rather a West European growth boom. Not for nothing one speaks of this period in West Europe as the "golden age of growth", which was "exportled", whereby the German economy presented a considerable material prerequisite because of its special strength in machine construction and the export of investment goods. But at the time, social benefits grew even faster than economic production and the German and West European welfare state reached its peak. Supporters of the concept of social market economy really noted and chastised the paradox, which consisted, in times of never before experienced real income, in that growth and therefore enormously increased possibilities of own provision measures, social benefits even grew in a disproportional way instead of decreasing. However, this was not able to change the facts, since it was relatively easy to finance continuously new socially motivated expenses due to constant high growth rates and since this was a proven instrument in politically motivated competition among parties to be favoured by voters. The latter also explains why a great part of social benefits were not actually useful for the poorest members of society in particular, but instead benefited above all the broad middle classes. In this connection, one only has to look at the index-linked pension, the home owner allowance and savings promotion, which all go back to the fifties. But in hindsight at least, it also becomes clear that the strong growth, which enabled a permanent expansion of the welfare state, could not last for ever. In effect, the process of catching up with the USA, which actually had made possible the comparatively faster growth in the first place, had to come to an end at some point and thus growth rates had to fall back to their long-term, for developed capitalistic macro-economies typical normal levels. That is exactly what happened in the course of the seventies. Since however, the relevant social expectations were not reduced also immediately – on the contrary, the stability and growth law just passed enhanced the idea that economic growth and the economic situation could be controlled politically in principle-, neither the drastic upward trend of wages changed at first, nor the political system's orientation towards reforms linked with constantly new state expenditure. Everything taken together could not be financed any longer because of the low growth rates, which resulted in the seventies becoming the decade of distribution struggles and therefore the years of inflation. In addition to the internal distribution struggles in Germany, there were also international ones, e.g. the USA, who were involved in the Vietnam War, increased the circulation of the key currency dollar unrestrictedly. In this connection, accesses to foreign resources led to the infamous "Dollarglut" and finally in 1973 to the final collapse of the system of fixed exchange rates. The struggle of distribution between industrial and oil producing developing countries resulted repeatedly in oil price shocks in the seventies. In terms of the Keynesian stability and growth law, the social-liberal coalition government under Chancellor Helmut Schmidt tried to get control of the numerous crises through repeated expansive economic programmes. In view of the lasting "stagflation" – as the state of relatively high inflation combined with comparatively low average growth rates was called – it was not possible to consolidate the state budget anymore and the public debt rose dramatically. Deficit spending (amounting to up to 6.5 per cent of the national income) played a role in the compression of company profits and became a risk for further economic development in itself. This situation finally led, initiated by the well-known "Lambsdorff-Paper", to the small domestic "change" in West Germany in 1982: through a constructive motion of no confidence, the Schmidt government was ousted, and supported by the liberal party FDP entering in the coalition, Helmut Kohl was elected Chancellor. Subsequently, a certain consolidation of state finances was achieved by turning away from Keynesianism in the eighties and inflation was controlled through a monetary inspired, money-supply-oriented policy on the part of the German Federal Bank. Primarily because of the implementation of the ambitioned EC single market programme inaugurated in 1986 through the Common European

Fußgängerzone in Ludwigshafen im Jahr 1978.

Pedestrian zone in Ludwigshafen in the year 1978.

Wirtschaftsgeschichte

explosionsartig an. Das „deficit spending" (in Höhe von bis zu 6,5 Prozent des Nationaleinkommens) trug zur Gewinnkompression bei den Unternehmen bei und wurde selbst zu einem Risiko für die weitere wirtschaftliche Entwicklung. Diese Situation führte schließlich, ausgelöst durch das bekannte „Lambsdorff-Papier", 1982 zur kleinen bundesdeutschen „Wende": Durch ein konstruktives Misstrauensvotum wurde die Regierung Schmidt gestürzt und mit Hilfe eines Koalitionswechsels der FDP Helmut Kohl zum Bundeskanzler gewählt.

In den achtziger Jahren wurde daraufhin durch die Abkehr vom Keynesianismus eine gewisse Konsolidierung der Staatsfinanzen erreicht und die Inflation durch eine monetaristisch inspirierte, geldmengenorientierte Politik der Bundesbank gebändigt. Vor allem infolge der Umsetzung des 1986 durch die Einheitliche Europäische Akte inaugurierten, ambitionierten EG-Binnenmarktprogramms kam es seit Ende der achtziger Jahre auch zu umfangreichen Deregulierungen in einzelnen, trotz Leitsätzegesetz und GWB bis dato nach wie vor mit staatlichem Segen kartell- oder monopolartig strukturierten Sektoren, z. B. beim Luftverkehr und in den Versicherungsmärkten, im Bereich der Telekom und Post, der Bahn und der Elektrizitätswirtschaft. Notabene erwies sich recht eigentlich erst dadurch und in der Rückschau, wie überreguliert wichtige Wirtschaftsbereiche in der viel gepriesenen Erhardschen Marktwirtschaft noch waren – was sich aber seinerzeit infolge der durch globale Faktoren bewirkten enormen Wachstumsdynamik nicht weiter negativ bemerkbar gemacht hat.

1989/90 traf die große weltpolitische Wende, nämlich der Zusammenbruch des sozialistischen Ostblocks, die Bundesrepublik völlig unvorbereitet. Bei der dadurch überraschend möglich gewordenen Wiedervereinigung der beiden deutschen Staaten wurden von der Bundesregierung schwere Fehler gemacht, die die wirtschaftlichen Probleme nicht nur in den neuen, sondern auch in den alten Bundesländern verschärften, nicht zuletzt durch die Notwendigkeit bis heute anhaltender Milliardentransfers von West nach Ost. Einer dieser Fehler bestand in der durch die Beschwörung einer historisch völlig falschen Analogie zwischen der Währungsreform von 1948 und der Währungsunion von 1990, die für Ostdeutschland ja ebenfalls eine Währungsreform darstellte, verstärkten Erwartung von „blühenden Landschaften" innerhalb von nur fünf Jahren bei den neuen Bundesbürgern, obwohl die Transformation einer jahrzehntelang völlig verstaatlichten Wirtschaft doch nur wenig mit der Wiedereinführung eines funktionierenden Geldes und dem Abbau staatlicher Bewirtschaftung in einer ansonsten von Privat-

Der seit 1951 produzierte Mercedes-Benz Typ 300 „Adenauer" war seinerzeit der größte und schnellste deutsche Serien-PKW. Glänzende Karossen im Mercedes-Benz-Museum zeugen von spannender Automobilgeschichte.

The Mercedes-Benz 300 called "Adenauer", produced since 1951, was the largest and fastest German serial car of its time. Shining limousines in the Mercedes-Benz Museum bear witness of a thrilling automobile history.

Act, there were also extensive deregulations in individual cartel or monopoly-like structured sectors, which still were tolerated by the state until then despite the Law of Basic Principles and the Competition Law, for example in air traffic and in the insurance branch, in the sectors of telecom and post, the railways and the electricity industry. Let it be noted, this only revealed in truth and in hindsight just how overregulated important economic sectors still were in Erhard's much praised market economy – a fact that did not have further negative effects at the time because of global factors that produced enormous growth dynamics.

Albeit, Germany was completely unprepared for the great change in world politics, namely the collapse of the socialist Eastern Block, which took place in 1989/90. The Federal Government made serious errors in the reunification of the two German states, which surprisingly became possible. These not only intensified economic problems in the new federal states, but also in the old ones, not least because it was necessary to transfer billions of euros from West to East, which is still ongoing today. One of these mistakes involved the assumption of a historically completely wrong analogy between the monetary reform of 1948 and the monetary union of 1990, which in fact represented a currency reform for East Germany. It increased expectations to see "green pastures" only within five years with the new German citizens, although the transformation of a decade-long completely state-owned economy only has little to do with the re-introduction of functioning money and the reduction of state-driven management in an economy normally characterised by private property. Because of the reunification, the Federal Republic of Germany today is one most suffering national economies in the OECD region because of unavoidable public burden. This fact is only compensated partly by the advantages that the introduction of the Euro brought the German economy with its relatively low rate of inflation when competing on the markets of partner countries, since these are accompanied with above-average real interest levels for the same reason.

From a historical perspective, however, there still results quite a positive forecast for the future of the German national economy, for:

1. Not the lower average-level growth rates since the mid seventies are an anomaly, indeed the extraordinary growth boom in the times before that was the great exception, which will not be repeated as far as anyone can judge.
2. The European economic region consists of economies that are on extremely different levels of development. On the whole, the German is one of the most developed ones. It has always been the fate of such national economies that their growth seems comparatively low, which is however unavoidable, when others are catching up economically – a process that ultimately also the German export trade is benefiting considerably.
3. Meanwhile, social expectations have adapted to present lower growth rates. Even the unions are prepared to accept cutbacks at long defended standards, as for instance the recent prolongation of working hours without additional pay in several companies showed.
4. In the meantime, deregulation and flexible working hours in production have, primarily through the influence of the EU, progressed relatively far. And the governing red-green coalition has also finally started to tackle reforms on the labour market, which had been put off far too long.

Wirtschaftsgeschichte

eigentum gekennzeichneten Wirtschaft zu tun hat. Die Bundesrepublik ist infolge der Wiedervereinigung heute eine der am stärksten unter unvermeidlichen öffentlichen Lasten leidenden Volkswirtschaften im OECD-Raum. Dies wird nur zum Teil kompensiert durch die Vorteile, die die Einführung des Euro der bundesdeutschen Wirtschaft mit ihrer relativ geringen Inflationsrate im Wettbewerb auf den Märkten der Partnerländer gebracht hat, zumal diese aus dem gleichen Grund mit einem überdurchschnittlichen Realzinsniveau einhergehen.

Aus historischer Perspektive ergibt sich dennoch eine durchaus positive Prognose für die Zukunft der deutschen Volkswirtschaft, denn:

1. Nicht die niedrigeren durchschnittlichen Wachstumsraten seit Mitte der siebziger Jahre sind eine Anomalie, vielmehr war der außergewöhnliche Wachstumsboom in der Zeit davor die große Ausnahme, die sich nach menschlichem Ermessen nicht wiederholen wird.
2. Der europäische Wirtschaftsraum besteht aus Wirtschaften auf höchst unterschiedlichem Entwicklungsniveau. Die deutsche ist insgesamt eine der am weitesten entwickelten. Es war von jeher das Schicksal solcher Volkswirtschaften, dass ihr Wachstum vergleichsweise gering wirkt, was jedoch unabänderlich ist, wenn andere wirtschaftlich aufholen – ein Prozess, von dem schließlich auch der deutsche Export nicht unerheblich profitiert.
3. Inzwischen haben sich die gesellschaftlichen Erwartungen an das niedrigere Wachstum angepasst, ja, selbst die Gewerkschaften sind bereit, Abstriche an lange verteidigten Standards hinzunehmen, wie z. B. die kürzlich erfolgte Verlängerung der Arbeitszeit ohne Lohnausgleich in verschiedenen Unternehmen zeigt.
4. Deregulierung und Flexibilisierung der Produktion sind, vor allem unter dem Einfluss der EU, inzwischen relativ weit gediehen. Und die regierende rot-grüne Koalition hat nun endlich auch die allzu lange aufgeschobenen Reformen am Arbeitsmarkt angepackt. ∎

Der Hamburger Hafen –
Symbol deutscher Wirtschaftskraft.
Port of Hamburg –
Symbol of German Economic Power.

Economic History

Mit der Marke Aspirin wurde die Bayer AG weltweit bekannt.

Diese Gebäude der Opel-Werke Rüsselsheim stammen aus den Jahren 1916–1929, Architekt war Paul Meißner.

The Bayer AG achieved worldwide fame with the brand Aspirin.

These buildings of the Opel Works in Rüsselheim date from the years 1916–1929; the architect was Paul Meißner.

Inserentenverzeichnis

*Acri.Tec Gesellschaft für
ophthalmologische Produkte mbH
Neuendorfstraße 20a
D-16761 Hennigsdorf b. Berlin
Telefon   +49 (3302) 202 6000
Telefax   +49 (3302) 202 6060
Internet   www.acritec.de S. 143

Adecco Personaldienstleistungen GmbH
Flemingstraße 20–22
D-36041 Fulda
Telefon   +49 (661) 93 98-0
Telefax   +49 (661) 93 98-100
Internet   www.adecco.de S. 86

ARWOBAU Apartment- und
Wohnungsbaugesellschaft mbH
Hallesches Ufer 74–76
D-10963 Berlin
Telefon   +49 (030) 25441-0
Telaefax   +49 (030) 25441-162
Internet   www.arwobau.de S. 121

ATS Gruppe
Bruchstraße 34
D-67098 Bad Dürkheim
Telefon   +49 (6322) 6 04-132
Telefax   +49 (6322) 6 04-290
Internet   www.ats-company.com S. 44

betandwin e.k.
Breitscheidstraße 20
D-02727 Neugersdorf
Telefon   +49 (3586) 77 17 17
Telefax   +49 (3586) 77 17 88
Internet   www.betandwin.de S. 123

Bindan-Gruppe
Bahnhofstraße 8
D-28816 Stuhr/b.Bremen
Telefon   +49 (421) 89 93-0
Telefax   +49 (421) 89 93-200
Internet   www.bindan.de S. 31

BIRD & BIRD Düsseldorf
Karl-Theodor-Straße 6
D-40213 Düsseldorf
Telefon   +49 (211) 20 05 60 00
Telefax   +49 (211) 20 05 60 11
Internet   www.twobirds.com S. 66

BIRD & BIRD München
Pacellistraße 14
D-80333 München
Telefon   +49 (89) 35 81 60 00
Telefax   +49 (89) 35 81 60 11
Internet   www.twobirds.com S. 66

BorgWarner Transmission Systems GmbH
Kurpfalzring
D-69123 Heidelberg
Telefon   +49 (6221) 7 08-0
Telefax   +49 (6221) 7 08-1 99
Internet   www.bwauto.com S. 95

Bosch Rexroth AG
Maria-Theresien-Straße 23
D-97816 Lohr am Main
Telefon   +49 (800) 99 33 222
Telefax   +49 (800) 99 33 111
Internet   www.boschrexroth.com S. 101

DB Zeitarbeit
Universitätsstraße 2–3a
D-10117 Berlin
Telefon   +49 (30) 25 35 67 00
Telaefax +49 (30) 25 35 67 20
Internet   www.db.de/zeitarbeit S. 87

Deutsche Post World Net
Charles-de-Gaulle-Straße 20
D-53113 Bonn
Telefon   +49 (228) 182-0
Telefax   +49 (228) 182-70 99
Internet   www.deutschepost.de S. 36

Die Region Nürnberg e. V.
Michael-Vogel-Straße 3
D-91052 Erlangen
Telefon   +49 (9131) 72 76 77
Telefax   +49 (9131) 72 76 55
Internet   www.metropolregion-nuernberg.org
           www.highqualityoflife.com
           www.existenzgruenderpool.de S. 134

DPD Deutscher Paket Dienst
GmbH & Co.KG
Wailandtstraße 1
D-63741 Aschaffenburg
Telefon   +49 (6021) 492 7074
Telefax   +49 (6021) 492 7099
Internet   www.dpd.net S. 12

EECH –
European Energy Consult Holding AG
Pöseldorfer Weg 36
D-20149 Hamburg
Telefon   +49 (40) 4 45 06 09-0
Telefax   +49 (40) 4 45 06 09-80
Internet   www.eech.de S. 100

Euler Hermes Kreditversicherungs- AG
Friedensallee 254
D-22763 Hamburg
Telefon   +49 (40) 88 34-0
Telefax   +49 (40) 88 34-77 44
Internet   www.eulerhermes.de S. 60

List of Companies

Epple Druckfarben AG
Gutenbergstraße 5
D-86356 Neusäß/Augsburg
Telefon   +49 (821) 46 03-0
Telefax   +49 (821) 46 03-200
Internet   www.epple-druckfarben.de   S. 128

Georg Maschinentechnik GmbH & Co. KG
Rheinstraße 18
D-57638 Neitersen
Telefon   +49 (2681) 804-0
Telefax   +49 (2681) 804-210
Internet   www.georg-gruppe.de   S. 135

Hansgrohe AG
Auestraße 5-9
D-77761 Schiltach
Telefon   +49 (7836) 51-0
Telefax   +49 (7836) 51-13 00
Internet   www.hansgrohe.com   S. 103

KSM Castings GmbH
Cheruskerring 38
D-31137 Hildesheim
Telefon   +49 (5121) 505-0
Telefax   +49 (5121) 505-345
Internet   www.ksmcastings.com.   S. 50

Lohmann GmbH & Co. KG
Irlicher Straße 55
D-56567 Neuwied
Telefon   +49 (2631) 34-0
Telefax   +49 (2631) 34-6661
Internet   www.lohmann-tapes.com   S. 94

MANAGEMENT ENGINEERS GmbH + Co. KG
Am Seestern 8
D-40547 Düsseldorf
Telefon   +49 (211) 53 000
Telefax   +49 (211) 5 300 300
Internet   www.Management-Engineers.com
S. 114

Motorola GmbH
Heinrich-Hertz-Straße 1
D-65232 Taunusstein
Telefon   +49 (6128) 70 700
Telefax   +49 (6128) 70 4900
Internet   www.motorola.de   S. 149

Möbelfolien GmbH Biesenthal
Bahnhofstraße 150
D-16359 Biesenthal
Telefon   +49 (3337) 48-0
Telefax   +49 (3337) 48-34
Internet   www.moebie.de   S. 67

Paracelsus-Kliniken Deutschland GmbH
Sedanstraße 109
D-49076 Osnabrück
Telefon   +49 (541) 66 92 0
Telefax   +49 (541) 66 92 189
E-Mail   info@pk-mx.de   S. 142

Premium Bodywear AG
Chemnnitzer Straße 36–38
D-09228 Chemnitz
Telefon   +49 (37200) 860-0
Telefax   +49 (37200) 860-314
Internet   www.olafbenz.com   S. 30

reinisch AG
Emmy-Noether-Straße 9
D-76131 Karlsruhe
Telefon   +49 (721) 66 377-0
Telefax   +49 (721) 66 377-119
Internet   www.reinisch.de   S. 76

SAP Deutschland AG & Co. KG
Neurottstraße 15a
D-69190 Walldorf
Telefon   +49 (800) 5343424
Telefax   +49 (800) 5343420
Internet   www.sap.de   S. 148

Simon Hegele Gesellschaft für Logistik und Service mbH
Hardeckstraße 5
D-76185 Karlsruhe
Telefon   +49 (721) 5 70 09
Telefax   +49 (721) 57 00 91 30
Internet   www.hegele.de   S. 120

Smurfit Deutschland
Tilsiter Straße 144
D-22047 Hamburg
Telefon   +49 (40) 6 94 43-272
Telefax   +49 (40) 6 94 43-157
Internet   www.smurfit.de   S. 102

Ticona GmbH
Professor-Staudinger-Straße
D-65451 Kelsterbach
Telefon   +49 (180) 5 84 26 62
Telefax   +49 (180) 2 02 12 02
Internet   www.ticona.com   S. 108

TRANSCOM WORLDWIDE
In der Steele 39a
D-40599 Düsseldorf
Telefon   +49 (211) 74 00 45 00
Telefax   +49 (211) 17 70 40
Internet   www.transcom-worldwide.com   S. 20

Vivanco AG
Ewige Weide 15
D-22926 Ahrensburg
Telefon   +49 (4102) 231-0
Telefax   +49 (4102) 231-160
Internet   www.vivanco.de   S. 122

Impressum/Imprint

Wirtschaftsstandort Deutschland
Business Location Germany

Verlag/Publishing House	EUROPÄISCHER WIRTSCHAFTS VERLAG GmbH Ein Unternehmen der MEDIEN GRUPPE KIRK AG Groß-Gerauer Weg 1–3 in D-64295 Darmstadt Telefon +49 (6151) 17 70-0 Telefax +49 (6151) 17 70-10 LeoPro +49 (6151) 17 70-48 E-Mail ewv@ebn24.com Internet www.ebn24.com
Herausgeber/Publisher	Christian Kirk ©
Realisation	Dieses Projekt wurde realisiert unter Mitarbeit der Autoren Wolfgang Clement, Dr. Angela Merkel, Jürgen R. Thumann, Michael Sommer, Dr. h. c. Ludwig Georg Braun, Hans Eichel, Roland Koch, Prof. Dr. Wolfgang Böhmer, Prof. Dr. Rudolf Steinberg, Prof. Dr. Karl Max Einhäupl, Joachim Broudré-Gröger, Prof. Dr. Utz Claassen, Hans-Georg Morawitz, Dr. Hanno Brandes, Albert Darboven, Béla Nikolai Anda, Prof. Regina Ziegler, Prof. Dr. med. Peter Sawicki, Wolfgang Niersbach, Prof. Dr. Christoph Buchheim, Christine Schuster (Schlussredaktion) sowie in der Organisation Jörg Plaacke, Melanie Becker, Daniel Süß und Monika Burger
Gesamtherstellung/Collect-run Production	MEDIA TEAM Gesellschaft für Kommunikation mbH
Chefredaktion/Editor-in-Chief	Heinz-Dieter Krage
Grafik & Satz/Graphics & Typesetting	Daniela Kraft, Eva-Maria Prinz, Steffi Sauermann-Schliebs, Lars Hintze, Katharina Jedral-Tomski, Jan Metzger, Jeannette Zahn, Christian Trott
Verantwortliche Übersetzerin/Responsible for translation	Asma Esmeralda Portales
Bildnachweis/Picture credits	Autoren der Artikel, porträtierte Unternehmen, Adam Opel AG; Alfred Harder, Weiterstadt; BASF; Bayer AG; BIS Bremerhaven Touristik; Bremer Touristik-Zentrale; DaimlerChrysler MediaServices und Konzernarchiv; Deutsche Messe AG; FAZ; FRAPORT AG; Giovanni Castell; Hafen Hamburg; Hannover Congress Centrum/Medienserver Hannover & Region; Humboldt-Universität Berlin; Messe Frankfurt GmbH; Partner für Berlin/FTB-Werbefotografie; Presse- und Informationsamt der Bundesregierung/Bundesbildstelle (Julia Faßbender); Presse- und Informationsamt des Landes Berlin; Scholvien/Berlin; Science Center Bremen; Siemens AG; Stadtarchiv Ludwigshafen; ThyssenKrupp AG; Tourismus+Congress GmbH FfM (Jochen Keute, Daniel Zielske, Frank Seifert); Universitätsklinikum FfM/Leipziger & Partner PR GmbH;
Computer to Plate	digigroup GmbH, Darmstadt
Druck/Papier/Printers/Paper	gedruckt in Deutschland auf 100 % chlorfreiem Papier mit Epple Druckfarben. Epple Druckfarben AG, Neusäß b. Augsburg
Vervielfältigung & Nachdruck/Reproduction & Reprints	Alle Rechte vorbehalten. Kein Teil dieses Buches darf ohne schriftliche Genehmigung des Verlages vervielfältigt oder verarbeitet werden. Unter dieses Verbot fällt insbesondere die gewerbliche Vervielfältigung per Kopie, die Aufnahme ins Internet bzw. andere elektronische Datenbanken und die Vervielfältigung auf CD. Verstöße werden rechtlich verfolgt. Redaktionsschluss: 11. Juli 2005
ISBN	3-938630-01-9, Ausgabe 2005/2006